THE CALIFORNIA DREAM

THE
CALIFORNIA
DREAM

DISCARDED

Edited by Dennis Hale and Jonathan Eisen

THE MACMILLAN COMPANY

New York

To the memory of Ambrose Bierce, who had the courage to leave.

"Come Stanford, let us sit at ease,
And talk as old friends do.
You talk of anything you please,
But I will talk of you."

Contents

CHAPTER III:
SOUTHERN CALIFORNIA COUNTRY

CHAPTER IV:
LIFE STYLES

A Word Before

"But I reckon I got to light out for the territory ahead of the rest, because Aunt Sally, she's going to adopt me and sivilize me, and I can't stand it. I been there before."

—The Adventures of Huckleberry Finn

THE TEMPTATION to run away to the West seems to trouble each generation of Americans, and ours is no exception. The promise of the West has always been the promise of escape, the chance to "light out" and start life all over, to be reborn. And of the western states, one seems to have kept that promise most faithfully. California has not only attracted the majority of the western immigrants, it has also attracted the most ambitious and the most dissatisfied. It is that land, and few others, that performs the magic of making "boosters" out of drifters; it is from there that the most extravagant reports are mailed to those left behind; and it is California that is rediscovered, about once every twenty years, by some happy (or loony) band of seekers who feel themselves extraordinarily lucky to have "found" such a marvelous place.

There is no denying California's attraction: descriptions of the state have always been lurid in the extreme, and most immigrants—and often chance passersby—have shown a remarkable willingness to become private tourist bureaus in order to attract even more immigrants and visitors. An early Spanish explorer wrote his king that California "was inhabited by robust dark women of great strength and warm hearts" who fought with weapons of gold, "and no other metal existed" in the land. Other reports told of "seven golden cities" and similar wonders. This alleged wealth attracted the interest of Spain, Great Britain, Russia, and Mexico, and California was for many years the point around which the great powers disputed their control of the New World. But each gave up when the reality failed to measure up to the expectation. The United States was about to begin her own exploration of California when gold was discovered, quite by chance, near Sacramento in 1848. Californians have been discovering treasures of every sort—both worldly and spiritual—ever since. The recent migration of thousands of young men and women fleeing conventional America is only the latest, and by no means the last invasion of a state whose motto is, appropriately, "*Eureka,* I have found it!"

California, as a hippy has put it, is a "whole new bag." That may, of course, be a self-fulfilling prophecy, born of the desire to escape and the state's tradition of discovery and innovation. Since California is as far as the seeker can go, he must decide either that he has found his Paradise, or wasted his time. The first is the more comforting illusion, and is supported by another characteristic of the state—its distance from the psychological center of America.

Most Americans are used to thinking of their country as lying within a triangle whose points are Chicago, Boston, and Miami, and of the rest as a sort of "ex-urb" lying on the periphery. California, especially, lies "away," across miles of unknown territory that most Americans (including many who live there) think of as a remote desert province of the East Coast. Beyond the plains, however, lies another land, and a curious mood of exile settles over the traveler from the East or Midwest as he crosses the Rockies and enters "this beautiful, sensuous Land of Mu by the Western Sea." It is easy to imagine why men thought they could get lost there. The frame of mind is suggested by one visitor, who remarked how odd it felt "to have the rest of the world over there [pointing toward China], rather than over there [pointing east]."

As air travel draws California closer, the psychological distance may diminish, as it certainly has, for example, between Europe and the East Coast. And as California grows closer to the "center" it may appear less alien, less bizarre; indeed, the conventional view that America will be tomorrow what California is today may be backwards: California may in fact be growing more like the rest of the country. At first glance, anyway, the state is more conventional than the visitor has been led to expect. Here are the people, the cars, the supermarkets, the hot-dog stands, the streets, the cracked sidewalks, the split-levels, the bouffant hairdos, and the neuroses one encounters everywhere in America.

But these are first impressions; after a while one notices something different about otherwise familiar objects: colors are deeper, metals are shinier, the air is cleaner, and the brilliant California sun seems to jump from every surface. Before long everyday scenes begin to look like Technicolor scenes. If the London fog can make the English "moody and introspective," what must the California sun do to the Californians? Certainly it was this infernal brightness that ruined the Beats: it is impossible to appear ashen and morose in California, even if one tries very hard.

The biggest surprise, however, is the people: no one believes in the "California dream" as intensely as the Californian. Conversations with a native reveal two things: first, that he believes California to be in some sense a "special" place requiring "special" rules; and second, that he is very conscious of being a Californian. Very few people are conscious of being Illinoisans or Dakotans, or even Texans or New Yorkers. But the Californian not only *believes* the ethos of his state, he *lives* it, and displays its main outlines in his everyday life. People "welcome" the visitor to California in precisely the same tone of voice used by a European greeting a tourist. They consider it your great good fortune to have arrived, and are doubly pleased if you agree.

Not everyone can consider his arrival in California to be a great good fortune. But because California is far away, both physically and psychologically, it has benefited from a process of self-selection that takes men who *want* to be far away and repels those who do not. The same process was at work on the earlier frontier—in Kentucky, for example—but in California it has continued steadily since the beginning of the nineteenth century. It will only begin to subside when technology diminishes the distance (and the differences) between California and the East.

Thus California was not simply the recipient of a mass migration, but of a certain type of migrant. The California-bound migrant was not fleeing religious or political persecution, and he did not suffer, in most cases, from actual want. He was not a member of an oppressed minority group breaking out of servitude and seeking, for the first time, a fair and equal opportunity. *He was, especially in the beginning, a failure,* and he sought, not liberty, but a second chance.[1] The continent, to paraphrase Ambrose Bierce, tipped, and everything that was not tied down rolled westward. The result was a continual upheaval, a constant shifting of cultural authority and experience, created by all the hopeful millions who went to California in search of their undefined "Something."

Now, there are two problems in a society bent on finding "Something." The first is that people seldom find what they are looking for; and the second is that they are driven to keep trying even when all hope is gone. The first difficulty is obvious. People whose searches have gone unrewarded possess a special bitterness toward those whose searches have been (or might be) successful: no one hates the Negro more than the okie, because the Negro will be free when the okie is still a slave. California is infested with broken men who came looking for gold and never found it; Hollywood, as Nathanial West knew, is where the losers go to die, and California, the graveyard of western man.

The second difficulty is the crueler of the two, and is directly related to what might be called California's "youth cult." The "quest" has always been the special province of the young; but in California it is also the moral duty of the citizen, enshrined in the state's motto and implied by all of its history; it is his reason for being, or, at any rate, his reason for being in California. The command is therefore explicit: stay young. The old do not dream dreams, and they do not go on quests. They collect social security checks and get sick. A society bent on fulfilling a perpetual dream, individually or collectively, must reject the aged, the infirm, and the "old at heart"; but in so doing it must also reject, even *obliterate,* its own past. And since all men age, all men are condemned, and the useful years of life are reduced (according to the current schedule) to thirty. What Tocqueville said of America is true especially of the West, that "not only does democracy make every man forget his ancestors, but it hides his descendents and separates his contemporaries from him; it throws him back forever upon himself alone and threatens in the end to confine him entirely within the solitude of his own heart."

---

[1] Major and important exceptions are the Chinese and the Negroes.

To be sure, this cult of novelty and youth gets an able assist from nature: California induces men to dream great dreams partly because it is so pleasant. In such a world, what could come between man and the Holy Grail? Unlike New England or the earlier frontier, where men came to look upon the world as unremittingly hostile, California presents an environment that is, usually, quite congenial. It encourages grand enthusiasms and great projects. It is, therefore, a state where politics is given an exalted status. Politics is the art of doing: men, and governments, are expected to accomplish things, to prove their worth by fulfilling some dream or plan of action. Californians are said to be "extreme," but it is probably more accurate to say that they are simply *excitable* in a way most Americans are not. It is significant in this regard that only in California does an amateur "club" movement give serious competition to professional politicians. Because everyone takes politics seriously, a variant of the "priesthood of all believers" is applied to a profession that is elsewhere considered beneath contempt or beyond comprehension.

This may explain the oft-noted "fragmentation of power" in California: the absence of strong traditional authority, the chaotic ideologies, the unpredictable electorate. California politics is "up for grabs" in the literal meaning of that phrase; no one, it is thought, has as yet tied power down or fenced it in with privilege, and a state that encourages men to dream also urges them to organize and to act.

But it offers them no guidelines, no well-worn paths, no venerable authorities. Every man is his own authority. It is perhaps a coincidence, but interesting, nonetheless, that the drug cult is stronger in California than anywhere else. For LSD is perhaps the ultimate application of the Protestant notion that the believer must be his own priest, and interpret the scripture as he sees fit. The shaggy-haired freak, curled in a corner gazing at a candle and communing with the Deity, may seem an alien figure in the land of the Rand Corporation and the Freeway. But if you listen very carefully you will hear him intoning an ancient and honorable, indeed, an official liturgy: *"Eureka, Eureka. I Have Found It!"*

But LSD is neither the beginning nor the end of our story. *The California Dream* begins with a chapter on what California *was* and how it got that way; Chapter II examines the formal politics of the state, past and present. Chapter III presents a discussion of Southern California, a subject (some say a state) all by itself.

The final chapter is a collection of "life styles," ranging from the mildly bizarre to the totally insane.

We would like to thank the people who helped us put this book together: Jerry Berman and Fred and Allison Kettering, for giving the editors a place to stay and for explaining some otherwise mysterious things; the Bancroft Library at Berkeley, for being such a good library; and finally, Alice Hale and Pat Finlay for advice, assistance, and general encouragement.

DENNIS HALE
JONATHAN EISEN

New York City
February, 1968

CHAPTER I

⁓

HISTORY AND
ANTECEDENTS

"Let us not imagine ourselves in a fool's paradise, where the golden apples will drop into our mouths; let us not think that after the stormy seas and head gales of all the ages, our ship has at last struck the trade winds of time. The future of our State . . . looks fair and bright; perhaps the future looked so to the philosophers who once sat in the porches of Athens. . . . Our modern civilization strikes broad and deep and looks high. So did the tower which men once built almost unto heaven."

Henry George

California: Notes of a Native Son*

WILSON CAREY MC WILLIAMS

NORMALLY, NATURE is mild in California, and the Pacific Ocean deserves its name. Yet the calm is deceptive: nature in California is neurotic, its apparent stability a mask for anguish and anxiety; drought and fire are her most frequent aggressions, but earthquake her constant menace. There is not a Californian who cannot tell you, with a certain perverse pride, where the faults run and which buildings will be likely to go in the next tremor.

The Pacific itself washes over an abruptly falling shelf, which may account both for its seeming "pacifism" and for the ominous feelings it provokes in the mind of the observer. Frost looked "Once by the Pacific" and saw a "night of dark intent." The phrase tells much. The regional literature of New England and the South, dark and gloomy and preoccupied with sin, arouses anxiety about the crimes of the *past*, ravening in the soul of man. The Pacific, by contrast, especially California's Pacific, arouses fears of man's *intent*, his dreams and his future, rather than his passions and his past.

California is a land of sepulchral visions; it calls up nightmares of human degeneration and extinction. Huxley saw them in the masses of condoms, flotsam from the Los Angeles sewers, washed up on the beaches of the South. Nathanial West felt the rage of "cheated men," with "fevered minds and emaciated bodies," furious

---

* Reprinted from *The Activist* (Fall, 1967), by permission of the editors and the author.

against a civilization which has told them to labor for a future that brought only age and impotence.

Yet consider the two anxieties: Huxley feared a sensuality become meaningless and lost to purpose; West feared a purpose so restrictive as to deny all delight. Nightmare, in California, is Protean in character.

But what is the real form of Proteus? California is, first of all, a place to which men move (a truth which is either trite or proverbial); and men move in response to symbols, ideas and images which are the foretaste of actuality. These symbols continue to exert a powerful influence on those who come to live in the state, shaping what they see and can perceive. More than any state, California is to its citizens what it is to the nation: a set of images, the largest Hollywood set ever created.

Most lands have been best known through the writings of travelers who have been able to escape patterns of understanding shaped by custom and self-ignorance. In California, however, the traveler still carries those patterns; he has created them, in fact, in a *state* of travelers. The objective observer is blinded by the same subjectivity as the resident. California can only be understood by those for whom the symbols, if they come at all, follow the land itself in the order of apprehension: it can only be known in all its dimensions by the native, or by those like him, from *within* and never from *without*.

To understand at all, the outsider must realize that he deals with a strange land, a new universe, and he must organize his thoughts in terms of the categories by which universes are understood; he must learn to study the four dimensions of California.

(1) LENGTH. The longitude of California places it in "the West," and the West as a region occupies a special place in the symbols of America. The West confronts its residents with the choice of becoming expatriates or of accepting defeat and "going back." We go "down South" (an image that is almost psychoanalytic) or "back East," but we move "out West," a phrase which invokes not only the great spaces but also the idea of escape from confinement, the constraint of the old regions.

All this is part of the new meaning which the four directions acquired with the discovery of the earth's sphericality. "Going west" suddenly became a new way of "going east," and the idiom translates to mean that leaving may be the means of coming home, that dying may be the means of being reborn. The West became an incentive to moving on fundamentally different from the infantilistic logic that led men "back East," back across the Atlantic to Britain, or, in past ages, on the crusades to Jerusalem.

The promise of the West, however, was established only by fixing it more firmly as the land of death, and the starkness of the American West only reinforced the image. One may feel called by the East which lies beyond, but the West itself remains a waiting area, a mortuary or a graveyard, for those who inhabit it. Promise and fear are tangled in complex ways that express themselves only too clearly in the social and political life of the West.

(2) BREADTH. The latitude and the circumstance of California make it a particular part of the West, however. California has always been set apart from her neighbors by the facts of climate. It is, of course, a warm state. Yet California is sharply different from the desert states and no less different from the dank, sub-tropicality of Florida. Being "Mediterranean," California is softer than the skeletal desert states, midway between them and Florida's vegetable excess. Yet the Mediterranean climate is associated with another image: that of the ancient world.

"Going west" in this case leads to a *new* East; it is not merely a devious route to the old one. The climate and the surroundings speak to antique memories which found confirmation in the feudal society of early California. That society Californians have always been eager to preserve in monuments and to inculcate in the young: one is confronted with the improbable image of militant Protestants eager to restore the missions; of the California Spanish school of architecture—feudal Spain re-created by modern technology.

There is more than Spain, of course, in the Mediterranean image. Spain is vital only to those whose feeble imaginations need some support in historic fact. Egyptology blossomed in San Diego and San Jose, and the Hellenic dream of Americans (revealed in their public buildings and banks across the continent) finds a natural setting in California.

The Mediterranean is a civilized image, not a raw one: ancient and not new. It helps account for the fact that "going to" California is more likely to mean going to *live* there than going for a vacation. The state has a permanence denied the other warm states, a human quality denied the rest of the West.

(3) DEPTH. Yet the first two dimensions only describe the boundaries of the state; they enclose its space without suggesting what lies inside. The depth of California is extraordinary: it is the high tower and the bottomless pit, Babel and Gehenna. The land

itself said as much, giving the state the highest and lowest points among the continental states and placing them so close together that they could hardly escape notice.

Partly, the depth of the state is the result of the conflict between the symbols of length and breadth, modern and ancient. Of course, California's depth is also due to the fact that a new state disorganizes old social patterns and leaves men without the protection of routine. California was not only new space, but new clime: the old patterns would not hold, and new ones were rarely compelling.

What remained was the fact of unsettlement and destabilization: freedom and threat combined; the chance to rise higher with the peril of falling further. Hence Carey McWilliams's definition of California as "the great exception," the end points of the curve, the departure from the norm.

Freedom, to put it simply, was not supported by social guarantees or customs. Freedom is a natural, sometimes a brutal, never a political fact. The freedom to do or to be has never been separated from the threat of punishment for doing or being. Drastic departures from what was the norm in the old states may arouse anxiety in those who have departed from the norm in a different way, and they may strike out with the violence of vigilante justice which does not change by being clothed, as it often is, in the robes of law.

The threat of punishment is less serious, perhaps, than the absence of support. At best, freedom is unmolested. Society feels no need to encourage or protect what is *done* with freedom. It is, like other "open societies," a system of *procedures*. Either it reacts violently to prevent a category of actions, or it is passively indifferent toward them, sometimes vacillating between the two. Yet it is always without substance, always without judgment as to the *aims* of action. And those who have broken with the safe base line of the old norms know that there is a subtle affinity between the high points on the curve and the low, between genius and insanity. Without support from society, the individual is forced to draw the line between the two for himself, a difficult task for those who are alone.

The task may paralyze action for a time, but it is likely to end in messianism, the belief that one has the truth once and for all, which is really a denial that there is any difference between genius and insanity, the assertion that what one walks is not a tightrope but a broad freeway.

California messianism, the constant theme of the state's history, is born partly from conflict within the state and partly from hope, but most often it is born from simple desperation. The great movements reflect them all, though in varying degrees. The radical right emphasizes conflict, the confrontation of old norms by new practice; the older cults reflect that conflict combined with desperation, a realization that the old society and the old standards are slipping away for good. The "Beat" movement of the late '50s reflected desperation pure; the Free Speech Movement and the liberal activism of the '60s tinged desperation with hope; the latest movements, the "hippies" of Hashbury, reflect the slow erosion of the hope which, oddly enough, finds its strongest recent expression in the riots at Watts and Hunter's Point.

(4) TIME. California messianism and California conformity arise from a similar source: the pre-Einsteinean dimension of the immigrant's symbolism, his lack of a sense of time. For the immigrant the continuity of time is broken and life—when it is not a lonely anticipation of death—is simply an endless present. Hence the California genius for improvisation, confronting each problem as it comes, answering it with a solution that adds to the difficulty of the next dilemma. Suburban development that seizes the best of the land and transforms it into piles of paperboard slimed together with asphalt, or that builds in the old watercourses that wash houses away when the flash floods come; houses tiered up hills without adequate foundations and sliding down in mud avalanches; the wild and almost aimless growth of freeways; the expanding cloud of polluted air hanging over what were intended, ironically, to be the "Pittsburghs of the West": these are only a few examples of the gimcrack improvisation that results from the lack of a sense of time.

The messianic movements do not interfere with such developments. The ferocious ideological debates of California politics, the savage cultural confrontations of her society are all artificial or superficial. The great moral issues of California politics like the U.N., capital punishment, "amorality" (in a myriad of forms), even "the University" have all been symbolic, like the perceptions of Californians themselves.

In one sense, they speak to the sense of possibility that is part of that perception; but they are too abstract, too disjointed, too little attentive to the material universe to exploit any of the chances that are open to men. The symbol-debates leave the possibilities of California life to be seized on by the great economic and social forces of the state, forces whose power is only the greater because they too are freed from the constraints of custom and tradition.

The real forces of California life, despite the beliefs of Californians and the nation, are not the cults, the radical right, the hippies, or the Watts rioters (to their credit, these last at least know as much). They are the Los Angeles *Times*, the Bank of America, the Sunkist Association, DiGiorgio, I.B.M., the aerospace and automobile industries, the Metropolitan Water District, P.G.&E., Southern California Edison, and so on. Arthur Samish, the old boss of the legislature, reflected their needs; so too did Clark Kerr and his concept of the "multiversity."

For a brief moment, the sovereignty of the great interests over California life was challenged by the revival of political action and political partisanship, but given the nature of California culture, that revival collapsed into a series of battles over symbols, which divided the parties and left the great interests the only survivors.

The power of these social and economic forces is the only stability that California possesses, their interests its bottom floor of certainty. Reagan, Yorty and their right-wing supporters can no more upset the system and the institutions it has created to serve its needs than could the liberal-left C.D.C. before them. To do so would require a more sophisticated understanding than either possesses, a more coherent analysis and vision of political things, and, most importantly, a sounder sense of time.

The distinctive genius of the West and of California in particular, one missed by almost all residents and observers, has not been freedom or openness. It has been social creativity. Debased or trivial in the expedientialism of improvisation, social creativity and what it implies—comprehension, organization, and planning —have been the logic of life in the West and especially in California. It began with water, on which depended life itself. It carried forward into the massive educational system which is the true motive power of California's economy. Then, however, the social forces which it had generated outran the ability of symbol-bound residents to understand or control, and social creativity was assigned the servile task of repairing the fabric when the interests left it rent, of building freeways for social power to drive its trucks over.

California is promise and not simply despair. Yet realization of the promise depends on the ability of men to pierce the thin veil of symbol and to see the possibilities inherent in collective political action; it requires not only vision and understanding, but the resources of allegiance and loyalty necessary to bind men together against process. The Free Speech Movement, in its high moment, said as much, before it fell away into low comedy.

Yet these conditions are what produced the despair of a Nathanael West. The culture of the immigrant, reinforced by the image of the nation, could not provide the sense of past, present, and future together which is the basis of political life and loyalty. And the culture of the immigrant has possessed itself of the home and the school and finds itself reflected—for whatever reasons of their own—in the mass media. Even the new natives could break through only by accident.

One might then have relied, however, on the slow power of the land, the almost entological necessity by which biological, material, physical life undermines, intrudes on, and overthrows the world of delusive symbols and compels the generation of truer ones. Modern America, however, and modern California in particular, has found in the technological engine a means of delaying and possibly of avoiding the powers of nature. The old cults used emotion-charged will to impose their delusions on themselves and the world around them; at some dim level they always knew as much. Technology now generates the pill, the oral contraceptive or LSD, which goes further on the road to escaping that awareness altogether. The two phantasms—Huxley's and West's—find confirmation in the two pills, and the gloomy prophecies are fulfilled.

Yet nature is more cunning than men, as she has showed more than once in California. Once she fought back with the sliding earth that brought down Mulholland's dam or the great quakes which leveled cities, and she may use these weapons again. Or, as Frost suggested, she may be conjuring new weapons as yet unsuspected, which may be dangers in the extreme, but which may also be the anvils for reforging the promise of California life.

California: Its Beginnings*

JOSIAH ROYCE

I. *The Philosophy of California History
During the Golden Days*

● ● ● Two VERY familiar errors exist concerning the California of the years between 1848 and 1856, both misconceptions of the era of the struggle for order. One of these errors will have it that, on the whole, there was no struggle; while the other affirms that, on the whole, there was no order. In fact there were both, and their union is incomprehensible, save as an historical progress from lower to higher social conditions. Both the mentioned errors find support, not in authoritative pioneer evidence, but in some of the more irresponsible reminiscences of forgetful pioneers, reminiscences that express little save a desire to boast, either of the marvelous probity, or of the phenomenal wickedness, of their fellows in the early days. Many pioneers seem to assume that, save their own anecdotes, no sound records of the early days are extant. Yet the fact is that, valuable as the honest man's memory must be, to retain and convey the coloring of the minds and moods of individuals and parties, this individual memory cannot be trusted, in general, either for the details of any complex transaction, or for an account of the whole state of any large and mixed community. And one finds this especially true when one reads some

* From *California: From the Conquest in 1846 to the Second Vigilance Committee in San Francisco* (Houghton Mifflin, 1914). Used by permission of the publisher.

of these personal reminiscences of the more forgetful California pioneers. In one mood, or with one sort of experience, the pioneer can remember little but the ardor, the high aims, the generosity, the honor, and the good order of the Californian community. A few gamblers, a few foreign convicts, a few "greasers" there were, who threw shadows into the glorious picture. But they could not obscure it. On the other hand, however, another equally boastful memory revels in scenes of sanguinary freedom, of lawless popular frenzy, of fraud, of drunkenness, of gaming, and of murder. According to this memory nothing shall have remained pure: most ministers who happened to be present gambled, society was ruled by courtesans, nobody looked twice at a freshly murdered man, everybody gayly joined in lynching any supposed thief, and all alike rejoiced in raptures of vicious liberty. These are the two extreme views. You can find numbers of similarly incomplete intermediate views. . . .

But these impressions are, as individual impressions, once for all doomed to be unhistorical. The experience of one man could never reveal the social process, of which his life formed but one least element. This process, however, was after all a very simple though widely extended moral process, the struggle of society to impress the true dignity and majesty of its claims on wayward and blind individuals, and the struggle of the individual man, meanwhile, to escape, like a fool, from his moral obligations to society. This struggle is an old one, and old societies do not avoid it; for every man without exception is born to the illusion that the moral world is his oyster. But in older societies each man is conquered for himself, and is forced in his own time to give up his fool's longings for liberty, and to do a man's work as he may, while in a new society, especially in one made up largely of men who have left homes and families, who have fled from before the word of the Lord, and have sought safety from their old vexatious duties in a golden paradise, this struggle being begun afresh by all comes to the surface of things. California was full of Jonahs, whose modest and possibly unprophetic duties had lain in their various quiet paths at home. They had found out how to escape all these duties, at least for the moment, by fleeing over seas and deserts. Strange to say, the ships laden with these fugitives sank not, but bore them safely to the new land. And in the deserts the wanderers by land found an almost miraculous safety. The snares of the god were, however, none the less well laid for that, and these hasty feet were soon to trip. Whoever sought a fool's liberty here (as

which of us has not at some time sought it somewhere?) was soon
to find all of a man's due bondage prepared for him, and doubtless much more. For nowhere and at no time are social duties in
the end more painful or exacting than in the tumultuous days of
new countries; just as it is harder to work for months on a Vigilance Committee than once in a lifetime to sit on a legal jury in
a quiet town.

What we have here to do is to understand what forces worked
for and against order in this community of irresponsible strangers,
and how in time, for their lonely freedom, was substituted the long
and wearisome toil that has caused nearly all the men of that
pioneer community to die before their due season, or to live even
today, when they do live at all, the life of poverty and disappointment. Let us name at the outset these forces of order and of
disorder.

II. *The Struggle for Order*

The great cause of the growth of order in California is usually
said to be the undoubtedly marvelous political talent of our race
and nation. And yet, important as that cause was, we must not
exaggerate it. The very ease with which the state on paper could
be made lulled to sleep the political conscience of the ordinary
man, and from the outset gave too much self-confidence to the
community. The truly significant social order, which requires not
only natural political instinct, but also voluntary and loyal devotion to society, was often rather retarded than hastened in its
coming by the political facility of the people. Their greatest calam-
ities they learned to laugh at, their greatest blunders they soon
recovered from; and even while they boasted of their prowess, and
denied their sins, they would quietly go on to correct their past
grievous errors, good-humored and self-confident as ever. A people
such as this are in the long run favored of heaven, although outwardly they show little proper humility or contrition. For in time
they learn the hardest lessons, by dint of obstinate cheerfulness in
enduring their bitter experiences, and of wisdom in tacitly avoiding
their past blunders.

Against order, however, worked especially two tendencies in
early California: one [was] this aforementioned general sense of
irresponsibility, and the other a diseased local exaggeration of our
common national feeling towards foreigners, an exaggeration for
which the circumstances of the moment were partly responsible.
The first tendency pioneers admit, though not in all its true mag-

nitude; the second they seldom recognize at all, charging to the foreigners themselves whatever trouble was due to our brutal ill-treatment of them.

As for the first tendency, it is the great key to the problem of the worst troubles of early California. The new-comers, viewed as a mass, were homeless. They sought wealth, and not a social order. They were, for the most part, as Americans, decently trained in the duties of a citizen; and as to courage and energy they were picked men, capable, when their time should come for showing true manhood, of sacrificing their vain hopes, and enduring everything. But their early quest was at all events an unmoral one; and when they neglected their duties as freemen, as citizens, and as brethren among brethren, their quest became not merely unmoral, but positively sinful. And never did the journeying pillar, of cloud by day and of fire by night, teach to the legendary wanderers in the desert more unmistakably by signs and wonders the eternal law, than did the fortunes of these early Californians display to them, through the very accidents of daily life, the majesty of the same law of order and of loyalty to society. In the air, as it were, the invisible divine net of social duties hung, and descending, enmeshed irresistibly all these gay and careless fortune-hunters even while they boasted of their freedom. Every piece of neglected social work they had to do over again, with many times the toil. Every slighted duty avenged itself relentlessly on the community that had despised it.

However, in the early days, there was also that other agency at work for disorder, whose influence is to blame for much, although not for all, nor even for most, of the degradation that the new state passed through. This was a brutal tendency, and yet it was very natural, and, like all natural brutality, it was often, in any individual man, a childishly innocent tendency. It was a hearty American contempt for things and institutions and people that were stubbornly foreign, and that would not conform themselves to American customs and wishes. Representatives of their nation these gold-seeking Californian Americans were; yet it remains true, and is, under the circumstances, a very natural result, that the American had nowhere else, save perhaps as conqueror in Mexico itself, shown so blindly and brutally as he often showed in early California, his innate intolerance for whatever is stubbornly foreign. No American of sense can be proud when he reflects upon these doings of his countrymen, both towards the real foreigners and towards those who were usually confounded with such, namely,

the native Californians. Least of all can a native American Californian, like the author, rejoice to remember how the community
from which he sprang treated both their fellow-intruders in the land,
and his own fellows, the born citizens of this dear soil, themselves.
All this tale is one of disgrace to our people. But it is none the
less true, and none the less profitable to know. For this hatred of
foreigners, this blind nativism, are we not all alike born to it?
And what but reflection, and our chance measure of cultivation,
checks it in any of us?

If we leave out the unprovoked violence frequently offered to
foreigners, we may then say that the well-known crises and tragedies of violent popular justice during the struggle for order were
frequently neither directly and in themselves crimes of the community, as conservative people have often considered them, nor
yet merely expressions of righteous indignation on the part of an
innocent and outraged society; but they were simply the outward
symptoms in each case of the *past* popular crimes of disloyalty to
the social order; they were social penalties, borne by the community itself, even more than by the rogues, for the treason of carelessness.

California: Character of the Population*

MARK TWAIN

I

T WAS IN THIS Sacramento Valley, just referred to, that a deal of the most lucrative of the early gold mining was done, and you may still see, in places, its grassy slopes and levels torn and guttered and disfigured by the avaricious spoilers of fifteen and twenty years ago. You may see such disfigurements far and wide over California—and in some such places, where only meadows and forests are visible—not a living creature, not a house, no stick or stone or remnant of a ruin, and not a sound to disturb the Sabbath stillness—you will find it hard to believe that there stood at one time a fiercely flourishing little city, of two thousand or three thousand souls, with its newspaper, fire company, brass band, volunteer militia, bank, hotels, noisy Fourth of July processions and speeches, gambling halls crammed with tobacco smoke, profanity and rough bearded men of all nations and colors, with tables heaped with gold dust sufficient for the revenues of a German principality—streets crowded and rife with business—town lots worth four hundred dollars a front foot—labor, laughter, music, dancing, swearing, fighting, shooting, stabbing—a bloody inquest and a man for breakfast every morning—*everything* that delights and adorns existence—all the appointments and appurtenances of a thriving and prosperous and promising young city—and *now* nothing is left of it all but a lifeless, homeless solitude. The men are gone,

* From *Roughing It* (Harper & Row, 1962). Used by permission of the publisher.

the houses have vanished, even the *name* of the place is forgotten. In no other land, in modern times, have towns so absolutely died and disappeared, as in the old mining regions of California.

It was a driving, vigorous, restless population in those days. It was a *curious* population. It was the only population of the kind that the world has ever seen gathered together, and it is not likely that the world will ever see its like again. For, observe, it was an assemblage of two hundred thousand *young* men—not simpering, dainty kid-gloved weaklings, but stalwart, muscular, dauntless young braves, brimful of push and energy, and royally endowed with every attribute that goes to make up a peerless and magnificent manhood—the very pick and choice of the world's glorious ones. No women, no children, no gray and stooping veterans—none but erect, bright-eyed, quick-moving, strong-handed young giants—the strangest population, the finest population, the most gallant host that ever trooped down the startled solitudes of an unpeopled land. And where are they now? Scattered to the ends of the earth—or prematurely aged and decrepit—or shot or stabbed in street affrays—or dead of disappointed hopes and broken hearts—all gone, or nearly all—victims devoted upon the altar of the golden calf—the noblest holocaust that ever wafted its sacrificial incense heavenward. It is pitiful to think upon.

It was a splendid population—for all the slow, sleepy, sluggish-brained sloths stayed at home—you never find that sort of people among pioneers—you cannot build pioneers out of that sort of material. It was that population that gave to California a name for getting up astounding enterprises and rushing them through with a magnificent dash and daring and a recklessness of cost or consequences, which she bears unto this day—and when she projects a new surprise, the grave world smiles as usual and says, "Well, that is California all over."

But they were rough in those times! They fairly reveled in gold, whisky, fights, and fandangoes, and were unspeakably happy. The honest miner raked from a hundred to a thousand dollars out of his claim a day, and what with the gambling dens and other entertainments, he hadn't a cent the next morning, if he had any sort of luck. They cooked their own bacon and beans, sewed on their own buttons, washed their own shirts—blue woolen ones; and if a man wanted a fight on his hands without any annoying delay, all he had to do was to appear in public in a white shirt or a stovepipe hat, and he would be accommodated. For those people hated aristocrats. They had a particular and malignant animosity toward what they called a "biled shirt." It was a wild, free, disorderly, grotesque society! *Men*—only swarming hosts of stalwart *men*—nothing juvenile, nothing feminine visible anywhere!

In those days miners would flock in crowds to catch a glimpse of that rare and blessed spectacle, a woman! Old inhabitants tell how, in a certain camp, the news went abroad early in the morning that a woman was come! They had seen a calico dress hanging out of a wagon down at the camping ground—sign of emigrants from over the great plains. Everybody went down there, and a shout went up when an actual bona fide dress was discovered fluttering in the wind! The male emigrant was visible. The miners said:

"Fetch her out!"

He said: "It is my wife, gentlemen—she is sick—we have been robbed of money, provisions, everything, by the Indians—we want to rest."

"Fetch her out! We've got to see her!"

"But gentlemen, the poor thing, she—"

"FETCH HER OUT!"

He "fetched her out," and they swung their hats and sent up three rousing cheers and a tiger; and they crowded around and gazed at her, and touched her dress, and listened to her voice with the look of men who listened to a *memory* rather than a present reality—and then they collected twenty-five hundred dollars in gold and gave it to the man, and swung their hats again and gave three more cheers, and went home satisfied.

Once I dined in San Francisco with the family of a pioneer, and talked with his daughter, a young lady whose first experience in San Francisco was an adventure, though she herself did not remember it, as she was only two or three years old at the time. Her father said that, after landing from the ship, they were walking up the street, a servant leading the party with the little girl in her arms. And presently a huge miner, bearded, belted, spurred, and bristling with deadly weapons—just down from a long campaign in the mountains, evidently—barred the way, stopped the servant, and stood gazing, with a face all alive with gratification and astonishment. Then he said, reverently:

"Well, if it ain't a child!" And then he snatched a little leather sack out of his pocket and said to the servant:

"There's a hundred and fifty dollars in dust, there, and I'll give it to you to let me kiss the child!"

That anecdote is *true*.

But see how things change. Sitting at that dinner table, listening to that anecdote, if I had offered double the money for the privilege of kissing the same child, I would have been refused. Seventeen added years have far more than doubled the price.

And while upon this subject I will remark that once in Star City, in the Humboldt Mountains, I took my place in a sort of long, post-office single file of miners, to patiently await my chance to peep through a crack in the cabin and get a sight of the splendid new sensation—a genuine, live Woman! And at the end of half an hour my turn came, and I put my eye to the crack, and there she was, with one arm akimbo, and tossing flapjacks in a frying pan with the other. And she was one hundred and sixty-five[1] years old, and hadn't a tooth in her head.

---

[1] Being in a calmer mood, now, I voluntarily knock off a hundred from that.

What the Railroads Will Bring Us*

HENRY GEORGE

UPON THE PLAINS this season railroad building is progressing with a rapidity never before known. The two companies, in their struggle for the enormous bounty offered by the Government, are shortening the distance between the lines of rail at the rate of from seven to nine miles a day—almost as fast as the ox teams which furnished the primitive method of conveyance across the continent could travel. Possibly by the middle of next spring, and certainly, we are told, before midsummer comes again, this "greatest work of the age" will be completed, and an unbroken track stretch from the Atlantic to the Pacific.

Though, as a piece of engineering, the building of this road may not deserve the superlative terms in which, with American proneness to exaggeration, it is frequently spoken of, yet, when the full effects of its completion are considered, it seems the "greatest work of the age" indeed. Even the Suez Canal, which will almost change the front of Europe and divert the course of the commerce of half the world, is, in this view, not to be compared with it. For this railroad will not merely open a new route across the continent; it will be the means of converting a wilderness into a populous empire in less time than many of the cathedrals and palaces of Europe were building, and in unlocking treasure vaults which will flood the world with the precious metals. The country west of the longitude of Omaha, all of which will be directly or

* From *The Overland Monthly* (October, 1868).

indirectly affected by the construction of the railroad (for other roads must soon follow the first), is the largest and richest portion of the United States. Throughout the greater part of this vast domain gold and silver are scattered in inexhaustible profusion, and it contains besides, in limitless quantities, every valuable mineral known to man, and includes every variety of soil and climate.

The natural resources of this country are so great and varied, the inducements which it offers to capital and labor are so superior to those offered anywhere else, that when it is opened by railroads —placed, as it soon will be, within a few days' ride of New York, and two or three weeks' journey from Southampton and Bremen, immigration will flow into it like pent-up waters seeking their level, and states will be peopled and cities built with a rapidity never before known, even in our central West. In the consideration of the effects of this migratory movement[,] of the economical, social and political features of these great commonwealths shortly to be called into vigorous being, and of the influences which their growth will exert upon the rest of the Union and the rest of the world[,] . . . a boundless and most tempting field for speculation is opened up; but into it we cannot enter, as there is more than enough to occupy us in the narrower range suggested by the title of this article.

What is the railroad to do for *us*?—this railroad that we have looked for, hoped for, prayed for so long?

Much as the matter has been thought about and talked about . . . there are probably but few of us who really comprehend all it will do. We are so used to the California of the stage-coach, widely separated from the rest of the world, that we can hardly realize what the California of the railroad will be. . . .

The sharpest sense of Americans—the keen sense of gain, which certainly does not lose its keenness in our bracing air—is the first to realize what is coming with our railroad. All over the state, land is appreciating—fortunes are being made in a day by buying and parcelling out Spanish ranches; the Government surveyors and registrars are busy; speculators are grappling the public domain by the hundreds of thousands of acres; while for miles in every direction around San Francisco, ground is being laid off into homestead lots. The spirit of speculation, doubles, trebles, quadruples the past growth of the city in its calculations, and then discounts the result, confident that there still remains a margin. And it is not far wrong. The new era will be one of great material prosperity, if material prosperity means more people, more houses, more farms and more mines, more factories and ships. Calculations based upon the growth of San Francisco can hardly be wild. There are men now in their prime among us who will live to see this the second, perhaps the first city on the continent. This, which may sound like the sanguine utterance of California speculation, is simply a logical deduction from the past.

After the first impulse which settled California had subsided, there came a time of stagnation, if not of absolute decay. As the placers one after another were exhausted, the miners moved off; once populous districts were deserted, once flourishing mining towns fell into ruin, and it seemed to superficial observers as though the state had passed the acme of her prosperity. During this period quartz mining was being slowly developed, agriculture steadily increasing in importance, and manufactures gaining a foothold; but the progress of these industries was slow; they could not at once compensate for the exhaustion of the placer mines; and though San Francisco, drawing her support from the whole coast, continued to grow steadily if not rapidly, the aggregate population and wealth of the state diminished rather than increased. Through this period we have passed. Although the decay of portions of mining regions still continues, there has been going on for some time a steady, rapid development of the state at large—felt principally in the agricultural counties and the metropolis, but which is now beginning to make itself felt from one end of the state to the other. To produce this, several causes have combined, but prominent among them must be reckoned the new force to which we principally and primarily look for the development of the future—railroads. . . .

It is not only the metropolis that is hopeful. Sacramento, Stockton and Marysville feel the general impulse. Oakland is laying out, or at least surveying, docks which will cast those of Jersey City, if not of Liverpool, into the shade; Vallejo talks of her coming foreign commerce, and is preparing to load the grain of the Sacramento and Napa valleys into ships for all parts of the world; and San Diego is beginning to look forward to the time when she will have steam communication with St. Louis and New Orleans on the one hand, and China and Japan on the other, and be the second city on the coast. Renewed interest is being taken in mining—new branches of manufacture are being started. . . .

The new era into which our state . . . has already entered [is] without doubt an era of steady, rapid and substantial growth; of great addition to population and immense increase in the totals of

the Assessor's lists. Yet we cannot hope to escape the great law
of compensation which exacts some loss for every gain. And as
there are but few of us who, could we retrace our lives, retaining
the knowledge we have gained, would pass from childhood to
youth, or from youth into manhood, with unmixed feelings, so
we imagine that if the genius of California, whom we picture
on the shield of our state, were really a sentient being, she would
not look forward now entirely without regret.

The California of the new era will be greater, richer, more
powerful than the California of the past; but will she be still the
same California whom her adopted children, gathered from all
climes, love better than their own motherlands; from which all
who have lived within her bounds are proud to hail; to which
all who have known her long to return? She will have more people;
but among those people will there be so large a proportion of full,
true men? She will have more wealth; but will it be so evenly distributed? She will have more luxury and refinement and culture;
but will she have such general comfort, so little squalor and misery;
so little of the grinding, hopeless poverty that chills and cramps
the souls of men, and converts them into brutes?

Amid all our rejoicing and all our gratulation, let us see clearly
whither we are tending. Increase in population and in wealth past
a certain point means simply an approximation to the condition
of older countries—the eastern states and Europe. Would the average Californian prefer to "take his chances" in New York or Massachusetts, or in California as it is and has been? Is England, with
her population of twenty millions to an area not more than one-
third of our state, and a wealth which per inhabitant is six or seven
times that of California, a better country than California to live
in? Probably, if one were born a duke or a factory lord, or to any
place among the upper ten thousand; but if one were born among
the lower millions—how then?

And so the California of the future—the California of the
new era—will be a better country for some classes than the California of the present; and so too, it must be a worse country for
others. Which of these classes will be the largest? Are there more
mill owners or factory operatives in Lancastershire; more brownstone mansions, or tenement-rooms in New York?

With the tendency of human nature to set the highest value
on that which it has not, we have clamored for immigration, for
population, as though that were the one sole good. But if this be

so, how is it that the most populous countries in the world are the most miserable, most corrupt, most stagnant and hopeless? How is it that in populous and wealthy England there is so much more misery, vice and social disease than in her poor and sparsely populated colonies? If a large population is not a curse as well as a blessing, how was it that the black-death which swept off one-third of the population of England produced such a rise in the standard of wages and the standard of comfort among the people?

We want great cities, large factories, and mines worked cheaply, in this California of ours! Would we esteem ourselves gainers if New York, ruled and robbed by thieves, loafers and brothel-keepers; nursing a race of savages fiercer and meaner than any who ever shrieked a war-whoop on the plains; could be set down on our bay tomorrow? Would we be gainers, if the cotton-mills of Massachusetts, with their thousands of little children who, official papers tell us, are being literally worked to death, could be transported to the banks of the American; or the file and pin factories of England, where young girls are treated worse than ever slaves on southern plantations, be reared as by magic at Antioch? Or if among our mountains we could by wishing have the miners, men, women and children, who work the iron and coal mines of Belgium and France, where the condition of production is that the laborer shall have meat but once a week—would we wish them here?

Can we have one thing without the other? . . .

. . . [I]t is certain that the tendency of the new era—of the more dense population and more thorough development of the wealth of the state—will be to a reduction both of the rate of interest and the rate of wages, particularly the latter. This tendency may not, probably will not, be shown immediately; but it will be before long, and that powerfully, unless balanced and counteracted by other influences which we are not now considering, which do not yet appear, and which it is probable will not appear for some time yet.

The truth is, that the completion of the railroad and the consequent great increase of business and population, will not be a benefit to all of us but only to a portion. As a general rule (liable of course to exceptions) those who *have,* it will make wealthier; for those who *have not*, it will make it more difficult to get. Those who have lands, mines, established businesses, special abilities of certain kinds, will become richer for it and find increased opportunities; those who have only their own labor will become poorer, and find it harder to get ahead—first, because it will take more capital to buy land or to get into business; and second, because as competition reduces the wages of labor, this capital will be harder for them to obtain.

What, for instance, does the rise in land mean? Several things, but certainly and prominently this: that it will be harder in [the] future for a poor man to get a farm or a homestead lot. In some sections of the state, land which twelve months ago could have been had for a dollar an acre, cannot now be had for less than fifteen dollars. In other words, the settler who last year might have had at once a farm of his own, must now either go to work on wages for someone else, pay rent or buy on time; in either case being compelled to give to the capitalist a large proportion of the earnings which, had he arrived a year ago, he might have had all for himself. And as proprietorship is thus rendered more difficult and less profitable to the poor, more are forced into the labor market to compete with each other, and cut down the rate of wages. . . .

And so in San Francisco the rise in building lots means that it will be harder for a poor man to get a house and lot for himself, and if he has none that he will have to use more of his earnings for rent; means a crowding of the poorer classes together; signifies courts, slums, tenement-houses, squalor and vice. . . .

To say that "Power is constantly stealing from the many to the few," is only to state in another form the law that wealth tends to concentration. In the new era into which the world has entered since the application of steam, this law is more potent than ever; in the new era into which California is entering, its operations will be more marked here than ever before. The locomotive is a great centralizer. It kills little towns and builds up great cities, and in the same way kills little businesses and builds up great ones. We have had comparatively but few rich men; no very rich ones, in the meaning "very rich" has in these times. But the process is going on. The great city that is to be will have its Astors, Vanderbilts, Stewarts and Spragues, and he who looks a few years ahead may even now read their names as he passes along Montgomery, California or Front streets. With the protection which property gets in modern times—with stocks, bonds, burglar-proof safes and policemen; with the railroad and the telegraph—after a man gets a certain amount of money it is plain sailing, and he need take no risks. Astor said that to get his first thousand dollars was his great-

est struggle; but when one gets a million, if he has ordinary pru-
dence, how much he will have is only a question of life. Nor can
we rely on the absence of laws of primogeniture and entail to
dissipate these large fortunes so menacing to the general weal. Any
large fortune will, of course, become dissipated in time, even in
spite of laws of primogeniture and entail; but every aggregation of
wealth implies and necessitates others, and so that the aggregations
remain, it matters little in what particular hands. . . .

Nor is it worth while to shut our eyes to the effects of this
concentration of wealth. One millionaire involves the existence of
just so many proletarians. It is the great tree and the saplings over
again. We need not look far from the palace to find the hovel.
When people can charter special steamboats to take them to watering places, pay four thousand dollars for the summer rental of a
cottage, build marble stables for their horses, and give dinner parties which cost by the thousand dollars a head, we may know that
there are poor girls on the streets pondering between starvation
and dishonor. When liveries appear, look out for bare-footed children. A few liveries are now to be seen on our streets; we think
their appearance coincides in date with the establishment of the
almshouse. They are few, plain and modest now; they will grow
more numerous and gaudy—and then we will not wait long for the
children—their corollaries.

But there is another side: we are to become a great, populous,
wealthy community. And in such a community many good things
are possible that are not possible in a community such as ours has
been. There have been artists, scholars, and men of special knowledge and ability among us, who could and some of whom have
since won distinction and wealth in older and larger cities, but who
here could only make a living by digging sand, peddling vegetables
or washing dishes in restaurants. It will not be so in the San Francisco of the future. We shall keep such men with us, and reward
them, instead of driving them away. We shall have our noble
charities, great museums, libraries and universities; a class of men
who have leisure for thought and culture; magnificent theaters and
opera houses; parks and pleasure gardens.

We shall develop a literature of our own, issue books which
will be read wherever the English language is spoken, and maintain periodicals which will rank with those of the East and Europe.
The *Bulletin*, *Times* and *Alta*, good as they are, must become, or
must yield to, journals of the type of the New York *Herald* or the

Chicago *Tribune*. The railroads which will carry the San Francisco newspapers over a wide extent of country the same day that they are issued, will place them on a par, or almost on a par in point of time, with journals printed in the interior, while their metropolitan circulation and business will enable them to publish more and later news than interior papers can.

The same law of concentration will work in other businesses in the same way. The railroads may benefit Sacramento and Stockton by making them work-shops, but no one will stop there to buy goods when he can go to San Francisco, make his choice from larger stocks, and return the same day.

But again comes the question: will this California of the future . . . possess still the charm which makes Californians prefer their state, even as it is, to places where all these things are to be found?

What constitutes the peculiar charm of California, which all who have lived here long enough feel? Not the climate alone. Heresy though it be to say so, there *are* climates as good; some that on the whole are better. Not merely that there is less social restraint, for there are parts of the Union—and parts from which tourists occasionally come to lecture us—where there is much less social restraint than in California. Not simply that the opportunities of making money have been better here; for the opportunities for making large fortunes have not been so good as in some other places, and there are many who have not made money here, who prefer this country to any other; many who after leaving us throw away certainty of profit to return and "take the chances" of California. It certainly is not in the growth of local attachment, for the Californian has even less local attachment than the average American, and will move about from one end of the state to the other with perfect indifference. It is not that we have the culture or the opportunities to gratify luxurious and cultivated tastes that older countries afford, and yet those who leave us on this account as a general thing come back again.

No: the potent charm of California, which all feel but few analyze, has been more in the character, habits and modes of thought of her people—called forth by the peculiar conditions of the young state—than in anything else. In California there has been a certain cosmopolitanism, a certain freedom and breadth of common thought and feeling, natural to a community made up from so many different sources, to which every man and woman had been transplanted—all travelers to some extent, and with native angularities of prejudice and habit more or less worn off. Then there has been a feeling of personal independence and equality, a general hopefulness and self-reliance, and a certain large-heartedness and open-handedness which were born of the comparative evenness with which property was distributed, the high standard of wages and of comfort, and the latent feeling of everyone that he might "make a strike," and certainly could not be kept down long. . . .

In a country where all had started from the same level . . . social lines could not be sharply drawn, nor a reverse dispirit. There was something in the great possibilities of the country; in the feeling that it was one of immense latent wealth; which furnished a background of which a better filled and more thoroughly developed country is destitute, and which contributed not a little to the active, generous, independent social tone.

The characteristics of the principal business—mining—gave a color to all California thought and feeling. It fostered a reckless, generous, independent spirit, with a strong disposition to "take chances" and "trust to luck." Than the placer mining, no more independent business could be conceived. The miner working for himself, owned no master; worked when and only when he pleased; took out his earnings each day in the shining particles which depended for their value on no fluctuations of the market, but would pass current and supply all wants the world over. When his claim gave out, or for any reason he desired to move on, he had but to shoulder his pick and move on. Mining of this kind developed its virtues as well as its vices. If it could have been united with ownership of land and the comforts and restraints of home, it would have given us a class of citizens of the utmost value to a republican state. But the "honest miner" of the placers has passed away in California. The Chinaman, the mill-owner and his laborers, the mine superintendent and his gang, are his successors.

This crowding of people into immense cities, this aggregation of wealth into large lumps, this marshalling of men into big gangs under the control of the great "captains of industry," does not tend to foster personal independence—the basis of all virtues—nor will it tend to preserve the characteristics which particularly have made Californians proud of their state.

However, we shall have some real social gains, with some that are only apparent. We shall have more of home influences, a deeper religious sentiment, less of the unrest that is bred of an adventurous and reckless life. We shall have fewer shooting and stabbing affrays, but we will have probably something worse, from which, thank God, we have hitherto been exempt—the low, brutal, cowardly rowdyism of the great eastern cities. We shall hear less of highway robberies in the mountains, but more, perhaps, of pickpockets, burglars and sneak thieves.

That we can look forward to any political improvement is, to say the least, doubtful. There is nothing in the changes which are coming that of itself promises that. There will be a more permanent population, more who will look on California as their home; but we would not aver that there will be a larger proportion of the population who will take an intelligent interest in public affairs. In San Francisco the political future is full of danger. As surely as San Francisco is destined to become as large as New York, as certain is it that her political condition is destined to become as bad as that of New York, unless her citizens are aroused in time to the necessity of preventive or rather palliative measures. And in the growth of large corporations and other special interests is an element of great danger. Of these great corporations and interests we shall have many. Look, for instance, at the Central Pacific Railroad Company, as it will be, with a line running to Salt Lake, controlling more capital and employing more men than any of the great eastern railroads who manage legislatures as they manage their workshops, and name governors, senators and judges almost as they name their own engineers and clerks! Can we rely upon sufficient intelligence, independence and virtue among the many to resist the political effects of the concentration of great wealth in the hands of a few? . . .

With our gains and our losses will come new duties and new responsibilities. Connected more closely with the rest of the nation, we will feel more quickly and keenly all that affects it. We will have to deal, in time, with all the social problems that are forcing themselves on older communities (like the riddles of a Sphinx, which not to answer is death), with one of them, the labor question, rendered peculiarly complex by our proximity to Asia. Public spirit, public virtue, the high resolve of men and women who are capable of feeling "enthusiasm of humanity," will be needed in the future more than ever. . . .

Let us not imagine ourselves in a fool's paradise, where the golden apples will drop into our mouths; let us not think that after the stormy seas and head gales of all the ages, *our* ship has at last struck the trade winds of time. The future of our State, of our nation, of our race, looks fair and bright; perhaps the future looked so to the philosophers who once sat in the porches of Athens—to the unremembered men who raised the cities whose ruins lie south of us. Our modern civilization strikes broad and deep and looks high. So did the tower which men once built almost unto heaven.

Kearneyism in California*

JAMES LORD BRYCE

I. *The Character of California*

WHAT AMERICA is to Europe, what western America is to eastern, that California is to the other Western states. The characteristics of a new and quickly developed colonial civilization are all strongly marked. It is thoroughly American, but most so in those points wherein the Old World differs from the New. Large fortunes are swiftly made and not less swiftly spent. Changes of public sentiment are sudden and violent. The most active minds are too much absorbed in great business enterprises to attend to politics; the inferior men are frequently reckless and irresponsible; the masses are impatient, accustomed to blame everything and everybody but themselves for the slow approach of the millennium, ready to try instant, even if perilous, remedies for a present evil.

These features belong more or less to all the newer and cruder commonwealths. Several others are peculiar to California—a state on which I dwell the more willingly because it is in many respects the most striking in the whole Union, and has more than any other the character of a great country, capable of standing alone in the world. It has a superb climate, noble scenery, immense wealth in its fertile soil as well as in its minerals and forests. Nature is nowhere more imposing nor her beauties more varied.

---

* From *The American Commonwealth* (1889).

It grew up, after the cession by Mexico and the discovery of gold, like a gourd in the night. A great population had gathered before there was any regular government to keep it in order, much less any education or social culture to refine it. The wildness of that time passed into the soul of the people, and has left them more tolerant of violent deeds, more prone to interferences with, or supersessions of, regular law, than are the people of most parts of the Union.

The chief occupation of the first generation of Californians was mining, an industry which is like gambling in its influence on the character, with its sudden alternations of wealth and poverty, its long hours of painful toil relieved by bouts of drinking and merriment, its life in a crowd of men who have come together from the four winds of heaven, and will scatter again as soon as some are enriched and others ruined, or the gold in the gulch is exhausted. Moreover, mining in this region means gambling, not only in camps among the miners, but among townsfolk in the shares of the mining companies. Californians of all classes have formed the habit of buying and selling in the mining exchanges, with effects on the popular temper both in business and in politics which everyone can understand. Speculation becomes a passion, patient industry is distasteful; there is bred a recklessness and turbulence in the inner life of the man which does not fail to express itself in acts.

When California was ceded to the United States, land speculators bought up large tracts under Spanish titles, and others, foreseeing the coming prosperity, subsequently acquired great domains by purchase, either from the railways which had received land grants, or directly from the government. Some of these speculators, by holding their lands for a rise, made it difficult for immigrants to acquire small freeholds, and in some cases checked the growth of farms. Others let their land on short leases to farmers, who thus came into a comparatively precarious and often necessitous condition; others established enormous farms, in which the soil is cultivated by hired laborers, many of whom are discharged after the harvest—a phenomenon rare in the United States, which is elsewhere a country of moderately sized farms, owned by persons who do most of their labor by their own and their children's hands. Thus the land system of California presents features both peculiar and dangerous, a contrast between great properties, often appearing to conflict with the general weal, and the sometimes hard-pressed small farmer, together with a mass of unsettled labor, thrown without work into the towns at certain times of the year.[1]

Everywhere in the West the power of the railways has excited the jealousy of the people. In California, however, it has roused most hostility, because no state has been so much at the mercy of one powerful corporation. The Central Pacific Railway, whose main line extends from San Francisco to Ogden in Utah, where it meets the Union Pacific and touches the Denver and Rio Grande system, had been up till 1877, when my narrative begins, the only route to the Mississippi valley and Atlantic,[2] and therefore possessed immense influence over the trade of the whole state. It was controlled by a small knot of men who had risen from insignificance to affluence, held nearly all the other railway lines in California, employed an enormous number of clerks and workmen, and made the weight of their hand felt wherever their interest was involved. Alike as capitalists, as potentates, and as men whose rise to gigantic wealth seemed due as much to the growth of the state as to their own abilities, and therefore to come under the principle which is called in England that of the "unearned increment," they excited irritation among the farming and trading class, as well as among the laborers. As great fortunes have in America been usually won by unusual gifts, any envy they can excite is tempered by admiration for the ability shown in acquiring them. The common people felt a kind of pride in the late Mr. A. T. Stewart, and perhaps even in that flagrant "monopolist," Mr. Jay Gould. But while these particular railway magnates were men of talent, there were also in California millionaires who had grown rich merely by lucky speculation. They displayed their wealth with a vulgar and unbecoming ostentation. They did not, as rich men nearly always do in the Atlantic states, bestow a large part of it on useful public objects. There was therefore nothing to break the wave of suspicious dislike.

Most of the western states have been peopled by a steady influx of settlers from two or three older states. Minnesota, for instance, and Iowa have grown by the overflow of Illinois and Ohio, as well as by immigration direct from Europe. But California was filled by a sudden rush of adventurers from all parts of

---

[1] "Latifundia perdunt Californiam," someone said to me in San Francisco.

[2] There are now four other transcontinental trunk lines, but two of them lie far to the north, and another belongs to the same group of men who have controlled the Central Pacific.

the world. They arrived mostly via Panama, for there was no transcontinental railway till 1869, and a great many came from the southern states. This mixed multitude, bringing with it a variety of manners, customs, and ideas, formed a society more mobile and unstable, less governed by fixed beliefs and principles, than one finds in such Northwestern communities as I have just mentioned. Living far away from the steadying influences of the eastern states, the Californians have developed, and are proud of having done so, a sort of Pacific type, which, though differing but slightly from the usual western type, has less of the English element than one discovers in the American who lives on the Atlantic side of the Rocky Mountains. Add to this that California is the last place to the west before you come to Japan. That scum which the westward moving wave of emigration carries on its crest is here stopped, because it can go no farther. It accumulates in San Francisco, and forms a dangerous constituent in the population of that great and growing city—a population perhaps more mixed than one finds anywhere else in America, for Frenchmen, Italians, Portuguese, Greeks, and the children of Australian convicts abound there, side by side with Negroes, Germans, and Irish. Of the Chinese one need not speak, for, though they numbered in 1880 some twelve thousand, have a large quarter to themselves, and have given rise to the dominant question in Pacific coast politics, they do not themselves join in any political movement, but mingle as little with the whites as oil with water.

California, more than any other part of the Union, is a country by itself, and San Francisco a capital. Cut off from the more populous parts of the Mississippi valley by an almost continuous desert of twelve hundred miles, across which the two daily trains moved like ships across the ocean, separated from Oregon on the north by a wilderness of sparsely settled mountain and forest, it grew up in its own way and acquired a sort of consciousness of separate existence. San Francisco dwarfed the other cities, for in those days Los Angeles had not risen to importance, and was a commercial and intellectual center and source of influence for the surrounding regions, more powerful over them than is any eastern city over its neighborhood. It was a New York which has got no New England on one side of it, and no shrewd and orderly rural population on the other, to keep it in order. Hence both state and city were, and in a sense are still, less steadied by national opinion than any other state or city within the wide compass of the Union.

These facts in Californian history must be borne in mind in

order to understand the events I am about to sketch.[3] They show
how suited is her soil to revolutionary movements. They suggest
that movements natural here are less likely to arise in other parts
of the Union.

II. *The Sand Lot Party*

In 1877 California was suffering from "hard times." The severe
commercial depression which began in the eastern states in 1873,
and touched the lowest point about 1876, had reached the Pacific
coast, and was aggravated there by a heavy fall in mining stocks.
The great Bonanza finds some years before had ushered in a period of wild speculation. Everybody gambled in stocks, from railroad kings down to maidservants. Stocks had now fallen, and
everybody was hard hit. The railroad kings could stand their losses,
but the clerks and shop assistants and workmen suffered, for their
savings were gone and many were left heavily in debt, with their
houses mortgaged and no hope of redemption. Trade was bad,
work was scarce, and for what there was of it the Chinese, willing
to take only half the ordinary wages, competed with the white
laborer. The mob of San Francisco, swelled by disappointed miners from the camps and laborers out of work, men lured from
distant homes by the hope of wealth and ease in the land of gold,
saw itself on the verge of starvation while the splendid mansions
of speculators, who fifteen years before had kept little shops, rose
along the heights of the city, and the newspapers reported their
luxurious banquets. In the country the farmers were scarcely less
discontented. They, too, had "gone into stocks," their farms were
mortgaged, and many of them were bankrupt. They complained
that the railroads crushed them by heavy rates, and asked why
they, the bone and sinew of the country, should toil without profit,

---

[3] The narrative which follows does not profess to be complete, for the
difficulty of procuring adequate data was very great. When I visited San
Francisco in 1881, and again in 1883, people were unwilling to talk about
the Kearney agitation, feeling, it seemed to me, rather ashamed of it, and
annoyed that so much should have been made of it (more, they declared,
than it deserved) in the eastern states. When I asked how I could learn the
facts in detail, they answered, "Only by reading through the files of the
newspapers for the years 1877–80 inclusive." Some added that there were
so many lies in the newspapers that I would not have got at the facts even
then. Failing this method, I was obliged to rely on what I could pick up
in conversation. I have, however, derived some assistance from a brilliant
article by Mr. Henry George, who was then a resident of San Francisco,
in the *Popular Science Monthly* for August, 1880.

while local millionaires and wealthy eastern bondholders drew large incomes from the traffic which the plough of the agriculturist and the pickaxe of the miner had created.

Both in the country and in the city there was disgust with politics and the politicians. The legislature was composed almost wholly either of officeseekers from the city or of petty country lawyers, needy and narrowminded men. Those who had virtue enough not to be "got at" by the great corporations, had not intelligence enough to know how to resist their devices. It was a common saying in the state that each successive legislature was worse than its predecessor. The meeting of the representatives of the people was seen with anxiety, their departure with relief. Some opprobrious epithet was bestowed upon each. One was, "the legislature of a thousand drinks"; another, "the legislature of a thousand steals." County government was little better; city government was even worse. The judges were not corrupt, but most of them, as was natural, considering the scanty salaries assigned to them, were inferior men, not fit to cope with the counsel who practiced before them. Partly owing to the weakness of juries, partly to the intricacies of the law and the defects of the recently adopted code, criminal justice was halting and uncertain, and malefactors often went unpunished. It became a proverb that you might safely commit a murder if you took the advice of the best lawyers.

Neither Democrats nor Republicans had done, or seemed likely to do, anything to remove these evils or to improve the lot of the people. They were only seeking (so men thought) places or the chance of jobs for themselves, and could always be bought by a powerful corporation. Working men must help themselves; there must be new methods and a new departure. Everything, in short, was ripe for a demagogue. Fate was kind to the Californians in sending them a demagogue of a common type, noisy and confident, but with neither political foresight nor constructive talent.

Late in 1877 a meeting was called in San Francisco to express sympathy with the men on strike at Pittsburgh in Pennsylvania. Their riotous violence, which had alarmed the respectable classes all over America, had gratified the discontented railroad operatives of California, then meditating a strike of their own against a threatened reduction of wages. Some strong language used at this meeting, and exaggerated by the newspapers, frightened the business men into forming a sort of committee of public safety, with the president of the famous Vigilance Committee of 1856, a resolute and capable man, at its head. Persons enrolled by it paraded the streets with sticks for some days to prevent any attack on the Chinese, but it was soon perceived that there was no real danger, and the chief result of the incident was further irritation of the poorer classes, who perceived that the rich were afraid of them, and therefore disposed to deal harshly with them. Shortly after came an election of municipal officers and members of the state legislature. The contest, as is the custom in America, brought into life a number of clubs and other organizations, purporting to represent various parties or sections of a party, among others a body calling itself the "Workingmen's Trade and Labor Union," the secretary of which was a certain Mr. Denis Kearney. When the election was over, Kearney declared that he would keep his union going, and form a workingman's party. He was Irish by birth, and though in business as a drayman, had some experience as a sailor, and held a master's certificate. He had borne a good character for industry and steadiness till some friend "put him into stocks," and the loss of what he hoped to gain is said to have first turned him to agitation. He had gained some faculty in speaking by practice at a Sunday debating club called the Lyceum of Self Culture. A self-cultivating lyceum sounds as harmless as a social science congress, but there are times when even mutual improvement societies may be dangerous. Kearney's tongue, loud and violent, soon gathered an audience. On the west side of San Francisco, as you cross the peninsula from the harbor towards the ocean, there was then a large open space, laid out for building, but not yet built on, covered with sand, and hence called the Sand Lot. Here the mob had been wont to gather for meetings; here Kearney formed his party. At first he had mostly vagabonds to listen, but one of the two great newspapers took him up. These two, the *Chronicle* and the *Morning Call*, were in keen rivalry, and the former, seeing in this new movement a chance of going ahead, filling its columns with sensational matter, and increasing its sale among workingmen, went in hot and strong for the Sand Lot Party. One of its reporters has been credited with dressing up Kearney's speeches into something approaching literary form, for the orator was an imperfectly educated man, with ideas chiefly gathered from the daily press. The advertisement which the *Chronicle* gave him by its reports and articles, and which he repaid by advising workingmen to take it, soon made him a personage; and his position was finally assured by his being, along with several other speakers, arrested and prosecuted on a charge of riot, in respect of inflammatory speeches delivered at a meeting on the top of Nob Hill, one of the steep heights which make San Francisco the most picturesque of American cities. The prosecution failed, and Kearney was a popular hero. Clerks and the better class of citizens now began to attend his meetings, though many went from mere curiosity, as they would have gone to a circus: the W.P.C. (Workingman's Party of California) was organized as a regular party, embracing the whole state of California, with Kearney for its president. The gathering on the Sand Lot to which all those "eager for new things," as the discontented class were of old time called, flocked every Sunday afternoon to cheer denunciations of corporations and monopolists, and to "resolute" against the rich generally, became a center of San Francisco politics, and through the reports of some newspapers and the attacks of others, roused the people of the entire state. The *Morning Call* had now followed the lead of the *Chronicle*, trying to outbid it for the support of the workingmen. There was nothing positive, nothing constructive or practical, either in these tirades or in the programme of the party, but an open-air crowd is not critical, and gives the loudest cheers to the strongest language. Kearney was not without shrewdness and address: he knew how to push himself to the front, and retain the reputation of rugged honesty; he always dressed as a workman and ran for no office, and while denouncing politicians as thieves and capitalists as blood-suckers, while threatening fire and the halter if the demands of the people were not granted, he tried to avoid direct breaches of the law. On one occasion he held a gathering beside the mansions of the Central Pacific magnates on Nob Hill, pointed to them and to the bonfire which marked the place of meeting, and while telling the people that these men deserved to have their houses burned, abstained from suggesting that the torch should be applied then and there. Another time he bade the people wait a little till his party had carried their candidate for the governorship of the state: "Then we shall have the control of the militia and the armories; then we can go down to the Pacific Mail Company's dock and turn back the steamers that come in bringing the Chinese."[4] Immense enthusiasm was evoked by these harangues. He was crowned with flowers; he was, when released from prison on one occasion, drawn in triumph by his followers in his own dray; newspaper reporters thronged around to interview him; prominent

---

[4] In an earlier agitation this company's yard was attacked, but the only person killed was a lad (one of the special constables defending it) whose gun burst.

politicians came to seek favors from him on the sly. Discontent
among the working class was the chief cause that made the new
party grow, for grow it did: and though San Francisco was the
center of its strength, it had clubs in Sacramento and the other
cities, all led by the San Francisco convention which Kearney
swayed. But there were further causes not to be passed over. One
was the distrust of the officials of the state and the city. The municipal government of San Francisco was far from pure. The officials enriched themselves, while the paving, the draining, the
lighting were scandalously neglected; corruption and political job-
bery had found their way even into school management, and liquor
was sold everywhere, the publicans being leagued with the heads
of the police to prevent the enforcement of the laws. Another was
the support given to their countrymen by the Irish, here a discontented and turbulent part of the population, by the lower class
of German immigrants, and by the longshoremen, also an important element in this great port, and a dangerous element (as
long ago in Athens) wherever one finds them. The activity of the
Chronicle counted for much, for it was ably written, went everywhere, and continued to give a point and force to Kearney's
harangues, which made them not less effective in print than even
his voice had made them to the listening crowds. Some think that
the monied classes at this juncture ought to have bought up the
Chronicle (supposing they could have done so secretly), and its
then editor and proprietor had been much maligned if he would
have refused to be bought up.[5] The newspapers certainly played
a great part in the movement; they turned the workingman's party
into a force by representing it to have already become one. Most
important of all, however, was the popular hatred of the Chinese.
This was so strong in California that any party which could become its exponent rode on the crest of the wave. The old parties,
though both denouncing Chinese immigration in every convention
they held, and professing to legislate against it, had failed to check

------

[5] This editor became subsequently famous over America by his "difficulties" with a leading Baptist minister of San Francisco. He had shot this
minister in the street from behind the blind of a carriage, and thereby made
him so popular that the W. P. C. carried him for their candidate for the
mayoralty. The blood feud, however, was not settled by this unintended
service, for the clergyman's son went soon after to the *Chronicle* office and
slew the editor. The young man was tried, and, of course, acquitted. He
had only done what the customary law of primitive peoples requires. It
survives in Albania and is scarcely extinct in Corsica.

it by state laws, and had not yet obtained federal laws prohibiting it. They had therefore lost the confidence of the masses on this point, while the Sand Lot Party, whose leaders had got into trouble for the ferocity of their attacks on the Chinese, gained that confidence, and became the "anti-Mongolian" party *par excellence.* Like Cato with his *Delenda est Carthago,* Kearney ended every speech with the words, "And whatever happens, the Chinese must go."

Meanwhile, where were the old parties, and what was their attitude to this new one? It is so hard in America to establish a new movement outside the regular party lines, that when such a movement is found powerful, we may expect to find that there exist special causes weakening these lines. Such forces existed in California. She lies so far from the Atlantic and Mississippi states, and has been so much occupied with her own concerns—even the War of Secession did not interest her as it did the country east of the Rocky Mountains—that the two great national parties have had a comparatively weak hold on the people. The Chinese question and the railroad question dwarfed the regular party issues. Neither party had shown itself able to deal with the former— both parties were suspected of having been tampered with on the latter. Both had incurred the discredit which follows every party in hard times, when the public are poor, and see that their taxes have been ill-spent. The Sand Lot Party drew its support chiefly from the Democrats, who here, as in the East, have the larger share of the rabble: hence its rise was not unwelcome to the Republicans, because it promised to divide and weaken their old opponents; while the Democrats, hoping ultimately to capture it, gave a feeble resistance. Thus it grew the faster, and soon began to run a ticket of its own at city and state elections. It carried most of the city offices, and when the question was submitted to the people whether a new constitution should be framed for California, it threw its vote in favor of having one, and prevailed.

"The hoodlums"[6] and other ragamuffins who had formed the audience at the first Sand Lot meetings could not have effected this. But the W.P.C. now got a heavy vote in San Francisco from the better sort of workingmen, clerks, and small shopkeepers. In the rural districts they had still more powerful allies. The so-called

---

[6] The term "hoodlums" denotes those who are called in Australia "larrikins," and in Liverpool "corner-boys," loafing youths of mischievous proclivities.

Granger movement had spread from the upper Mississippi states into California, and enlisted the farmers in a campaign against the railroads and other "monopolists" and corporations. To compel a reduction of charges for goods and passengers, to prevent the railroad from combining with the Panama Steamship Company, to reduce public expenditure, to shift more taxation on to the shoulders of the rich, and generally to "cinch" capital—these were the aims of the Granger Party; nor will anyone who knows California think them wholly unreasonable. The only way to effect them was by a new constitution, not only because some could not have been attained under the then existing constitution (passed in 1849 and amended in several points subsequently), but also because the people have more direct control over legislation through a convention making a constitution than they have over the action of a legislature. The delegates to a convention go straight from the election to their work, have not time to forget, or to devise means of evading, their pledges, are less liable to be "got at" by capitalists. They constitute only one house, whereas the legislature has two. There is no governor to stand in the way with his veto. The rarity and importance of the occasion fixes public attention. Thus a new constitution became the object of the popular cry, and a heavy vote in favor of having it was cast by the country farmers as well as by decent working people in the towns just because it promised a new departure and seemed to get behind the old parties. As often happens, the "good citizens," who ought to have seen the danger of framing a new constitution at a time of such excitement, were apathetic and unorganized.

Next came, in the summer of 1878, the choice of delegates to the convention which was to frame the new constitution. The Workingman's Party carried many seats in the convention, but its nominees were mostly ignorant men, without experience or constructive ideas.[7] Among the lawyers, who secured a large representation, there were some closely bound by business ties to the

---

[7] Anecdotes were still current three years afterwards of the ignorance of some of the delegates. When the clause prohibiting any "law impairing the obligation of contracts" (taken from the federal Constitution) was under discussion, a San Francisco delegate objected to it. An eminent lawyer, leader of the California bar, who recognized in the objector a little upholsterer who used to do jobs about his house, asked why. The upholsterer replied, that he disapproved altogether of contracts, because he thought work should be done by hiring workmen for the day.

great corporations and therefore disposed to protect the interests of these corporations, as well as those of the legal profession. In justice to many of them it must be added that their respect for the principles of the common law and for sound constitutional doctrine made them do their best to restrain the wild folly of their colleagues. However, the workingmen's delegates, together with the more numerous and less corruptible delegates of the farmers, got their way in many things and produced the surprising instrument by which California was thereafter governed.

III. *The New Constitution*

An able Californian writer gives the following account of the constitution of 1879:

The new Constitution adopted in May, 1857, made radical changes in almost every department of the Government. It completely changed the judicial system, and thereby rendered necessary an alteration of almost all the laws relating to civil and criminal procedure. It revolutionized the working, and to a great extent the scope of the legislative department, lopping off special and local legislation, and obliging the objects heretofore obtained by such legislation to be covered by general law. As a part of this revolution, it required a new plan of county, township, and city organization, with the idea partly of forcing the same general laws upon all local governments, and partly of investing such local governments with power to legislate for themselves. But the main underlying spirit of the new instrument was an attack upon capital under the specious name of opposition to monopolies. To use an expressive Californian phrase, capital, and especially accumulated capital, wherever it was found, was to be "cinched."[8] With this object in view, cheap labor was to be driven out of the country, and corporations so restricted and hampered in their operations as to be unable to make large profits. The cry was that there were unjust discriminations on the part of the railroads, and extortionate rates on the part of water and gas companies; that vicious practices were indulged in by mining corporations; that fair day's wages for fair day's labor could not be obtained; that rich men rolled in luxury, and that poor men were cramped with want. It may be admitted that there were some grounds for these complaints. But it does not follow that capital was any more tyrannical or corporations more unconscionable than by their very nature they are compelled to be.[9]

---

[8] "Cinching" is drawing tight the girths of a horse.

[9] Mr. Theodore H. Hittell in the *Berkeley Quarterly* for July, 1880.

Some of the above points, and particularly the changes in local government and in the judicial system, lie rather outside the scope of the present narrative, and I therefore confine myself to inquiring how far the objects aimed at by the Sand Lot Party were attained through the constitution whose enactment it had secured. They and the Grangers, or farmers' party, which made common cause with them, sought to deal with four questions in which lay the grievances chiefly complained of by discontented Californians. These were—

> The general corruption of politicians, and bad conduct of state, county, and city government.
> Taxation, alleged to press too heavily on the poorer classes.
> The tyranny of corporations, especially railroads.
> The Chinese.

Let us see what remedies the constitution applied to each of these. The cry of the Sand Lot Party had been: "None but honest men for the offices." To find the honest men, and, having found them, to put them in offices and keep them there, is the great problem of American politics. The contributions made to its solution by the convention of 1879 were neither novel nor promising. Its main results may be summed up under the four heads above-mentioned.

1. It restricts and limits in every possible way the powers of the state legislature, leaving it little authority except to carry out by statutes the provisions of the constitution. It makes "lobbying," i.e., the attempt to corrupt a legislator, and the corrupt action of a legislator, felony.
2. It forbids the state legislature or local authorities to incur debts beyond a certain limit, taxes uncultivated land equally with cultivated, makes sums due on mortgage taxable in the district where the mortgaged property lies, authorizes an income tax, and directs a highly inquisitorial scrutiny of everybody's property for the purposes of taxation.
3. It forbids the "watering of stock," declares that the state has power to prevent corporations from conducting their business so as to "infringe the general well being of the State"; directs the charges of telegraph and gas companies, and of water-supplying bodies, to be regulated and limited by law; institutes a railroad commission with power to fix

the transportation rates on all railroads and examine the books and accounts of all transportation companies.
4. It forbids all corporations to employ any Chinese, debars them from the suffrage (thereby attempting to transgress the fifteenth amendment to the federal Constitution), forbids their employment on any public works, annuls all contracts for "coolie labor," directs the legislature to provide for the punishment of any company which shall import Chinese, to impose conditions on the residence of Chinese, and to cause their removal if they fail to observe these conditions.

It also declares that eight hours shall constitute a legal day's work on all public works.

When the constitution came to be submitted to the vote of the people, in May, 1879, it was vehemently opposed by the monied men, who of course influence, in respect of their wealth, a far larger number of votes than they themselves cast. Several of the conservative delegates had, I was told, abstained from putting forth their full efforts to have the worst proposals rejected by the convention in the belief that when the people came to consider them, they would ensure the rejection of the whole instrument. Some of its provisions were alleged to be opposed to the Constitution of the United States, and therefore null. Others were denounced as ruinous to commerce and industry, calculated to drive capital out of the country. The struggle was severe, but the Granger Party commanded so many rural votes, and the Sand Lot Party so many in San Francisco (whose population was then nearly a third of that of the entire state), that the constitution was carried, though by a small majority, only 11,000, out of a total of 145,000 citizens voting. Of course it had to be enacted as a whole, amendment being impossible where a vote of the people is taken.

The next thing was to choose a legislature to carry out the constitution. Had the same influences prevailed in this election as prevailed in that of the constitutional convention, the results might have been serious. But, fortunately, there was a slight reaction, now that the first and main step seemed to have been taken. The Republicans, Democrats, and Sand Lot Party all ran "tickets," and owing to this division of the workingmen's and the Granger vote between Kearneyite candidates and the Democrats, the Republicans secured a majority, though a small one. Now the Republicans are in California, as they would themselves say, the moderate and conservative party, or as their opponents said, the party of the rich and the monopolists. Their predominance made the legislature of 1880 a body more cautious than might have been expected. Professing hearty loyalty to the new constitution, the majority showed this loyalty by keeping well within the letter of that instrument, while the workingmen and farmer members were disposed to follow out by bold legislation what they called its spirit. Thus the friends and the enemies of the constitution changed places. Those who had opposed it in the convention posed as its admirers and defenders; while those who had clamored for and carried it now began to wish that they had made its directions more imperative. The influence and the money of the railroad and the other great corporations were of course brought into play, despite the terrors of a prosecution for felony, and became an additional "conservative force" of great moment.

Thus a series of statutes was passed which gave effect to the provisions of the constitution in a form perhaps as little harmful as could be contrived, and certainly less harmful than had been feared when the constitution was put to the vote. Many bad bills, particularly those aimed at the Chinese, were defeated, and one may say generally that the expectations of the Sand Lot men were grievously disappointed.

While all this was passing, Kearney had more and more declined in fame and power. He did not sit either in the constitutional convention or in the legislature of 1880. The mob had tired of his harangues, especially as little seemed to come of them, and as the candidates of the W.P.C. had behaved no better in office than those of the old parties. He had quarrelled with the *Chronicle*. He was, moreover, unfitted by knowledge or training to argue the legal, economical, and political questions involved in the new constitution, so that the prominence of these questions threw him into the background. An anti-Chinese agitation, in which the unemployed marched about San Francisco, calling on employers to discharge all Chinese workmen, caused some alarm in the winter of 1879–80, but Kearney was absent at the time, and when he returned his party was wavering. Even his prosecution and imprisonment on a rather trivial charge gave only a brief revival to his popularity. The W.P.C. was defeated in a city election in March, 1880, by a combination of the better class of Democrats with the Republicans, and soon after expired.

When I was in San Francisco in the fall of 1881, people talked of Kearney as a spent rocket. Some did not know whether he was in the city. Others said that the capitalists had rendered him harmless by the gift of a new dray and team. Not long afterwards he went East, and mounted the stump on behalf of the Labor party in New York. He proved, however, scarcely equal to his fame, for mob oratory is a flower which does not always bear transplantation. Though he lived till 1906, he was never again a leading figure in Californian politics, and was, indeed, in 1883, no longer deemed a force to be regarded. And now, as the Icelandic sagas say, he is out of the story. . . .

Honest Men and Grafters*

GERTRUDE ATHERTON

ALL THINGS BEING relative, San Francisco for some fifteen or twenty years after the housecleaning given it by the Vigilance Committee of 1856 was a peaceful and decent city. But, as ever, its citizens ceased to be alert to any but their personal affairs, particularly during the Comstock madness; and, logically, the body politic, unprotected by renewed vaccination, fell an easy prey to the insidious and venomous microbes of the underworld; and before the city realized that its system was even relaxed, "run down," it had broken out virulently in several places. Nor did the hostile swarms confine their activities to the police, the professional politician, the municipal organs generally; eminent citizens were infected—and they are still fumigating themselves.

Following the denunciations of the Sand-Lotters, which no one attempted to refute in toto, there was a reaction in favor of the upper classes, owing to the intemperate excesses of the W.P.C. and the new constitution they were instrumental in foisting upon California. But in the course of the next fifteen years many besides the proletariat were awake and alarmed at the dangers threatening the city. The Wallace grand jury was impaneled in August, 1891. The exposures of this body, after investigations made under the

---

greatest difficulties, so securely were the malefactors intrenched, proved a system of wholesale bribery and corruption by corporations, legislators, and supervisors.

For some years San Francisco had been dominated by "bosses," the most notorious and shameless of whom was "Blind" Boss Buckley. (The others are too contemptible for more than a passing mention.) All of them, and Buckley in particular, were experts in every form of extortion, oppression, and demoralization of their army of human tools. The investigations of the Wallace grand jury startled complacent San Francisco, and Buckley fled to return no more; but there was little improvement in conditions until another sudden awakening of the civic conscience swept Mr. James D. Phelan into the mayor's chair in 1897.

One of the crying needs of San Francisco was a new charter granting enlarged powers to the mayor, for the exercise of which he would be directly responsible. As the case stood he might be an angel of light, but his hands were tied; the legislature passed nearly all laws for San Francisco, and behind that august body of sea-green incorruptibles the "machine" could hide and shift responsibility as it listed.

Mr. Phelan at once appointed a committee of one hundred citizens to draft a charter; and, what was more to the point, he put it through. It provided for a responsible government, civil-service reform, and home rule, and declared for municipal ownership of those public utilities, light, water, transportation, so preyed upon and debauched by the municipal council, which had the power to fix the rates.

Mr. Phelan was mayor of San Francisco for five years, and, in the estimation of any impartial student of that politics-ridden town, was the ablest and most energetic in her annals. It would be an insult to add that he was honest if he were not a San Franciscan, and the temptation to do so is irresistible, because California officials who are able, energetic, and honest are so rare that they should have at least plaster statues while alive; to be bronzed over or not, as an impartial and discriminating posterity shall advise.

Mr. Phelan stood firmly with the people against the bosses, exposed the fraudulent specifications of the lighting monopoly, and saved the people three hundred thousand dollars a year; defended the city from pillage at the hands of the supervisors, among other amounts, diverting two million dollars from reaching their itching

palms by "blocking jobs"; raised the standard of the pay of laborers in the city's employ; and gave back to San Francisco in public
gifts many times his salary as mayor.

Our rich men of late years have been so culpably negligent of
San Francisco's interests, so long as their own have prospered,
that too much emphasis cannot be laid upon Mr. Phelan's sleep-
less and practical concern for his city, quite apart from his munif-
icent donations and his unostentatious help to so many in private
life, and his presentation to the city of the best of its statues. His
father made the fortune which he inherited and doubled, and if
he had chosen to devote all his energies to business, or even if it
had been his disposition to loaf, no one would have been surprised
or critical. Nor, oddly enough, would he have made one-tenth of
the enemies he accumulated while striving to clean up San Francisco. If he had been poor and originally obscure he would have
been forgiven, for Americans seem to understand and forgive ambition and public efforts in the impecunious; but in new communities, at least, symptoms of civic decency in a rich man are
regarded with alarm as a new and mysterious germ which may
prostrate the entire order. When the symptoms develop into aggression they are for stamping the traitor out of existence. All
sorts of mean motives are ascribed to him, the press sneers and
vilifies, he falls a victim to the cartoonist, and only his friends
and solid money respect him. If he survives and pursues his un-
deviating way this phenomenon is due to two causes only: his
staying-powers and the basic common sense of the American people. As Abraham Lincoln once remarked, "You can fool, etc."

During the last two years of Mr. Phelan's incumbency there
were serious labor troubles. Capital assumed a hostile attitude to
large bodies of workingmen striking not only for more pay, but
for recognition of the union; and labor in turn becoming still more
hostile, the two camps, even after the "Teamsters' Strike" was
settled, remained armed and bristling. The result was the rise of
Abraham Ruef and his creature, Eugene E. Schmitz.

Ruef was a little ferret-faced, black-eyed French Jew, of abilities so striking that he could have become one of the most re-
spected and useful citizens in the history of San Francisco had he
not deliberately chosen the "crooked" role. Sentimentalists cannot
argue in Ruef's case that "he never had a chance." He was of
well-to-do parents, he finished his education at the University of
California, graduated into the law, and had a lucrative practice
from the beginning. But although his worst personal indulgence

was "candy," he was one of the most innately vicious men this country has spawned, and one of the most destructive incubated by poor San Francisco.

The stiff-necked attitude of the Employers' Organization, which denied labor's right to unionize, gave Ruef his opportunity. He skilfully engineered his friend Schmitz, an imposing, bluff, and hearty person, and a real man of the people, having been a fiddler in a local opera company, into the mayor's chair with little or no difficulty. The class line was as sharply drawn as the earthquake fault, and the proletariat and his sympathizers outnumbered the others and voted with entire independence of party lines. They wanted a labor–union man; to his bias otherwise they were indifferent. This fine figurehead at the prow, Ruef began to build up his machine.

The board of supervisors during the first two years of the Schmitz incumbency continued to be the decent men natural to Mr. Phelan's administration; for even Ruef, with his brilliant if distorted talents for organization, could not upset the work of an honest mayor as quickly as he had hoped. But he went on fomenting class hatred to his own advantage and that of Schmitz, and simultaneously they grew rich by grafting on vice, forcing that class of establishments euphemistically known in San Francisco as "French restaurants" to pay an enormous tribute, under threat of revocation of license.

When in the elections of 1905 Schmitz was found to have lost strength with the Labor–union party, always prone to fickleness and suspicion, and to have polled a heavy vote in capitalistic districts, citizens shrugged their shoulders and "guessed" that the stories of the Ruef–Schmitz machine, holding up corporations and rich men for large sums before granting franchises, were true. The *Evening Bulletin,* true to its traditions, and edited by Fremont Older, of the genuine militant brand, had been thundering for some time against the police board and the administrative boards of the machine, which were making no visible use of the money raised by taxation for specific purposes. The police board could be bought by any violator of the law who came to it with the price in his hand. But the result of the elections furnished Mr. Older with new and forked lightning; the heavy vote polled for Schmitz was in the wrong quarter, and the board of supervisors were Ruef's tools, chosen from the dregs of the workingclass, men with no inherited ideals to give them moral stamina, and utterly unable to resist temptation in the form of the large sum that would

fall to each after Ruef and Schmitz, having "gouged" some impatient corporation, had divided the lion's share. Then once more
the citizens of San Francisco "sat up," awake to the new perils
that threatened their battered city.

But although the Ruef–Schmitz machine looked as formidable
as an invading horde of locusts in Kansas, and grew more arrogant
every day, more contemptuous of public opinion, it had its weak
spots. Ruef in January, 1906, made the irretrievable blunder of
putting an honest man in office. Apprehending that Schmitz was
losing his hold on the Labor–union party, he permitted William
A. Langdon, superintendent of schools, and possessing a large
following in labor circles, to be elected district attorney. When he
made the discovery that Mr. Langdon was quite honest and nobody's creature, his amazement and wrath would have been ludi-
crous if they had not been pathetic.

No sooner had Mr. Langdon taken the oath of office than he
began a series of raids on the various gambling institutions which
paid a heavy tribute to the machine but flourished nevertheless.

Of course, San Francisco has always been a gambling city.
It is in the marrow and braincells of her people, whether their
blood ancestors were "Forty-niners" or not, and as there is no
evil out of which good may not come, it is the source of their
superb powers of bluff, their unquenchable optimism, and their
indomitability under the most harrowing afflictions. When, after
the earthquake and fire of 1906, the world was startled to learn
that the people of San Francisco were planning to rebuild before
the ashes were cold, David Belasco said to a reporter, "The Californians are bully gamblers!"

Therefore, when Mr. Langdon made it manifest that he pur-
posed to put an end to the industrial manifestation of the race
spirit, there was not only a terrific howl from his victims, but the
well-regulated citizens themselves were amazed. Mr. Langdon,
however, paid as little attention to one as to the other. He brought
down the heavy hand of the law on the Emeryville racetrack (the
most sordid and wholly abominable in the West), and upon the
slotmachine, that lucrative partner of the saloon and the cigar-
stand. In the ordinary course of events he would be crippled for
funds; legal investigation and prosecution were necessary, and the
coffers of the city were in the robber stronghold. But Ruef had
discovered some time since that there was another dark cloud on
his horizon and that in the middle of it was a star. And while the

star directed a cold and hostile gleam on Mr. Ruef, it was the bright hope of the district attorney.

Rudolph Spreckels it was who proved to be the nemesis of Ruef. This very remarkable young man had left his father's roof when a boy of nineteen, taking the part of a brother whom he believed to be a victim of parental injustice. Then he proceeded to make his own fortune; and, having that special group of brain-cells which constitute the talent for making money, he was, in the course of a few years, one of the richest men in the community. Until 1903 business and the enjoyment of life in a quiet way occupied him fully, but by Abraham Ruef—unwitting savior of his city!—his eyes were opened to the needs and perils of San Francisco.

Ruef, with the serene confidence of the congenitally corrupt that every man has his price, approached the young financier with a particularly abominable plan for enriching himself at the expense of the city, and Mr. Spreckels suddenly woke up. His enlightenment was completed by Mr. Phelan and Fremont Older. He applied himself to a thorough study of existing civic conditions, and was horrified to discover that for viciousness and general rottenness San Francisco could vie proudly with the worst cities of ancient or modern history.

He was emphatically the man for the hour. He was young, rich, energetic, honorable, implacable, ruthless, and tenacious. Mr. Phelan could help him with advice and money, but he had made too many enemies among the grafters of all classes during his five years as mayor to be an effective leader. Mr. Spreckels was greeted as a sort of knight of the Holy Grail; for in the beginning, when his sole intention was to crush the Ruef–Schmitz machine and imprison its chiefs and tools, he was acclaimed by even that capitalistic class that later accused him of every contemptible motive and trait revealed in the course of human history.

Ruef also made his investigations and discovered that Mr. Spreckels had built his fortune honestly, and was, therefore, unbribable. This, of course, was before 1906, and when the anachronistic Mr. Langdon grasped the reins carelessly tossed him by the idol of the Labor party, it became immediately apparent that if the machine would not furnish the money for the investigations and reforms Mr. Spreckels would. Moreover, Mr. Phelan, Mr. Older, and Mr. Spreckels had secured the services of Attorney Francis J. Heney, and induced President Roosevelt to give them the services of Detective Burns, then employed by the United States.

Then came the earthquake and fire of April, 1906. The reader may remember that old melodrama, "The Silver King," and the escaping convict who, watching the train on which he had escaped blazing from end to end with its imprisoned victims—he being almost the only survivor—falls on his knees and thanks God. Picture Mr. Ruef as he watched San Francisco burning. The crippled millionaires, including Mr. Phelan and Mr. Spreckels, would be occupied with their own affairs for years to come. He and Schmitz were free. So profound a student of human nature was Mr. Ruef.

An hour or two after the earthquake, when it became apparent that a large part of San Francisco would burn, the pipes of the water system being broken and thirty fires having started simultaneously, Mr. Downey Harvey, a grandson of the "War Governor," John G. Downey, and himself a citizen of wealth and influence, went down to Mayor Schmitz's office and suggested that immediate measures be taken for the protection of the city and the relief of the homeless—who were already fleeing to the Presidio and the hills beyond the city. Everybody on that terrible day was either at a pitch above the normal or hopelessly demoralized. Schmitz, being a musician, had a temperament; consequently he was in the upper register. Morally supported by the "Committee of Fifty" that he called together at Mr. Harvey's suggestion, he proved himself as admirable an administrative officer as if life had groomed him to be a symbol of all the civic virtues. In truth, he was a weak man of good intentions, but putty in the hands of a man like Ruef.

Mr. Phelan, during the first day or two, was busy in actual rescue work and in carrying dynamite in his car for the purpose of blowing up buildings—a vain attempt to prevent the spread of the fire. But he was elected chairman of the Citizens' Finance Committee, and to him as great a compliment was paid as to Mr. Coleman in 1878. Congress voted a million and a half dollars for the relief of San Francisco, but hesitated to send it via Ruef–Schmitz. When, however, President Roosevelt was informed that Mr. Phelan had been made chairman of the Citizens' Finance Committee, he sent him the money personally. The President also issued a proclamation directing the people of the United States to send their contributions to Mr. Phelan, chairman of the Citizens' Finance Committee; and the corporation growing out of this committee received all the supplies and approximately $10,000,000 in money.

Mr. Phelan as well as Mr. Spreckels and Mr. Harvey, and all the other men on the committee, neglected their private affairs for months, and the refugees were housed on the hillsides either in tents or cottages, fed, clothed, and generally taken care of. Ruef accepted the temporary domination of the committee with apparent philosophy, and himself opened an office just beyond the burned district, obviously adjusting matters for his legal clients. In reality he was looting right and left, preying upon the women of commerce, the bootblacks, the newsboys, the small shopkeepers, upon every class, in fact, to which his tentacles had reached during the years of his autocracy.

But Mr. Spreckels did not forget him nor his ultimate object for a moment. Heney, when he promised his services, was still engaged in exposing the Oregon land frauds, but he was free in June. Then he came to town, and with him Detective Burns. This was only two months after the disaster; but although Ruef was surprised, he was not particularly apprehensive; he did not believe that they could make any headway in the existing conditions.

In October sufficient evidence of extortion in the matter of the French restaurants had been accumulated to warrant District Attorney Langdon announcing that a general investigation would begin at once. He appointed Mr. Heney assistant district attorney.

This was six months after the earthquake. Men never alluded to it any more. The women still talked nothing but earthquake and fire; but the men talked only insurance and rebuilding. They went about dressed in khaki and topboots, exhilarated by the tremendous call upon their energies, and with all the old pioneer spirit reincarnated and intensified by the consciousness that they were about to build a great city, not merely using its site while "making their pile" to dissipate at a gambling-table or carry elsewhere. And this time they wanted a decent city. Schmitz, resting on his labors, had gone to Europe, and they had no intention of reelecting him.

Ruef was thoroughly frightened. But he was ever a man of resource; he suddenly played one of the boldest coups in the history of any city. Mr. Langdon was off campaigning for the governorship; T. H. Gallagher, president of the board of supervisors, was acting mayor, and, of course, a creature of the Chief. He was ordered to remove Langdon from the district-attorneyship on the

ground of neglect of duty and appoint Abraham Ruef. The city
held its breath and then emitted a roar of indignation; it was quite
patent that San Francisco was not as selfishly absorbed as Mr.
Ruef had believed. The impudence of this plot to dictate the personnel of the proposed grand jury may be the better understood
when it is remembered that the city had just been informed officially of Mr. Ruef's iniquities and that he would be subjected to
prosecution. But this attempt to balk justice was summarily defeated; Judge Seawell, of the Superior Court, held that as the
district attorney represented the people as a whole, the mayor had
no jurisdiction over him.

After this events proceeded rapidly. On November 10 Judge
Thomas F. Graham appointed a grand jury to investigate the con-
dition of the city. It was known as the Oliver grand jury, Mr. B. F.
Oliver having been elected foreman. The other members were:
Maurice Block, C. G. Burnett, Jeremiah Deasy, Dewey Coffin,
Frank A. Dwyer, E. J. Gallagher, James E. Gordon, Alfred Greene-
baum, Morris A. Levingston, Rudolph Mohr, W. P. Redington,
Ansel C. Robinson, Christian P. Rode, Mendle Rothenberg, F. G.
Sanborn, Charles Sonntag, Herman H. Young, Wallace G. Wise.

It will be observed that five members of the Oliver grand jury
were of the same race as Ruef; in fact, practically every denomi-
nation was represented. Many of these men had close affiliations
in the social and business world with "eminent citizens" they were
forced later on to indict; but never did an investigating body do its
work more thoroughly and impersonally.

Like Mr. Spreckels, they met with encouragement at first, their
original and avowed purpose being to "get" Ruef, Schmitz, and
the supervisors, without whose consent no franchise could be
obtained.

It had been common talk for at least two years that every man
and corporation with capital to invest or some new industry to
launch was "held up" by the board of supervisors before they
could proceed. Capital of every sort was grafted upon the moment
it sought new outlets, and rich men in condoling with one another
had ceased to comment upon the miseries of San Francisco in general. Therefore, the Oliver grand jury, as well as Mr. Heney and
Detective Burns, thought that it would be an easy matter to obtain
affidavits from these distinguished victims which would go far
toward convicting the malefactors. At that time they had not a
thought of prosecuting the "higher-ups." But, to their amazement,
the rich men, individually and collectively, swore that they never

had been approached, never had paid a cent of graft money. In the terminology of the hour, they refused to "come through." It looked as if the grand jury could not gather evidence enough to convict the machine of anything but the tribute levied on vice.

Then it was that Mr. Heney and Mr. Burns and his detectives changed their tactics. They offered immunity to the supervisors if they would give the information necessary to convict not the bribed, but the bribers. They agreed, and the grand jury was enabled to find indictments not only against Ruef and Schmitz, but against Patrick Calhoun, president of the United Railroads, and his manager, Thornwall Mullaly; the finance committee of the San Francisco Gas and Electric Company; the agent of the Parkside Realty Company; the Home Telephone; the Pacific Telephone, and the Prize-fight Trust.

It is only possible here to give a brief account of the two principal trials. To quote from the Denman report:

The supervisors' testimony gave the grand jury the facts as to the passing of the ordinances, the payment of the money by Gallagher to various supervisors, and the payment of the money from Ruef to Gallagher. The chain of evidence, however, stopped at Gallagher's testimony that Ruef paid him the money in all but the Pacific Coast Telephone briberies, and no further evidence was discovered against the mayor in connection with the French restaurant extortions. The question then arose as to the advisability of treating with Ruef to secure the evidence as to the method by which the moneys came from the quasi-public corporations . . . it became apparent that without this man's testimony the many bribe-givers whose enrichment by the large profits of such undertakings made them equally if not more dangerous to society, would not only escape the penalty which was their due, but that even their names would not be discovered and written in the "detinue book" of the city's suspicious characters. Besides, without Ruef's assistance, the conviction of Schmitz, with the resultant change in the mayoralty, the police, and other muncipal boards, seemed impossible. The district attorney had his choice in this dilemma. He could leave the mayor and his administrative boards in power, discover nothing regarding the profit-takers from briberies, and content himself with a mere change in the supervisors and a long term of imprisonment for Ruef, or he could reasonably expect the conviction of the mayor, the cleaning up of the city government, the obtaining of a complete revelation of the grafters "high up" as well as the "low down," and the possible conviction of some of them. The district attorney chose the latter alternative and bargained with Ruef. . . . A written contract was finally signed whereby Ruef agreed to tell fully and unreservedly all he knew of the briberies and to plead guilty to certain of the French restaurant extortion cases, and the district attorney agreed to use the power of his office to procure him immunity as to the other charges.

Complete immunity never was promised.

Schmitz was tried and found guilty on Ruef's testimony, and convicted on June 13, 1907. He was subsequently released on a technicality. Although Ruef had pleaded guilty to accepting bribes during his own trial, he also escaped the penalty under the decision which freed Schmitz.

Sixteen supervisors had confessed to receiving bribe-money from their president, Gallagher, who, of course, confessed that he got it from the Chief. Ruef was again indicted and made desperate efforts to escape prosecution, including a change of venue. All devices failing, he ran away. His friends, the sheriff, the coroner, and the police force failed to find him, but an elisor named by the court unearthed him. It was then that he bargained with the district attorney.

But Ruef, after promising to "come through" (in which case he would have been prosecuted for the French restaurant cases alone), fell into a panic as he reflected upon the condign punishment sure to be visited upon him did he betray his powerful associates; he resolved not to "snitch"—to quote once more from the elegant vocabulary of the moment—and attempted to pretend confession while admitting nothing.

But Heney was far more agile of mind than the now distracted Ruef. He caught him lying and exposed him. The immunity was canceled, and he was brought to his second trial in the bribery transactions, August 26, 1908. These trials—financed by Rudolph Spreckels—were conducted in Carpenter's Hall in Fulton Street, just beyond the burnt district, and before Judge Lawlor.

The chief witness against Ruef was the president of the board of supervisors, T. H. Gallagher. On April 29, 1908, his house in Oakland was wrecked by dynamite, but the witness whose life was sought survived and gave his testimony. The man who placed the bomb testified that he was employed by a henchman of Ruef.

This attempt at murder had been preceded by the kidnapping of Fremont Older, whose thunders in the *Bulletin* had never ceased. Naturally, statements crept into those inflammatory columns that were not wholly substantiated. One day Mr. Older accidentally printed a libel. He made amends on the following day, but he had given the enemies of the prosecution one of the chances for which they had been lying in wait. The libeled man had Mr. Older indicted in Los Angeles. Mr. Older ignored the summons, knowing well that if he went to Los Angeles he would remain there until the trials were over.

On October 27, 1907, he was lured by a false telephone message into a quiet street and forced, by several men, into an automobile, which dashed through and out of the city. The muzzle of a "gun" was pressed against Mr. Older's side; but he was wise enough not to struggle. A southbound train was boarded at a way-station, and Mr. Older shut up in a drawing room. One of the kidnappers was an attorney for the United Railroads, R. Porter Ashe, a son of the Dr. Ashe, friend of Terry and other "Law and Order" men of 1856, who so bitterly opposed the Vigilance Committee.

The plot did not succeed. The hue and cry was raised by suspicious friends in San Francisco, and Mr. Older and his kidnappers were traced. The authorities in Santa Barbara were appealed to, and when the train arrived in the morning the party was commanded to appear in court, and Mr. Older was released. The net result of this episode was the "reform" of the spelling of the word "kidnapped," which, as may be imagined, was overworked. It is now spelt—and presumably pronounced—by the California press, kid*naped*.

In November, 1908, an attempt was made on the life of Mr. Heney. The San Francisco newspapers, with the exception of the *Bulletin* and the *Call*, by this time were indulging in furious attacks on the various members of the prosecution, and upon Heney in particular. The attacks were necessarily personal, as they would not have dared to defend Ruef, even had they been so inclined, but no doubt they were actuated by fear that Heney's hectoring methods would surprise the names of the "higher-ups" from the defiant Ruef, now in his third trial. Their diatribes, assisted by cartoons, were held responsible for the attempted murder of the assistant district attorney; but the general opinion is that the man was a hired assassin. His name was Haas. There was little doubt that attempts were being made to "fix" the jury; and, as this man had boasted that he soon would be able to live in luxury, Heney succeeded in getting him off the third jury by exposing the fact that Haas had sojourned in a State's prison for forgery. He was altogether a miserable specimen of humanity. On the 13th of November he slipped up behind Mr. Heney in the crowded courtroom and fired a pistol-bullet into his head, just before his right ear.

Heney's mouth happened to be open. The ball passed between the skull and jaw and exhausted its strength in the soft lining at the back of the mouth, finally lodging in the bone of the jaw on the opposite side.

There was great excitement in Fulton Street that day. The old-time crowds were there, wrought up to the point of hysteria, and there was much speechmaking and talk of lynching. But it ended in no overt attempt to frustrate the law, and Haas meanwhile had been rushed to jail in an automobile. When searched, no other weapon was discovered, but that night he was found dead from a derringer wound in his head. Whether the derringer had been concealed in his shoe or whether it had been passed to him in his cell with orders to use it, or whether he was murdered, will probably never be known. He certainly knew too much to be permitted to stand the "third degree."

Heney was ill from the shock, although his only permanent disability was deafness in one ear. The prosecution of the Ruef case was continued by Matt I. Sullivan and Hiram Johnson, one of the ablest lawyers in San Francisco, and in full sympathy with the prosecution.

Probably Ruef himself was not more astonished, when he actually was convicted and sentenced to fourteen years in the penitentiary, than San Francisco, so long accustomed to the miscarriage of "justice," particularly when the prosecuted was a rich man. But Ruef, at least, was out of the way.

The next sensational trial was that of Patrick Calhoun, a gentleman of variegated record, handsome appearance, and fascinating personality, who had honored San Francisco with his citizenship for several years and was now president of the United Railroads. There is no space to devote to this trial, which was spun out over many weary months. He wanted an overhead trolley system, and obtained the franchise from the Ruef–Schmitz machine. His best friends never denied in private conversation that he had paid over at least two hundred thousand dollars, although he denied the charges in toto when, after indictment by the grand jury, he was brought before the bar. Witnesses disappeared, the jurymen were bribed, and copies of the reports of the government's detectives were stolen. It was impossible to convict him legally.

The bringing of Calhoun to trial was the signal for a disruption of society rivaling that caused by the Civil War. So many of the men whose families composed society were in danger of a similar indictment that they naturally herded together; and Mr.

Calhoun being a social ornament, the wives were as vehement in his support as their husbands. Mrs. Spreckels, who enjoyed a brilliant position at Burlingame, the concentrated essence of California society, suddenly found herself an outsider. So did Mrs. Heney, who was a member of one of the old southern families. Mr. Phelan also was ostracised; and the few people of wealth and fashion that stood by the prosecutors were for a time in a similar plight. One wife of a suspected millionaire and personal friend of Calhoun went so far as to demand the politics of her guests as they crossed her threshold. And among all there was a bitterness unspeakable.

But although Calhoun could not be convicted, nor the few others that were brought to trial, the prosecution at least accomplished a moral fumigation. The first evidence of this was the election to the mayoralty, after the deposition of Schmitz, of Dr. Edward Robeson Taylor. The second was the triumphant personal campaign for governor of Hiram Johnson. The whole state had followed the trials, condemned the grafters, and made up its mind to elect the best men to office. Of course, that high pitch of enthusiasm does not last; and as Dr. Taylor refused to build up a machine of decent men, the next mayor was an objectional person named P. H. McCarthy. He disgusted the Labor party, however, and they helped to elect Mr. Rolph, the present mayor, with whom all parties are as satisfied as they ever are with any one.

The most interesting event which followed the graft prosecutions and their direct results was the passing of the Woman's Suffrage Bill in 1911. Conservative people and the liquor trust fought the campaign successfully in San Francisco; but the women, who had taken motors and visited practically every farmer and hamlet in the state, won with the country vote. What changes they will make in the moral conditions of the state remain to be seen, but there is no question that the campaign and its encouraging result have awakened the minds of the California women and developed them intellectually. They read better books, take an interest in public questions, quite ignored before, are making constant attempts to improve the condition of the poor women and children; and at the San Francisco Center of the Civic League some great or pressing question of the day is discussed by the best authorities obtainable. Its weekly meetings are patronized by hundreds of women, and all men invited have long since found it quite worth their while to attend.

California, cleaned up as thoroughly as may be, is flourishing and happy, secure in the fact that with her enormous grain supply

and orchards and vineyards and cattle ranges, her thousand healing springs, she never can go bankrupt, no matter how hard the
times, and that her perennial beauties will bring many hundreds
of thousands of dollars into the state annually: the tourist never
deserts California, and her winter cities in the south are always
crowded by the people of the eastern states that dread the cold
of their own winters, and by those from the mountain states of the
Northwest, who long for sea air and low altitudes. No matter what
happens in the world beyond the Rocky Mountains or the Pacific
Ocean, her orange groves bear their yellow fruit, her skies are
bluer than Italy's, her people are idle and luxurious and happy in
the warm abundant south, or bustling, energetic, and keenly alive
in San Francisco—which is no more California than Paris is France.
She is the permanent resort of cranks, and faddists, and extremists,
and professional agitators and loafers, but they are in the minority
despite their noise. As a whole the state is one of the most de-
pendable, patriotic, and honorable in the Union, and has produced
great personalities, eminent and good men, and brilliant and gifted
minds out of all proportion to her age. May the fools and extremists never wreck her!

CHAPTER II

❧

POLITICS
ON THE EDGE
OF THE WORLD

EPIC, or Politics for Use*

LUTHER WHITEMAN AND SAMUEL L. LEWIS

By 1933, California at last knew there was a depression, although it is doubtful if the actual physical suffering and malnutrition were as great in the Golden State as elsewhere. One does not die of cold in California; recorded cases of actual starvation were few; homeless men who poured into the state at the approach of winter constructed shacks from old boards and tin cans at the edge of every city dumpheap; food of some sort was usually available. Citizens were more than usually sympathetic and generous, and the charitable organizations and county and city welfare bureaus did their best.

On the other hand the foreclosures of mortgages and the tax sales reached terrifying numbers, particularly upon ranches and homes in the southern part of the state. These foreclosures aroused the citizenry to desperation. It was not so much the sufferings of the working class, employed or unemployed, that really gave rise to Upton Sinclair's EPIC as it was these foreclosures, although in Los Angeles County, at the time of EPIC's nativity, half a million people were on relief. Sinclair states that in the first four months of 1933 Los Angeles county relief agencies took on 63,000 new persons as objects of charity. In the months of May, June and July, there was added another 75,000, with each case involving 4.3 persons—322,500 new dependents upon charity. A very large

---

* From *Glory Roads* (Thomas Y. Crowell Co., 1936). Used by permission of the publisher.

proportion of these were of the whitecollar class, were or had been small property owners. Under the iniquitous terms of the trust-deed laws of the state, almost nine thousand foreclosures were made in Los Angeles county in the first seven months of 1933, of property valued at more than $52,000,000. This showing was worse for Los Angeles county than for most of the state. Los Angeles became known as one of the black spots of the nation, but it was a difference in degree only. Farm after farm passed into the possession of the banks in all the great valleys of the state. The widespread Bank of America, through its affiliated California Land Corporation, was selling foreclosed property when it could be sold at all, at distress prices.

The state finances were in a serious condition. Governor Rolph had taken office in 1931 when there was a surplus of $24,000,000 in the treasury; in 1934 there was a deficit of $65,000,000. The stage was all set for the appearance of an Avatar. All that was needed was a *man* with a *plan*. Sinclair was that man; EPIC was the plan.

Robert Wagner, editor of Hollywood *Script*, drew an emblem, a bee with widespread wings under which was the legend, "I produce, I defend." This emblem appeared as stickers on thousands of windshields, on countryside fences and in vacant doorways: "I produce, I defend." Cynics later commented that it should have been a wasp with the motto, "I sting, I buzz."

Under the California State Primary Law anyone can become candidate for office on any party simply by filing notice of candidacy, by filing a petition signed by a hundred voters who must, however, have registered as members of the party under which the candidate is running. Sinclair changed his lifelong affiliation from the Socialist Party to the Democratic, and his campaign for Governor was on.

It was some weeks before the heavy business interests of the state, particularly in the north, took the movement seriously. It was looked upon as a noisy project of intellectual left-wingers. Sinclair had been in the political arena before and nothing serious had ever come of it. It did not occur to the "interests" that Sinclair, a candidate on the Socialist ticket was one thing, and that Sinclair, a candidate on the Democratic ticket was another. He understood the difference perfectly, with all the acumen of a firstclass advertising man.

Then, too, how could the political bosses and party hacks know that the Time had come, that a new age was about to be born, that a California miracle was now overdue. It is of course doubtful even whether Sinclair himself took his campaign in the beginning very seriously; it was really "good copy," something more to write about and write about it he did.

Between the writing of "I, Governor of California," which began his campaign, and "I, Candidate for Governor, and How I Got Licked," which ended the campaign, "Epic Answers," "Immediate Epic," and "The Lie Factory Starts" were published, as well as weekly contributions to the publication, *Epic News*. Soon after his defeat in November 1934, there appeared "We, People of America," in which he propounded EPIC miracles for all of the United States—EPIC no longer stood for "End Poverty in California," it now signifies, "End Poverty in Civilization." Every EPIC book seems to call for one more.

Early in the campaign he paid San Francisco a visit as guest speaker of the Western Athenaeum which meets monthly in the huge, almost deserted Fairmont Hotel which for years has crowned San Francisco's famous and ritzy Nob Hill. At Athenaeum meetings intellectually minded socialites and politicians mingle with socially minded intelligentsia and artists; many come in evening dress and none appear poor. The policy of the organization is so broad as to make the broadest "liberal" appear to be almost bigoted. Without making the slightest endeavor to learn anything about EPIC or even to consider that Sinclair had been a torch bearer in the Socialist Party, the club invited him to come before them, and the doors were closed on an overflow meeting long before the appointed hour. San Franciscans were sure they were going to hear the illustrious author of *Main Street* and other equally famous books!

One of the broadcasting companies provided a Pacific Coast hookup; the usual musical entertainment and introductory talks were cut short and a breathless four hundred listened to the great Sinclair and liked it. They liked it when he belabored them for having full stomachs when thousands were starving; they liked it when he offered them a program a little over their heads, and therefore pleasing to good Californians; they loved his wit, his easygoing humor, his rapid fire repetition of facts and statistics; they admired his tribute to themselves; but most of all they hailed him when some communists tried to break up the meeting and challenge him forthright to debate. A glance, some pointed arguments, some daring challenges and the communists began beating a retreat (some of the communists, by the way, were in evening clothes!) amid a shower of boos and cheers.

The temporary chairman of the evening, the senior judge of

the San Francisco bench, warmly thanked Mr. "Lewis" [sic] for
the splendid talk. The bourgeoisie, petit and grand, began dream-
ing of invitations to the Governor's Inaugural Ball. Very soon the
names of not a few appeared on EPIC letterheads or invitations
to EPIC meetings. "*I, Governor*" had not visited San Francisco
in vain.

Sinclair was undoubtedly qualified for some sort of leadership.
He was fearless, he had been in crusade after crusade against economic slavery, and willingly exposed his own person when the
situation demanded. There had been the steel mill and Colorado
coal-center crusades. He had been arrested for reading the Constitution of the United States on private property in southern California, and had been held incommunicado for eighteen hours by
the Los Angeles police.

One of Sinclair's hobbies was his interest in cooperative colonies. The cooperative movement has existed in some form or
other in the state of California ever since it entered the Union.
Colonies based on Rochedale or socialistic principles have for the
most part been unsuccessful, the principal reason being not opposition from banks or capitalists but the individualistic attitudes of
members. Sinclair himself is perhaps just as much of an individual-
ist realistically, as he is a cooperator, idealistically.

During this period the California agricultural districts were
torn with especially violent strikes. The Imperial Valley at the
southern end of the state lies below sea level, and the richness of
its soil is comparable to that of the delta of the Nile. It is cropped
continuously all the year round and during the summer months its
climate is an inferno. The vast fields of lettuce, melons, cotton,
etc., are worked only by Mexicans and a sprinkling of Hindus
and Japanese. Imperial Valley has been called a feudalistic empire.

The large landholders and their shopkeeping adherents brook
no interference by outside labor leaders. All strangers were suspect.
General Glasscock, former Chief of Police of Washington, D.C.,
visited the valley on a more or less official inspection. He was
escorted to the Arizona state line by vigilantes and told not to
return.

In the lettuce sheds of Salinas in western California, the Filipinos, who form the bulk of the workers, went on strike in 1934.
Their meetings were disturbed by Vigilante Clubs and their headquarters burned. There was no small amount of violence in this
region. Many white workers, however, stood shoulder to shoulder
with the Filipinos; class lines proved stronger than racial distinctions.

Psychological California did not conceive that any group might strike voluntarily to better its economic position or conditions. All strikes were due to Communists or communist propaganda. Communism must be suppressed at all costs. In the cotton pickers' strike in Kern County armed "Minute Men," to save their homes from the starving Mexicans on strike, fired into a cluster of shelter tents killing several and wounding more. Strike leaders afterwards charged under the State Syndicalism Act went to San Quentin. No vigilante was convicted of anything serious during 1934.

In San Francisco came the general strike. This began with a long smoldering trouble on the waterfront not yet ended. This waterfront strike extended simultaneously over the ports of the Pacific Coast and Gulf states. It was called revolution, and the eyes of the world for a week were turned on California.

This general strike had been inevitable since the governor of California had called out the militia after a day of riot and killing on the waterfront. The frantic efforts of the President's Mediation Board, conservative labor-leaders, and public officials had been in vain. Riot and murder had resulted from an attempt of the San Francisco Industrial Association to "open the port." The San Francisco Industrial Association is an organization formed some years ago to counteract the power of the San Francisco unions and to maintain San Francisco as an "open shop" city.

The coming of troops broke the longshoremen's strike. Labor's answer was the general strike. Its effect was immediate and devastating. Its total cost, and the costs of the strikes that precipitated it, ran into many millions.

Almost at once the streets were swept clean of taxicabs and trucks. Restaurants, soft drink parlors, barber shops, cleaners and dyers, closed their doors. Laundries and theaters shut down. Hotels barred their portals to all except registered guests. Service stations, after a run in which all sales records were broken, one by one hung up signs, "No more Gas." Thousands of automobiles were stranded with empty tanks in their garages. Grocery stores and wholesale provision markets were soon emptied by a frightened populace. Streetcars stayed within their barns. Trains out of the city were jammed. Factories were shut down as their essential supplies were withheld by the paralysis in transportation.

The strikers formed a General Strike Committee, whose avowed purpose was to police the city, provide emergency services, assure food for all, and generally assume the direction of essential services normally under the control of their employers. It should be noted, however, that no strike was called in the baking industry

nor among the milk distributors. Milk and bread were never for
a moment unavailable. The strike committee issued permits, and
had placards printed to attach to the windshields of trucks, facili-
tating the distribution of food and supplies to hospitals, orphan-
ages, old people's homes, and so on. This committee announced
that San Francisco was "not to be starved" and arranged for limited amounts of trucks to pass the pickets at the city gates. It issued
permits to physicians to secure gasoline and provided that trucks
supplying certain designated gasoline stations should not be mo-
lested. It ordered nineteen restaurants to open their doors, and all
day long the next day citizens stood in line at the doors of these
eating places.

Every attempt was made by the civil authorities to disregard
and countermand the control assumed by the strike committee.
The military tore the strike permits from provision trucks when
these trucks appeared within their lines. Barricades were built by
the militia; young National Guardsmen were herded into trucks
pointing their guns indiscriminately at all passersby, ready to shoot
when the order was given—but it was never given. It was evident
the authorities would almost have preferred that hospitals should
go without provisions than be supplied under a union permit.

The Communists put on a few sympathetic parades of their
own and on them the forces of conservatism were unleashed. From
one end of the state to the other they were scattered. Their headquarters were wrecked, their printing presses and libraries destroyed. They were beaten by police and many of the younger even
sought to be martyrs. The jails were filled and a cry came for
deportations.

The tension of all these strikes aroused the masses to the need
of a leader. There appeared no leader in sight other than Upton
Sinclair. The strikes redounded to his political benefit; liberals and
left-wingers who had hitherto opposed the erstwhile Socialist rushed
into the EPIC camp; Sinclair should be their generalissimo.

Sinclair was no longer the Socialist with a mission to lead
strikers or read the Constitution on vacant lots. He was now a
Democrat engaged in a crusade, not in a class war. His entire interest and his movement was based on the needs of the actual and
the potential unemployed. This interest in the unemployed was
avowedly a middle class feeling; these unemployed were on the
taxpayers' backs. It was the taxpayers that Sinclair offered to
succor. Sinclair, when asked whether he would have called out
troops in case of a general strike, answered that if he had been

governor there would have been no strikes. He would have settled the difficulties before they reached this point.

Minnesota, which *elected* a radical governor, was not so fortunate.

As the campaign progressed cells known as EPIC clubs, were formed in every community. Before the primary campaign had ended, two thousand clubs had been organized, half a million booklets distributed and thousands of speeches made. To the astonishment and dismay of the old line politicians Sinclair developed an entirely new technique, hitherto unknown in the political field —he was able to secure not only enormous collections at mass meetings but ultimately was able to charge admission to political rallies. Political war horses admiringly stated, "he is the greatest politician of us all."

Sinclair first called for the "return of unemployed to the land." He believes that "for a very small outlay we can have the best agricultural land in the State, already under cultivation and equipped with machinery for operation." He proposed that land colonies be established for the unemployed. "These colonies will be run by the State *under expert supervision*"—this last requirement, apparently an element of EPIC democracy, to some looked very much like a "German work colonies" scheme; to others it appeared like a new brand of communism.

He proposed to grow every kind of fruit and vegetable, and with true Los Angeles spirit, states that "there are 25,000 useful and beautiful plants that can be grown in California." Elsewhere he comments on the fact that there is now an abundance of these 25,000 plants and that the capitalistic economy is to destroy them to hold up the price system. Why did it not occur to Sinclair that his genius might have been applied to working out some system of distribution instead of concentrating upon production schemes? Elsewhere he states "one should put an end to the private control of credit, which is the tap-root of our troubles." Just how the production of more goods and commodities could destroy this *taproot*, he has never explained.

The EPIC land colonies differed in one important respect from the self-help communities, a difference which is profoundly psychological and at least partially Californian. Whereas in the barter and cooperative groups education in cooperation is an integral part of the program and policy, not to be distinguished from economic activity, the EPIC plan called for a planned economy first, the principles of it to be taught afterward. "These land colonies were to have motion picture theaters and lecture halls where *we* can explain the principles of cooperation." (Italics ours.) Apparently our economic recruits were to be thrown into battle and be taught the elements of military science afterwards!

Within the colonies all was to be clean and prophylactic. He states: "that the workers [now] have to live in squalid surroundings and be ignorant and dirty" just because "our present class system takes that for granted."

For the unemployed city factory worker he had a similar scheme. The *state*, which with "*I, Governor*," would be that all-powerful, all-wise institution, was to take over the "thousands of factories which are idle or half idle and start them up." "A simple enabling act by the Legislature would give us the right to do this.

"Let us begin with the absolute necessities, of course. Let us take laundries, bakeries, canneries, clothing and shoe factories, cement plants, brick-yards, lumber-yards. Let us construct a complete industrial system, a new and self-maintaining world for our unemployed, in which they will live, having as few dealings as possible with our present world of speculators and exploiters." These factories were to have dealings only with the land colonies.

Did he envision an island of planned state-owned and directed economy in a capitalistic sea? At times he gives the impression that the unemployed would be supported under a supplemental economy without necessarily greatly altering the present system. At other times he states that the EPIC program would ultimately result in the substitution of a new type of society for profiteering capitalism. In his public appeals, however, he stated that one great purpose of EPIC was to take the load off the taxpayers' backs by having them relieved of demands to support relief rolls, etc.

On the Republican side, previous to the August, 1934, primaries, were four candidates, each in his own way a figure. Frank Merriam, now governor that Rolph was dead, stood for election. He was determined to win, even if he had to swing away from the extreme right. He let his opponents attack his old record; "he was out after a new one," the voters could decide.

Supervisor Quinn of Los Angeles County had the support of Hearst and of almost nobody else. Ex-Governor C. C. Young, supposed leader of the Hiram Johnson progressives, had refused to pardon Mooney, and had been none too favorable to labor during his term of office; he lost a large bulk of his followers to young Raymond Haight who, besides being a candidate in the Republican primaries, had a monopoly on the Progressive and

Commonwealth party tickets. After the primaries, ex-progressive C. C. Young stood shoulder to shoulder with Merriam. Raymond Haight, who had previously been State Commissioner of Corporations, had to campaign almost alone against two giants, Merriam and Sinclair, in the final run-off.

On the Democratic side the outstanding figure was George Creel, husband of Blanche Bates, New Dealer and representative of the N.R.A., and a comparative newcomer into northern California. He was supposed to be leader of the Rooseveltian middle of the road progressives, and more or less had the blessing of James Farley.

While there were eight candidates on the Democratic ticket, all told, the only others of importance were Justis Wardell who represented the strictly California traditions and was at one time closely allied with the Al Smith faction, and Milton K. Young, party nominee of 1930.

In the beginning of the campaign complications were threatened in the person of Sheridan Downey of Sacramento, law partner of progressive State Senator Inman, and who was supposed to occupy a position to the left of Creel, and to the right of Sinclair. He had written a book called *Onward America* in which he had vigorously belabored Wall Street as the source of all evil. Downey had a strong backing among the farmers of northern California, members of the Grange. He was looking for a movement, had investigated the possibilities of Social Credit, and was somewhat chagrined by Sinclair's hat being in the ring. He knew Sinclair was bound to draw the support of the progressives and liberals, upon which his own candidacy depended. Sinclair was too well known in those circles and had a genius for publicity while Downey was hardly known and without financial backing.

Some friends of Downey urged him to withdraw. Others persuaded him to join with Sinclair on the best terms procurable. Downey flew to Los Angeles and attempted to persuade Sinclair to withdraw in *his* favor. The upshot was that Downey became candidate for lieutenant-governor on the EPIC ticket. No little strength of the EPIC movement in California can be attributed to Downey's connections. In the November election he polled close to two hundred thousand more votes than Sinclair received, just being nosed out by the Republican, Hatfield. . . .

The C.D.C.: Yearning for Community*

WILSON CAREY MC WILLIAMS

Spring, 1960

THE DELEGATES to the recent Issues Conference of the California Democratic Council felt victory in the air: temporarily, at least, the "old party" professionals have capitulated and there is unity among California Democrats on terms set by the amateur clubs. Until November there will be no enemies but Republicans.

State Senator Hugh Burns, last seen in pursuit of subversives, graced the C.D.C. platform, perhaps managing a wry smile when another recent convert to the cause of liberalism and civil liberty, Senator John F. Kennedy, delivered an attack on the N.D.E.A. oaths. Around Burns clustered the state legislators, many owing their seats to the C.D.C. and familiar with its conventions, others its old foes, looking as if they doubted that this could be the right hall. And the delegates greeted their defeated opponents with magnanimity: Burns received correct, if unenthusiastic applause when introduced, no mean feat in a body which booed the mere mention of Lyndon Johnson. Victors in their own eyes, the delegates could afford generosity.

The C.D.C. gimmick has been organization. It has been no more effective than reform movements elsewhere, and its techniques are the same: the suburban housewife is its staple precinct worker. Two facts, however, make California different. First is the

---

* From the *SLATE Newsletter* (Spring, 1960). Used by permission of the author.

simple fact that there are more suburbanites: the constituencies that reform touches are more important. Second, and more important, is that C.D.C. has had no opposition: there never was a Democratic "organization" in California. Roosevelt's victories were based on the Depression and an anemic old-line Democracy, and ultimately destroyed both: the Olson administration came to power late (1938) and left early after one term leaving little mark on the state, and the clubs provide the first real "organization" that California Democrats have ever possessed.

A C.D.C. convention is a fantastic social universe, a Middle-Eastern bazaar of political psychology. Followers of General Holdridge, incredibly aged supporters of abstinence and vegetarianism crossed paths with the pension lobby of George McLain, with odd sectarians who feared the growth of Mormonism, and bar-owners turned libertarian under the new purity of California's Alcoholic Beverage Commission. The Progressives of 1948 were there in some strength, recovering slowly from the taint of schism and heresy; mothers concerned with strontium-90; leaders of the A.D.A.; one found all of the flotsam of American liberalism gathered as by an irresistible tide.

Students were there in hordes, from colleges and from the local high schools, learning what insiders looked like and being vicariously "in" themselves, sharing the dominant sentiment for Stevenson but quite unable to understand why one might support a candidate who might also lose an election. In the cheaper hotels, one could chat with a lobby of "Socialists" who knew Marx only through the anthologies of Sidney Hook and whose "ideology" was an imperfectly focused discontent; or, one could join a group around one of the liberal professors who tend, these days, to quote Burke and to bask in a metaphysical despair so dark as to black out the possibility of real disaster, the old optimism in a new form.

The dominant elements were, however, the suburban professionals and their wives (and often, their children) and the urban, middle-class representatives of minority groups (normally without children). For the first, ennui and isolation are the moving forces leading to political involvement. But it is not enough to call their motives "social." A large part of political motivation always has been, from the days when "games of chance, bars and brothels" became the staples of the American machine. In the old days, however, the machine provided concrete diversions, specific recreations which men valued, which they lacked the means to enjoy, and for which they were delighted to exchange their votes. Suburbia is different: sex and alcohol are not diversion but routine, part of the evening round of "California living," almost at the level of obligation. It is boring; purposeless; as bureaucratic and impersonal as the organizations of which most are a part. C.D.C. is a desperate striving to find something else, to discover community and a political universe.

The Negro, or the Mexican-American, is different. The minority delegates, almost all middle-class, aspire to the leadership of their respective groups. They speak, eloquently, for the excluded, and with undoubted sincerity, but for them politics is a drive for status and professional advance. These, in fact, are the would-be new professionals, the new Irish, for whom politics is still a matter of clear and definite goals, of local grievances and general solutions.

The white C.D.C. leader is a "professional" too, in a way: he devotes his labor to political life. Yet he is normally a success at another profession first; he comes to politics because he finds success a bit hollow. Moreover, he is very likely to be a prisoner of his own cant, to deny his professional status and to denounce "office holders" and "politicians." (There is, however, a growing segment of C.D.C. leaders who have adopted a "realistic" mode. Themselves products of the suburban middle-class, and victorious through C.D.C. efforts, they are sensitive, affection-starved men, who protect themselves by a rhetoric so savage as to be unreal; the old bosses, who knew they relied on the loyalties of men, were far wiser, in speech at any rate.)

Apart from its members, the C.D.C. is "issues." These are fundamental, the justification of the clubs' claim to offer a higher variety of politics. Yet it was striking how easily an "issue" was adopted as a plank by the C.D.C. if it sounded reasonably liberal: two alternate delegates in a committee were normally enough to obtain inclusion if they were determined. The C.D.C. does not select issues, it embraces them with a blinding promiscuity; it loves them all, sure that each is but an additional proof of its own virtue.

The leaders of the convention were concerned to live down the charge that the C.D.C. is unconcerned with the big economic issues like water and power. In fact, the only real debate in the conference raged around Governor Brown's dubious compromise water bill. But the dispute did not really interest the delegates: if anything, it bewildered them, as a departure from the normal pattern, a unanimous, stolid approval of what-all-good-liberals-agree. It drowned the loudest *cri de couer* in waves of indifference and let it go at that. That much is revealing: the C.D.C. is certainly not ideological politics, for no ideology would be indifferent to water and power and the C.D.C. is.

Liberalism in the modern sense is not doctrine, it is sentiment; it is a vague congregation of symbols, feelings and impulses, given such coherence as it possesses by that vaguest of all political potpourris, the New Deal. It is American to the core, a great swelling warm-heartedness, a humaneness touched with secular piety, a colossus of well-meaning. Liberalism, like conservatism, has become a "state of mind" and not a very inspiring one at that.

The C.D.C. yearns after community, for a place for the liberal in an alien world. Yet its political leaders and writers do not discuss community. Whatever community is found lies in opposition, once directed against the Republican administration and this year safely against the Republican national administration, but which year after next must come home in schism within the party and the C.D.C. itself. Witness the fact that in counties and congressional districts with Democratic majorities, membership in the clubs is small; numbers of delegates come from massively Republican districts like Santa Monica. Loving thy neighbor is not a C.D.C. maxim, for if you love him—or even agree with him—the clubs may seem superfluous; distaste for most of those who are close at hand is the basis of unity among the few who share it.

Here, after all, are five thousand delegates from a state of millions, who never see one another save in passing at the great conventions; behind them are a hundred thousand and more club members, each closer in proximity and life to relatives, work associates and even neighbors than to the club members whose life he shares for an hour or two a week, at most. The emotion of the C.D.C. is derived from its body of symbols, and association with those symbols enlivens the personal life of each member, but the members remain strangers to each other.

The C.D.C. is based on an insecurity in relations between men which is understandable in those who have only begun to feel gingerly outside the walls of isolation. Yet its symbols bar any further progress. They are, after all, impersonal, and since the members are concerned to find an inter-personal environment, the symbols stir little fervor or conviction. The C.D.C. is religion without prophecy, emotion without *eros*. Hence the references which every speaker felt compelled to make to the power, the accomplishments, the invincibility of the C.D.C. itself: without these, little remains, and the C.D.C. will have trouble surviving any defeat.

Partly, one can pass this off as the result of sophistication. Yet that impression disappears when the general meeting of delegates hears a major address. The members of C.D.C. are not true believers but they would like to be, and show as much in their facile enthusiasms and eager excitements. It responds to the stylized cliches with applause without cue: "the principles of the New Deal," "freedom of speech," "the United Nations," and especially, "Civil Rights."

Of course, these things ought to be applauded, but they were cheered in the most tawdry verbal contexts, in the most pedestrian settings. Senator Hubert Humphrey was the delight of the conference. He promised not to yield an inch on civil rights and they were enraptured by his courage (how many segregationists are there in the C.D.C.? Or, for that matter, in Minnesota?). He denounced loyalty oaths and they were impressed by his sincerity (the Humphrey–Douglas Bill? The old, witch-hunting days in Minneapolis?). He referred to every liberal program since 1932, demanding more of the same and they were impressed by his originality, just as his citations from John Kenneth Galbraith seemed the essence of erudition, and his ability to defend both widespread disarmament and efforts to close the "missile gap" was taken as evidence of broad vision.

The C.D.C., despite the permanent anxiety of some academics, could not be "totalitarian." It is generous, and ineffably—even intolerably—humanistic. Yet the C.D.C.'s humane imbecility is no answer to the dilemmas of American, or even of Californian politics. The face of C.D.C. is that of a grinning infant, a pituitary giant whose slowly developing brain will never keep pace with the growth of its loins. The C.D.C. is little better than noble savagery in the civil state.

The last of the political men may be passing, as the last of the statesmen seems to have done already. Rousseau gave no place in his ideal state to the legislator, but he presumed that there would be citizens to take his place. Unfortunately, there is little in the Brave New World of the C.D.C. to lead one to such a hope. And without statesmen, political men, or citizens, there is little indeed which remains of political life.

Robert Scheer Trims His Beard*

ROBERT KUTTNER

May, 1966

IN CALIFORNIA, the Left has learned the utility of operating through the Democratic Party by means of an anomaly called the California Democratic Councils. And so it is that in Berkeley, where the New Left seems frequently too reminiscent of the Old Left, a peace candidate named Robert Scheer is making a serious bid for Congress. He is managing to preside over a loose coalition of older Bay Area progressives, the more moderate element of the Vietnam Day Committee, a raft of leftish Cal sophomores, and some rather queasy ADA types like this reporter. Scheer is one of a dozen congressional candidates in this incredible state who are calling for an end to the Vietnam war. About half of them actually stand a chance of winning the Democratic nomination. In Scheer's case the platform also includes such goodies as support for the grape strike, Berkeley free speech, conservation, and a massive overhaul of the mess which calls itself Oakland.

Scheer was born in New York, and became active in Left politics while doing graduate work at the University of California in Berkeley. He coauthored a book on Cuba, and a widely read pamphlet for the Center for the Study of Democratic Institutions entitled "How the U.S. Got Involved in Vietnam." Folklore has it that Berkeley radicals "don't trust anyone over thirty," and

---

* From *The Activist* (May, 1966). Used by permission of the editors.

Scheer, therefore, is twenty-nine, to the dismay of his more conventionally minded campaigners.

But to understand Scheer, it is necessary to consider another California anomaly, *Ramparts* magazine, of which Scheer is Foreign Editor. *Ramparts* was founded four years ago as a liberal lay Catholic magazine: it has since shed much of its Catholicism, and acquired an extremely talented staff and a slick layout which its perennial four paid advertisements suggest it can't afford. It has made headlines with articles and exposés by Scheer, and by ex-Green Beret Don Duncan (an enigma even to his *Ramparts* associates). A week after the Oakland study which Scheer directed, the mayor and the police chief resigned. More recently, Scheer worked on the exposé of C.I.A. involvement in the Michigan State Vietnam Project. *Ramparts* is difficult to place: it seems to take more joy in its iconoclasm than its radicalism, though it is clearly on the Left. Three of the California peace candidates for Congress are from the *Ramparts* staff: Publisher Ed Keating; Stanley Scheinbaum, who was former head of the M.S.U. project; and Scheer. Don Duncan, now an official staff member, was very nearly a fourth.

It would be difficult to make a case that a *Ramparts* cabal is trying to take over the California Democratic Party, though that wouldn't be so bad. Scheer's candidacy, ironically, was first suggested by Vietnam Day Committee activists last year after the death of the Free Speech Movement, when a new radical project was being sought. Since then, after the troop train sit downs, marches, and the departure of much of the moderate Left from V.D.C. ranks, the Vietnam Day Committee has reached the point of semi-opposition to Scheer, and the Scheer campaign has almost approached the margin of respectability. But not quite. And the saga of how this process came about is an interesting lesson in the ways of American politics.

The incumbent in California's seventh congressional is Jeffery Cohelan. By any reckoning, Cohelan is on the liberal wing of the Democratic representation in Congress. His voting record places him on the "second tier" of House liberals, behind Ryan, Katsenmeier, Burton, and a very few others. Cohelan will not go so far as to take roll-call stands against appropriations for the Vietnam war or the House Un-American Activities Committee, but his ADA record is well over 90 percent; he has been outspoken on the need for farm labor reform, and was one of seventy-eight House liberals who sent a letter to Johnson urging caution in

Vietnam. Aesthetically, however, Cohelan is not a radical. He began his career as a milk-wagon driver, rose within Teamster ranks, and was elected to Congress in 1958 with wide labor and C.D.C. backing. Whereupon, for some inexplicable reason, he cast one of his first votes in favor of Landrum–Griffin, which his Teamsters hold against him to this day.

But organized labor in the East Bay is well within the Johnson fold, and the A.F.L.–C.I.O. Committee on Political Education (COPE) endorsed a slate of establishment Democrats which differed almost totally from the one put forward by the local C.D.C. Labor remains the pillar of Cohelan support. In short, the incumbent has been described as an enlightened hack, who liberals, in normal times, would be glad to get. However in this age of consensus, Cohelan is a Johnson man, and, give or take an escalation, he supports the war.

This winter, Scheer and his wife marched to Cohelan's office with a number of V.D.C. partisans demanding, among other things, that Cohelan introduce an impeachment resolution, and that he immediately return to his district and debate the war with the V.D.C. Shortly afterwards, Scheer was astute enough to maintain that, while he continued to welcome V.D.C. support, he was by no means a "V.D.C. candidate." This, in turn, caused the first wave of criticism from the V.D.C., for whom a decision to register and vote in the Democratic primary had been trauma enough; some sparks flew, but by and large the V.D.C. was still behind Scheer. Scheer's organization developed autonomously, but with exaggerated dependence on the campus community. For a while tactical decisions as well as press conferences shifted to *Ramparts'* San Francisco offices rather than the Berkeley campaign head-quarters. V.D.C. leader Jerry Rubin began as campaign manager, but increasingly has been isolated from the center of things, and from the campaign's tone in general.

Black Backlash

A major event of the political year in California was the battle to depose C.D.C. president Simon Cassady. Cassady, iron-ically, was originally proposed by the moderate wing of the volun-teer federation. However, his outspoken criticism of the war and of Johnson personally brought pressure upon him both locally and from Washington. C.D.C.'s future effectiveness was seriously called into question; Governor Brown stated that he would not seek C.D.C. endorsement. Cassady was finally narrowly defeated in a vote of confidence, but the price of keeping the organization intact was a strong resolution against the war, and a new president who, though less forceful, largely shared Cassady's views.

The local C.D.C. nominating convention in the East Bay met only two weeks after Cassady's ouster; Bay Area delegates had been among the strongest Cassady backers, and nine out of ten had walked out following the vote of no confidence. In addition, something like 150 Scheer supporters had joined local C.D.C. clubs in order to secure the C.D.C. nomination for him. As it turned out, this was quite unnecessary, for he received the convention's endorsement by well over three hundred votes. However the charge of "packing" gave Cohelan a handy excuse to decline the C.D.C. nomination before he lost it, and to disavow the organization. Cohelan reconnoitered the district a few weeks before the convention, and issued a statement saying that the local Democratic party had been infiltrated by alien elements who were using it for their own sinister ends. The local press—the *Berkeley Gazette* and the redoubtable *Oakland Tribune*—have managed virtually to avoid mentioning Scheer's candidacy except when an incident appears to discredit him. (A benefit party for the campaign was raided by police for "selling liquor without a license," and this got headline coverage.) Cohelan's statement likewise made the headlines; it is a difficult feat of journalism to give front page publicity to a denunciation without ever mentioning what is being denounced, but the *Berkeley Gazette* managed it—overt bias, in favor, for once, of a liberal democrat, and perhaps that is progress.

Scheer's presence dominated the C.D.C. convention. He delivered a powerful speech, which set a radical tone for the gathering, and produced some unexpected side effects. Byron Rumford, the veteran Negro assemblyman who pioneered fair employment and fair housing legislation, was denied endorsement in his bid for the state Senate. Rumford was backing Cohelan in exchange for COPE support. His one challenger, a very parody of a politician who began his address with a toothy "Hi, friends," jumped on the Scheer bandwagon, and almost received the convention's backing. Oakland's other congressman, a do-nothing Democrat, was passed up in favor of backing no one. The day had an unreal air about it. Here was a local Democratic party gathering; its tone was truly radical, and for a moment, one felt as if this were not a peculiar accident, but the normal pattern of grass-roots American politics. The meeting opened with the Pledge of Allegiance—a loyalty oath which somehow seemed awfully incongruous. This was followed by a sheepish rendition of the "Star-Spangled Banner." It reminded me of watching the London May Day parade in 1964 and thinking: the same happy fringe as in America, but this crew is preparing to form the next government! Scheer backers were so euphoric, so spontaneously unorganized that no one bothered to give consideration to such bourgeois notions as ticket-balancing. It was simple—the most radical candidates were endorsed, and perhaps the gathering was so utterly free from prejudice that nobody noticed that all were white. The result was something of a Black Backlash, which continues to haunt Scheer.

Respectability?

It is very difficult to decide just when the campaign first began to smell of respectability. Since the convention, Scheer has had the look of a candidate who believes he has a chance. Even at the convention, the minority of Scheer backers who appeared in beards and bluejeans looked more like they were there to disrupt the meeting rather than to back the favorite. The campaign has undergone an embourgeoisment, but one largely of style. By taking itself seriously, it has grown to resemble most other political campaigns—in everything but its message. The four store front offices do not betray much of Scheer's radicalism. The north Oakland office, in the ghetto, is hopelessly middle-class. The photographs of poverty displayed in the windows are Negro, but the faces inside the office are white.

There is still a lingering schizophrenia. Most of the literature and speeches are designed for a mass public, yet a number of workers continue to radiate an aura of "Come the Revolution . . ." Scheer himself has been a tireless and increasingly impressive campaigner. He has made himself thoroughly familiar with the Oakland maze, and addresses daily meetings of formal and informal groups. He appeared as a keynote speaker at the Berkeley rally which opposed the granting of an honorary degree to Ambassador Goldberg. Scheer suggested Fulbright instead; the university, he said, had missed a tremendous opportunity. Scheer has become impeccably informed about the brutality, inconsistency, and futility of the Vietnam war; his speech, like others, was moving, but the praise for Fulbright was no longer incongruous. Nor was there any talk of impeaching President Johnson.

Recently, Scheer refused to speak at a carelessly organized V.D.C. "Street Demonstration," which turned into a free-for-all, for which the V.D.C. leadership shared legitimate blame with the police. He was roundly denounced for his absence. His is a radicalism minus a certain gratuitous defiance, the propensity for "instant crisis" which has been the less positive side of the Berkeley Movement. A moderate faction of the Californians for Liberal Representation (CLR), whose endorsement Scheer sought and got, expected a brash kid, and came away from his speech surprised and impressed. The Scheer campaign began as a pure protest; lately, it has decided that the *election* of a radical candidate might be of some significance as well. In the early days of the campaign, the mere suggestion that this might be a (however utopian) goal met scornful derision. Estimates as of late April put Scheer's primary strength from 30 to 40 per cent.

Scheer began his candidacy as a V.D.C. partisan, which prevented him from being taken terribly seriously by many outside the defiant left. Moreover, he appeared a good deal younger than twenty-nine, and his style of oratory was something of a less articulate cross between Jean Shepherd and Paul Krassner. Somehow, without the aid of a P.R. outfit, but through what must be innate political sense combined with the logical dynamics of an electoral campaign, Scheer's venture has undergone significant changes. Whether these changes are seen as maturation or moderation depends upon where you sit, but most agree that they are for the better.

A recent poll reported that two out of three Americans said they would be more inclined to support congressional candidates who favor a negotiated settlement to the Vietnam war. Scheer has been accused by the V.D.C. of scenting power. This is not quite fair. He has simply observed—consciously or not—that support can be won or lost on matters of style and personal emphasis, support which the aesthetic Left would reject out of spite. Scheer's posters on the commuter busses, forced on a reluctant transit company, read: "Stop the War/Rebuild our Cities," not "Get out of Vietnam/Crush the Establishment." A matter of emphasis, and perhaps a sellout of sorts, but one that may prove in the June seventh primary that opposition to radicalism is more on grounds of style than content. And after all, Scheer still hasn't shaved his beard—though it is neatly trimmed.

The Economics of Extremism*

CAREY MC WILLIAMS

L ABOR UNIONS in California have been compelled by the nature of the economy of the state to federate, to seek alliances, and to found assemblies. The second largest state in the union, California is a highly developed economic area. All forms of economic activity are embraced within its borders. Its high level of cash farm income; the value of its mineral and forest products; its fisheries and oil fields; its canning and processing industries— these and other factors have served to make it an economic empire in itself. Since it is not one thing economically, but many things, labor has been compelled to reach out, to expand the area of organization, and to consolidate its gains. The labor market is as large, as interrelated and as interdependent as the state's economic activities. In such an economic area, nothing less than complete organization can possibly safeguard the interests of labor.

In California, also, agriculture has a unique relation to industry which arises from the dependence of agriculture on the export market and the accompanying reliance upon the processing, handling, and transportation industries. The very nature of many California crops brings a host of industries into close and intimate relation with agriculture. In 1948, some 6,352 trucks were used in transporting produce from the Imperial Valley alone, which

---

* From *California: The Great Exception* (A. A. Wyn, 1949). Copyright © 1949 by Carey McWilliams. Used by permission of the author and publisher.

83

suggests the reliance of agriculture upon transportation. In fact, it is often difficult to classify a particular industry in the state as being primarily "agricultural" or "industrial." The type of labor used in many agricultural operations shades off imperceptibly into the type of labor used in the handling and processing industries. The interdependence of so many industries has naturally encouraged labor to achieve, if possible, total organization.

For many years the economic life of the state has been dominated by two urban centers, San Francisco and Los Angeles, and the existence of these two competing centers has tended to divide the state into two major economic areas. The fact that large agricultural and tributary areas have been so highly dependent upon two major urban areas has given the urban areas an enormous power to influence labor relations in their respective hinterlands. The determination of labor policies in these two urban areas has affected labor policies throughout their respective regions; conversely, control of labor policies in the tributary areas is vital to control of labor policies in the urban centers. If the two major urban centers had not been highly competitive, each might have been able to ignore or to tolerate conditions in the hinterland areas which were inconsistent with or tended to undermine urban labor policies; but they have never been able to afford this tolerance.

The rivalry between the two centers, moreover, has always been accentuated by the fact that San Francisco was vitally dependent upon its port; whereas Los Angeles was late in developing a man-made port. The close relation between the Port of San Francisco and California agriculture can be shown by reference to the principal commodities which were exported through the port in 1938. Agricultural products totaled $75,744,046; other extractive products, such as wood, bulk oil, etc., totaled $44,276,-415; and other products $19,599,524. So far as the economic activity of the northern and central portion of the state is concerned, the Port of San Francisco is the bottleneck. On more than one occasion, therefore, control of the San Francisco waterfront has carried with it, as a rich prize, indirect control over a large part of the economy of the state. Just as the waterfront has been the scene of innumerable labor struggles, so San Francisco labor subsidized the fight to organize Los Angeles, for to the extent that commerce and industry shifted to Los Angeles the advantage of waterfront control was weakened. Labor had to expand, therefore, in order to protect what it had achieved.

A large part of the California labor market has always been seasonal in character. Employment expands and contracts in the canning, processing, and handling industries as it expands and contracts in agriculture. The casual nature of waterfront employment invests it with some of the characteristics of a seasonal labor market. Faced with this situation, unions have been compelled to extend their control over the entire labor market; in fact the fight to control the *supply* of labor has been, perhaps, more important than the struggle to raise wages or to improve working conditions. For precisely the same reason, employers have strenuously resisted every attempt by labor to control the entire labor market. With seasonal employment being of such crucial interest, it is extremely important, from the employer's point of view, that the labor market should be kept unorganized and fluid. Seasonal industries in California cannot tolerate any interruption in work schedules. Peaches must be picked at a certain time; they must be processed on schedule; and they must be shipped on time to reach distant markets.

In short, the nature of the state's economy has always catapulted labor and capital into an intense struggle for control of the labor market. Since the labor market is as diverse as the products produced, both sides have sought to gain strength by combination. They have reached out, also, for allies and have constantly sought to enlist the public on their side. It has been the compulsion to reach out and control *related* lines of economic activity that accounts for the continued emphasis which the California labor movement has always placed on such weapons as the secondary boycott, the sympathetic strike, and "hot cargo" tactics. To keep the Chinese relegated to the unskilled trades, California labor made the first extensive use of the boycott in this country. The union label, which has long since become part of labor's arsenal of weapons, was first used in California. These various weapons, the boycott, the union label, the refusal to handle "hot cargo" and so forth, have been of great importance in a state whose economy was so interrelated and interdependent as that of California's.

The same compulsions have driven both labor and capital in California to achieve, in their respective fields, total integration. "Labor unions and employee groups," reads the report of the La Follette Committee, "have been driven to cooperate with one another to a greater degree, perhaps, than in any other section of the nation." The same, of course, is true of the employer groups. The Ship Owners' Protective Association of the Pacific Coast, formed in San Francisco in 1886, was the first association among employers to be formed in this country for the exclusive purpose of dealing with labor. Not only was industry quick to use the collective approach to labor problems in California, but employer associations are almost as old as the trade union movement itself. California has always had a pattern of organized anti-unionism. Industrial employers in the state have been more solidly arrayed, as a class, against labor than in any other state. To such an extent has this been true that, with the formation of the Board of Manufacturers and Employers in San Francisco in 1893, the day of the independent, isolated businessman in labor relations was gone. From 1900 to 1940, the Merchants and Manufacturers' Association in Los Angeles coerced the small industrialist and businessman into following the labor policies which its directors had decided upon. In no respect is this control-by-association more strikingly illustrated than in the "license system" which the Industrial Association of San Francisco used to wreck the building trades unions in 1921. Under this system, every contractor had to agree in writing to operate an open shop before the material dealers would furnish him with materials and supplies. Confronted with this type of united opposition, unions have been compelled to resort to extraordinary tactics in order to survive.

Labor's Curious Ducklings

The major paradox about the labor movement in California consists in the fact that a powerful labor movement should ever have arisen in a state which, prior to 1900, was largely non-industrial. Yet by 1900 San Francisco was recognized as not only the most tightly organized city in America but as the stronghold of trade unionism in the United States. Obviously the labor movement in California must have included elements which are not ordinarily thought of as part of labor. In California there were three such elements: the small shopkeeping element; a large section of the rural population; and a sizable element of what today would be called "white collar" workers. How was it that these elements became allies and, in some cases, integral parts of the labor movement?

The answer is to be found in Camp's statement that the fear of Chinese competition in California "brought about the rise of such a great wave of emotional class consciousness that it swept obscure opportunists into public office." But it did more than sweep opportunists into office; it drove thousands of shopowners, farmers, and clerical workers into the camp of organized labor. If the gold rush had not brought a tidal wave of white settlers to California, it is altogether possible that the whites might have formed a tightly knit plantation-like economy based on the use of Chinese labor; but the whites were too numerous in relation to the Chinese to form a ruling clique. The alternative was to organize and thereby force the Chinese into the undesirable positions. A better alternative, of course, would have been to organize the Chinese also, but the language and cultural barriers were too great to make this a feasible alternative. It was, in any case, the threat of competition from Asiatic labor that made for solidarity and invested labor in California with a political power far stronger than it has ever possessed in any other state.

The potency of anti-Chinese agitation as "an emotional class consciousness" consisted in the fact that it tended to fuse with class lines. At an early date, J. Ross Browne reported that he could find "among the influential and respectable class" little antagonism to the Chinese. "The objections against them," he said, "are purely of a local and political character and come from the lower classes of Irish." By and large, the upper classes consistently favored unrestricted immigration; the lower classes as consistently opposed it. By utilizing this unity of feeling against the Chinese, labor was able to build the most powerful alliances. Nor was anti-Oriental agitation a passing phase in California politics; in various phases it persisted for seventy years or longer. It goes without saying, of course, that this movement had some extremely ugly implications; but it was certainly the force that held labor together.

After 1900 anti-Japanese agitation was used for the same purpose as anti-Chinese agitation had been used over a period of thirty years, i.e., to build a powerful labor movement. From 1900 to 1910 a union charter in California was, in some respects, primarily significant as an authorization to engage in anti-Japanese agitation. The Japanese represented a more potent threat to the lower middle class and middle class than the Chinese for they demonstrated a remarkable ability to move up into the self-employed and farm-owner category. The threat of this competition, real or imagined, drove thousands of people into labor's ranks not only in the cities but in the small towns and rural areas. After 1900, as one labor journal put it, the unions experienced a "Pentecost breeze." In fact it is doubtful if any state ever felt the ardor for organization that then prevailed in California. All sorts of occupations and callings were organized and charters were "signed for and hung in meeting houses until they covered the four walls." But, as this same labor journal pointed out, "very few of these unions were trade unions. . . . The labor council gathered under its wings a most varied collection of eggs and hatched some curious ducklings and labeled them trade unions." As one reads through lists of unions formed during this period one notices butchers, barbers, bakers, picture frame makers, cloak-makers, tailors, milk wagon drivers, art glass blowers, blacksmiths, and many similar occupations which usually fall into the "little business" category.

Ordinarily there is no more inveterate if misguided opponent of organized labor than the small shopkeeper. It is the history of small shopkeepers that they are usually more capitalistic than the capitalists. They are also notoriously chauvinistic; in fact it was their tendency toward chauvinism that brought them into the California labor movement in droves. Many of these elements, of course, were never thoroughly integrated with the labor move-ment and they began to drop out as the anti-Oriental agitation passed out of the control of the labor leaders. These were the elements that kept some of California's most corrupt "labor" politicians in power for many years, thereby bringing great dis-credit to the labor movement.

Regardless of the price that labor ultimately paid for its espousal of the anti-Oriental movement, there can be little doubt that this movement, from an opportunistic point of view, paid great dividends to labor. In 1911, 39 out of 49 labor measures placed before the state legislature were adopted and a similar record was made in 1913 and 1915, with the result, as Dr. Cross has pointed out, that "California took a prominent place among states interested in conserving the welfare of the workingclass"— that is, the non-Oriental workingclass.

The Pattern of Violence

Since labor was totally engaged with capital from the earliest date, it is not surprising that the history of labor in California should be a history of labor's strenuous and often violent thrusts for power, and of the equally violent counterrepression invoked by capital. It has been this periodic outbreak of class warfare on a large scale which has been so largely responsible for the continued political instability of the state. Even in those periods in which labor has held the upper hand, fear of the expected and inevitable counterattack from the organized anti-union forces has driven labor to seek still further power. "Cease fire" orders have been given from time to time but until the federal government began to intervene in labor relations there was no real peace between capital and labor.

Without going into the full details, it can be said that there have been four major labor–capital battles in California. The first, which occurred in the period from 1886 to 1893, had its genesis in a determined effort on the part of the employers to break the power of the unions. In 1886 there had been a serious waterfront strike, which is generally taken to mark the beginning of San Francisco's famous waterfront warfare, and an important strike by the brewery workers. In both cases, the contest had quickly developed into a fight between *groups* of unions and *groups* of employers. The employers were particularly disturbed by the formation in 1891 of the Coast Seamen's Union, a truly remarkable labor organization and the first stable organization of its kind to be formed in the world. Embracing the entire Pacific Coast, the union was centrally directed from San Francisco with agents in every west coast port. Wherever the coasting sailor went, into whatever port, his membership card was recognized and he enjoyed the same protection as every other sailor in that port.

There had also occurred, in 1890, a bitter fight between the Iron Trades Council, a federation of metal workers, and an employer organization known as the Engineers' and Foundrymen's Association. In each case, an issue had been fought out between a group of unions on the one hand and a particular employers' association on the other. The employers, therefore, decided to form an all-inclusive employers group—the Board of Manufacturers and Employers formed in 1891—and to break up, if possible, the combinations of unions that had developed. This particular struggle culminated in a second waterfront strike in 1893 which labor lost largely because the explosion of a bomb on Christmas Day in front of a non-union boarding house, killing eight men and wounding many others, alienated public support. As a consequence of this defeat, the unions of San Francisco were, for the time being, largely destroyed or at least demoralized to the point where little unity or strength remained. This first battle, therefore, resulted in an unqualified victory for capital.

But, by the turn of the century, California was again booming. The Spanish–American War, the annexation of Hawaii, the gold rush to Alaska, and other factors stimulated a flurry of industrial activity in the state. Both sides, of course, immediately began to prepare for a resumption of the earlier battle. In this case the unions took the offensive since they feared that the employers were plotting another systematic campaign against them. In a great organizing campaign the number of union members was doubled in a year. The State Federation of Labor was formed in 1901, and the City Front Federation, a loosely knit federation representing some 13,000 waterfront workers, came into being the same year. The employers promptly formed an all-inclusive employers' group, the Employers Council, and proceeded to raise a war chest of $250,000 which was precisely the amount the City Front Federation had in its treasury.

The second great struggle began on July 30, 1901, when the waterfront workers struck, but the situation quickly developed into a tangle of sympathetic strikes as the two great contending forces moved into action. For three months the harbor was crippled. In the course of this strike, five men were killed and three hundred assaults were reported. The violence was so great that both sides seem to have exhausted themselves and a mutual cessation of hostilities was finally negotiated without either side having won a clear-cut victory. In effect, however, the unions won this round because they emerged from the battle stronger than when they had entered it. "There is a kind of fighting which makes the enemy stronger," reported Ray Stannard Baker at the time, "and that was the method of the San Francisco Employers' Association. It was an example of how *not* to combat unionism." A few weeks after the strike was called off, the Union Labor Party won a smashing political victory in San Francisco and remained in undisputed control of the city administration for a decade. In the wake of this strike, in fact, San Francisco emerged as the first "closed shop" city in America.

The third great battle developed shortly after the outbreak of the first World War. The war, of course, immediately brought about a sharp increase in the volume of cargo moving through the port and both sides promptly squared away for another slugging match. In 1916 the longshoremen went on strike, bottling up some $2,500,000 in exports. As in the prior struggle, the farming and business interests of the hinterland demanded that the San Francisco employers' group should break the strike. The murder of a striking longshoreman on June 21 seemed, for a few days, to tip the scales of public opinion in favor of the unions. But, while the strike was still on, the tragic Preparedness Day bombing took place (on July 22) in which some ten people were killed and forty seriously injured. Out of this fateful event, of course, came the infamous frame-up of Tom Mooney. The bombing threw the weight of public opinion against the unions, the strike was lost and, at the height of the excitement, the city adopted an anti-picketing ordinance by a vote of 73,993 to 68,570.

Following its earlier victory in 1901, organized labor in San Francisco had decided that the time had come to organize Los Angeles, "the open shop citadel of America." Just how important this organizing drive was, in terms of protecting the closed shop in San Francisco, can be shown by the fact that in 1900 San Francisco had 66 per cent of the total organized trade union membership of the state by comparison with 6 per cent in Los Angeles. In 1910, 65 per cent of the trade union strength was in San Francisco and only 8 per cent in Los Angeles. Viewing open shop Los Angeles as a threat to everything it had achieved in San Francisco, the labor movement proceeded to raise nearly $500,000 for an organizing campaign. There the trouble started on May 19, 1910, with a strike of brewery workers, followed by a strike of metal workers and of Mexican workers on the street railway. To break these strikes, the Merchants' and Manufacturers' Association drafted an anti-picketing ordinance which is known in the labor histories as the model for all the anti-picketing laws and ordinances in the country.

Within a few weeks after the adoption of this ordinance on July 16, 1910, over 470 workers had been arrested; but, almost as fast as they were arrested, Los Angeles juries acquitted them. This particular struggle culminated in the dynamiting of the Los Angeles *Times* on October 1, 1910, in which twenty-one men lost their lives. This dreadful explosion, and the plea of guilty which the McNamara brothers entered a year later, set the cause of labor back for at least two decades in Los Angeles. Previously uncompromising in their anti-union attitude, the open shop employers of Los Angeles used this event in a most spectacular and devastating manner to swing community sentiment to their narrow purposes. What the dynamiting of the *Times* was to Los Angeles, the Preparedness Day bombing was to San Francisco: both events symbolized a crushing defeat for the labor movement.

All this while, however, there was another "labor movement"

in California spearheaded by an outlaw, revolutionary organization, the Industrial Workers of the World. There was only one delegate from California at the meeting in Chicago on June 27, 1905, at which the I.W.W. was formed but, by 1910, the wobblies had eleven locals in the state and nearly a thousand members. It was Local No. 66, which Frank Little had organized at Fresno, that launched the first of the famous wobbly free speech fights in California. The campaign opened with an outdoor meeting on October 16, 1910, at which Frank Little, one of the speakers, was arrested and given a jail sentence by a jury which he contemptuously referred to as "composed of Bourgeois cockroaches and real estate grafters." In subsequent meetings, first ten, then fifteen, then twenty-five, and fifty people were arrested and, finally lawless elements in the community burned the wobbly headquarters. Fire hoses were used by irate police in an unsuccessful effort to keep the arrested wobblies from singing in jail. The campaign was finally settled, six months later, by the appointment of a mediation committee and at least a partial vindication of the right of free speech was secured.

The wobblies, of course, were quite free of the chauvinism that prevailed in the California labor movement at this time. They repeatedly attacked the "yellow peril" agitation and sought, without too much success, to organize Mexican field workers and other minority groups. Although many of the labor leaders of California of this period were of foreign birth, most of the wobbly leaders, ironically, were Old Americans with names like Dunn, Ryan, Olson, Sherman, and Eaton. The wobblies had real influence with the casual and seasonal workers of California, notably the waterfront workers, the lumberjacks, and the field and cannery workers. Their informal organization, the tactic of organizing on the job, the use of quick strikes, and the roving and migratory nature of the organization itself, made the wobblies effective pioneers in the effort to organize seasonal and casual workers.

Following the Fresno free speech fight, San Diego adopted on January 8, 1912, an ordinance limiting the right of free speech. The wobblies promptly moved in and launched a sensational fight to have the ordinance revoked. Although they had not more than fifty members in San Diego, it has been estimated that nearly 5,000 people took part in this campaign. Michael Hoy, a wobbly, was kicked to death in jail and another member, Joe Mikolash, was shot and killed. When jailings failed to break the spirit of the wobblies, a vigilante mob aided by police rounded up several hundred men, made them "run the gauntlet," beat them with clubs and fire hoses, and drove them out of town. The issue reached such a pitch of excitement that Governor Hiram Johnson sent Harris Weinstock to San Diego to make an official report and investigation. In part because of this excellent, clear-headed report, the wobbly campaign was finally successful and the right of free speech was vindicated.

The wobbly campaign in California came to a climax with the famous Wheatland "hop pickers' " riot of August 3, 1913, in which four people were killed.

Some 2,800 hop pickers, representing a wide diversity of nationalities, had been recruited by ads for work on a ranch owned by one of the largest employers of farm labor in the state. The pickers included a large number of women and children. On arriving at the ranch, the pickers found that the wage rates varied from day to day, depending on the number of pickers on hand, and that the "bonus"—that was advertised—was actually a "hold-back" forfeited if the worker left the job. Widely distributed, the ads had brought in about one thousand more pickers than were needed. Average daily earnings were found to be about 90¢ or $1. The conditions at the camp may be indicated by the fact that eight small toilets had been built to accommodate 2,800 people and that there were no separate toilets for women. The riot was touched off when law enforcement officials attempted to break up a protest meeting that a group of wobblies had called on the rancher.

To the wobbly movement, the Wheatland Riot had much the same significance that the Preparedness Day bombing and the dynamiting of the *Times* had for the labor movement; the three events, in fact, were part of a much larger pattern of violence in industrial relations. The Wheatland Riot is of great historic importance for it marked the beginning, in a sense, of intense labor strife in California agriculture. There had been earlier incidents, of course, but this case focused national attention for the first time on the miserable plight of seasonal field workers in California. Out of this incident came the prosecution of Richard Ford and Herman Suhr, both of whom were convicted in one of the most famous "labor trials" in the state's history. Along with Tom Mooney, J. J. McNamara, and J. B. McNamara, "Blackie" Ford and Herman Suhr acquired legendary fame as "labor martyrs." In the context of this chapter, the Wheatland affair is of importance for two reasons: it marked the extension to agriculture of the pattern of "total engagement" that had long characterized labor relations in California; and it emphasized, once again, the manner in which repressive employer tactics consistently precipitated radical protests.

In a broad historical sense, the third chapter of labor violence in California came to its climax with the adoption on April 30, 1919, of the Criminal Syndicalism Law. Although Idaho has the unenviable distinction of having adopted the first statute of this kind, the California act received the most notoriety because it was more widely enforced than any similar legislation. Criminal syndicalism acts in the other states soon became "dead letter" statutes but the California act was systematically enforced. In a five-year period following its adoption, 504 persons were arrested, bail was usually set at $15,000, and 264 of those arrested were actually tried. At least thirty-four cases, arising under this act, went to the appellate courts. Of those arrested, 164 were convicted and 128 of these were sentenced to San Quentin Prison for terms which ranged from one to fourteen years. The emphasis given the enforcement of this act in California is not surprising for its adoption represented the culmination of seventy years of intense anti-union activity on the part of employer groups. It was, in effect, the logical end-product of the "total engagement" between capital and labor in California.

The fourth "engagement" took place in the 1930's and involved, first, a recrudescence of the waterfront warfare which had become more or less endemic in San Francisco, and, second, a series of great strikes in agriculture. Between January 1, 1933, and June 1, 1939, approximately 180 agricultural strikes were reported in California; farm labor strikes were reported, in fact, in thirty-four of the fifty-eight counties of the state. All in all, some 89,276 workers took part in these strikes for which no parallel of any kind can be found in the history of American labor. Civil and criminal disturbances were reported in 65 of the strikes, with hundreds of arrests, 14 "violent" strikes, several deaths, and considerable property damage. The ferment of these years reached its climax with the "general strike" in San Francisco, July 16 to 19, 1934, which was called to protest the killing of two waterfront workers on "Bloody Thursday," July 5. Although the general strike collapsed, the waterfront workers won a great victory which was followed up, one year later, with the formation of the Maritime Federation of the Pacific. As much as anything else, perhaps, it was this upsurge in labor activity, following the suppressions of the period from 1910 to 1924, that brought about the election of Governor Culbert L. Olson in 1938 whose first official act was the issuance of a pardon for Tom Mooney. The fourth round, in short, was won by labor and, with the adoption of the National Labor Relations Act in 1936, the labor movement achieved a new maturity and succeeded, at long last, in breaking the power of the employer organizations and in organizing "open shop" Los Angeles. . . .

Another America: The Grape Strike in California*

EDGAR Z. FRIEDENBERG

I N SEPTEMBER, 1965, there began in Delano, California, a
strike whose impact on the evolution of labor relations in this
country, and on the quality of American democracy, is likely to
be out of all proportion to the number of people, strategic importance of the industry, or bread-and-butter issues involved.
This is the strike called against the local grape-growers by the
independent National Farm Workers Association, and the AFL–
CIO Agricultural Workers Organizing Committee. Both are new
organizations. Though the most active leaders of AWOC have
grown old in the labor movement, AWOC itself was founded in
1959; NFWA was started in 1962 by Cesar Chavez, a native
Californian from Brawley, in the Imperial Valley, whose childhood and youth were spent in a series of agricultural labor camps.

Agricultural workers are today the most helpless and deprived
labor force in the country, and by a margin that readers accustomed to present-day industrial conditions can hardly imagine.
These workers have never been effectively unionized. Partly for
this reason they have been excluded from nearly all legislation
that guarantees the rights of workers and establishes collective bargaining machinery in industry. Agricultural workers are still treated
under law as if they worked on family farms, under the genial
supervision of the farmer and his bountiful wife. This is not justi-

* Reprinted from *The New York Review of Books,* March 3, 1966.
Copyright © 1966, The New York Review. Used by permission.

fiable in any part of America today; in California, where agriculture has been big business since long before Steinbeck wrote *The Grapes of Wrath* and Carey McWilliams reported on *Factories in the Field*, it is absurd.

Added to their legal disabilities are those imposed on agricultural labor by the way it is recruited, administered, and housed —limitations which, however, are less applicable to the grape industry than to the "stoop-labor" crops of truck gardens, like melons or lettuce. In these crops, which are highly seasonal, workers are usually not employed directly by the grower at all, but by labor contractors who recruit them through publicly operated employment offices, or simply hire them off the streets of Skid Row at dawn and load them into trucks or old school buses for the trip to the fields. For longer or more remote jobs the workers are lodged in camps located on company property and inaccessible except by trespass or the owner's permission.

The difficulties of organizing agricultural workers and getting them into a position to improve their lot are therefore enormous. They are usually disfranchised and virtually unschooled—Chavez, who got as far as the eighth grade by heroic efforts, attended forty schools to do it.[1] Organizers cannot approach them either at work or afterwards, since the camp may be their only home. They are politically powerless and often apathetic; the growers have great political influence at all levels.

Administratively, too, the problems are overwhelming. As Henry Aderson, chairman of Citizens for Farm Labor—an organization including labor and civil rights leaders, university professors, and other Californians—observed in a broadcast on KPFA last December 3:

. . . a strike presupposes the existence of some sort of framework, some sort of ground rules, for negotiation. It presupposes the existence of collective bargaining machinery. There is no such machinery in agriculture. Not more than one in a hundred California farm workers is represented by anyone, in any meaningful sense. There is no way to find by whom farm workers would like to be represented, if anyone. No one has a list of workers who are "attached" to the grape industry; where they live; or anything which needs to be known if there is to be any sort of contract covering them. These are some of the consequences of the fact that agriculture is excluded from the Labor-Management Relations Act of 1947 (Taft–Hartley) and from the jurisdiction of the National Labor Relations Board.

---

[1] Truman E. Moore, *The Slaves We Rent* (Random, 1965), p. 130.

The grape industry, however, presents several features that make it a promising place to begin trying to organize agricultural workers. Grapes are not quite as seasonal as most truck garden crops. Like all crops, they have to be harvested; but they also have to be pruned and sprayed, and sprayed, and sprayed throughout the season. This means that grape-production relies, in part, on a comparatively stable, less migratory labor force, with potential political power if the workers can be got to register. The grape industry makes little use of labor contractors; growers hire directly, which means that negotiations will be that much simpler if they can ever be got under way. Grape-tending, by and large, requires skill and dependability. It is not a job for casual laborers; "winos" may depend on the grape industry to keep them going, but the industry cannot depend on them to keep it going. This makes workers who strike more difficult to replace.

Striking under these conditions amounts primarily then to trying to persuade grape-workers not to work for the struck growers. This task has two main aspects. First, it is necessary to build *esprit de corps* among local groups of workers and potential workers; then, it is necessary to picket the fields in order to try to dissuade new recruits, or old employees who have decided to remain loyal to the employer, from scabbing. Building group spirit, however, requires great resourcefulness when dealing with a labor force as ethnically varied as grape-workers, who are primarily of Mexican and Filipino stock, but who also include more exotic elements, like one camp full of Yemenites I observed, whose quarters were festooned with highly decorative signs in Arabic.

Picketing is likewise difficult when the workers are brought directly to the employer's property in his own trucks and lodged in its midst; and when the growers find it comparatively easy to obtain restraining orders from familiar and understanding local authorities, even though these orders may be vacated at the next level of appeal. I observed one such picket; and found it an extremely moving experience but not, I should judge, a particularly effective one in getting anybody to quit pruning grapes. Picketing begins at dawn, when workers move out into the fields; but the pickets move in motorcades from one operation to another. At the location I observed, two miles or so out of Delano, about a dozen picketers were drawn up on the far side of a narrow county road while workers' and growers' automobiles were parked on the field side. This picket had been dispatched from Chavez's organization, and bore NFWA's splendid barbaric device—a black eagle on a scarlet ground, with the single word HUELGA (strike). There were some banners, but most of these were circular, wooden signs on long rods that looked like the emblems carried in the grand procession in *Aida*. The young men who composed the picket marched slowly and with great dignity; while a stout and forceful young woman addressed the fields across the road in Spanish through a portable loud-hailer.

But only three or four pruners were visible in the field— whether because the strike was succeeding there, or because the field-bosses had moved the pruners back onto the land and out of earshot, as they often do when a roving picket arrives, I do not know. The growers' representative, a young man in a black sombrero, paced up and down the roadside opposite and tended his own public address system, that was being run from the battery of his car and played light music. The intent was to drown out the speech the young woman was giving; but the effect, I thought—since I couldn't understand it, anyway—was rather to set it off, like the musical portion of the sound track of a foreign movie. But what contributed most to the emotional impact of the scene was its saturation by police. To protect the peace of Tulane County . . . from these ten or twelve people who glowed with composure, restraint, and determination, there was a deputy sheriff in his paddy wagon—which here, as is usual in California, is an ordinary station wagon made sinister by removing the inside handles of the rear doors and erecting a heavy metal screen above the front seat—and two cruising patrol cars that drove back and forth along this tiny stretch of road. They were accompanied by two little unmarked red trucks that the picket captain told me belonged to the grape corporation, whose function I cannot grasp unless it was to remind the police to do their duty impartially. The deputy sheriff, an unusually civil servant, did walk over and bid the pickets a genial good morning, observing that it was going to be a nice day, which it was, in many respects. (On other occasions, several of the pickets informed me, the day had been marred by considerably more aggressive behavior by some of the sheriff's colleagues.)

To plan and conduct this complex enterprise, making the most of limited resources and avoiding the continual danger of internal conflict, requires leadership of a very high order, and self-discipline among a great many hard pressed people. This is particularly true because of the severely contrasting styles of NFWA and AWOC. Both are chaired locally by impressive and able men. But Cesar Chavez designed and built his own organiza-

tion, and its approach is something new to American labor. Larry
Itliong, the courtly regional director of AWOC, bears the burden,
and occasionally receives the support, of the entire structure of
American organized labor. So far, organized labor has behaved
rather ambiguously about the grape strike. Walter Reuther has
delivered $10,000 to the Delano strike fund, and pledged to sup-
port it in the future at the rate of $5,000 per month. Longshore-
men have immensely heartened the Delano leaders by refusing to
load grapes from struck vineyards on ships for export. But the
Teamster's Union would have given the strike far more decisive
support if it had refused to truck the grapes out of Delano; and
it hasn't. Drivers sometimes observe the picket line *pro forma*,
parking outside it and leaving the actual crossing of the line to
be done by employees of the grower who bring the grapes out to
the truck. And, indeed, there is a question whether such refusal
by the Teamsters would be illegal under the Taft–Hartley Act,
complicated by the fact that agricultural workers are excluded
from it.

What the AFL–CIO has provided unstintingly is a procession
of dignitaries giving speeches. AWOC's headquarters are in the
Filipino Hall, a shabby, battleship-clean building with an auditorium, a few offices, and a soup kitchen. During the day, idle
workers sit around watching television or chatting; there are grave,
curious children; and a crew of women preparing delicious and
abundant food which they graciously invited a friend and myself
to share. The atmosphere is precisely that of a church social;
even the sign at the entrance to the chow line advising that "none
will be turned away," though active pickets have precedence, is
written in gothic script. The hall fills for the evening meal, with
gentle, dignified Filipino farm workers. Then, at six-thirty, the
meeting begins, and goes on till nine o'clock—and, suddenly, the
audience, though addressed by Mr. Itliong from the chairs as
"Brother" or "Sister," finds itself at the equivalent atmospherically
of a Democratic rally in the Bronx. Inspirational greetings are
given by the heads of Ethnic-American Associations, down from
San Francisco on a visit, along with an official from the SNCC
office, or a young civil-rights lawyer, in bluejeans. Mr. Itliong's
superior in AWOC, Al Green, also down from the city, comes
on as the horny-handed veteran of the labor movement that he
genuinely is, reminding one how times have changed. The
favorite daughter of the Delano strike, Mrs. Anne Draper,
Regional Director of the Union Label Department of the Amal-
gamated Clothing Workers of America, AFL–CIO, speaks un-

abashedly to the workers as her children—"the best children any mother could have"—and they are utterly delighted. No one has worked more devotedly for *La Huelga* than Mrs. Draper, and she is both indefatigable and very bright. To an ex-Brooklynite like myself, her style suggests rich chicken soup in an inexhaustible cauldron of tough, shiny, stainless steel. This sort of meeting goes on nearly every night, and most of the distinguished guests tell the workers they can't lose. The effect is of watching a new play of Bertolt Brecht, more ironical than most.

Hometown Boy

At 102 Albany Street, in a little grocery store converted to offices at the corner of two dirt roads southwest of town, Cesar Chavez has established the very different headquarters of the National Farm Workers Association. . . . NFWA also runs a meal service for its pickets, and pays those on actual duty; stockpiles food and clothing for them and their family, and pays rent, and, when it can, car payments. It runs a credit union for its members, who pay $3.50 a month, and publishes, for $2 a year, a sprightly illustrated fortnightly called *El Malcriado* in two editions, Spanish and English. It supports a satirical troupe called *El Teatro Campesino*, that puts on sketches and playlets. But its most notable accomplishment was to obtain from the Office of Economic Opportunity a grant of $267,887 for "a plan for sending out cadres of trained workers to collect basic facts about farm workers' lives and also to instruct the marginal workers in better money management and developing their communities."[2] Chavez, on being informed of the grant, immediately requested that the money be withheld until the strike had been settled, so that NFWA could not be accused of using it as a war chest; and this has been done. Nevertheless, the Delano City Council has officially complained of the grant, characterizing Chavez in a resolution as ". . . well known in this city, having spent various periods of his life in this community, including attendance at public schools, and it is the opinion of this Council that he does not merit the trust of the Council with regard to the administration of the grant."[3]

This opinion of the Delano City Council differs, apparently,

[2] San Francisco *Sunday Examiner and Chronicle*, Sec. 1, p. 7, October 17, 1965.

[3] *The Movement* (published by SNCC of California) Boycott Supplement.

from that of Stephen Spender. On a bulletin board in the barren
outer office at 102 Albany there is pinned, along with maps and
instructions to pickets, and a list of grocery and laundry items
needed for the strikers' depot, a holograph copy of a poem by
Spender inscribed "for Cesar Chavez" and reading, familiarly;

> *I think continually of those who*
> *were truly great*
> *Who from the womb remembered*
> *the soul's history. . . .*

It is strange that the Delano City Council should have advanced an argument that tends to establish Chavez as a hometown
boy, since real resentment of the strike centers, as with the Civil
Rights Movement in the South, on the issue of outside interven-
tion. Thus, the *Delano Record* for January 11, 1966, has two
headlines: DEMAND FOR DELANO GRAPES JUMPS ("Delano area
grape grower Jack Pandol says national publicity from the union
efforts has helped to boost the sale of Delano grape products.
. . .") and CATHOLIC BISHOP SCORES PRIEST FOR "PERFORMANCE"
HERE—an account of the condemnation by the Bishop of Mon-
terey-Fresno of the Reverend James Vizzard, S.J., Director of the
Washington, D.C., office of the National Catholic Rural Life
Conference "and his intrusive associates" for coming to Delano
and speaking in support of the strike. A broadside sheet entitled
FACTS FROM DELANO, bearing no date or attribution, that was
given me by a grower on my request for publications expressing
their viewpoint, features a statement signed by the Delano Min-
isterial Association and even Protestant ministers individually,
stating that the Association ". . . has not fostered nor does it
encourage any ecclesiastical demonstration or interference in the
farm labor situation." This sheet also reproduces a report from
the *Delano Record* that the Delano chapter of Community Service
Organization:

. . . deplores sincerely the civil rights movement that has become the
prevailing issue in the former local labor dispute in our community.
We sympathize with the plight of the farm worker or any other worker
in those areas where poverty exists and where they are exploited, but
we feel that these conditions are not prevalent in the Delano area.
Delano CSO through experience knows that living conditions of farm
workers in our area are far more adequate than those of the poor
living in the ghetos [sic] of our large cities.
We feel that the outside elements invading our city are performing

a dis-service to the well-being of our community by creating adverse conditions and feeling of animosity among the citizenry that have not existed in our city for the past 25 to 30 years.

This statement created a hassle when it was published; for Cesar Chavez was trained in various CSO operations, and left the organization amicably when he felt that it was emphasizing urban problems too much to provide scope for his interests in farm labor. CSO is primarily a Mexican-American social action group that functions in California along the self-directing lines laid down by Saul Alinsky; and at a special meeting in Fresno the organization repudiated the action of its Delano chapter by endorsing the grape strike.[4] Nevertheless, the Delano chapter's statement about working conditions in the area seems to me justified. Chavez's choice of Delano as a proving ground for his approach to the organization of agricultural labor follows the highly sophisticated revolutionary principle that successful revolt starts with the richest of the poor—the poorest are too abject, vulnerable, and apathetic. Even around AWOC I heard few expressions of discontent with the money grape-workers were now earning, which comes close to the $1.40 per hour they want—though there was widespread belief that wages would immediately fall if the strike failed.

On my way north from Delano, I stopped in the neighboring community of Earlimart to interview Mark Zaninovich, Jr., who, two years earlier, had been vice-president of the student body at the University of California, Davis, and who is some twenty years my junior, but who recently took over from his father the management of one of the major grape companies in the state, which is regarded as a leading opponent of the strike. I had not previously met Mr. Zaninovich, and he clearly perceived that I was sympathetic to *La Huelga*. But he received me with flawless, though formal, courtesy and spent more than two hours at the close of an exceptionally busy day driving me over grape fields— his own, and those of other growers—showing me anything I cared to see. He was plainly torn between his conviction that I would be suspicious of anything he selected to point out and his shrewd hunch that I was too ignorant to know what to ask him to show me. But once I got used to the idea of riding over unmarked dirt roads in a beat-up truck with a mobile telephone in it and a sticker reading "I fight poverty; I work" on the bumper, we got along well enough.

---

[4] *El Malcriado*, 25, p. 4.

What I wanted to see was the camps the workers are lodged in; and Mr. Zaninovich showed me three, all different, with different owners. I found them appalling; but not because they were physically squalid. None was that. And none suggested any form of oppression—though one did bear on its woodwork the marks of a recent fire-bomb that had rendered two bedrooms uninhabitable.

What was appalling was the conception of the kind of life that is good enough for a human being that underlies the very design of these camps. The first one Mr. Zaninovich showed me belonged to his own company; and he apologized for its age and shabbiness. As soon as his company could afford it—and, despite the strike, they were running a little ahead of schedule on their operations—they planned to build one like the next camp he would take me to; his company didn't own it, but it was brand new and a model of what such a camp might be.

It was a horrible place. The Zaninovich camp had not been bad; it was weathered, but clean, and rather suggested an old-fashioned tourist court of the early days of motoring. The new place was air-conditioned and centrally heated, steam burst aggressively out through the doors of its ample shower rooms. But it was still a long, concrete building whose central corridor was lined with doors that do not reach the floor. Each little room houses two men. Nobody had turned on the electric light in the corridor, which was illuminated only by the light of dusk coming under the stall-like doors. This is not, in the ordinary sense, a temporary dwelling. Migrant workers move from one such camp to another, following the crops; many have no other home than such a camp all their adult working lives. This, as Mr. Zaninovich truly said, was one of the best in the country; but nobody accustomed to an ordinary American life—even a poor man's life—could design such a structure for the use of other human beings unless he believed that they ought to accept a pattern of life so impoverished as to suggest a different species. In the next, and last, camp that we stopped at, Mr. Zaninovich asked one of the workers he knew and was on friendly terms with if he would mind showing me his room. The man at first demurred with a giggle because he had "awful things" in it; then flung the door open. The walls were lined with commonplace nude pin-ups and the bed had a cheap scarf on it with a similar design. The only awful thing was that the man was in his thirties, and this was the best he had, except when he made a visit to his home, in Yemen.

Meanwhile, he was saving his money to retire there ultimately, a wealthy man. It was, as Mr. Zaninovich said, a classic example of a man bettering himself economically by his own efforts.

I thought of this man; comparing him to the people I had been with earlier on the picket line; and it occurred to me that they seemed the only people I had seen in months who seemed positively happy and free from self-pity. In their response to me, they had been friendlier and more open, by far, than most of the people I met; though my speech and manner must have struck them as very unlike their own. I wondered why they had trusted me; then I realized that, of course, they hadn't. It was themselves they had trusted; such people do not fear strangers. Whether he wins La Huelga or not, this Cesar Chavez has done or, rather, has taught his people to do for themselves. Nothing I know of in the history of labor in America shows as much sheer creativity as NFWA, as much respect for what people, however poor, might make of their own lives once they understood the dynamics of their society. The cardinal sin of labor leaders, indeed—their special form of *accidia,* not of pride—is pomposity. If NFWA becomes sinful, it will be in quite a different way. I don't know the exact title of this sin, but an example of it would be restoring to all of us our common speech, and reconstructing the Tower of Babel.

The Organizer's Tale*

CESAR CHAVEZ

IT REALLY STARTED for me sixteen years ago in San Jose, California, when I was working on an apricot farm. We figured he was just another social worker doing a study of farm conditions, and I kept refusing to meet with him. But he was persistent. Finally, I got together some of the rough element in San Jose. We were going to have a little reception for him to teach the *gringo* a little bit of how we felt. There were about thirty of us in the house, young guys mostly. I was supposed to give them a signal— change my cigarette from my right hand to my left, and then we were going to give him a lot of hell. But he started talking and the more he talked, the more wide-eyed I became and the less inclined I was to give the signal. A couple of guys who were pretty drunk at the time still wanted to give the *gringo* the business, but we got rid of them. This fellow was making a lot of sense, and I wanted to hear what he had to say.

His name was Fred Ross, and he was an organizer for the Community Service Organizations (CSO) which was working with Mexican-Americans in the cities. I became immediately really involved. Before long I was heading a voter registration drive. All the time I was observing the things Fred did, secretly, because I wanted to learn how to organize, to see how it was done. I was impressed with his patience and understanding of people. I thought this was a tool, one of the greatest things he had.

It was pretty rough for me at first. I was changing and had to take a lot of ridicule from the kids my age, the rough characters I worked with in the fields. They would say, "Hey, big shot. Now that you're a *politico*, why are you working here for 65 cents an hour?" I might add that our neighborhood had the highest percentage of San Quentin graduates. It was a game among the *pachucos* in the sense that we defended ourselves from outsiders, although inside the neighborhood there was not a lot of fighting.

After six months of working every night in San Jose, Fred assigned me to take over the CSO chapter in Decoto. It was a tough spot to fill. I would suggest something, and people would say, "No, let's wait till Fred gets back," or "Fred wouldn't do it that way." This is pretty much a pattern with people, I discovered, whether I was put in Fred's position, or later, when someone else was put in my position. After the Decoto assignment I was sent to start a new chapter in Oakland. Before I left, Fred came to a place in San Jose called the Hole-in-the-Wall and we talked for half an hour over coffee. He was in a rush to leave, but I wanted to keep him talking; I was that scared of my assignment.

There were hard times in Oakland. First of all, it was a big city and I'd get lost every time I went anywhere. Then I arranged a series of house meetings. I would get to the meeting early and drive back and forth past the house, too nervous to go in and face the people. Finally I would force myself to go inside and sit in a corner. I was quite thin then, and young, and most of the people were middle-aged. Someone would say, "Where's the organizer?" And I would pipe up, "Here I am." Then they would say in Spanish—these were very poor people and we hardly spoke anything but Spanish—"Ha! This *kid*?" Most of them said they were interested, but the hardest part was to get them to start pushing themselves, on their own initiative.

The idea was to set up a meeting and then get each attending person to call his own house meeting, inviting new people—a sort of chain letter effect. After a house meeting I would lie awake going over the whole thing, playing the tape back, trying to see why people laughed at one point, or why they were for one thing and against another. I was also learning to read and write, those late evenings. I had left school in the 7th grade after attending sixty-seven different schools, and my reading wasn't the best.

At our first organizing meeting we had 368 people: I'll never forget it because it was very important to me. You eat your heart out; the meeting is called for 7 o'clock and you start to worry about 4. You wait. Will they show up? Then the first one arrives.

By 7 there are only twenty people, you have everything in order, you have to look calm. But little by little they filter in and at a certain point you know it will be a success.

After four months in Oakland, I was transferred. The chapter was beginning to move on its own, so Fred assigned me to organize the San Joaquin Valley. Over the months I developed what I used to call schemes or tricks—now I call them techniques—of making initial contacts. The main thing in convincing someone is to spend time with him. It doesn't matter if he can read, write or even speak well. What is important is that he is a man and second, that he has shown some initial interest. One good way to develop leadership is to take a man with you in your car. And it works a lot better if you're doing the driving; that way you are in charge. You drive, he sits there, and you talk. These little things were very important to me; I was caught in a big game by then, figuring out what makes people work. I found that if you work hard enough you can usually shake people into working too, those who are concerned. You work harder and they work harder still, up to a point and then they pass you. Then, of course, they're on their own.

I also learned to keep away from the established groups and so-called leaders, and to guard against philosophizing. Working with low-income people is very different from working with the professionals, who like to sit around talking about how to play politics. When you're trying to recruit a farmworker, you have to paint a little picture, and then you have to color the picture in. We found out that the harder a guy is to convince, the better leader or member he becomes. When you exert yourself to convince him, you have his confidence and he has good motivation. A lot of people who say OK right away wind up hanging around the office, taking up the workers' time.

During the McCarthy era in one Valley town, I was subjected to a lot of redbaiting. We had been recruiting people for citizenship classes at the high school when we got into a quarrel with the naturalization examiner. He was rejecting people on the grounds that they were just parroting what they learned in citizenship class. One day we had a meeting about it in Fresno, and I took along some of the leaders of our local chapter. Some redbaiting official gave us a hard time, and the people got scared and took his side. They did it because it seemed easy at the moment, even though they knew that sticking with me was the right thing to do. It was disgusting. When we left the building they walked by themselves ahead of me as if I had some kind of communicable disease. I had been working with these people for three months and I was very sad to see that. It taught me a great lesson.

That night I learned that the chapter officers were holding a meeting to review my letters and printed materials to see if I really was a Communist. So I drove out there and walked right in on their meeting. I said, "I hear you've been discussing me, and I thought it would be nice if I was here to defend myself. Not that it matters that much to you or even to me, because as far as I'm concerned you are a bunch of cowards." At that they began to apologize. "Let's forget it," they said. "You're a nice guy." But I didn't want apologies. I wanted a full discussion. I told them I didn't give a damn, but that they had to learn to distinguish fact from what appeared to be a fact because of fear. I kept them there till two in the morning. Some of the women cried. I don't know if they investigated me any further, but I stayed on another few months and things worked out.

This was not an isolated case. Often when we'd leave people to themselves they would get frightened and draw back into their shells where they had been all the years. And I learned quickly that there is no real appreciation. Whatever you do, and no matter what reasons you may give to others, you do it because you want to see it done, or maybe because you want power. And there shouldn't be any appreciation, understandably. I know good organizers who were destroyed, washed out, because they expected people to appreciate what they'd done. Anyone who comes in with the idea that farmworkers are free of sin and that the growers are all bastards, either has never dealt with the situation or is an idealist of the first order. Things don't work that way.

For more than ten years I worked for the CSO. As the organization grew, we found ourselves meeting in fancier and fancier motels and holding expensive conventions. Doctors, lawyers and politicians began joining. They would get elected to some office in the organization and then, for all practical purposes, leave. Intent on using the CSO for their own prestige purposes, these "leaders," many of them, lacked the urgency we had to have. When I became general director I began to press for a program to organize farmworkers into a union, an idea most of the leadership opposed. So I started a revolt within the CSO. I refused to sit at the head table at meetings, refused to wear a suit and tie, and finally I even refused to shave and cut my hair. It used to embarrass some of the professionals. At every meeting I got up and gave my standard speech: we shouldn't meet in fancy motels, we were getting away from the people, farmworkers had to be organized. But nothing happened. In March of '62 I resigned and came to Delano to begin organizing the Valley on my own.

By hand I drew a map of all the towns between Arvin and Stockton—eighty-six of them, including farming camps—and decided to hit them all to get a small nucleus of people working in each. For six months I traveled around, planting an idea. We had a simple questionnaire, a little card with space for name, address and how much the worker thought he ought to be paid. My wife, Helen, mimeographed them, and we took our kids for two or three day jaunts to these towns, distributing the cards door-to-door and to camps and groceries.

Some 80,000 cards were sent back from eight Valley counties. I got a lot of contacts that way, but I was shocked at the wages the people were asking. The growers were paying $1 and $1.15, and maybe 95 per cent of the people thought they should be getting only $1.25. Sometimes people scribbled messages on the cards: "I hope to God we win" or "Do you think we can win?" or "I'd like to know more." So I separated the cards with the pencilled notes, got in my car and went to those people.

We didn't have any money at all in those days, none for gas and hardly any for food. So I went to people and started asking for food. It turned out to be about the best thing I could have done, although at first it's hard on your pride. Some of our best members came in that way. If people give you their food, they'll give you their hearts. Several months and many meetings later we had a working organization, and this time the leaders were the people.

None of the farmworkers had collective bargaining contracts, and I thought it would take ten years before we got that first contract. I wanted desperately to get some color into the movement, to give people something they could identify with, like a flag. I was reading some books about how various leaders discovered what colors contrasted and stood out the best. The Egyptians had found that a red field with a white circle and a black emblem in the center crashed into your eyes like nothing else. I wanted to use the Aztec eagle in the center, as on the Mexican flag. So I told my cousin Manuel, "Draw an Aztec eagle." Manuel had a little trouble with it, so we modified the eagle to make it easier for people to draw.

The first big meeting of what we decided to call the National

Farm Workers Association was held in September, 1962, at Fresno, with 287 people. We had our huge red flag on the wall, with paper tacked over it. When the time came, Manuel pulled a cord ripping the paper off the flag and all of a sudden it hit the people. Some of them wondered if it was a Communist flag, and I said it probably looked more like a neo-Nazi emblem than anything else. But they wanted an explanation, so Manuel got up and said, "When that damn eagle flies—that's when the farmworkers' problems are going to be solved."

One of the first things I decided was that outside money wasn't going to organize people, at least not in the beginning. I even turned down a grant from a private group—$50,000 to go directly to organize farmworkers—for just this reason. Even when there are no strings attached, you are still compromised because you feel you have to produce immediate results. This is bad, because it takes a long time to build a movement, and your organization suffers if you get too far ahead of the people it belongs to. We set the dues at $42 a year per family, really a meaningful dues, but the 212 we got to pay, only 12 remained by June of '63. We were discouraged at that, but not enough to make us quit.

Money was always a problem. Once we were facing a $180 gas bill on a credit card I'd got a long time ago and was about to lose. And we *had* to keep that credit card. One day my wife and I were picking cotton, pulling bolls, to make a little money to live on. Helen said to me, "Do you put all this in the bag, or just the cotton?" I thought she was kidding and told her to throw the whole boll in so that she had nothing but a sack of bolls at the weighing. The man said, "Whose sack is this?" I said, well, my wife's, and he told us we were fired. "Look at all that crap you brought in," he said. Helen and I started laughing. We were going anyway. We took the $4 we had earned and spent it at a grocery store where they were giving away a $100 prize. Each time you shopped they'd give you one of the letters of M-O-N-E-Y or a flag: you had to have M-O-N-E-Y plus the flag to win. Helen had already collected the letters and just needed the flag. Anyway, they gave her the ticket. She screamed, "A flag? I don't believe it," ran in and got the $100. She said, "Now we're going to eat steak." But I said no, we're going to pay the gas bill. I don't know if she cried, but I think she did.

It was rough in those early years. Helen was having babies and I was not there when she was at the hospital. But if you haven't got your wife behind you, you can't do many things.

There's got to be peace at home. So I did, I think, a fairly good job of organizing her. When we were kids, she lived in Delano and I came to town as a migrant. Once on a date we had a bad experience about segregation at a movie theater, and I put up a fight. We were together then, and still are. I think I'm more of a pacifist than she is. Her father, Fabela, was a colonel with Pancho Villa in the Mexican Revolution. Sometimes she gets angry and tells me, "These scabs—you should deal with them sternly," and I kid her, "It must be too much of that Fabela blood in you."

The movement really caught on in '64. By August we had a thousand members. We'd had a beautiful ninety-day drive in Corcoran, where they had the Battle of the Corcoran Farm Camp thirty years ago, and by November we had assets of $25,000 in our credit union, which helped to stabilize the membership. I had gone without pay the whole of 1963. The next year the members voted me a $40 a week salary, after Helen had to quit working in the fields to manage the credit union.

Our first strike was in May of '65, a small one but it prepared us for the big one. A farmworker from McFarland named Epifanio Camacho came to see me. He said he was sick and tired of how people working the roses were being treated, and he was willing to "go the limit." I assigned Manuel and Gilbert Padilla to hold meetings at Camacho's house. The people wanted union recognition, but the real issue, as in most cases when you begin, was wages. They were promised $9 a thousand, but they were actually getting $6.50 and $7 for grafting roses. Most of them signed cards giving us the right to bargain for them. We chose the biggest company, with about eighty-five employees, not counting the irrigators and supervisors, and we held a series of meetings to prepare the strike and call the vote. There would be no picket line; everyone pledged on their honor not to break the strike.

Early on the first morning of the strike, we sent out ten cars to check the people's homes. We found lights in five or six homes and knocked on the doors. The men were getting up and we'd say, "Where are you going?" They would dodge, "Oh, uh . . . I was just getting up, you know." We'd say, "Well, you're not going to work, are you?" And they'd say no. Dolores Huerta, who was driving the green panel truck, saw a light in one house where four rose-workers lived. They told her they were going to work, even after she reminded them of their pledge. So she moved the truck so it blocked their driveway, turned off the key, put it in her purse and sat there alone.

That morning the company foreman was madder than hell and refused to talk to us. None of the grafters had shown up for work. At 10:30 we started to go to the company office, but it occurred to us that maybe a woman would have a better chance. So Dolores knocked on the office door, saying, "I'm Dolores Huerta from the National Farm Workers Association." "Get out!" the man said. "You Communist. Get out!" I guess they were expecting us, because as Dolores stood arguing with him the cops came and told her to leave. She left.

For two days the fields were idle. On Wednesday they recruited a group of Filipinos from out of town who knew nothing of the strike, maybe thirty-five of them. They drove through escorted by three sheriff's patrol cars, one in front, one in the middle and one at the rear with a dog. We didn't have a picket line, but we parked across the street and just watched them go through, not saying a word. All but seven stopped working after half an hour, and the rest had quit by mid-afternoon.

The company made an offer the evening of the fourth day, a package deal that amounted to a 120 per cent wage increase, but no contract. We wanted to hold out for a contract and more benefits, but a majority of the rose-workers wanted to accept the offer and go back. We are a democratic union so we had to support what they wanted to do. They had a meeting and voted to settle. Then we had a problem with a few militants who wanted to hold out. We had to convince them to go back to work, as a united front, because otherwise they would be canned. So we worked—Tony Orendain and I, Dolores and Gilbert, Jim Drake and all the organizers—knocking on doors till two in the morning, telling people, "You have to go back or you'll lose your job." And they did. They worked.

Our second strike, and our last before the big one at Delano, was in the grapes at Martin's Ranch last summer. The people were getting a raw deal there, being pushed around pretty badly. Gilbert went out to the field, climbed on top of a car and took a strike vote. They voted unanimously to go out. Right away they started bringing in strikebreakers, so we launched a tough attack on the labor contractors, distributed leaflets portraying them as really low characters. We attacked one—Luis Campos—so badly that he just gave up the job, and he took twenty-seven of his men out with him. All he asked was that we distribute another leaflet reinstating him in the community. And we did. What was unusual was that the grower would talk to us. The grower kept saying, "I can't pay. I just haven't got the money." I guess he must have found the money somewhere, because we were asking $1.40 and we got it.

We had just finished the Martin strike when the Agricultural Workers Organizing Committee (AFL–CIO) started a strike against the grape-growers, DiGiorgio, Schenley liquors, and small growers, asking $1.40 an hour and 25 cents a box. There was a lot of pressure from our members for us to join the strike, but we had some misgivings. We didn't feel ready for a big strike like this one, one that was sure to last a long time. Having no money —just $87 in the strike fund—meant we'd have to depend on God knows who.

Eight days after the strike started—it takes time to get 1,200 people together from all over the Valley—we held a meeting in Delano and voted to go out. I asked the membership to release us from the pledge not to accept outside money, because we'd need it now, a lot of it. The help came. It started because of the close, and I would say even beautiful relationship that we've had with the Migrant Ministry for some years. They were the first to come to our rescue, financially and in every other way, and they spread the word to other benefactors.

We had planned, before, to start a labor school in November. It never happened, but we have the best labor school we could ever have, in the strike. The strike is only a temporary condition, however. We have over 3,000 members spread out over a wide area, and we have to service them when they have problems. We get letters from New Mexico, Colorado, Texas, California, from farmworkers saying, "We're getting together and we need an organizer." It kills you when you haven't got the personnel and resources. You feel badly about not sending an organizer because you look back and remember all the difficulty you had in getting two or three people together, and here *they're* together. Of course, we're training organizers, many of them younger than I was when I started in CSO. They can work twenty hours a day, sleep four and be ready to hit it again; when you get to be thirty-nine it's a different story.

The people who took part in the strike and the march have something more than their material interest going for them. If it were only material, they wouldn't have stayed on the strike long enough to win. It is difficult to explain. But it flows out in the ordinary things they say. For instance, some of the younger guys are saying, "Where do you think's going to be the next strike?"

I say, "Well, we have to win in Delano." They say, "We'll win, but where do we go next?" I say, "Maybe most of us will be working in the fields." They say, "No, I don't want to go and work in the fields. I want to organize. There are a lot of people that need our help." So I say, "You're going to be pretty poor then, because when you strike you don't have much money." They say they don't care about that.

And others are saying, "I have friends who are working in Texas. If we could only help them." It is bigger, certainly, than just a strike. And if this spirit grows within the farm labor movement, one day we can use the force that we have to help correct a lot of things that are wrong in this society. But that is for the future. Before you can run, you have to learn to walk.

There are vivid memories from my childhood—what we had to go through because of low wages and the conditions, basically because there was no union. I suppose if I wanted to be fair I could say that I'm trying to settle a personal score. I could dramatize it by saying that I want to bring social justice to farmworkers. But the truth is that I went through a lot of hell, and a lot of people did. If we can even the score a little for the workers then we are doing something. Besides, I don't know any other work I like to do better than this. I really don't, you know.

Reagan, Ex-Radical*

ANDREW KOPKIND

RONALD REAGAN is selling out. Not completely, or immediately, or even obviously; the politician's art, like the actor's, is to make things seem what they are not. But disbelief cannot be willingly suspended forever, and in the great back lot of Reagan country, the most perceptive of his followers are beginning to realize that his "Creative Society" is not the plot they had expected.

Reagan wrote (or at least read) the original script during his excruciatingly long campaign for the Republican gubernatorial nomination and the subsequent duel with Pat Brown. As treatments go, it was expensive; the whole affair cost Reagan's backers about $5 million. In outline, Reagan developed a catalogue of the Devil's works in modern America: big government, high taxes, bureaucratic waste, crime in the streets, the new (for him) economics, and those aspects of health, education, and welfare policy which seem to contradict the Protestant ethic.

It was not a bad list. The issues were real, even if crudely defined, and the two-term Democratic administration had for the most part failed to deal with them. Fearful and a little hysterical, the Democrats attacked not only the inadequacy of Reagan's proposals, but also the legitimacy of the issues and his motives for stating them. It became liberal heresy even to acknowledge the oppressive effects of centralized bureaucracy, or the threat of so-

---

* From *The New Republic* (July 15, 1967), Copyright © 1967, Harrison-Blaine of New Jersey, Inc. Used by permission.

cial upheaval, or the inequality of the tax system, or the consequences of a no-win war in Asia. The most they could offer were four more years of ambiguous, probably irrelevant, minutely incremental "improvement." Reagan saw that most voters were in no mood for tolerance. He offered them a vision of a revolution, and he articulated their deepest concerns. If it added up to much less than a program and hardly more than a complaint, it still worked to win him the governorship last November by a million votes.

On the surface, Reagan seemed to have a mandate for sweeping systematic change. He was at the head of an army of ideological infantrymen; they had all watched him on TV the night in 1964 that he had made his big pitch for Barry Goldwater, and they knew that some day he would take command himself. Now he was Goldwater's reincarnation, only smoother and warmer and somehow more believable. The location and composition of Reagan's army were crucial for its victory. Where it's *at* is the glassy, grassy flatland suburbs beneath the mountains, where even the palm trees are imported.

Here are nine million people with a life rich and full of everything except meaning. Families are "units," salaries are paid in "K's" (i.e., kilodollars, on the analogy of kilowatts, as in the phrase, "I'm making 12 K a year"), and there is good medical evidence that kidneys are swimming-pool shaped. Certainly everything else is. The inhabitants belong to a new working class, not a new middle; they are wage-slaves in air-conditioned sweat shops, with no ILGWU in sight. They have jobs which give them almost enough money, almost enough status, almost enough security, and absolutely no sense of creation or purpose (not for nothing a "creative" society appeals strongly). They are programmers, systems analysts, chain-store dentists, servicers, processors, and plasticized professionals with neither past nor future. They have no more sense of participation in the product of their labors than an assembly-line worker who affixes a screw (or hits a button which affixes a thousand screws) feels in a finished Mustang.

One theory holds that Southern Californians have the attitudes they do because they are so content; they allow no threats to the happiness they derive from their property. It is more likely that they are miserable, even if they would not put it in those terms. They can't manage the credit payments, they wonder why their kids blow pot, they don't understand the war, they stall on the freeways and choke on the smog.

Reagan and his organizers saw (as the Democratic liberals did not) that the mega-people of Southern California are potentially radical, not merely status-quo minded. They don't want more; they want different. Reaganism—the successor and refinement of Goldwaterism—made sense to millions of people precisely because it was a movement.

But Reagan as a political campaigner bound himself in a coalition that made radical politics difficult. The infantrymen supplied the precinct work and (some) vote power. Reagan, however, needed more than that, and as his campaign grew more costly and more serious he turned to the traditional sources of power. Like Goldwater, Reagan had threatened the economic and social interests of the big corporate managers. They wanted expansion, government manipulation of the economy, labor peace, satisfied minorities, and international tranquillity (or at least low-cost hostility). In California, as elsewhere, most of the nationally oriented economic forces had fallen in with the Johnson campaign.

Search for Alternatives

In the early days of the primary campaign, that same business bloc, and its political allies, avoided Reagan like poison. There was a frantic search for alternatives: first, Senator Thomas Kuchel, then former San Francisco Mayor George Christopher. But Kuchel shrank from the fight, and Christopher—who finally ran in the primary—came too late with much too little. When it was over, Reagan moved to include part of the "moderate" force in his campaign, as Goldwater had never effectively done. But Reagan could hold out the best promise of all—winning. Those with money and influence knew that if they joined Reagan early enough, they could ultimately direct the course of his administration. As one Republican legislator, an early and dedicated opponent of Reagan, explained: "We all campaigned for Ronnie. Hell, the guy was going to win, so we might as well have some voice. He bought that."

As he took office, Reagan was still thinking more of the infantry and the rich entrepreneurs who had financed his campaign, rather than the come-lately forces on the margins of the team. His inauguration was an emotional visionary production staged at midnight in the capitol. Above the dome flew a tattered state "bear flag" which a wounded soldier had carried home from Vietnam. Inside, Reagan spoke of the "miracle" of (small-r) republican government, where "every man, woman and child becomes a shareholder with the first penny of tax paid." There were echoes of the Kennedy inaugural mixed in with some very contemporary rhetoric about participatory democracy:

The path we will chart . . . demands much of those chosen to govern, but also from those who did the choosing. [It] turns away from any idea that government and those who serve it are omnipotent. It is . . . impossible to follow unless we have faith in the collective wisdom and genius of the people. . . . Government will lead but not rule, listen but not lecture. It is the path of a Creative Society. . . . If this is a dream, it is a good dream. . . . Let this day mark the beginning.

The beginning, in fact, came a few days later, and in a way it was also the beginning of the end. The first decree of the Creative Society was (in the form of an offhand remark by the finance director) a recommendation that the budget for the nine University of California campuses and the eighteen state colleges be drastically reduced. The university regents had requested $278 million in state funds; Reagan proposed $196.5 million. Furthermore, Reagan wanted students to pay tuition for the first time in modern history; not much—just a few hundred dollars or so, as a token of their participation in the expensive program of higher education. The regents, the college trustees, and the academic "community" reacted with instant fury. The cuts, they said, would reduce university enrollment by 22,400 students (90,000 are expected in September), and might necessitate the closing of three campuses. The colleges would be similarly crippled. University President Clark Kerr and College President Glenn Dumke retaliated by closing all admissions for the next term, in order to bring the impact of the cuts home.

Students marched, faculties raged. *The Los Angeles Times*, perhaps more than any other single institution the epitome of the California "establishment," roundly attacked the governor whose election it had, a bit reluctantly, supported.

"Governor Reagan jumped most heavily on the University, possibly because of public resentment over disorders on the Berkeley campus," a *Times* editorial said. (It did not say that the paper had helped prepare that resentment.) It called the cuts "false economy," and a "repeal" of the semi-sacred Master Plan of Higher Education. "No substantial reductions will be possible in the higher-education budget if the quality of such education is to be maintained and expanded."

If Reagan had appeased the people, he had also alienated the major economic interests. California corporatism, perhaps more than any other state's, relies heavily on the production of technicians and intellectuals to support its "infrastructure." Huge technological parks go up around every new campus, the better to feed off the state-subsidized resources. California's agri-business, the richest in the country, owes much to the technology developed in subsidized research.

Either Reagan had completely misunderstood the nature of the power structure in California, or he really thought he could bring it to its knees. As if the budget cuts and the tuition plan were not bad enough, he compounded the antagonism by helping the regents out-flank Clark Kerr, and then fire him from the university presidency. Reagan deserves only a measure of blame, but it was hard to separate the internal politics of the affair from Reagan's pattern of "attacks" on the educational system. For a while, Reagan rode the hobby horse of anti-intellectualism; the state, he said, should not be "subsidizing intellectual curiosity." There were too many silly courses, like the one at Davis which taught students how to demonstrate and burn the governor in effigy (it actually was a seminar in the history of nonviolent change). But in the end, all the attacks were pointless. The regents voted against tuition, Reagan began "revising" his budget recommendations to a point where they were only $10 million from the regents' figure, and he hardly said another word—publicly or at regents' board meetings where he sits—about higher education.

Bloodied and only slightly bowed, Reagan still had one or two more revolutionary acts to attempt before retiring. His second massive budget cut was in the administration of mental hospitals. Their population had been declining (40 per cent in three years), largely because of improved therapy and the use of outpatient clinics. Reagan proposed elimination of 3,700 jobs at the hospitals, the closing of fourteen state outpatient clinics, and the assumption of community mental health care by county centers. The state would save $17.7 million (although there would be an added burden on property taxpayers, as there would if those who were denied or could not afford to go to the university and colleges went instead to community junior colleges).

Again the established interests reacted violently. "First, Reagan stood in the schoolhouse door," an economist said later, "then he stood in the nuthouse door." Reagan was accused of reviving the "snake pit" and of disregarding the unfortunates of society. The

Times, which had originally commended the cuts, called Reagan's plan to give some patients the work of fired employees "repugnant."

Slowly, and with elaborate rationalization, Reagan began to cave in on mental health as he did on higher education. His executive assistant, Philip Battaglia, announced that eight hundred jobs previously eliminated would be restored. Instead of firings, there would be "phasing out." Reagan then developed a new interest in community health care, and declared that it was not he but those who wanted to maintain the old "warehouse" style of hospital care who were responsible for the snake pits.

A Prophetic Mission

Both education and mental health were right-wing issues, but Reagan had more in mind than political pandering. He felt he had a prophetic mission to cut the budget, and 57 per cent of the cutable funds are lodged in those two areas (83 per cent are in education and welfare as a whole). Reagan's ideas on finances were not original. Governor James Rhodes began a similar program in Ohio in 1963, and sold the package in modified form, to Governor Romney in Michigan and Governor Dan Evans in Washington. Shortly after his inauguration, Reagan met with Rhodes' finance director, Richard Krabach, who explained how he had fired five thousand state employees, slashed Ohio's budget 9.1 per cent across the board, and set up a volunteer task force of businessmen to review state operations, resulting in savings of $68 million.

Reagan and his finance director, a Los Angeles management consultant named Gordon Paul Smith, loved the ideas. They quickly followed suit, upping the stakes in proportion to California's needs. They ordered budget cuts of 10 per cent for all agencies, trimmed more off education and welfare, froze employment at current levels (eliminating 4,514 new jobs), and appointed their own task force of two hundred businessmen, most of whose names were kept secret because (the chairman said) "a lot of people will try to contact them to try to sell things . . . and tell them how to conduct the study."

Reagan promised to "squeeze, cut and trim" the budget, and after a tremendous expenditure of energy he came up with a low, low $4.6 billion figure, slightly higher than Pat Brown's last effort (although Brown later added more funds). But one thing led to another, and before Reagan was through, he himself had added another $434 million—for a state low-income medical plan, for property tax relief for local school districts, and for much of what he had (in his inaugural speech) attacked as "just goodies dreamed up for our supposed betterment." On June 30, just before the midnight deadline, he signed a $5.93 billion budget, $38 million larger than he had even proposed. He felt compelled to make only relatively small blue-pencil vetoes, and only token cuts in the education figure.

Reagan was discovering, rather late in the first reel, that the "goodies" served the interests of the big free enterprisers as well as the creeping socialists—and perhaps there wasn't that much difference between them. The technology companies, the aerospace industry, and to some extent the banks and utilities have more than a passing concern with social services. In many cases, they are eager to get into the market themselves. Under the Brown administration, the (lagging) aerospace corporations began developing ambitious programs to analyze and direct pollution control, highway projects, prison reform, welfare, crime reduction, and of course education on all levels. To restrict expansion in those areas, Reagan would have to risk alienating the men who run (and, eventually, the stockholders who own) Litton Industries, or the Bank of America, or the big data processors. In the modern corporatist state it is impossible to separate out the powers in business from those in health, education, and welfare. For example, Dr. (of medicine) Franklin Murphy, the chancellor of UCLA, is also one of the most influential directors of the Ford Motor Company, and sits on the boards of such diverse companies as McCalls and Hallmark.

So Reagan was stuck with the biggest budget in the history of any state in the nation, and to finance it he came up with the biggest tax increase—$946 million—that any governor had ever proposed. Like his original budget, it was weighted, although not entirely devoted, to the interests of his new working class base. It called for a 98 per cent ("temporary") rise in income taxes, to come primarily from the upper brackets. There was an 18 per cent rise in corporate taxes, and a 10 per cent increase in the tax on banks. Reagan called for an increase in the sales tax (to 5 per cent) but he also extended it to commercial purchases of gas and electricity, and to other business sales (he succeeded in infuriating the big agricultural packers by advocating a tax on containers). Moreover, he refused to eliminate the cumbersome business inventory tax (each year firms have to pay taxes on the value of their stocks), and he kept his promise to relieve the local property tax burden by giving state subsidies. He refused to include a provision for withholding income tax on a regular basis; people ought to "feel" the pain of taxes, he said.

The Moderates' Program

"Moderate" Republicans and Democrats in the legislature responded by submitting their own tax plan, which would get things back on a proper footing again by concentrating on hitting the poorer people in the society. The moderates' program would also include sales and corporation tax increases, but it would eliminate the inventory tax and substitute an across-the-board 60 per cent surcharge on income tax, instead of the complex formula Reagan wanted. And it would institute withholding.

The tax bill was still in legislative committee last week, but Reagan was ready to cave in on the essential matter of the income tax, and he was willing to suspend the plan for property tax relief. Slowly Governor Reagan was becoming a good liberal corporatist.

It would be a mistake to see Reagan as a neo-populist reformer, doing battle with the fat cats in the interests of the poor. Although some of those attitudes seem to crop up in every California administration since Hiram Johnson's, there is ample evidence that Reagan does not much care about the poor. His base was simply the not-rich. His welfare program is almost nonexistent. He wants to close many of the centers which Brown set up after the Watts revolt to centralize state services. To get people off the welfare dole, a very progressive objective, he would rely almost entirely on the kind of job training and placement service set up by H. C. "Chad" McClellan in Watts. McClellan, a former president of the National Association of Manufacturers and an Eisenhower undersecretary of Commerce, thinks that private enterprise can clean up poor Negroes, change their "attitudes" and their accents, and give them decent jobs in the mainstream economy. He claims to have turned the trick with fully half of the unemployed in the Watts "curfew" area. But his statistics, not to mention his assumptions, are open to broad attack and a great deal of suspicion, and it is hard for most antipoverty workers to believe that his kind of program can make a difference; probably not more than 5 per cent of those on welfare are "employable" in any significant sense.

Reagan made McClellan director of employment. The idea of a NAM president overseeing the labor market was a good example of Reagan's early appointment philosophy. His savings and loan commissioner had been a consultant to the council of savings and loan banks; his real estate commissioner was an open advocate of repeal of the fair housing law; an appointee to the Board of Education (later withdrawn) was a San Diego doctor who had overthrown a local school board in a recall election on a platform of prayers for the classroom; the agricultural commissioner was a rancher and member of the Right to Work Committee; the labor commissioner is a businessman, and the industrial relations commissioner is a former corporation executive and management consultant. His clemency commissioner is a former assistant DA in Oakland who made brief (and minor) headlines last year by helping the House Un-American Activities Committee prepare its case against the Berkeley war protestors. Some of Reagan's appointments were more reasonable; he made many good choices in areas of conservation and resource development—highly important to the hemmed-in basin-dwellers in the Southland. But the overall statistics are revealing: of Reagan's first 30 appointees, 11 were ranchers and 12 were financial types.

It is hard to place all the appointees in a single political bag, but many legislators—who watch the appointments closely—get the impression that there are two groups, and that a change has come about from the early "team" members to the later. The first represented the interests of the Southern California ideologues; they were for budget cuts, low taxes, slight economic manipulation. Many were big businessmen, but their interests were either personalistic or confined to the state. Reagan's original advisers were wealthy Southern California entrepreneuers: Holmes Tuttle, a Ford dealer; Henry Salvatori, a Goldwater financier and an oil industry man; the late Cy Rubel, president of a local oil company; and filmland egotists without number. Reagan had some support from the big utilities, the banks and the savings and loan companies, all of which are heavily regulated and traditionally throw their weight around the politics of both parties. Reagan has begun to please them more and more; he recently spoke quite out of turn for a telephone rate increase, which won't sit well with old friends in the suburbs. The aerospace, electronics, and national manufacturing industries had to be convinced that Reagan would look out for them. After a while, he started sending them signals. His budget was expansionist, and so was his tax bill. He gave in on the deepest cuts for education and on tuition, and he promised a scholarship program if tuition ever goes through. He backed down on mental health, and he seemed uninterested in pushing for legislation that might be considered anti-union, or anti-civil liberties, or anti-civil rights (he will agree to "modification" instead of repeal of the Rumford open housing law). He consolidated his gains with the corporatists, finally, by filling up the survey "task force" from their ranks.

"The education and the mental health things were just sops to those right-wingers down South," one liberal Republican legislator said privately a few weeks ago. "He stopped that kind of stuff a while ago. Now he throws them a few words or promises, and his political maneuvers don't mean much. He'll still talk about riots, and capital punishment, and the beatniks, and pornography, but he's finking out on his shock troops. Ronnie's people don't want the right-wing around them. Spencer and Roberts [the PR firm that handled Reagan's campaign] culled the kooks out of the campaign structure, and they're isolated. Some of the organized Right here—and all of it outside California—still think they've got a man on a white horse. But a lot of his fanatics are disillusioned, and some are jumping on the Wallace-for-President bandwagon."

The most prominent dropout has been State Senator John G. Schmitz, the one "avowed" Birch Society member in the senate, who represents part of Orange County, the Bavarian heartland of Reaganism. Utterly shattered by the governor's budget and tax program, he declared it "a tragic end to the brightest hope on the American political scene today," and a betrayal of "the campaign promises which Governor Reagan kept during the first two months of his administration." Sighing the long sad sigh well known to so many on the Left who have seen their heroes turn away from the gates of paradise, Schmitz predicted that "many of the best of our citizens may never again be willing to trust the word of a seeker or holder of high political office."

A Kind of Hubert Humphrey

So Ronald Reagan turns out to be a kind of Hubert Humphrey of the Right, and for the same familiar reasons. He keeps the ideological rhetoric flowing, and he may fool himself by promoting programs he feels will do "some good" and take a "first step" toward the old radical objective. But his main function is to disarm his most trusting troops, by adopting their words and never giving them the goods. He rationalizes his own position by calling himself a pragmatist, and may even believe that he is working from the inside. But he is out for himself alone.

For Reagan, like Humphrey, that means national power. Reagan is campaigning for the Presidency, as anyone can see, and he is mending all the fences in sight. After a bad start, he is even cosying up to the legislature, which had its doubts. One Republican said recently, "there are three big phonies in politics in this state—Sam Yorty [mayor of Los Angeles], Max Rafferty [education superintendent] and Ronald Reagan. At least Yorty and Rafferty are politicians." Reagan is getting along better with Assembly Speaker Jesse Unruh, a brilliant politician of questionable allegiance, who is the leading Democrat extant in the state. Since flexibility and moderation are still new to him, Reagan may have some stylistic difficulties. Last month he flip-flopped so openly on the abortion issue (he finally signed a reform bill) that one right-wing opponent of the measure left the Reagan camp in disgust. "That guy's such a good actor," he said, "he plays Pat Brown better than Pat Brown."

Reagan has made his peace with Tom Kuchel, but it was not easy for either man. Reagan supported Kuchel's primary opponent in 1962; Kuchel supported Christopher against Reagan, and "went fishing" in the general election. Now Reagan wants party unity more than anything. He told a distinctly hostile convention of right-wing Republicans recently that they should support the "candidates chosen by the entire party in the primary," and avoid "narrow sectarianism" at the risk of going down in a "blaze of glorious defeat." The same group had very nearly accused Kuchel of treason. Reagan's men are quietly telling the big-money sources to boycott Max Rafferty's campaign to oppose Kuchel in the Senate primary next year.

Reagan's aids are practically falling over themselves preparing the presidential strategy. They like this scenario: the already deflated Romney boom collapses, and his support goes to Rockefeller. Percy can't get enough exposure quick enough to get a boom going. Nixon loses a few crucial primaries, Reagan does well in Nebraska and Oregon and he consolidates the middle and right of the party. Those are the people who work hardest and vote in greatest numbers. Goldwater and the western governors (eleven of the thirteen in the region are Republican) swing to Reagan, and he goes into the convention battling with Rockefeller. There, it will be a tough contest, but if worse comes to worst, Reagan will accept the vice-presidential nomination. Nationally, it would be a strong ticket, and even California liberals would be attracted.

"Of course," one legislator said not long ago, "I'm for Reagan for vice president. We all are. Anything to get him out of California."

Black Friday:
A Beginning for the Student Movement*

DAVID HOROWITZ

T HE SPRING TERM at the University of California began with the excitement of the Chessman case, but that was soon superseded by compelling events of national and international scope. The campaigns for the presidential nominations began gathering momentum, winds of a new summit meeting were growing stronger, and suddenly, in April, accounts of student demonstrations in Turkey and Korea were making the headlines. One photograph, in particular, of Korean students being hosed by government police, appeared on the front page of *The Daily Californian*, as an un-noted portent of the future.

On April 26, 1960, the papers reported that the House Committee on Un-American Activities had issued subpoenas for hearings to be held May 10–12 (subsequently changed to May 12–14) in City Hall, San Francisco. At the University of California in Berkeley, a meeting was called by a twenty-five-year-old teaching student assistant in economics to discuss possible action to protest the appearance of this committee which had done such unwarranted damage to innocent members of the community the year before.

An account of this meeting was printed on the front page of *The Daily Californian,* informing the students that an ad-hoc

---

* From *Student* (Ballantine, 1962). Copyright © 1962, David Horowitz. Used by permission of the publisher.

Students for Civil Liberties organization had been formed by the
participants and that plans for a petition campaign, a picket, and
a rally in Union Square, San Francisco, on the opening day of
the hearings had been made. The petition was an immediate success, gaining 1,000 signatures in three days, while similar petitions
against the Committee were circulated and signed by 300 members
of the faculty at the University of California and 165 members of
the faculty at San Francisco State.

Meanwhile, the news that Douglas Wachter, an eighteen-year-
old sophomore at the university, had been subpoenaed, served to
arouse a considerable amount of campus interest. An interview
with Wachter was accompanied by a series of editorials disapprov-
ing of the Committee's tactics, and urging students to make themselves familiar with the Committee's actions.

On Thursday morning May 12, an unofficial student picket
circled City Hall (the official picket was not scheduled to begin
until after the noon rally). Members of this line distributed to
newcomers the following instructions printed by the Students for
Civil Liberties:

The purpose of the picket line is to protest the invasion by the
HUAC of privacy of individual belief and its free expression, and to
gain support from the public for the abolition of this Committee. We
strive to achieve respect for the dignity of man. Thus, we must act in
accordance with this ideal if we want others to respect it. All persons
who participate in this line are expected to show good-will and to be
polite, calm, and reasonable to everyone, including police, hecklers,
the public and other picketers. Do not show anger and do not use
abusive language; do not respond to hoots, jeers, or derogatory language. Do not debate with the public. Questions about the group and
its activities, especially from the press should be directed to monitors,
who are wearing white arm-bands initialed with a black "M." Monitors are in charge of maintaining the order of the picket line, and
you are expected to carefully follow their directions. If you cannot
abide by the decisions of the monitors or if you cannot remain nonviolent in character and in deed, please withdraw quietly from the
line. All who wish to demonstrate against the HUAC are welcome to
join the line. Remember, your conduct must reflect the ideals for
which we are demonstrating.

Meanwhile, several hundred other students had lined up with
the general public to be admitted to the hearing room. Just before
the hearings began over 150 people carrying special white cards
were allowed to enter the hearing room ahead of those who had

been standing in line. When these people had gone in, about seventy-five of those standing in line were admitted.

During the noon hour, when the Committee was in recess, the students held their rally in Union Square. State Assemblymen Philip Burton and John A. O'Connell, and Canon Richard Byfield of Grace Cathedral spoke against the Committee along with two student speakers. The crowd, which numbered a thousand, then proceeded to City Hall to join the picket.

Inside the City Hall trouble was brewing. Only a few of the seventy-five students (who were not white card holders) were allowed to re-enter the hearing room. This new restriction increased the resentment of those who had been standing in line all morning and chants of "Let us in! Let us in!" went up. Inside the chamber some of the students joined in the chants and then some of the witnesses themselves began to chant "Open the door! Open the door!" On orders from the Committee, police charged the witnesses and began dragging them from the room. The white card holders pummeled them as they were drawn away and shouted "Get the bastards out! Send them back to Russia!"

The students began to sing "The Star Spangled Banner." The white card holders remained seated, shouted, and hissed. Outside, Sheriff Matthew Carberry appeared in plain clothes, and called for quiet. Immediately there was silence. The sheriff requested the students to leave or at least maintain quiet so that the courts could function. Although not all of the students left, those who remained acquiesced and were quiet.

The newspapers carried the story of this incident on their front pages, playing it up as a "riot," much to the dismay of the students. Beside a picture of Archie Brown being ejected were phrases like "Riotous demonstrators disrupted . . . a wild, uproarious scene . . . 200 student partisans massed in the corridor outside were working themselves into a frenzy. . . ." With these words, the whole object of the picket which had walked peacefully around the hall the entire day was defeated.

The student leaders were well aware that even though no picket had been planned for the next day (Friday) the newspaper stories had insured that an even larger crowd would inevitably line up outside the chamber door seeking admittance. They therefore decided that a picket should be held and an attempt made to convince those inside the City Hall to give up their protest against the white cards and come out. They also decided to contact the police and ask them to make waiting lines outside the room so that the crowd would be more controllable. The police told them that it was a public building and they couldn't tell people what to do.

On Friday morning the white card holders again walked by the line into the Committee room, and this time only twenty of the several hundred students in the line were allowed to go in. Resentment, naturally, was high and for the rest of the morning the crowd chanted and sang songs in the City Hall rotunda, just outside the room where they had vainly sought admittance.

The following account of what went on inside the rotunda was written by Fred Haines, KPFA reporter who recorded the actual events for his station: "Shortly before the noon recess I was standing on the police side of the barricade recording the chanting of the students who were by now jammed into the limited space in the rotunda. Sheriff Matthew Carberry came up to the barricade from the police side and asked for attention. The conversation which ensued was not an easy one for the Sheriff. He had been asked, he said, by the presiding judge of one of the Superior Courts which was convened on the floor above to quiet the demonstration—the previous afternoon the court had been adjourned because of the noise—and he told them that they were placing themselves subject to arrest by continuing to demonstrate although they could remain in the building if they were quiet. He assured them that a 'representative group—sufficient number' of students would be admitted for the afternoon session. He told them to return at two o'clock—the hearings reconvened at one. He offered to discuss the matter in his office, next week. And he promised to be 'available all day,' and in the building.

"An assistant of some sort kept valiantly trying to get the Sheriff away to take care of some kind of business, but not before the following exchange with one of the student leaders took place —the young man told the Sheriff that they *would* discontinue the demonstration for the noon hour.

" 'We will cooperate,' he said, 'and if they cooperate with us at two—and let us in—on equal come basis—then at two o'clock, you'll hear from us again, at two o'clock. Sheriff, is that right? We shall cooperate with you. Until two o'clock. And if you keep your promise, and let everybody go into that hall, on a first-come, first-served basis, we'll cooperate. But if we're kept out of here, if we're kept out of here . . .'

" 'I have nothing to do with admissions,' the Sheriff interjected. 'I told you that.'

" 'I know that, I'm sorry. If, at that time, we find out that all law enforcement agencies, including the Committee, which says it is a law enforcement agency, will allow people to go into that hall on a free and democratic basis—that is, first-come, first-served— *we* will cooperate with the law enforcement agencies. However, I would suggest to the group . . .'

"Sheriff Carberry broke in, saying, 'I promise you full cooperation.'

"And the young man continued, '. . . if the law enforcement agencies, either true, or,' gesturing toward the Supervisors' Chambers, '*not* so true, do not cooperate with us, that we do organize, that we do use our free assembly, our right to petition. We do it orderly, but we do it loudly. Are you with me?' he finished, turning into the crowd.

"They were. No further demonstrations occurred during the noon hour, and many of the crowd left the building, as I did for lunch.

"I returned shortly before one, filled with misgivings. Inside the building again, I found that the group of students had nearly doubled; they had jammed the tiny rotunda and had overflowed onto the wide mezzanine landing that lay seven steps below it on the opposite side from the Supervisors' Chambers. Still others straggled down the imposing flight of granite steps that led all the way down to the main floor of the building.

"Halfway up the stairs I met one of the Cal students who had organized the picket line outside the building. 'I'm afraid there's going to be trouble,' he told me. 'We can't find anybody to talk to . . .'

" 'Is Carberry here?' I asked.

" 'His office says he's out to lunch and won't be back until two. We've been trying to get someone from the Mayor's office all morning, but he went to lunch in Burlingame . . .'

" 'Isn't there anyone else in charge?' I asked.

" 'Mike McGuire,' he said, 'he's an inspector for the red squad.'

"Another student broke in to ask who McGuire was, and I described him briefly. 'That's what I thought,' he said. 'We've been asking the cops who's in charge and they said McGuire. So we asked this guy if he was McGuire and he wouldn't tell us—I suggested there might be trouble because all these people expect to get in and he just flipped. He shouted, "Are you threatening me? Get the hell out of here!" And I thought he was going to hit me.'

" 'We're going to try to get as many of them inside as possible with white cards,' the picket monitor said. 'We'll send four people in for each one we've got, and then one guy can come back out with the pass and we'll send in four more. We're trying to talk people into getting out of the building and on to the picket line where they belong, too. Other than that I don't know what to do.'

"Exercising my press privilege, I took a station immediately behind the center barricade on the police side. The word went through the crowd to form a line, and, with a few exceptions, they managed to get into a rough approximation of a line, four abreast. The 'Friends of the Committee' gathered just to the right of this line, among them a number of the demonstrators who had some-how acquired the privileged white cards. As I watched, McGuire opened a way through the center barricade and began to admit the white card holders one at a time; for a moment the waiting crowd paused, and then an angry roar went up. Those in the rear, who were half-way down the stairs and couldn't see what was going on began to edge forward, and in the resulting crush began to press the flimsy sawhorse barricade toward me and the police officers, who leaped forward to hold it. Angry cries of 'Hold it! Stop pushing!' came from those in front; the barricade held and the police pushed it back to its original position. 'Let's wait and see what they're going to do!' someone called out.

"The barricade back and the crowd quiet, McGuire suddenly noticed that the white card holders, who were still filing through, included in their number some students—he lunged forward and grabbed one of them roughly. The student wrenched himself free, shouting angrily, 'I've got a white card!' McGuire, taken aback, let go and seized another by the lapels of his jacket—this young man thrust a 35 mm camera in McGuire's face and tripped the shutter. Again McGuire let go, and several students managed to slip into the chambers.

"Then an officer came out of the chambers and announced loudly, 'Room for five more!' The response from the crowd was immediate, loud, and angry. 'Nobody go in!' some called out, but five people did manage to get in, although with some difficulty because of the crush in the suddenly explosive crowd.

"Another officer came out of the chambers, spoke to McGuire, and several more were admitted. One of them, a girl who had been standing at the opposite end of the barricade from the entry, chat-ting with one of the uniformed officers, was led by this officer the length of the sawhorse to the opening, and the crowd obeyed his order to move back from the barricade to let her pass.

"Already the singing was beginning again, raggedly at first, but with greater volume as more and more took up the song. There was only one last move: the picket monitors and others began passing the word to sit down on the floor—Here and there individuals began to sit down, then groups, until finally the whole central part of the crowd was seated. Only two girls remained standing by the flanking pillars in front of the central barricade; I could see all the way across the rotunda to those standing by the seven shallow stairs that led to the landing behind them.

"Four or five minutes had passed since the doors were closed on the expectant crowd, and the crisis was safely over. I supposed the police might begin wholesale arrests shortly, but the possible eruption of violence had been neatly averted, with the vast majority of the crowd safely self-immobilized on the floor.

"Moments later, an attorney who was representing two of the witnesses made his way across the rotunda and arrived behind the barricades just in time to see McGuire opening one of the hydrants. He ran to the officer, shouting, 'You can't do this to these kids.' McGuire shrugged him off. An officer behind the center barricade picked up the nozzle of one of the fire hoses which had been unrolled from the floor and pointed it at several students sitting just beyond the barricade. 'You want some of this?,' he shouted. 'Well, you're going to get it!' One of the young men waved at him and kept on singing. A trickle dripped from a nozzle, a spurt, bubbly with air—and then the hose stiffened with the full pressure of the water, which blasted into the group of seated demonstrators.

"The rotunda seemed to erupt. The singing broke up into one gigantic, horrified scream. People fled past me as I ran forward, trying to see what was going on; a huge sheet of spray, glancing off one of the granite pillars, flashed through the air in front of me, and I retreated. It was impossible to comprehend everything that was going on. Those who stood up within ten feet or so of the hose were simply knocked down again by the force of the water, tumbling head over heels on their still seated friends. Others stood, found no place to run, their way blocked by bodies, and so sat down again. Some huddled together for protection. A second tongue of water licked out in a long arch over the barricades, and through the spray and confusion I saw that McGuire himself was manning the nozzle.

"Everything happened too fast to get more than a vague, over-all impression of struggling bodies and the two silvery whiplashes

of water exploding against backs and heads and faces—and a
crazy-quilt of disconnected impressions: John Burke, with whom
I was slightly acquainted, stepping gingerly through the water
flowing across the treacherously slippery floor, he trying to change
the plates in his press camera and I trying to flip the cartridge in
my tape recorder—both of us nodding politely as we pass. Another
acquaintance, an ex-RAF pilot in the U.S. on a Commonwealth
Scholarship, who had attended the hearings with an idea of writing
on them for the *Manchester Guardian,* twisting under the blast
of the water, his elegantly tailored suit matted against his back and
his hair splayed out in a sodden halo around his head. A lawyer,
in the building on other business, who ran out, angrily protesting
the hosing, hit full in the face with a blast from the hose. A news-
man near me yelling, 'Where's our photographer?' over and over
again. A demonstrator trying to shield the heads of two girls with
his soggy suede jacket while a stream of water battered against
the base of his skull for what seemed minutes on end. A girl, so
expressionless she might have been daydreaming, standing at the
pillar next to the barricade and watching a stream of water pour
out past her; no place to go, nowhere to hide, unable to move,
she waits . . . the officer sees her, brings the hose behind her, and
rakes it up her body—slowly—from heels to head at a range of
about two feet. Three, four, then five of the demonstrators clawing
their way toward the barricade in an insane attempt to rush the
police—but they stop two or three yards away, turning their backs
to the water blast, and, linking arms, they try to build a human
wall to shield the others.

"It couldn't have lasted long, but it seemed forever. It was
impossible to grasp; it couldn't be happening. It seemed more like
a bad surrealist film than an actual occurrence, and it was so
absurd I couldn't even think about it. I rethreaded the cartridge in
my tape machine and began recording, automatically and somewhat dazedly, an account of what I was seeing.

"Throughout the hosing you were relatively safe if you stayed
in the wings of the rotunda, the area between the massive main
pillars and the elevators, and I did, cradling the tape machine in
my arms against the spray. Every time I tried to move in closer
to the scene I would be driven back by the flying water. In the
opposite wing I could see other onlookers, newsmen and passersby, gazing out on the scene like tourists. As the final touch of
lunacy I discovered afterward that I had replaced the microphone
plug—which kept falling out as I fumbled with the cartridge—in

the machine upside down, and I spent the first couple of minutes babbling into a dead mike.

"And the two streams of water faltered, fell away, and, after a moment, stopped completely. I waded out into the rotunda to see what was going on. Nothing. It was all over. All seemed almost still and silent. Somewhere in the crowd of sodden, bedraggled students a single voice began to sing, 'We shall not, we shall not be moved . . .' Another voice took it up, and another, and presently all were singing, filling the rotunda with a sound that was almost jubilant. There was some sort of activity behind the barricades, but it seemed to be just aimless milling about—I noticed that there were a lot more police officers than I had thought. In addition to the dozen or so who'd been on duty there all day, there were another twenty clad in the helmets, jackets, and jackboots of the motorcycle troops.

"For the first time I had a moment to think, to take stock of the situation. How incredibly stupid and aimless it was: during the past few minutes they'd dumped thousands of gallons of water inside a public building, causing several thousand dollars worth of damage (not counting whatever human injury there had been). And they had accomplished nothing. Perhaps 50 people out of 200 or so had fled, but they surely could have achieved the same end if they had quietly and matter-of-factly begun placing people under arrest—and now they had 150 people wet, angry, and injured, most of whom were rooted to the spot and determined to make as much noise as ever before. But my thoughts were conditioned by the assumption that the police had given up the attempt to dislodge the demonstration.

"The center barricade was shoved to one side, and Inspector McGuire began to line up the motorcycle officers in the breach. Now, I thought, they'll do what any sensible person would have tried first—they'll begin arresting them. But once again I was wrong. There was a shout of 'Let's go! and the phalanx of officers lumbered forward into the crowd of seated demonstrators, clubs swinging wildly. Once again the refrain of 'We Shall Not Be Moved' broke up, disintegrating into a terrified shriek. The students were hauled to their feet, knocked down again, pushed over each other, kicked, and clubbed in the onslaught. A girl was hauled to her feet and thrown back to the floor on her face. Another demonstrator rolled in the water on the floor in pain. An ex-Army officer who considered himself only a spectator was struck across the arm, and when he tried to retreat toward the elevators he was seized and thrown violently into the crowd of demonstrators, the officer yelling, 'Get back there where you belong, you Commie!' Some of the students were thrown back toward the doors of the Supervisors' Chambers, where other officers seized them and slapped them around or beat them—one of these was held completely off the floor by several officers while another beat him across the legs with his nightstick. When the attorney who had tried to stop McGuire from turning on the hoses again attempted to intervene, he was grabbed by both arms and an officer threatened to strike him—when he protested that he had to represent clients, he was thrown against the doors and then pushed through. (Inside he came across all three of San Francisco's police commissioners, none of whom seemed at all perturbed about the melee outside. One answered the attorney's protests by telling him, 'You run the Communist party—we'll run the police.')

"Another student who had been beaten behind the barricades was thrown bodily back over the sawhorses into the lake of bloody water running on the granite floor. Yet another, a student who had managed to avoid being hosed by watching from the wings, was seized by his arms, lifted off his feet, and held dangling while a third motorcycle trooper struck him repeated in the stomach with his club; when he finally lost consciousness he was thrown across the rapidly clearing rotunda and down the seven steps at the rear to the part of the mezzanine which served as a landing between the rotunda and the great granite staircase that fell by 37 steps to the floor below. He lay there bleeding and unconscious in the water. Closer to where I stood in the wings one of the injured demonstrators was trying to get to his feet when he was kneed by a motorcycle officer who charged into him full tilt, knocking the boy sprawling across the floor. Half falling, half skidding, he tumbled some thirty feet across the floor, past my feet, and down the steps to the first landing where he lay groaning and clutching his stomach.

"I'd had enough. I too retreated to the landing for fear I would be attacked as well.

"Although many had fled, there were still some 50 or 60 people gathered on the landing. Most of those who still hoped to escape, either by going around the mezzanine or risking the descent of the stairs which were flowing with water like an indoor waterfall, had their way cut off by police officers, who forced them to return to the landing. One student had made the main floor already but was intercepted by a police officer who seized him roughly; a girl nearby who tried to intervene was struck in the face by the officer's club. Another had slipped and fallen on the stairs, and an officer below shouted at him, telling him to get back up to the landing, which he did.

"Most of the demonstrators on the landing had again resumed their seated position at the frantic urging of some who apparently feared the result of a mass exit down that hazardous staircase. Here and there the young people clustered around those who were hurt, trying to give them some aid.

"The moments that followed were curiously quiet, another of those strange lulls which were so absurd they seemed almost hallucinatory. Several feet away from me a girl bent over one of the injured boys sobbing hysterically and pleading with any policeman who came within earshot to get an ambulance. Up in the rotunda one of the plainclothesmen stood quietly rocking on his heels and toes in the water, one hand behind his back, the other holding a toothpick, with which he introspectively poked at his teeth, looking for all the world like a man waiting for a bus. Erwin Goldsmith, who had been inside with Dale Minor taping the hearings for KPFA, finally managed to get out of the chambers and he stood beside me for a moment as I recorded a description of the scene. When I finished he pointed to an elaborate, wrought-iron electric light stand close by. 'Don't touch that thing,' he said. 'In this water it'll fry you.' We didn't say anything else—there didn't seem to be much to say. I realized for the first time that my shoes, socks, and pants legs were soaked through from the two or three inches of water that was now pouring down the stairs and over the edge of the landing. Nearby a young girl leaned against a pillar staring at nothing in particular; when I looked a second time she was still staring, only this time I noticed she was softly crying.

"Minutes passed, and still nothing happened. The police had brought the barricades forward and lined them along the top of the seven steps to the rotunda, but, for the moment, that was the only action they took. The students had begun to sing and chant again, chanting 'Mr. Willis, we're still here!' again and again. Looking across the wide chasm which lay beyond the landing, I saw that hundreds of people had gathered quietly on the mezzanine and floors above to watch what took place.

"Then the hoses started again—again with no conceivable reason. The students were seated, unable to offer any violence if they wanted to, and none would have been permitted to leave (many had tried). This time few of the demonstrators seemed to mind as much. Most resignedly squatted under jackets or whatever protection they could muster, with their backs to the hoses. Some, in a foolish attempt at bravery, tried to face the hoses and hold their picket signs aloft for all to see, but half-a-minute of hosing in the face could either cure them of the first notion or drown them, and the water blasted the poster paint lettering right off the signs, and then the signs off the sticks. Again some of the young men went to the fore to form a human wall against the water, and through it all they continued to sing.

"I marveled at the casual gratuity of it all. If there was no reason for turning the hoses on the first time, there was even less now. Why? What good did it do? These officers who directed the pounding streams of water at the young peoples' heads for no reason at all—weren't they good men, who loved their wives and children the way most men do, men who were, like other men, sometimes charitable and generous and upright and even, perhaps, tender? How could they have been brought to such a pitch of fear and hatred that they could engage in this gratuitous cruelty without compunction, without pity?

"As abruptly as the hoses had been turned on they were again turned off. The students rose to their feet and faced the barricades as they sang 'The Star Spangled Banner' with both dignity and pride. One of them had raised his fist over his head in defiance, thought better of it, and changed the gesture into the famous 'V-for-Victory' sign of World War II. Others noticed it and followed suit until the dripping crowd seemed to blossom out with the sign. But I saw why the hoses had been turned off: on the main floor below two squads of motorcycle troopers reappeared (I hadn't noticed they'd left the rotunda above), marching in single file up the stairs. The singers were still faced toward the rotunda when the officers arrived at the head of the stairs, and as they finished the final chorus of the National Anthem the police began clearing a pathway through the crowd and the students courteously moved aside for them.

"Their intention was to remove the 50 or 60 remaining demonstrators from the building. There were six large elevators thirty feet away from the stairhead, and more elsewhere on the floor, but the police chose a different method: they began throwing the demonstrators down the stairs one by one. They were gentler at first, two officers trying to slide a demonstrator down a step or so at a time, but one trooper started a dangerous precedent by grabbing a young Negro by the ankles and pulling him down the stairs on his back, with his head and spine striking every step. Then other officers began grabbing the young people by any convenient part of the clothing or body and half hauling, half throwing them down the long staircase. Those who linked arms were clubbed apart and taken down like the others. One girl was dragged part way down by her hair, another was thrown down over half the length of the stairway in one long tumble. Almost all were thoroughly stunned, in a state of shock, paralyzed, or unconscious by the time they reached the bottom—later, many were unable to tell me how they had gotten out of the building.

"Some of the officers seemed to find great amusement in the debacle, and called encouragement to each other, 'Step on him! Break his legs!' Others were clearly appalled and pleaded with the students to walk down and avoid injury. One girl who had attempted to leave before the second hosing but had been refused passage by the police stood near me, apart from the demonstrators, weeping hysterically until an older officer in a regular uniform took her by the arm and led her down the stairs holding on to the banister. Most of them, however, were afraid to walk down —some who had tried had been knocked down before they reached the bottom, and one young man had been knocked down and his hand clubbed on the balustrade until he let go to be pushed down the stairs. By and large it was safer to keep sitting and let yourself be dragged down.

"At the bottom of the stairs the demonstrators were picked up by other policemen, including some of the plainclothesmen (one of whom was wearing a palm sap) who were marching those who were still conscious through a corridor of spectators. Those who were unconscious were dragged out by the collar, some with their hands still jammed tightly in their pockets. But no resistance was tolerated. Those who tried to sit down again on the main floor were handcuffed and jerked to their feet by the bracelets. One student who was struggling in the grip of six motorcycle troopers was bashed on the head with a nightstick to quiet him. One girl, her arm twisted so tightly behind her back by the officer who was escorting her from the building that she was doubled over, fainted, and another girl who came to help was smacked across the teeth with a club.

"I saw one case of student violence; a tiny blonde girl, perhaps five feet three inches tall, furiously attacked a trooper who was roughly handling her girlfriend. He easily fended her off, but she did succeed in socking him once or twice. (She was never arrested.)

"Meanwhile, only a handful of demonstrators awaited removal at the head of the stairs. A girl pleaded hysterically with them to get up and leave. 'What do you think this is accomplishing?' she demanded. 'Let's not have any more people hurt.' After a moment of indecision, the last defenders of the right to attend a public hearing of a government body straggled to their feet and gingerly made their way down the stairs and out of the building to the taunts and jeers of the spectators. Some of these had edged their way out on the landing from the mezzanine in order to see what was going on near the door. They seemed almost unanimously in favor of the police, some of them even gloating over specific acts of brutality they had seen. 'What about Hungary?' they called, and 'If you wanna fight, why not go fight in Tibet?' I felt sick. Hate, suspicion, ignorance and fear ruled the day.

"But inside the building the show was over. It seemed fairly safe by now, but just in case I held my press card out in front of me and clutched the balustrade tightly on my way down. I shouted 'Press!' at any officer who glanced at me, just in case.

"The next day, Saturday, as was to be expected, the picket swelled to a considerable size, while several thousand people gathered to watch from across the street. Towards the end of the day, a crowd gathered in front of the City Hall (the police had closed the inside of the building) chanting and shouting at intervals. Four individuals were arrested for offering various provocations to the police, but the presence of the mounted officers made any danger of mob action remote. The majority of the students remained on the picket line as they had two days before.

"Some weeks later, the charges against 62 of the 63 defendants arrested on Friday (4 others were arrested on Saturday) were dropped. At this time, 58 of the students issued a statement which said:

" 'We appreciate Judge Axelrod's courage which has insured the triumph of justice and good sense. The defendants have been vindicated. Encouraged by the court's action, we shall continue our opposition to the HCUA. It is now doubly clear that public protests against it are in accord with American justice.

" 'The House Committee denies the rights to which we as defendants were entitled before the courts: namely, to be fully represented by counsel, to know the evidence on which charges are based, and to cross-examine accusers. In denying these rights, the House Committee denies due process of law. It smears because it cannot prove, holding up to public attack people who are not allowed to defend themselves. We oppose this. We opposed it when the committee conducted its hearings in San Francisco on May 12, 13, and 14. We acted as citizens aware of our duty to protest any violation of individual rights.

" 'Nobody incited us, nobody misguided us. We were led only by our convictions, and we still stand firmly by them.

" 'We shall continue our opposition to the committee. We thank those who have had the courage to stand with us, and invite the community of which we are a part to join us.

" 'From our efforts to abolish the committee, we shall not be moved.' "

The Philosophy of Clark Kerr*

BRUCE PAYNE, DAVID WALLS, AND
JERRY BERMAN

T ODAY there are two words that describe and characterize the common bond among the majority of American intellectuals; those words are *confusion* and *concern*. As truly political men, we are concerned about our common life, with respect to both its meaning and its purpose. We desire to act and yet we cannot seem to answer the question "For what?" Purposes do not appear as "self-evident" in the age of impersonal government and mass organizations. The meaning of the American political consensus seems to blur. For instance, we rightly insist on protecting liberty, and yet the meaning of liberty seems interchangeable with the meaning of alienation and loneliness. Americans have always pursued "prosperity," but today they find that prosperity is not necessarily interchangeable with happiness. In the end we often find ourselves unable to act or to read meaning into life. With Paul Goodman, we find more and more that we are "growing up absurd."

Few men in American life are more concerned with the present and future of American society than Clark Kerr, president of the University of California and past chairman of the Institute of Industrial Relations at the Berkeley campus. Not only has he given much time to research the present trends of the American community, but he has set down his ideas and findings in several

---

* From *The Activist* (1962). Used by permission of the editors.

pamphlets, articles, and his most recent book, *Industrialism and Industrial Man*. (Besides these important contributions, Clark Kerr has served the public as a labor management arbitrator.)

Whereas most of us are confused and concerned about the prospects for America, Clark Kerr claims to know this future in many of its more important aspects. More importantly he believes this future is "necessary" and "logical," and, more profoundly, an improvement over the present state of American life. Since it is a better future for Americans, we are encouraged at least explicitly to act in accordance with the prophetic vision and help make it a reality. Not the vision of the philosopher or moralist, but the vision of the social scientist—making predictions and calculations on the basis of known facts—is the presumed meaning of Clark Kerr's future society.

History, says Kerr, reveals "a pattern to all the apparent chaos" about us. It is the "process of industrialization." Once a country begins to industrialize, its history can follow only the logic of industrialism, which is "designed to be the ever-lasting thread of the future." In Kerr's opinion there is no turning back and there is no alternative to industrialism once a country has chosen to industrialize.

We become suspicious of this interpretation of history when we discover that the end of industrialization is "pluralistic industrialism" for all countries. The nature of this "good industrial society" happens to be the *American* answer to the questions of industrialization and the basis of the decisions by the American industrial elite. Pluralistic industrialism turns out to be the result of American culture, ideology, and organization.

In America the cause and legitimacy of industrialization can be ascribed only to "liberty." Time and again Kerr defines liberty as "the absence of restraint" and the right to "act as you please," which are our common notions of liberty. America in the Declaration of Independence happened to desire "happiness." Happiness, declares Kerr, is prosperity. Prosperity is the promised land for which we make sacrifices. From this seed industrialism begins and continues to be the essence of American history. From this viewpoint Americans did not contract for an equal opportunity to live and develop their potentials, but rather their agreement was based on a desire to gain "satisfactions" from "wealth." Upon this desire, rational or irrational, there has been built the industrial complex we know today. For Kerr there is no use being concerned for what we have given up in exchange for this age of large, impersonal organizations and mass society. There is no escaping the logic of industrialization.

Although the general trend toward industrial society is clear and seemingly irresistible, Kerr argues, the exact characteristics of the new order are not inevitable. To predict, one must first choose. What is chosen and what is required by the "logic of industrialism" is often unclear, but it is certainly clear that Kerr prescribes the kind of society that he predicts.

This new society is to be a society of the "managers and the managed." "Everywhere there develops a complex web of rules binding the worker into the industrial process, to his job, to his community, to patterns of behavior."

These rules cover every aspect of economic life. They are to be devised by the managers, who are the leaders of the "New society, the vanguard of the future." Interestingly enough, the managers are also to perform the "role of protest," though it is to be a "more restricted and passive role."

Some of the specific features of this society might be pointed out. Religion, custom, and tradition, Kerr and his associates argue, will eventually be destroyed by industrialism. Some traditional institutions will be preserved, but most of them will not. Agriculture for instance, is not a way of life to be preserved, but will become rather an industry with a single purpose of the production of food in the most efficient possible manner. This stands in striking contrast to the words emblazoned over the doors of the Agricultural Hall on the Berkeley campus. Only a few hundred yards from Kerr's office in the modern University Hall, these words state the historic aim of the School of Agriculture:

TO RESCUE FOR HUMAN SOCIETY
THE NATIVE VALUES OF RURAL LIFE

The family, too, is to change in character. The destruction of the institution of the extended family seems already to have taken place in advanced industrial societies like our own. "There is no place for the extended family in the industrial society; it is on balance an impediment to requisite mobility." The function of the nuclear family is constricted. It is to be "largely a source of labor supply, a unit of decision-making for household expenditures, and a unit of cultural activity."

This sort of family is necessary to provide the society with the mobility required by constantly changing occupations and places of work. Certain jobs become obsolete in industrial society, and retraining will be necessary.

The point of this argument is that Kerr intends to argue quite seriously that the "web of rules" is the only force holding society together. These rules of the game determine the division of labor and the power relationships in the society, and for Kerr, these are the primary factors in the society.

What this society means to individuals is broadly defined in the study. Regarding the worker, the author states that "in his working life he will be subject to great conformity imposed not only by the enterprise manager but also by the state and by his own occupational association. For most people any true scope for the independent spirit on the job will be missing."

There is to be little danger of strife between the managers and the managed, for most of the members of society will have both types of roles. Moreover, *there will be little cause for strife*. The economic wants of the people will be more and more satisfied, though never fully, since aspirations will rise proportionally.

More importantly, there will be little conflict because all the basic questions have been answered. A consensus will have been developed around the goals of production efficiency and individual self-interest that will allow conflict only at lower levels. Society has achieved consensus and it is perhaps less necessary for Big Brother to exercise political control. Nor in the Brave New World need genetic and chemical means be employed to avoid revolt. There will not be any revolt anyway, except little bureaucratic revolts that can be handled piecemeal.

Under this system, ideology and politics (and Kerr seems characteristically to make little distinction) become "bureaucratic gamesmanship." Politics is still seen as conflict, but that conflict will be over narrower issues. "It will be less between the broad programs of capital and labor and of agriculture and industry; and more over budgets, rates of compensation, work norms, job assignments."

Nineteenth-century Utopians would have found little which is original in Kerr's new society. It is fundamentally identical with the managerialism of St. Simon, the militarized capitalism of Bellamy, and even, perhaps surprisingly, with the old Marxian dream of a society where "the government of persons is replaced by the administration of things"—because under its beneficent aegis persons have been reduced to things. . . .

Students will be particularly interested in the position of education in the new society. Even after accepting industrialism's goal of prosperity, one might well feel there is a certain inconsistency in having a leading theoretician of industrial organization as the president of one of the nation's leading universities. It is disconcerting to realize that these two roles are not seen as contradictory in the least by Kerr. As the "handmaiden of industrialism," education has itself become a leading industry. Kerr considers education to be a functional imperative to an order based on technology. As there is a "relatively smaller place for the humanities and the arts," the system of higher education becomes keyed to the production of specialized careers—professionals, technicians, and managers.

The principal functions of education are to train the bulk of the population to "receive instructions, follow instructions, keep records," and to train the managers, engineers, and civil servants to operate this system. The increasing importance of the funds obtained for research activities adds to the need for patterning the university more along the lines of the industrial organization. Each participant has his carefully delineated role within the "great web of rules," the authority allotted out to each person is carefully subordinated to the principle of efficient productions and control.

Kerr is well aware that intellectuals and students can often be most disruptive to the carefully laid plans the managerial bureaucracy has for the new society. Since Kerr assumes the goals of society are already embodied in the things that be, students and intellectuals "are by nature irresponsible . . . not fully answerable for consequences. They are as a result never fully trusted by anybody, including themselves." Especially by Clark Kerr, we are tempted to add. At the same time the conflict within societies takes place increasingly in the realm of ideas. Thus the student can be a "tool as well as a source of danger," in these intellectual skirmishes. Even so Kerr also remarks that "in some cases students may be taught things they must 'unlearn' if they are to make good production workers."

Kerr's history as president of the University of California suggests how he proposes to control this apparently natural tendency of some students to refuse to see education as merely another technical procedure designed to fit them to a specialized niche in the process of production. In October, 1959, the "Kerr directives" were first promulgated under the guise of being a liberalization of university policy toward political activity. A quick series of "clarifications" removed certain of the more objectionable provisions— such as restrictions on the power of the academic senate and such obviously unconstitutional provisions as qualifications on the freedom of students to lobby in the legislature on matters concerning the university. While the directive did certainly liberalize certain rules on political speakers and the distribution of literature, the attempt to codify the regulations on the student government amounted to a severe reduction in the actual scope of its traditional authority. The old restrictions had originated in the political stress of the thirties and the later period of McCarthyism. Under a principle of "salutary neglect" they had been enforced only intermittently.

By the fall of 1961 the major points of the clarified directives seemed to establish two general policies: (1) an "open forum" for discussion of public issues; and (2) "limited purpose" student government. The open forum was tested at the UCLA campus by an invitation to Dorothy Healy, former chairman of the Communist Party of Southern California, to speak on the campus. At this time an old graduate of the Berkeley campus promised the university a million dollar trust fund on the condition that no members of the Communist Party be allowed to use University facilities. President Kerr immediately stated that it had been the policy of the Board of Regents since 1944 to prohibit Communists from speaking on the campus on the grounds of "incompatibility with the educational ends of the University." This line of reasoning becomes more comprehensible if one assumes the end of the university education to be the production of individuals with the particular skills required by the existing industrial order more than the preparation for citizenship and training in distinguishing truth from error.

The "limited purpose" nature of the student government revolves around the "on campus–off campus" distinction and the question of the right of student government to represent the interests of the students whenever this may be opposed to the interest of the administration. The National Student Association has held that these distinctions indicate a grave misunderstanding of the student community. To limit student government to "on campus" issues, narrowly defined, is to deny that students have any common interests whatsoever outside the price of cheeseburgers in the cafeteria and the type of background music to be played in the student union. This reasoning parallels Kerr's concern for

protecting the individual from the associations to which he belongs
—be they labor unions, professional societies, or student bodies.

At the bottom of Kerr's theoretical concern for restricting the
scope of student government is his concept of the "absolutism
of the group," the strangely vague process through which the individual is tyrannized by these intermediary organizations between
himself and the state. There seems to be a definite, if curious,
relation between Kerr and defenders of the "Beat Generation" who
maintain that man can gain some portion of freedom and attain
a certain measure of human virtue only in isolation, never through
acting in concert with other men.

The most recent addition to the Kerr directive was announced
to the students this past year. Student political groups (YD's,
YR's, YAF, SLATE, etc.) are forbidden to use the campus for
their business meetings on the grounds that the university's charter states that the university must be kept free of "political and
sectarian influence." The Kerr administration does not recognize
the argument that it is precisely when they yield to the pressure
of small but vocal elements in the state—as by exiling campus
politics—that they place themselves subject to political influence.
But it is not to be expected that the university would recognize
any obligation to encourage student participation in politics. Kerr
believes it is sufficient to allow these groups to sponsor speakers
on campus. In a manner very consistent with the rest of his system of "liberal pluralism," Kerr refuses to admit the necessity of
connecting thought with political action.

The new society of industrial pluralism, while requiring a
great degree of conformity in the work individuals do, is designed
to increase their degree of individual freedom. "The great new
freedom, it is argued, may come in the leisure of individuals.
Higher standards of living, more leisure, more education, make
this not only possible but almost inevitable. This will be the happy
hunting ground for the independent spirit. Along with the bureaucratic conservatism of economic and political life may well go a
New Bohemianism in the other aspects of life."

This is not an unusual sort of argument, particularly in America. One assumption behind it is that men are motivated primarily
by self-interest, and that freedom is the ability to do as one likes.
It is an argument in the Madisonian tradition, and a number of
fairly standard criticisms may be applied to it. With many others,
we would challenge this idea of irresponsible freedom. The freedom to do what one feels he ought to do, the freedom to do one's

duty, are concepts which argue against the one-sided view that man is no more than a self-interested beast. And certainly freedom for economic self-interest can hardly hold much meaning for individuals in an economy of abundance.

Further comments at the end of *Industrialism and Industrial Man* remind us that the arguments made by Kerr and his associates go far beyond the arguments of the eighteenth-century liberals.

The new slavery and the new freedom go hand in hand. Utopia never arrives, but men may well settle for the benefits of a greater scope for freedom in their personal lives at the cost of considerable conformity in their working lives. If pluralistic industrialism can be said to have a split personality, then the individual in this society will lead a split life too; he will be a pluralistic individual with more than one pattern of behavior and one dominant allegiance.

The new system, then, involves not only a division of the society, but the division of the individual. The separation of the parts of an individual's life prevents any one part from having overriding importance. Kerr has argued in the past that groups are dangerous because they tend to interfere with individual freedom. The aim, therefore, is to prevent any one group or institution from having any great part of the loyalty of an individual. It may be worth noting that loyalty is not a word that one finds often in the works of President Kerr. When it does appear, in fact, it is usually found to be "loyalty to the plant," or something similar.

Kerr rejects, notably, any idea of civic or political loyalty. His citizen is a "private citizen" and not a public one. For civic or political loyalty demands that the individual integrate his diverse roles into a whole personality, just as it demands that he accept responsibility for the whole political society. This fact lies behind Aristotle's dictum that man is a "political animal," one who discovers himself and his being only through political society. Loyalties, in Kerr's argument, are specialized, fragmented into "roles"; they reflect Kerr's complacency regarding the individual of split or multiple personalities. A man is, Josiah Royce argued, what he is loyal to, and he urged nineteenth-century Americans to "be loyal to loyalty," and to the idea of the whole man. Kerr rejects politics and civic loyalty because he rejects man as such. He accepts a "system" in which men are only parts, and schizophrenic parts at that.

Challenging this system, we would argue that it carries with it a great potential for destroying itself, and with terrible results for the citizens who make it up. We are convinced that at least for most people, this system would not create the "happy hunting ground of the independent spirit." It would rather lead to a heightened sense of alienation, both from the society itself and from other individuals. It is that very lack of a sense of control over one's own environment that has produced such feelings in America. It seems, moreover, that the closer we move toward the industrial society, the more we find ourselves faced with boredom and apathy and alienation.

A little reflection reminds us that these feelings are dangerous. Bored and alienated people do surprising and destructive things to escape their sense of boredom. They are seldom moved, but when they are, the bitterness produced by years of unsatisfied needs may vent itself in reckless fury.

Whether such destruction results or not, however, makes little difference if the feelings of the individuals in the system are as we have argued. Kerr's system throws the individual back completely on himself, with no serious support or loyalty from any group or idea except the "web of rules." Intermediate loyalties between those to family and to nation are destroyed or rationalized in the terms of self-interest. Kerr argues that his "system" makes "Big Brother" unnecessary. It is too efficient to need him—a kind of rationalized 1984. Yet when the groups between the individual and the state become so specialized and remote as to lose all meaning, when the individual loses all sense of a "public," Big Brother is not far off. For the isolated individual is unable to act with his fellows to control the system. Convinced of his own isolation, he can acquire the sense that the "system" is concerned for him and for his welfare at all only by a fevered personal identification with an "ego-ideal," with the Messianic chieftain who is at once "one" with the citizen and elevated far above him. "Big Brother" arises when man can no longer find brothers of his own.

It should not be thought that the basic themes in the predictions and prescriptions for the new society are the creations of President Kerr and his associates. The basic choices have been made and are being made by the populace, even in Kerr's eyes. We dislike President Kerr's picture of education and the new society intensely, but we are forced to admit that this picture is true to the standard of American fears of loyalty and prejudice against politics. The American people have believed in self-interest, and many of them sense that this ethic has cheated them. As yet, however, they have been unable, in all but a few instances, to substitute a new one.

Yet there is at least one ideal that still survives in our society, although it has been a part of our civilization for more than eight hundred years. That ideal is a university, a community of scholars bound together by the search for knowledge and truth, and feeling a responsibility to their society. That ideal declares that teaching and learning are more important than economic self-interest, and where that ideal has been a reality, some men have been able to face the future with self-confidence and hope.

We believe the defense of that vision and the attempt to make it a reality are profoundly important. For in fact, the vision is losing to Kerr's adherents, and not only losing in California. The defeat of the vision of the university is, of course, only part of the general social process of which Kerr is both analyst and advocate. But students have a special duty to combat that process on their own part of the battlefield: the university campus. "History" may be moving in the way Kerr believes it to be. *Brave New World* or *1984* may be the destiny of men in some ultimate sense. We do not believe that this must be the case. But in any event there is all the difference in the world between resisting any such trend and advocating it, between hoping to postpone 1984 to 2025 and hoping to establish it, as Kerr seems to, in 1975.

The Politics of Outrage*

MICHAEL PAUL ROGIN

I WOULD LIKE to explain my students to the friends of my parents. My students? The Berkeley kids who participated in or supported the Free Speech Movement. At Berkeley explanations were not needed. Most of the faculty one cared about supported the kids' demands and sympathized with their style. As for the others, individual exceptions aside, they generally fell into two groups. Some represented the old university: paternalistic, conservative old-timers absorbed by their loyalty to the institution. Others were part of the multiversity—younger, ambitious manipulators with institute connections, practiced in the uses of the university. No identity problems for me here.

Besides, one knew the kids; one taught them. There were the children of intellectuals, radicals, or New York Jews. There were those from the Jewish ghettos, in Los Angeles and the San Fernando Valley. Here there was some cultural explanation. But most impressive were the girl from a lower-middle class Protestant Alameda family, the son of Greek immigrants from San Jose. Where did these nineteen-year-olds get their sensibilities; how did they know so much? To get to learn from sixteen of the best of them, as I was fortunate enough to do during the year of the Berkeley revolt, was a remarkable experience. Of course, many were not so serious nor so impressive as the best. Maybe the total

* From *Commonweal* (April 8, 1966). Used by permission of the publishers.

milieu contained too much studied innocence, too much Gemein-schaft, to suit my taste. But this was, overall, a remarkable, dedi-cated, creative bunch of kids.

The friends of my parents: old socialists and trade unionists, nice Jewish ex-radicals from that older radical generation. Now they work for the government, or in the trade union bureaucra-cies. But the anecdotes remain, the nostalgia is powerful, the words to the "International" are still remembered. I liked these people; I admired them. In a corner of my mind as I participated in a small way in the Berkeley revolution, was the thought of the anecdotes I could contribute, the pedigree in radicalism I had earned. So when I came back to Washington for the summer (not New York, the city of the 1930's, but Washington, with its union headquarters and government bureaus; already something was wrong), when I came back east for the summer, I had something to bring—stories, commitments, things to fulfill my tradition, things to make me feel at home.

But the East is a long way from Berkeley. There we heard much about the civil rights movement's public war against racism, little about its private quarrels. Here those quarrels dom-inated civil rights discussions. There one conversed about the basic moral questions; here it was a matter of Washington manip-ulation and congressional pressure politics. One knew that the old radicals here did not share one's own attitude toward Vietnam, but one had not expected quite so untroubled an atmosphere; again tactics preempted the discussions. Certainly one knew there were differences between one's parents' friends and one's students. But one was hardly prepared for the distrust, the confusion, even the rage directed against the young radicals. One was quite cer-tain that had there been no obscenity incident at Berkeley, the old radicals would have had to invent it, so pleased were they to find a legitimate outlet for their suspicions. Though the four-letter word fracas received little support from FSM leaders and rank-and-file, it demonstrated to the old radicals the childish irration-ality of the movement.

But neither the Free Speech Movement nor current political stances always distinguished the young radicals from the old ones. Consider Irving Howe, radical spokesman for the old Left, quite sound on the FSM, but vitriolic on the new Left in general. Like others who still consider themselves Socialists, he is perhaps closer to the ex-radicals than to the new ones. This is not to minimize Howe's political differences with other members of the old generation. Even less do the students present a unified, political line. But as one read more articles, participated in more conversation, a basic fact became clear. There were two styles of politics here, one for the old Left, one for the new, and these styles were mutually incomprehensible. Dialogues could occur only among the generations, not between them. One would take sides in the dialogues, of course. Often on specific issues agreement and disagreement crossed generational lines. But there remained a gulf between the older generation of Jewish Socialists and the SNCC–FSM radical youth. To comprehend the feeling about life which separated the generations, one had to return to the matter of style.

Style and Meaning

Consider the churches. Today they signify Negro protest in the South, white support in the North, ministers killed in Cleveland, nuns marching in Montgomery. Who could have imagined them leading the social struggles of the 1930's? The Church—that meant Spain, that meant southern autocracy in the textile communities, that meant opiates to the masses. For those days saw the struggle of one class against another. The classes had interests. One supported some interests against others. The Church (a vested interest) was conservative. The radicals had other ideas. They were after power; they were going to reorganize society. Reason was on their side; emotion stood in their way. The Left of the 1930's was a discursive Left. It knew what it wanted. Today it would like to know what the kids want. It strongly doubts that they know what they want.

The kids are an outraged Left. Official society nauseates them. (One, who works in the District library, left his job for two days to march in the Washington Vietnam demonstrations. He returned from jail to find A.W.O.L. stamped on his record. "What kind of a place is this where they have to use army terms?" Not something one expects from a bourgeois institution; not something one organizes to fight against; these kids live every day with a renewed sense of shock.) Their style is closer to Protestant religious dissent, Negro and white, than to the discursive Jewish, secular radicalism of my parents' generation. It is just the 1930's style of politics—interest politics, calculation politics, structured, power politics—against which they rebel. Those who try to be practical, who think in terms of consequences, do not wind up changing society, say the kids. They rather wind up in the smaller and more conservative realm of Washington salons. And the kids point to the degeneration of the old Left as their example. They rather begin by divorcing themselves, personally, from the hypocrisy, corruption, and decay of the visible world. They create separate communities; they take a moral stand. And the physical insistence of these communities has consequences in the official world, far greater consequences, say the kids, than the calculated decisions of old-politics. Thus, not to plan consequences is the best way to be effective.

Now there is immediate and there is historic truth in this. Perhaps in other societies and in other times the Left has been rational, the Right emotional. But the American Left has always contained a strong feeling that to begin to think, to plan, to calculate, to be practical (for these are all synonyms in America) is to take the first step on a one-way street toward accommodation. One finds this in the politics of Abolitionism, of Populism, of IWWism. As a political mood, it is akin to the literature of nostalgia, innocence, and illusion (Mark Twain, Sherwood Anderson, John Cheever). In the confident world of the 1930's, such politics and such literature was quixotic; certainly, as the Bolsheviks used to say, it had nothing in common with Marxism. And American intellectuals in the 1950's continually ridiculed the fear of being corrupted by reality. Surely one knew by now that purity, and anti-intellectual purity at that, had nothing to do with politics.

But one learned something else in the 1950's; one learned from Irving Howe a lesson he has more recently neglected—that in a conservative and corrupt society the price of political involvement may be conservatism and corruption, that in such a society art, literature, and moral criticism perform essential political functions. And when a civil rights movement began to emerge in the late 1950's, it emerged out of that instinct—and demonstrated that moral indignation could be an effective political weapon. Berkeley taught us this again, concretely and immediately. From the seizure of the police car until the faculty resolution two months later, most of us on the faculty were practical; we thought about consequences, we sought compromises and deals. The FSM—led by civil rights activists, not scions of the old, radical political groups—had only one tactic. It presented with its bodies the validity of its demands. The strength of its moral position was its winning political weapon. The police invasion of Sproul Hall, provoked by the students, finally mobilized the faculty, too, around principle. Until then we were wrong; they won because they were right.

Of course there was more strategy to it than that, in Berkeley as in civil rights. There were, after all, the bodies; surely this was pressure politics in its most literal sense. But the approach of the new Left toward the problem of bodies only increases the distance from the old generation. For the 1930's bodies meant numbers, political power. For today's Left bodies are strategic, but they are also expressive. Bodies connote rhythm, beat, total involvement. Consider the music—not the hymns of protest, produced as much by the old radicals as by the young ones—by Bob Dylan and the Beatles. Much more could be said about the Beatle mood, the Dylan mood, but I stop with a grosser observation. Never before have the young intellectuals and the young masses liked the same music. Here, in this contact, hope seems to lie. SNCC, SDS, orient toward the most deprived masses, Negro and white. When have these masses marched in demonstrations? When have they desired to get out of Vietnam? When has their radicalism been more than nihilistic; when has it not been assuaged by cars and televisions? Still, there is the feeling, symbolized by the music that if only one could tap the vitality of the masses, one could transform America. Not the classes in their relation to the means of production but the masses in their lack of relation to the hypocrisy and sophistication, the ambition and oppressiveness, of the Great Society. Here the new Left finds the potential for something more spontaneous, more real, than the life of the respectable world.

Such a dream has American roots—Wobbly, Populist, even Jeffersonian. Perhaps more striking is the parallel with the *Narodnya Volya*, the young Russian intellectuals who Went to the People in the 1870's. Almost certainly the new Left's dream, badly stated, is as quixotic and sentimental as the Russians' was. Equally certainly such a dream produces the Fannie Lou Hamers, who speak with a voice close to SNCC's, far from New York and Washington.

Masses Replace Classes

No wonder the old radicals do not feel at home. Before them is a politics of virtue not skill, of morality not interests, of innocence not sophistication. Where they organized pressure, the new Left promotes spontaneity. Outrage replaces reason, masses replace classes. Certainly the old radicals have changed, are more comfortable now; but they were never like this. Still, in one important way their attitudes differ from those they held in their youth. Far more pro-American than they used to be, the old radicals are perhaps most angered by the anti-Americanism of the kids. And they do raise an embarrassing question. For how can a politics of moral indignation be so effective in an immoral society? Let us approach the answer obliquely.

Consider the admiration felt for Hannah Arendt by the young intelligentsia of the Left. Miss Arendt is not a favorite of the old radicals. For Irving Howe and Lionel Abel she is simply an obfuscating conservative. Indeed, several years back *Dissent* gleefully printed an attack by Arendt on the civil rights movement. But the kids had barely reached puberty in 1957; they have not read that piece. They have read instead *The Human Condition*, maybe *On Revolution* and *Eichmann in Jerusalem*. They share with Arendt a revulsion at interest politics; they long with her for a politics of examination and community. But there is more to it than that. In the Eichmann book the point of contact is perhaps clearest, for Arendt's prescription for the Jews is similar to SNCC's politics for the Negro.

The horror of Nazism, as she sees it, lay partly in the Jewish response—the cooperation of the leadership, the failure of the Jews to refuse to compromise with evil. Had they only extricated themselves completely from the Nazi tentacles, hundreds of thousands of Jews, perhaps millions, would not have died. For the kids America is also an evil society; the Negroes must not corrupt and destroy themselves by participating in it. This is Arendt's argument applied to America. But surely it is absurd to equate America with Nazi Germany, or the fate Negroes would suffer by cooperating with Johnson to the fate of the Jews. According to this line of thinking, if Arendt's attack on cooperation makes some sense, SNCC's is apocalyptic.

Exactly the reverse is true. For Arendt's argument depends on the view that the Nazis had to disguise from themselves what they were doing. Eichmann vomited at the sight of violence and was a mild, little man; only as a bureaucrat could he be a murderer. The balance of Nazi terror depended on abstraction; the job of the Jews was to strip the veils from the Nazi atrocities. And so the inevitable conclusion from the premise about the Jews and the premise about the Nazis: if only the Jews had spoken out, had made visible the horror of the Nazi terror, the Nazis would have let up. It is the wish of the child, that if he lets himself go and is as angry with his parents as he feels, they will stop hurting him. The trouble was, the Nazis were already facing themselves. As Norman Podhoretz writes, "No person could have joined the Nazi party, let alone the S.S., who was not at the very least a *vicious* anti-Semite . . . no person of conscience could have participated knowingly in mass murder."

The politics of SNCC, of Berkeley, of Hannah Arendt are a politics of outrage and moral purity. But the point is not the obvious one, that such a view is virulently anti-American (or anti-Nazi). Rather to believe that exposing hypocrisy (or murder) will stop the hypocrite from lying, the murderer from killing, indicates considerable faith in the attacked authority; appalling in the case of the Nazis, which is why *Eichmann in Jerusalem* is ultimately a frightening book. Perhaps not so absurd in the case of official America. To put it more precisely, insofar as the Establishment lives on an ideology of morality, it cannot permit itself to be exposed as immoral. One hears in Washington that at least Johnson (at this writing) hasn't machine-gunned all the Dominican rebels. However, the Dominican invasion was only possible because Johnson does not think of himself as a murderer. About Johnson Arendt is right; he can be an imperialist because his ideology disguises him from himself. His ideology, his abstractions, therefore, provide leverage for those opposed to his actual policies. The leverage is most effective where, as in civil rights, the ideology is unambiguously democratic. It is the Establishment's need for moral clothing, not merely its fear of disorder, which renders powerful the moral weapons of the young radicals. Hence to expose hypocrisy is to force action.

The politics of exposure is simply one more thing beyond the comprehension of the old Left. For in the twenties and thirties the enemy admitted what he was; he had to be conquered, not exposed. In the mass society the kids see, the enemy is in all of us, and must be exorcised. For the new Left conscience *is* the political arena, instilling guilt the political *weapon*. When the young radicals face the corruption in themselves, they force those in power to face it in *themselves*. That is the most political thing they can do.

This Calvinist atmosphere makes the old radicals very angry. They are caught between the expurgated guilt of the young and the exposed guilt of the Establishment. They do not like being made to feel guilty and hypocritical. (They do their jobs, work for liberal causes, involve themselves in the day-to-day politics of official America. Perhaps they have been seduced by comfort and fame; perhaps they are not doing enough.) The old radicals do not like a radicalism that works religiously, on the insides. They like to know where they stand. They would like to be left alone. They would like to know what the kids want; then, like parents, they could satisfy them and quiet them down.

I went to college in the fifties, when things were no longer simple (except in foreign policy). It was a dulling experience, that disappearance of good guys and bad guys; I learned to play chess. The radicalism of the sixties reasserts the reality of good and evil, but it enacts a morality play, not a western movie. For the aim of the kids is not to confront the bad guys on a battlefield, but rather to expose the evil in others, preserve the good in themselves. If the old radicals rely on the Establishment in their way, the young ones do the same in theirs. Both stances are the product of the weakness of a substantial left in America. Sometimes I imagine myself faced with America before the CIO, say around 1910. I could work in the AFL unions or support the IWW—Victor Berger or Bill Haywood. Which would I choose? For me it is a question, though I know where my sympathies lie. For the radical generation I teach, as for that which taught me, it is not.

Berkeley and the University Revolution*

SHELDON S. WOLIN AND

JOHN H. SCHAAR

I.

DURING THE recent crisis on the Berkeley campus, the favorite quotation among the cognoscenti was Marx's aphorism that great historical events occur twice, "the first time as tragedy, the second as farce." Two years ago, the Berkeley campus was shaken by a series of events culminating on December 2, 1964, with a mass sit-in by the students, followed by mass arrests. What might have been a tragedy was averted by the faculty resolutions of December 8, 1964, which recognized the fundamental political principles for which the students had contended. The faculty declared that there should be no university regulation of the content of speech or advocacy, and only such regulation of the time, place, and manner of political activity as was needed to prevent interference with normal university functions. The crisis began over constitutional rights, and the faculty had responded with a constitutional solution.

When the old administration was replaced, first by the interim regime of Martin Meyerson and then by the new administration of Roger Heyns, all of the auguries were favorable. In outlook the new chancellor was liberal, and in action he was committed to the

---

* From *The New York Review of Books* (February 9, 1967). Copyright © 1967, The New York Review. Used by permission.

principle of consultation. He appointed to his staff several professors who were prominent in the struggle for the resolutions of December 8. Unlike previous chancellors, he was not harassed by outside meddling, either from the state-wide university administration or from the Regents. During the past year, for example, President Kerr kept a prudent distance from Berkeley controversies.

November 30, 1966, Berkeley students again sat in; police were again called to the campus, and on December 2 the students voted to strike against the university. Had 1964 really been farce and was 1966 to end as tragedy? Although there are coincidences in chronology between the events of 1964 and those of 1966, the settings differed in important ways. The crisis of 1964 extended over several months, thus allowing the contestants time to formulate fairly coherent positions. The crisis of 1966 erupted suddenly, catching all parties off-guard. This was most evident in the case of the faculty, which, unprepared and without a position, was reduced to a promiscuous search for consensus. In 1964 the politics of the Free Speech Movement had a kind of radical purity: the students focused on political objectives and pursued them with an idealism similar to that of the heroic phase of the civil rights movement. In 1966 student political orientations had been shaped by the growth of "New Left" doctrines, by participation in the congressional campaign of Robert Scheer, by continuous protests against the Vietnam War, and by endless disputes with the administration concerning political rights and due process on campus. Thus, in 1964 the students claimed "constitutional rights"; in 1966, they demanded "student power." Also, between 1964 and 1966 the graduate teaching assistants organized into a trade union and many of them took a certain pride in their worker status. "The issue here," explained the student president of the union during the crisis, "is working conditions. As long as the police are used in this way, we can't work." Along with the unionists another and more exotic element entered the movement: the cool and hippy culture of Telegraph Avenue with its distinctive blend of student and non-student styles. In 1964 the politicos had been impatient with and distrustful of the hippies; at the very end of the 1966 crisis Mario Savio, who had been the student leader of FSM in 1964 but was now a non-student leader of the new alliance, gave a benediction calling for a "coalition between student politicos and hippies." Thus by 1966 a new culture had come into being, one which escapes the categories of the settlement of 1964.

Of all the differences, the most striking was the difference in mood. In 1964 the campus had a wealth of idealism and hope; the FSM had been good-natured, ironical, and humorous. In the months before the present crisis, the campus was tired, humorless, and disillusioned. During and after the crisis it was, above all, fearful. Not only had internal battles taken their toll, but the outside world had become more menacing. Governor Reagan had made the Berkeley campus a major campaign issue and had promised to establish an investigating commission headed by John McCone, former director of the CIA.

If there is tragedy in the making it will not be merely the result of what state politicians may do in the future, but of what the university has failed to do in the recent past. During the past two years, the campus has grown more and more distracted by political controversy. But the underlying causes are not being searched out. Until they are, political questions will continue to bedevil the campus, for all the worry and despair which arise from a fundamentally deranged community are being poured into the political arena. The behavior of faculty, students, and administrators reminds one of Santayana's fanatic, who redoubles his energy as he loses sight of his goal.

This is not to say that there are no genuine questions concerning political activity on campus. It is only to say that those questions have assumed disproportionate significance. Nor is it to say that the principles of 1964 were incorrect or unimportant. They spoke to real needs, and subsequent events have shown that too many people, on and off the campus, never understood or accepted them. It is only to say that 1964 brought not a hopeful peace but an uneasy truce; not a solution of the basic moral and intellectual questions, but only an opportunity, thus far unused, and now rapidly disappearing, for facing those questions.

Over the past two years the truce was often strained, and on several occasions nearly broke down. Increasing numbers of students began to doubt the administration's loyalty to the principles of political freedom. Students felt that they were not given a fair voice in the formulation of the rules governing political activity. A year-long effort to revise the constitution of student government, so as to give more autonomy, came to nothing when the new constitution was brusquely termed "illegal" by administration spokesmen. At the request of the House Committee on Un-American Activities, the university handed over the names of student political leaders without their knowledge and consent, and when an Oakland taxpayer sued the university to make those names available to any citizen, the university's lawyer sided with the taxpayer in court. The chancellor frequently expressed his disgust with the quality of the political meetings held in Sproul Plaza (symbolic home of 1964's Free Speech Movement) and talked about removing the rallies to some less conspicuous corner of the campus. The Vietnam Day Committee and the administration were constantly at loggerheads, and many students came to feel that the administration hated the VDC's doctrines and style more than it loved principles of political freedom. A student who excoriated one of the deans was threatened with punishment. These and similar events brought the students to the point where they had little trust in the bureaucracy.

The resolutions of 1964 spawned a generation of pettifoggers who argued furiously over such matters as the precise size and location of tables, the distribution of literature, the regulation of parades, and the size of posters. As the issues grew more legalistic, the passions aroused grew more intense, and the disputants less capable of self-examination. For one antic moment in 1965, Berkeley was without a chancellor and the statewide University without a president. Both resigned when a puckish demonstrator hoisted a banner bearing the terrible four-letter word. The demonstrator maintained that the Word stood for Freedom Under Clark Kerr, but everyone else insisted that the struggle was over rules and that there was nothing funny about it.

Gradually a certain mood and a certain political style began to dominate campus life. The mood was one of hostility and despair; the style one of confrontation. The two sides met as adversaries in a hopeless game, and, to a remarkable degree, both accepted the same definition of the rules of the game. Both sides agreed that the overall character of the contest was political, that the action took the form of a battle, with a winner and a loser, and that confrontation was the appropriate style of behavior.

Thus, the students theorized that they were confronting a "power structure" bound by strong and subtle links to the larger power structures of state and nation. The objectives of the national power elite were empire abroad and the suppression of dissent at home. The university administration's target was "the student movement," which stood for peace, civil rights, and radical social change. Hence, if the administration won, the children of light lost. During the struggle every administration move had to be probed for its "real" meanings. This view, obviously, made no allowance for mistakes, accidents, or common stupidity, let alone for good will.

The administration had its own version of the power elite theory: in its view the university's troubles were the work of a hard core of non-student agitators, plus a small number of student activists, who persistently abused the generous freedoms allowed on campus. Their goal was either to wreck the university or take it over. The "silent majority" of unpolitical students and a few hundred unrealistic faculty members had been duped by the agitators, thereby aggravating the administration's task.

Starting from these shared premises, relations between the combatants followed ritual patterns and ritual forensics. Each side was helplessly dependent on the other. Each could predict the other's tactics. Trapped by theory, neither had the freedom to deal radically with the fundamental malaise of which the endless controversies over rules were only symptoms.

Thus, when the administration proposed moving the Free Forum, with its mass rallies and raucous microphone, from Sproul Plaza to a less visible part of the campus, the students "knew" that this was another move to escalate the campaign against student dissent. The chancellor predictably replied that the Forum in Sproul Plaza fostered "a style of speech that is often vicious in intent, dishonest, laced with slander and character assassination, indifferent to evidence and truth, contemptuous of disagreement, and often charged with hatred." The microphone was "primarily an organizational weapon. . . . Its frequent use is coercive and its main target is the University itself." The students responded that the administration's standard of style was all too clear: just as the administrators admired a desk free of clutter, so too they desired a campus free of dissident students.

The administration asserted that the mass rallies and agitation were making the campus "unstable," even "ungovernable." While retreating from its intention of moving the microphone, the administration warned that "the days of doing business on this campus by coercion . . . are over." The students agreed that the question was one of power, and that the microphone and the Forum were their essential weapons. They countered the administration's conception of power as the ability to enforce rules by demanding greater student participation in rule-making and adjudication. Inevitably, they raised the banner of "Student Power"—inevitable, because authority had disappeared and only power mattered. Each side saw any action of the other as an "escalation" of the conflict, to which a "response" must be made.

The sterility of the shared premises became manifest in the self-contradictory aims announced by each side. Ever since 1964, the students had castigated the university for its bureaucratism, its maze of rules, and its intricate procedures. Now they were demanding additional rules, new procedures, and more machinery. Having first attacked the machine, the students next complicated its structure, and were now demanding a greater part in running it. No administration theorist was able to see that here, proposed by the students themselves, was a "final solution" to the student question: administrators and students, working together, might construct a machine capable of swallowing 27,500 students forever.

The administration caught itself in a different trap. A huge and complex campus necessarily looks to the Administration as the continuing center of energy and direction, especially when that campus must face profound tasks of reform within and hostility without. The faculty is incapable of sustained action. But instead of directing the energy and idealism generated by 1964 toward reconstruction, the administration insisted that the primary problem was order. While faculty members and students pleaded for new directions, the administration replied that it was so absorbed with the "fallout" from the Plaza that reform had to await the solution of the political problem. It seems never to have occurred to the chancellor and his many assistants that they had formulated the problem in such a way that it could not be solved. Order, as they defined it, was unattainable. Short of a repudiation of the December 8 resolutions, which would have brought instant chaos, there was no conceivable way of exorcising the student activists, of preventing students and non-students from mingling, or of lessening the deep revulsion against the corruptness of American society, and the horrors of Vietnam. The administration's deepest intellectual and moral failure was its failure to understand that it was directing an educational community. Its deepest psychological and political failure was lack of political foresight: it was willing to use force— even outside police force—to secure order, but it was silent as to how it would then gain the future trust, cooperation, and enthusiasm of those whom it had determined to pacify.

There was, then, a fatal logic in this politics of confrontation, in this academic reenactment of game theory. Once the premises were set, a showdown was inevitable; the more rationally each side acted out the shared premises, the more profoundly irrational would the final outcome be. All that was needed was a triggering event.

II.

For some years the Navy has been coming to campus to recruit future sailors. In early 1965, when the Navy set up a recruiting table, students picketed it. They also submitted a formal complaint to the administration, asking why governmental agencies should enjoy privileges on campus not accorded to other non-student organizations. The administration took no action.

On November 28, 1966, the Navy again set up a recruiting table in the lobby of the Student Union building. The executive vice-chancellor claims that elected student officers consented to the placing of the table, but the chief student officers have flatly contradicted this assertion, saying that in fact they had advised against it.

For two days the Navy quietly performed its duty, but the Students for a Democratic Society (SDS) were working too. They were planning an action which would simultaneously oppose the war in Vietnam and show the inequity in the administration's application of the rules governing the use of campus facilities by off-campus organizations. Their method was to set up a table for the dissemination of material opposed to the war and the draft. This table would be placed beside the Navy table, and it would be manned by a non-student. At the same time, students would form a picket around the Navy table.

On Wednesday morning, November 30, a non-student (a lady member of an anti-draft organization) asked the dean of students for permission to set up her table. Her request was refused. Nonetheless, she returned to the Student Union building and set up a table alongside the Navy's with a sign offering "Alternatives to Military Service." Shortly after noon, the SDS pickets arrived and formed their line.

Soon after the pickets came the police, and also the reporters and cameramen. The scene quickly attracted a fair-sized crowd, some sympathetic to the demonstration, some opposed, and some just curious.

At this point, a campus policeman told the anti-draft lady that she would have to leave. After a brief argument she agreed, and the police started to carry her table through the crowd. Many by-standers loudly protested the removal of the table, and several tried to grab it, making the police jerk it from their hands. Just then, a former football player shoved through the crowd, apparently in an attempt to clear a path for the police. Several students shouted at the football player to stop pushing people around. The football player turned, and, according to several witnesses, struck a student in the mouth. When the person who was struck lunged at his attacker, he was restrained and led away by policemen. The crowd grew resentful and apprehensive. In order to reduce confusion and the possibility of more violence and arrests, several students urged the crowd to sit down. Within moments, some seventy-five or one hundred people sat down around the Navy table, jamming the lobby of the Student Union. They began discussions about the arrest and about the Navy's special privileges.

Around 1 P.M. some notables began to arrive, including the president of the student body, the vice-chancellor for student affairs, and Mario Savio, Berkeley's most famous non-student (Savio was denied re-admission to Berkeley for passing out leaflets on campus while not a student).

The vice-chancellor told the demonstrators that he was willing to talk with the students, but not under coercion, and that unless the crowd dispersed he would declare the assembly unlawful. Campus policemen closed all entrances to the lower lobby of the Student Union building, permitting people to leave but not to enter. Three officers also barricaded the stairway leading to the main floor, preventing the persons in the main lobby from joining those in the lower lobby. The three officers were slowly being pushed down the stairs when the barricade broke and students poured into the lower lobby.

Order was soon restored, and the discussions continued. The demonstrators agreed to disperse if the anti-draft table were permitted to remain, if no charges were pressed against the student who had been led away by the police, and if no disciplinary actions were taken against the demonstrators. The vice-chancellor agreed to let the table remain if the student manned it, but he said that he could not promise amnesty for the demonstrators, and that the case of the arrested student was out of his hands. Further discussion produced no agreement. The vice-chancellor declared the assembly unlawful and left. The demonstrators stayed.

While all this was going on downstairs, a crowd of several thousands had formed outside the building and in its main lobby. A degree of organization and leadership emerged among the demonstrators. The talk turned to "student power," the sins of the administration, and the failures of the faculty. "Happy Birthday" was sung for Mario's year-old son, and when the Navy left about 4 P.M., the demonstrators gave them a hearty "Anchors Aweigh."

Shortly before 6 P.M., some twenty or thirty off-campus police entered the locked building. The demonstrators inside had no way of knowing the policemen's intention: did they intend to arrest only a few, or were they going to carry everyone away, in a reenactment of 1964? The police, holding warrants signed by the executive vice-chancellor, arrested six persons, all non-students, on charges of trespassing and creating a public nuisance. Chaos threatened when the police attempted to drag the first person from the crowd of seated protestors. Some persons shrieked in alarm. Others shouted abusively at the officers, and pulled at their arms and legs, getting hit and kicked in return. The other arrests were accomplished without incident. None of the six resisted. Among those arrested were Savio and Jerry Rubin, local leader of the VDC.

Administration spokesmen have offered a very different account of these events. The executive vice-chancellor was reported in the student newspaper as saying that the six were arrested because they played "the key role" in the sit-in. In an official statement to the faculty and staff, he said that "the demonstration today was initiated and led by non-students in direct defiance of University regulations." On the other hand, three faculty eye-witnesses, in a signed document, have reported that "none of the six seemed involved as initiators," that one of the six did not speak throughout the demonstration, and that "two others participated minimally if at all. When confronted with these statements, one of the chancellor's assistants said that the administration had put up with "eighteen months of activists' blackmail" before moving against the students. The chancellor himself, addressing the Academic Senate, stated that the whole thing began when "non-students attempted in violation of our rules to set up a table. . . ." He referred to other recent "provocations," and concluded that "we are dealing, then, not with a single incident but with a chronic situation."

These administration statements overlooked certain critical distinctions among the groups of people involved in the early stages of the disturbance: (1) the non-student who set up the anti-war table but was not arrested; (2) the students who, after seeing one of their number struck, sat in; and (3) the six arrested non-students, who, by no account, initiated or organized the demonstration. It appears that the administration, acting on its "outside agitator" theory, was out to get these people, even if that meant calling police onto the campus and committing a possible injustice against individuals.

As the police van moved away, another violent encounter took place. Hundreds of students jammed the street around the van. They were swept aside by a phalanx of policemen. Many persons were shoved and clubbed, some severely. Three students were arrested for interfering with the police.

The Student Union building was now unlocked, and the demonstrators outside were able to join those inside. They began a marathon mass meeting. By 10 P.M. the crowd had grown to around three thousand, jammed into a large ballroom. Many speakers stressed the futility of trying to negotiate reasonably with the administration over questions of political activity. The executive vice-chancellor appeared for about a half hour to answer questions. The hostile audience clearly considered his statements to be evasive or even false, and he was loudly hooted. Savio, who had returned after posting bail, was the last speaker of the evening. He recounted the unsuccessful efforts of individuals to gain due process during the last two years, and described a student strike as the "least disruptive way of pressuring the Administration." At 1 A.M. the students voted, nearly unanimously, to strike. The campus community was offered coffee and rebellion for breakfast.

The next day (December 2, two years to the day after the mass sit-in and arrests of 1964) a rally of about eight thousand confirmed the decision and accepted the demands of the strike: that police must never be called on campus to "solve" political problems; no disciplinary action against participants; off-campus individuals and non-commercial groups should have privileges on campus equal to those enjoyed by governmental agencies; disciplinary hearings must in the future be open and conducted according to the canons of due process; discussions must begin toward the creation of effective student representation on rule-making bodies. The Teaching Assistants' union, the student government, and (later) the student newspaper all supported the strike. Chancellor Heyns, who had been away, returned to an embattled campus.

Throughout the rest of the week the strike and mass rallies continued. Groups of faculty met frequently to discuss the issues and prepare for the forthcoming meeting of the Academic Senate. The chancellor declared himself opposed to the strike and refused to meet with representatives of the strikers.

The strike itself was well organized, but there are no reliable estimates concerning its effectiveness. Although there are a marvelous range and variety of political groups on the Berkeley campus, there was little factionalism or doctrinal infighting apparent in the conduct of the strike. For some time now most campus political groups have united in a loose confederal structure, called the Council of Campus Organizations, for the purpose of doing battle with the administration over issues concerning the legitimacy of the rules governing political activity. Hence, the many organizations participating in the strike had a pre-established system of discussion and communication. Perhaps the two most powerful new forces on the campus political scene are the Teaching Assistants' union and the Free University of Berkeley. The former has a membership of about four hundred graduate teaching assistants, and is affiliated with the AFT. The union voted to strike, supported it to the end, and supplied many of its leaders. The Free University is a "counter-institution" offering courses in everything from psychedelics and modern painting to Marxism and the theory and practice of imperialism. Some 250 persons are in some sense enrolled in the Free University, and some of the strike's leaders are closely associated with it. The strikers quickly elected an executive committee and a negotiating committee, proving once again that Berkeley students have a trained capacity for political organization and action. They can produce a manifesto and arrange a demonstration at a moment's notice. Many of the students have become impressive political speakers and tacticians. While the campus administration intones the language of community, it is the students who have been actually building community among themselves. Although there are student leaders, there is no permanent clique which can manipulate the students. The movement waxes and wanes, leaders come and go, as the situation changes. When the right conditions appear, thousands of students with a shared orientation can be mobilized within hours. If the administration tries to destroy this community by chopping off its head, it may find itself battling a Hydra.

The [Academic] Senate meeting of December 5 opened with an address by the chancellor. He reaffirmed his opposition to the strike, rejected amnesty for rule violators, called the rules "fair and equitable," argued that present hearing procedures met "the highest standards of judicial fairness," and asked for confidence from the faculty. The Senate debated and approved by a vote of 795 to 28, with 143 abstentions, a compromise, omnibus resolution. On the one hand, the Senate called for an end to the strike and affirmed "confidence in the Chancellor's leadership." On the other hand, it urged amnesty for students who had violated rules during the course of the strike. The Senate declared that tactics of "mass coercion" and the use of external police, except in extreme emergency, were both inappropriate to a university. The resolution also asked that new avenues be explored for increasing student participation in rule-making and enforcement, and called for a faculty-student commission "to consider new modes of governance and self-regulation in the University."

Unlike December, 1964, no one was enthusiastic about the result. Many faculty members wanted a more outspoken condemnation of the decision to bring the police on campus. A smaller number was disappointed that the Senate had not even discussed the matter of the arrest of the six non-students. A near majority, sick of the turmoil and persuaded that it had been caused by a few trouble-makers, narrowly failed to pass a "hard" resolution supporting the chancellor without reservation. No one spoke in defense of the students. Only a few dared to challenge the official theory that a small band of subversives had caused the trouble. None dared to say openly what many had declared privately, that the administration's decision to call in the police was more than a mistake, it was a crime. The fragile compromise in the resolutions caused the faculty liberals to abstain from vigorous debate for fear that the resolutions would be mutilated by amendments. Consequently, the speeches were made by faculty conservatives and many were harsh. One compared the Berkeley demonstrators to the Nazi students who had driven the non-Nazi professors from Germany. Another member finished his long speech by declaring in exasperation that he didn't want to hear any more arguments, only a vote of confidence in defense of order and authority.

It is doubtful that the chancellor was pleased by resolutions which coupled police action with the student strike and condemned them both; nor could the faculty declaration for amnesty be viewed by him as other than a rebuff. The students interpreted the resolution as final evidence of faculty unreliability. "The faculty cannot solve our problems," declared a student manifesto. "They did not choose to implement the December 8 Resolution, and [they have] demonstrated their inability to deal . . . with the educational ills of the University." Thus the faculty managed to disappoint itself, the administration, and the students.

The next day the Board of Regents met in emergency session. Regent Edwin Pauley, who had declared that "if people on the payroll can't understand their conditions of employment they shouldn't be there, and I'm for getting rid of them," introduced a resolution calling for retroactive punishment of striking Teaching Assistants and faculty. It was defeated and a substitute was passed that supported the chancellor, refrained from punishing the students, and condemned the "interference" of "outsiders." "The Regents support all necessary action to preserve order on all campuses of the University." Separating the student strikers from their supporters among the Teaching Assistants and faculty, the Regents produced the only unequivocal action of the week, a resolution that radically redefined the nature of academic freedom and tenure. Henceforth, "University personnel . . . who participate in any strike or otherwise fail to meet their assigned duties, in an effort to disrupt University administration, teaching, or research, will thereby be subject to termination of their employment . . . denial of re-employment, or the imposition of other appropriate sanctions." Obviously, the Regents had sown the seeds of future controversy.

Meanwhile the politicians of the state were angrily demanding that the striking faculty and Teaching Assistants be dismissed. The governor-elect warned the students "to obey the prescribed rules or get out. . . . The people of California . . . have a right to lay down rules and a code of conduct for those who accept that gift [of public education]." The president *pro tem* of the Senate advised Reagan that all that the university needed was "a new president and some regents with more guts than liberalism." The Speaker of the Assembly, and sometime Chubb Fellow of Yale, who had gotten his investigating committee from the 1964 crisis, made his usual statesmanlike suggestion: instead of appointing a new commission, the Governor should appoint the former CIA head to the Board of Regents. As of this writing, a bill has been introduced into the state legislature which would drastically reduce the powers of the Regents and place the university under closer legislative control.

The strike dragged to a close that evening and a haggard faculty and student body prepared for finals. In their last mass meeting, the students found a measure of joy and humor—graces sadly lacking this time. Half the joy was relief: they had been naughty, but hadn't gotten spanked too hard, at least not yet. There also emerged at the rally a spontaneous coalition between the hippies and the political activists. While the Teaching Assistants, like good trade unionists, sang "Solidarity Forever" in one room, the hippy–activist coalition sang "The Yellow Submarine" in another, and promised that next term they would "blow the Administration's mind." Instead of resorting to such "square" tactics as strikes and sit-ins, they might clog the machine, mock its logic, and drive its operators out of their minds by such tactics as flooding the deans with thousands of petitions, misplacing their identity cards, returning books to the wrong libraries, flocking to the student medical clinic for all manner of psychosomatic complaints, and wearing masks to class. It is impossible to anticipate how the chancellor will respond to that escalation.

III.

It is doubtful whether the strike settled anything. Surely it added to the legacy of bitterness and anxiety. Perhaps it provided the jolt needed to start the university on the work of self-examination which it has so far shirked. More likely, Berkeley will enter an era of strong solutions—an obsession with total control, possibly a purge of dissident elements. That way may bring peace, but it will be the peace of intellectual and moral torpor.

The only hope for the university lies in replacing the narrow and fatal premises which have produced the present impasse with others more appropriate to the general social situation in which the university now stands. That social situation is one that can be called revolutionary in the sense that while the forces of change gather momentum, the society cannot find the appropriate response either in thought or act.

The troubles which beset American society are unprecedented and paradoxical. Stated broadly, our condition is one of widespread affluence, growing social expectations, scientific and technological dynamism, extensive welfare programs, and a high degree of formal democracy. In spite of all this, there is pervasive contempt for the very system which has given its members more comfort and leisure than any society in history. There is in this progressive, tolerant, and literate society a frightening lack of intellectual loyalty and spontaneous affection for the system. Above all, there lurks the fear that behind the greatest concentration of economic, scientific, and military power in history there is a moral weakness so thoroughgoing that when the society faces a substantive problem, such as racial discrimination, its cities are thrown into turmoil, or when it becomes embroiled in a foreign policy misadventure, its political creativity is limited to throwing increasing military might against a small country in a cause whose hopelessness rises in direct ratio to the violence employed.

Historically, revolutions have been occasions for attempting something new in the political world: a new vision of society, a new concept of authority, a new ideal of freedom or justice. We are accustomed to think of revolutions as arising out of poverty and injustice, exacerbated by the governing class's refusal to "modernize"—France of 1789, Russia of 1917, China of 1945. But the revolution brewing in America, this richest and most advanced of societies, is different. It is nourished by a sense of failure rather than hope. Our physical success is accompanied by spiritual despair. America is proving that modern man can create powerful and rich societies in which the rate of change is so intense that men cannot endure it, let alone master it. The paradox of our revolutionary condition, then, is the existence of despair, disaffection, and contempt within a society that is prosperous, progressive, and democratic.

Berkeley is the perfect example of the kind of university which a democratic and progressive society might be expected to produce. Its faculty is distinguished, its students highly selected, and its facilities superb. Like the society around it, the university is dynamic and growing, and it can claim excellence in science and professional training. Despite these achievements, it is a university whose administrators find ungovernable, whose educational leaders find unreformable, and whose students find unliveable. For two years its life has been marked by an enervating anxiety and hostility which cannot be dismissed as "a failure in communication." The melancholy truth is that there is no widely shared understanding about the meaning and purpose of the institution. Lacking the unifying force which flows spontaneously from common understandings, the system is held together by a bureaucratic organization whose weakness is exposed whenever it is directly challenged.

This is partly the result of Berkeley's legacy as a public university, a legacy which contrasts with the traditional idea informing the ancient public universities of Europe, as well as the private universities and colleges of this country.

The striking difference between the traditional university and the modern public university is best seen in the small place assigned to administration in the former. The older university could flourish with a "housekeeper" administration because of one basic presupposition: that a genuine and autonomous community of scholars existed to be served. The modern public university, however, was born in a state of dependence on the outside society, and in most instances, the administration was created first. It never had the chance to become a community. Its survival depended upon public support and administrative power, not on the moral and intellectual fellowship of its members.

The public university adheres to a conception of knowledge which differs greatly from that of its ancestors. The knowledge it produces must be useful to the social and economic interests of an expanding society. At Berkeley, there are installations, institutes, and laboratories in which trained experts develop knowledge in such fields as naval medicine, sanitary engineering, space science, marine food products, nuclear weapons, mining, and range management. The demand for all these services is strong and growing. But it goes without saying that there is no irresistible demand that the university preserve the knowledge and experience of the past or encourage reflection on the intangibles of the good life. The old idea of the university as a community of conservants has been pushed aside by the Baconian vision of knowledge as power. But practicality has not by itself created the ideal of knowledge which now threatens all universities, public or private. The notorious concern of most faculties with publication and research is directly related to the requirement that a scholar be "original." He must turn up novelties of fact or theory, and his novelties must pay off, either because they are practical or because they "generate" further research. Knowledge is no longer associated with wisdom, or with the fruits of contemplation or rediscovery. It is not guided by reflection, but fired by the hope of a "breakthrough." This conception of knowledge brings a new pace to academic life: the researcher is forever racing to the frontiers where the future beckons. He must continuously invent new concepts, models, and techniques. The greatest sin lies not in being trivial, but in appearing old-fashioned.

At Berkeley these concerns amount to an obsession. It is virtually official doctrine that the ruthless pursuit of productivity is the key to Berkeley's rapid rise to a position where it is no longer just "another state university," but can compare with such renowned institutions as Harvard.

The assumption that a university is a place where knowledge is "pursued" and "cumulated" seems harmless enough until its effects are considered. This approach entails destruction of and contempt for the old, and for the fuddyduddies who profess it. The perfect illustration of the new spirit is the popularity of Whitehead's battle cry among social scientists: "A science which hesitates to forget its founders is lost." Forgetting and destroying are necessary preconditions for productivity; he travels fastest who travels lightest; he travels lightest who sheds civility, tradition, and care for the common culture of the intellect.

The new conception of knowledge produces human casualties as well. In departments throughout Berkeley there are endless macabre discussions, amounting to ritual murder, about the older professors left stranded alongside the main stream of research. Young men are ready, but the old men are protected by tenure. The curiosity is that the superannuated professor is probably in his thirties.

The competitive ethos of the modern research-oriented university has created "dysfunctional" or "deviant" human types, to use the current idiom. These are, lamentably, the very types which were "functional" in the traditional university. Foremost among them is the teacher. The teacher who is threatened is not the one who loves to be surrounded by admiring undergraduates and who makes a cult of non-writing, but rather the one who naively believes that teaching and research can be creatively combined. But, as an academic member of the Berkeley administration responsible for promoting educational reform has said, "A professor's bread is buttered by his relationships within his field, and they are established by research. You don't get an international reputation for giving a great course at Berkeley." Nor need the academic face a Kierkegaardian choice between teaching and research. Numerous agencies are eager to pay for the professor's "released time" from the classroom so that he can pursue his research free from the distractions of teaching. In some fields, it is tacitly agreed that the professors who carry normal teaching loads are those whose research is not so valuable as to justify their giving full time to it.

If the teacher is "dysfunctional," the student is worse. To the jet-age frontiersman he is a distraction and an anomaly, except when he is an apprentice researcher. Most graduate students present few problems, for they have been "socialized" and can even instruct their seniors in the art of grantsmanship. Those undergraduates and graduates who are left outside the system and who feel hurt and betrayed have formulated their own counter-idea of knowledge. Against the professionalism of the insiders, they proclaim the primacy of passion, subjectivity, and openness. Knowledge which is not obviously related to their immediate personal needs and situations is irrelevant. To be relevant, knowledge must speak *now* to *their* needs. The ancient values of detachment and disinterested inquiry are seen as evasions of responsibility; or, worse, as typifying the vice of "objectivism" which transforms thought and feeling into alienated objects and serves as an ideological figleaf for a corrupt establishment.

It would be a foolish man who, given the complex problems

confronting the modern university, would claim to have a new constitution in his pocket. Nevertheless, certain things are clear. If some thing of the traditional idea of the university is to be salvaged, there must be revitalization of a common culture and a lessening of the centrifugal tendencies of specialization. It must be recognized that the pursuit of knowledge can take forms incompatible with the unique cultural and educational character of the university. This is not to say that the university should turn away from new modes of knowledge and inquiry and lovingly cultivate all that is precious and old. A creative tension between tradition and innovation should be the guiding principle.

It has become clear that the University of California is no longer viable in its present form. The whole vast state-wide complex, with its centralized bureaucratic apparatus of control, should be decentralized toward something like a "Commonwealth of Campuses" model, but it is unlikely that this will happen. Two years ago, a committee appointed by the Regents proposed that the state-wide system be devolved into a looser alliance of largely autonomous campuses. After creating a brief sensation, the report was conveniently forgotten. The best hope for the future lies in devising ways to reintegrate faculty and students around smaller structures which are allowed genuine powers of decision-making and broad opportunities for educational experiments. If smaller communities are to be established, there must be serious open-minded discussion of the possibilities of student participation in a far broader range of university matters than hitherto.

At this moment, the Academic Senate is considering a concrete proposal to establish a student–faculty commission to explore ways of improving "the participation of students in the formulation of educational policies, including measures for the improvement of teaching." The proposal lays special emphasis on the need to develop "patterns of student–faculty cooperation" at the departmental level.

These proposals move in the direction recently suggested by President Kerr. In a newspaper interview of a month ago, he described Berkeley's steps toward educational reform as "somewhat too conservative." He also said that "the University of California had the most restrictive policies [regarding political activity] of any university I've ever known about, outside a dictatorship." He also declared "that this is a generation that wants to participate" and "there ought to be 100, or 1,000 opportunities" for it to do so.

In contrast, too many faculty members have resisted trying

to understand the contemporary student and have indulged themselves, instead, in grotesque analogies between Berkeley and Latin American-style universities or Nazi youth movements. These spectral analogies, like the outside agitator theory, are appeals to fear and rest upon the belief that men can be frightened into order.

Today's student finds himself in a world of complexity and change, of exciting possibilities and ominous threats, of uncertain landmarks for personal conduct and all too certain prescriptions for success in the straight world. He sees a world whose promise is constantly violated by destruction, discrimination, and cruelty. In an older and simpler age he would have entered the university with greater confidence and stability, for many institutions would have helped prepare him for adulthood. But family, church, neighborhood, and school have now declined in effectiveness and where they once contributed to his confidence, they now reinforce his uncertainty. Consequently, the student is led to demand more from his university experience than ever before. Such students embarrass the university for the same reason that Kierkegaard embarrassed Christendom: by the purity of their demands. They want the university to be a place where education and knowledge are pursued out of love for the pursuit itself. They are in revolt against all that is remote and impersonal in human relations. They want an educational community whose members will look at each other, not one in which relationships are defined by rules and treated as simple problems of order and compliance. Because they take the democratic ideal seriously, they want a voice in the decisions which shape their lives. It is these students who provide hope.

Opportunities for creative change still exist at Berkeley, but the problems are profound, reflecting as they do the sickness of our society and the disaffection of a whole generation. This time the campus must face the future with a fuller appreciation of the radical nature of the reforms needed.

The Cold War and the University of California*

MARK SHECHNER

T HE COLD WAR is an American institution, perhaps the most powerful institution we have, not only because of the physical and economic power behind it but also because of its status in American mythology. The office of the President promotes it, the economy depends upon it, political figures rise to power on it, our relations with other countries are controlled by it—there is scarcely a person in the country whose life is not touched by it. It is in some respects *the* American ideology; it is the sole *raison d'être* for innumerable acts of Congress, presidential directions, for national acts of unusual benevolence and unspeakable barbarity. The Cold War's effect upon the American university has been a profound though not entirely an unambiguous one. For if the Cold War has brought to the surface of American life the worst of our chauvinism, it has also been the cause and occasion of a massive national introspection and a consequent recognition that all has not been well with our lives.

In the universities, both faces of the Cold War have made themselves manifest. Some universities no longer distinguish truth from "national defense" because their values derive ever-increasingly from the role they are playing in the defense establishment. The modern university has indeed arisen to "meet the challenge of the Cold War" and not to have done so in some manner would have been preposterous. The Cold War is real and the survivability

* From *Frontier* (August, 1966). Used by permission.

of a university is unquestionably related to its ability to perceive and come to terms with what is real. But what is worth questioning is the way in which the university has responded and the manner in which the Cold War has helped to establish such priorities that the life of the mind is for some no longer easy to separate from the business of the government. Some schools that have hitherto lacked an independent sense of purpose have latched onto the "national purpose" and tried to build a reputation on the proceeds.

Evidence that the relationship between military needs and academic functions compromises many of the universities involved is eminently available. Among the most recent and most highly publicized manifestations of the scholar-soldier ethos (or "Fishel's syndrome") have been the famous Michigan State project in Vietnam, the army's now-defunct-but-not-entirely-forgotten Project Camelot which was a grand scheme to employ social scientists in massive numbers to predict and influence revolutionary activity in Latin America, and the University of Pennsylvania's Project Spicerack which is presently engaged in biological warfare research. But these are only the most obvious services that universities today are performing; the relationship between the military and the campus is not totally definable in terms of these three functions.

In most schools, for MSU is still an atypical example of university response, the reaction has been more ambiguous. Every major campus no doubt has its complement of Cold War planners, its weapons designers, game theorists, counter-insurgency tacticians, and propagators of doctrinaire anti-communism. But for once there is money enough available for research of *all* kinds. The army has money enough to support research in brain chemistry or soil behavior or the value of ammonia as a fuel or wave diffraction; the Office of Naval Research can sponsor research in radio astronomy, statistics, differential equations, the behavior of molecular and atomic beams, or language learning; the Air Force Office of Scientific Research too has great sums of money to spread around. Whatever the motives of the various federal sponsors may be and whatever advantages may accrue to the military from the sponsorship of scientific research, the boon to science itself has been incalculable.

Of the slightly more than $2 billion spent in American colleges and universities in 1965 for research and development, $1.6 billion was provided by the federal government. One meaning of this fact, at least in terms of its force in defining the societal role of the American university, has been suggested by Clark Kerr in his *Uses of the University:*

It is interesting that American universities, which pride themselves on their autonomy, should have taken their special character as much or more from the pressures of their environment as from their own inner desires; that institutions which identify themselves either as "private" or as "state" should have found their greatest stimulus in federal initiative; that universities which are part of a highly decentralized and varied system of higher education should, nevertheless, have responded with such fidelity and alacrity to national needs; that institutions which had their historical origins in the training of "gentlemen" should have committed themselves so fully to the service of brute technology.

One of the oldest children of this relationship that Kerr has called a "common-law marriage" is the intellectual entrepreneur, the scientist whose home university is little more than a boarding house, a place to hang his contract. Last year Gerard Piel, publisher of *Scientific American,* complained of the "new *condottieri,* mercenaries of science and scholarship hooded with doctorates and ready for hire on studies to contract specifications." It is not so unusual nowadays for a high-powered researcher to spend several days a week as a high-priced consultant for industry or the government and make two to three times his university salary in fees. The ramifications of this are many and serious. In an article in *Scientific American* for July, 1965, Dael Wolfle pointed out the tendency of this massive availability of outside money to weaken a professor's ties with his university and to break down those integrative forces that give a university its own character and purpose and make it more than just a laboratory complex around which famous men rent large houses. For the big researcher, the maintenance of good relations with Washington and private foundations is more lucrative and professionally satisfying than his ties with his own university administration.

Another unfortunate but inevitable result of massive federal spending for research is that education, most markedly undergraduate education, is being severely downgraded. The big researchers who spend much of their time traveling, drafting proposals and sitting on committees have little time for teaching, but their ability to land the big contracts makes them both valuable properties for universities on the make and models for graduate students who, impressed by the successful style of their mentors, prefer research to teaching assistantships.

But most important and most ominous is the strong military cast to research today—and this is true even of basic research. Last year, in reviewing Jerome Wiesner's *Where Science and Politics Meet* for the *New York Review of Books,* James Newman complained that areas of study in which the military can perceive no relevance to its needs whatever are permitted to drink at the public trough because they are vaguely thought to strengthen our "defense posture" or be in the "national interest."

The University of California is, because of its size and the degree of its indebtedness to federal funding agencies, a good focus for a study of the ways in which federal–educational relationships operate, how the values of one institution shape another and how the whole culture in which they both exist is shaped by that relationship.

The university's annual expenditure on organized research (at least for fiscal year 1964–65) is around $337 million, far higher than the amount spent by any other state university or land-grant college. Research volume for the school next in line, University of Chicago, is about $142 million, less than half the California total, while the third-ranking school, Cornell University, spends only some $55 million a year. The major portion of UC's giant research budget is the $235 million AEC appropriation for the operation of three major research and development facilities: Los Alamos Scientific Laboratory, Lawrence Radiation Laboratory (Berkeley and Livermore), and the Nuclear Medicine and Radiation Biology Laboratory at UCLA. The "Current Fund Income" section of the university's 1964–65 *Financial Report* shows how the massive AEC contracts (for Special Federal Research Projects) compare with the university's budget as a whole.

Student fees and tuition	$ 33,800,000
State of California	180,666,000
United States of America	95,411,000
Endowment income	7,666,000
Gifts and private grants	10,282,000
Sales and services	2,013,000
Organized activities	
Hospitals and clinics	16,768,000
Other	2,375,000
Other sources	5,294,000
Auxiliary enterprises	23,922,000
Total	$378,197,000
Special federal research projects	$237,642,000
Total current income	$615,839,000

These figures mean that around 54 per cent of the university's total income for fiscal year 1964–65 derived from the federal government.

Money from a Variety of Sources

The bulk of the university's federal funds come from a few agencies that have a particular interest in higher education—some, like the National Science Foundation (NSF) tend to be concerned with the process of education; others, like the National Aeronautic and Space Administration (NASA) or the air force, are more inclined to be interested in the product. A partial inventory of the University of California's major supporters in Washington yields the following:

AEC (exclusive of the special federal research projects)	$ 5,964,911
Department of Defense (DOD)	
Air Force	$ 3,567,952
Army	1,765,291
Navy	10,724,002
Other	842,499
Total DOD	$ 16,899,744
National Institutes of Health (NIH)	$ 38,813,976
National Science Foundation (NSF)	16,109,988
National Aeronautics and Space Administration (NASA)	6,304,016
Agency for International Development (AID)	2,005,409

Of the slightly more than $337 million spent last year for research on UC campuses or university-managed research facilities about $297 million was federal money, a ratio which is consistent with the national average.

The most obvious and most portentous component of that research expenditure is the money spent for the operation of the country's largest nuclear weapons research-and-development laboratories—the Los Alamos Scientific Laboratory in New Mexico and the Livermore branch of the Lawrence Radiation Laboratory. All, or certainly almost all the nuclear and thermonuclear weapons in America's arsenal today were designed and assembled either at Livermore or Los Alamos. Los Alamos boasts, in fact, of having fabricated 90 per cent of this country's atomic weapons, and it is reasonable to assume that a large part of the remaining 10 per cent are Livermore devices. Los Alamos, as everyone knows, was the site of the World War II Manhattan Project which, under the direction of former Berkeley physics professor J. Robert Oppenheimer, designed and tested the first atomic bomb near Alamogordo, N.M., and made the bombs that were dropped on Hiroshima and Nagasaki. Livermore was set up by the AEC in 1952 specifically so that Edward Teller could have his own laboratory in which to work on the hydrogen bomb.

Los Alamos and, to a lesser degree, Livermore, are legacies of an earlier heroic age whose great scientists, in the light of history, have come to be regarded as great men as well. It is perhaps an accident of history that E. O. Lawrence was in Berkeley in 1930 when he invented the cyclotron, but from this event there issued a series of consequences which have bound the University of California tightly to its heroic past. In the early thirties, with men like Lawrence and Oppenheimer as a nucleus, a small but talented group of young physicists and chemists, Nobel Prize winners and winners-to-be, came together on the Berkeley campus. Among the physicists were Luis Alvarez, Edwin McMillan, and Emilio Segre. The cadre of young chemists included J. W. Kennedy, Arthur C. Wahl, and Glenn Seaborg. For them Lawrence's new particle accelerators were the realization of the old alchemist's fantasy of transmuting one element into another.

When the war broke out the UC Radiation Laboratory was turned into an industrial laboratory and set to work separating the fissionable uranium isotope, U-235, from its non-fissionable matrix material, U-238. In 1942 the almost-complete 184″ cyclotron was refitted and put to work on uranium separation; the UC Radiation Laboratory was the first laboratory in the country to produce fissionable uranium in large quantities.

Early on the morning of February 24, 1941, Seaborg, McMillan, and Wahl, using the 60″ cyclotron of the old Crocker Laboratory, isolated and identified plutonium. As a result of these early investigations in Berkeley, the Plutonium Project of the Manhattan Engineer District was set up under A. H. Compton at the University of Chicago to explore the military potential of the new element.

In January, 1943, after it had been decided that the bomb was to be built in New Mexico, the University of California contracted with the Manhattan Engineer District of the War Department to administer Los Alamos personnel and procurement from a purchasing office in Los Angeles. Thirty-one months later, on July 16, 1945, at Alamogordo the first atomic device, which Oppenheimer had inexplicably dubbed Trinity, was detonated and less than a month later, August 6, Hiroshima was bombed.

After the war most of the scientists who had built the Trinity bomb went back to their university campuses and Oppenheimer yielded his post as director to Norris Bradbury and it seemed for a while, in 1946 and '47, that Los Alamos might well close. But the advent of the first Cold War pressures in Eastern Europe and the unexpected explosion of an atomic bomb by Russia in 1949 revived Los Alamos and the race to build up an atomic stockpile began once again—still under the managerial auspices of the University of California which was now under contract to the new civilian AEC.

Enter the "Father" of the H-Bomb

The history of the Livermore laboratory is the history of Edward Teller's efforts to get the country rolling on the H-bomb. It came into existence as a result of his frustration over having to work with hostile colleagues and a hostile administrator, Norris Bradbury, at Los Alamos. Teller had tried, three times in fact, starting in 1951, to get the General Advisory Committee of the AEC to approve a second thermonuclear weapons laboratory and was three times refused. But early in 1952, when the University of Chicago began making plans to build such a laboratory for the air force, the AEC relented and that summer Teller had his workshop in Livermore where his friend E. O. Lawrence had already established a small research facility. For the director of the laboratory, Lawrence and Teller decided upon Herbert York, "a young physicist who was full of vitality, good humor and common sense" and whose secret love was space travel. "In his home," Teller fondly recalls in *The Legacy of Hiroshima,* "he had a beautiful picture of the moon and its craters."

Center of Atomic Development

Thus, from 1930 to the present a massive structure of atomic installations, both military and non-military, has grown up within and around the University of California. The imposing hill complex of basic research facilities behind Strawberry Canyon in

Berkeley is all that most people ever see, though it makes up, in relation to the whole bulk of the UC–AEC atomic establishment, the visible ninth of the nuclear iceberg. Below the waterline lie what are probably the greatest nuclear weapons research-and-development laboratories anywhere in the world.

As distant now as Lawrence's invention may seem, it was quite clearly responsible for the presence, in Berkeley, of a great array of talent and equipment when the war began and consequent upon that fact was the inevitable result of the university's playing a major role in the Manhattan Project. The Los Alamos laboratory today still devotes about half of its total effort to research and development of military hardware; not only nuclear but conventional weapons are designed and tested at its facilities in New Mexico and Nevada. But it has diversified its activity and presently is engaged in such things as reactor design for atomic rocket propulsion and has sent into orbit six satellites of the Vela-Hotel series which are aimed at detecting nuclear tests in outer space.

Livermore, too, is primarily a developer of weapons though that aspect of its work is publicly subordinated to its non-military operations such as the well-publicized Project Plowshare which is dedicated to finding peaceful uses for atomic explosions. But out of a Lawrence Radiation Laboratory budget of $140 million in fiscal year 1964–65 (including the Berkeley branch) Plowshare received $6 million, while 64 per cent of the total budget, or $90 million, was spent on weapons.

While the university administers these laboratories, handles their hiring, firing, buying, selling, bookkeeping and cleans their sidewalks, it exerts little if any influence over their life or thought. The free exchange of knowledge is inimical to the world behind the chain-link gates of secrecy and security. In complete contradistinction to a university campus which is, at least in theory, an open forum, knowledge in the UC weapons laboratories is strictly compartmentalized and access to it controlled by the criterion of "need to know." Nor do the laboratories and their directors feel at all obliged to discuss openly their activities with critical citizens who raise important questions. In 1960, a local pacifist exchanged letters with Dr. Harold Brown, then head of the Livermore laboratory, now Secretary of the Air Force, informing him that he intended "to be in the area of your facility for a nonviolent direct action protesting the continuation of nuclear weapons research." The pacifist, Samuel R. Tyson, concluded his letter with this request:

We hope it will be possible to have a chance to talk with you during this period so we all may have a chance to exchange verbally some of our motivations.

Brown's answer concluded with a refusal to interview the demonstrators and a statement which reflects the mentality of every maker of weapons who has ever thought his own work had at last made war unthinkable:

As to your request to talk with me during this period, I think that such a discussion in the environment of "direct action" demonstration could not lead to a calm weighing of the issues. I must therefore decline to engage in such a meeting.

However, I am glad to give the following personal views on the Laboratory's work. I think we would agree that maintaining peace and freedom is the most vital objective of people of good will. I believe that our work on nuclear weapons has been one of the most important factors in preventing a catastrophic war. It has also helped to maintain free institutions against the threat of piecemeal aggression. It is because I believe that these ends will continue to be served by our work that I consider the laboratory's efforts to be so important.

Sincerely yours,
(S) Harold Brown

Vast Development of Weapons

As a result of the historical importance, relative antiquity and public character of its ties with these laboratories, the university has been able to present a potentially critical public with an open and above board *fait accompli,* thereby preempting the kind of criticism that would normally follow an expose. Thus it has been that in a time of student protests against germ-warfare research at the University of Pennsylvania and an uproar over a comparatively small CIA engineering contract at Stanford, a relatively radical and activist student body in Berkeley has raised not so much as a whisper of complaint about their school's central role in the fabrication of the most powerful arsenal of weapons in human history.

A Series of Unanswered Questions

But though the university acknowledges its stewardship of weapons design and its maintenance of secret research, it seems not particularly willing to respond candidly to critical queries about them. This past May I asked university Vice-President Earl Bolton

a series of questions about various programs, functions and public
acts of the university such as the nature and function of the uni-
versity-operated Naval Biological Laboratory in Oakland, the assumptions that underlay the Berkeley-based Brazil Development
Assistance Program and the presentation of the Shah of Iran with
an Honorary Doctorate of Humane Letters at UCLA in June,
1964. The main thrust of the questions, however, was in the
direction of determining the character of the university's attitude
toward these laboratories. These questions were submitted as
follows:

As a statement of my general purpose in asking these questions I
wish to point out that I am not out to rake up muck so much as to
discover to what extent this university, which is so obviously a model
for public universities throughout the country, has an independent
sense of values which distinguishes it from the surrounding community—and to what extent the values of this university are determined
at any particular moment by whatever fund or agency is willing and
able to pay for the services of the institution. I am predisposed to
think the latter state of affairs is the rule rather than the exception
and as matters stand today, with so much money being spent by the
federal government in this and other universities for the purpose of
"meeting the challenge of the Cold War," we are being gradually but
inexorably transformed into tools and weapons of that war. But unlike the Michigan State effort in Vietnam which was so incredibly
clumsy and far out as to predestine its own failure, our own involvement with the military and other mission-oriented agencies is a quiet,
tastefully conducted relationship which is so much a part of our landscape that we are hardly aware of it and thereby it is so much more
of a problem for being so much less blatant.

After World War II, the Regents of the University briefly considered dropping their wartime arrangement with the War Department for the administration of the Los Alamos Scientific Laboratory
but apparently never did so. Today we find ourselves administering
two scientific laboratories at Livermore and Los Alamos whose primary mission is weapons research and development. With regard to
these laboratories I would like to ask the following questions:

1. What advantages accrue to the University from this managerial
   service? Are there scientific advantages, economic advantages,
   advantages in matters of academic prestige and public acclaim
   that the University derives from these labs?
2. Does the University envision any limits to the kinds of services
   it can in good conscience provide for society? For example, if
   the University of California were offered a lucrative contract
   by the Defense Department to manufacture machine guns,

would it refuse and if so, insofar as it already participates in the manufacture of weapons, what reason would it give for refusing?

3. Do you personally see any contradiction between the University's role as a community of scholars and a market-place of ideas on the one hand, and its maintenance of a regime of security and secrecy in some of its facilities? Do you think the University's role as a supporter of democratic and libertarian principles is in any way rendered less credible by its support of secret research and its past connections with a fundamentally anti-democratic organization, the CIA?

Bolton's reply was not unexpected:

After a careful review of these questions, I find that they are not capable of being answered without a long preliminary review of the underlying assumptions and, in some cases, the factual inaccuracies, upon which the questions are based. Your predisposition to mistrust the University's motivations and your conviction that the University is susceptible to external and, in your view, sinister influences make it virtually impossible for us to communicate in a meaningful way on this subject.

There is a moral here and it lies in the reasonable assurance that Bolton's reply could hardly have been otherwise for the questions can in fact be answered without "a long preliminary review of the underlying assumptions" only by mission-minded men, like, for example, Harold Brown, for whom the dictum "knowledge is power" means the same thing as its permutation "power is knowledge." What this failure to reply suggests is that the relationship between the university and these laboratories is nothing so much as a habit which, for historical and sentimental reasons compounded by a "gee-whiz" attitude toward science, is no longer available for critical scrutiny though there is every reason to be critical of it.

Some Influence Is Inevitable

The university has insisted that safeguards have been established to protect the academic community from "contamination" by the laboratories and no doubt many precautions are observed to make sure that they do not exert undue influence over education and campus policy. But even if the laboratories themselves, with their ethic of secrecy and service, do not directly affect campus life, there is some reason to suspect that the university's almost filial ties with the AEC itself may control, to some immeasurable extent, the institution's stance toward both the community as a whole and its own faculty.

Aside from the contractually established bonds, the true nature and strength of the UC–AEC relationship is essentially unknown. There are undoubtedly secret channels through which favors flow and obligations recirculate but more important are the actual physical presences of the Berkeley hill complex that cast a shadow over the campus and the giant weapons laboratories whose unseen mass radiates a certain unseen influence.

The university's conspicuous refusal to take a stand in behalf of its own clear interest during the long fight between the Pacific Gas and Electric Company and various civic groups (of which some UC professors were members) over the proposed building of a nuclear power plant on Bodega Head in Sonoma County brought up a host of questions the university would prefer were left unasked.

One most disturbing aspect of the Bodega affair was the inability of those civic groups that fought the PG&E reactor to engage UC personnel as consultants. At a public meeting held November 10, 1962, in Santa Rosa, Dr. Richard Sill, a physicist at the University of Nevada outlined the problem:

Let us examine the procedure you as citizens could go through to decide whether the site selection was in error. First of all there is the question pertaining to the effects of radioactivity placed in your environment by normal operation of the reactor. In addition an evaluation of the usual hazards associated with the experimental design or size—in this case size more than anything else—of the reactor or with the possible malfunction of the reactor from renewed activity of the San Andreas fault. With regard to this type of technical problem, you would probably seek out the advice and consultation of a nuclear engineer, a nuclear physicist who had specialized in reactors for power for research, or a health physicist, or a nuclear chemist. Such a man could be found in one of a very limited number of places such as—in the near vicinity—the University of California, the Lawrence Radiation Laboratories of the University of California, the Atomic Energy Commission, one of a few other universities sufficiently large to have such a man on their staff, the military forces, or perhaps the large utility companies that are either in the atomic field or going into it. But when you try and hire the man, then you find you have difficulty. You will discover that he cannot or will not work for you, or if he does he cannot or dare not reach conclusions opposite to the official policies of his particular organization and ultimately of the AEC. The difficulty is that one of these highly specialized scientists can only work for one of a limited group of employers. If he rocks the boat too much, he may be pushed overboard. In addition, of course, military security is frequently involved. The chances are, and I am only guessing here, that a really intensive examination of reactor safety is still classified under military or AEC security.

. . . What all this says is that no open controversy or independent study on the technical aspects of the problem is available to the ordinary citizen. *You cannot find out for yourself.*

The Missing Man from Livermore

Following Dr. Sill's speech that evening Dr. Thornton Sargent of the Donner Laboratory read a paper on the subject of past reactor accidents. The report originally was to have been read by a man from Livermore who at the last minute had declined to attend the meeting. David Pesonen, moderator of that meeting, remarked about the incident, "He said he couldn't tell me the reasons, but he thought I could guess."

The six-year-long battle over Bodega Head formally ended in October, 1964, when PG&E gave in for purely geological reasons—the proposed site was extremely close to the San Andreas fault—and announced it was withdrawing its plans to build a reactor on the site. As a consequence, the university's new Bodega Marine Biology Laboratory has been assured that the ecology of the areas will be, at least in the near future, unimpaired. The university since then has acknowledged its interest in the area when it empowered Professor Ralph Emerson last December to testify officially before the State Parks Commission that the university did not welcome commercial development of the land but rather preferred that the state buy it from the present owner, PG&E, and make a state park of it. But that was, many people feel, six years too late—reputations are not so easily resurrected. As yet the state has not moved to purchase the land which PG&E is leasing to Sonoma County under a contract with a thirty-day cancellation clause. Should the company decide in the future that a new reactor design can meet the needs of the site and propose once more to build, it will be of no small interest to see whether or not the university finds itself again stricken by the old paralysis.

It is felt by some that the Bodega Head incident is either inconclusive or, at best, a matter having more to do with the university's special relationship with the AEC—whose chairman, Glenn Seaborg, was former chancellor at Berkeley—than the Cold War in general. In the narrow sense this is true but it is doubtful whether, in a larger sense, such a familial relationship would have developed outside the context of the Cold War. This mutual dependency of the university on government agencies for funds and of those agencies on the university for technical assistance and trained manpower has never been so great as in the post-World War II era and the Cold War is directly responsible for this. As a result, the university has become increasingly a resource which is there to be tapped by buyers in need of a product and has come to feel that it owes its sponsors a certain amount of service. When the buyer is the federal government and its vision of the world a vision of an eternal struggle against the hundred-headed enemy of communism, then scientific inquiry is in danger of becoming harnessed to military ends and the universities must face the temptation of being co-opted into the military as tactical aids to the national purpose. To Congress already, the distinction between the scientist and the soldier is becoming blurred; when congressmen talk of scholarship, the language they use is often the language of weaponry:

> To do their job in assisting the nations defending themselves against Communist subversion, U.S. military personnel—and the people who are being aided—must understand the motivations of the enemy, its weak points and its strengths. Behavioral sciences research helps to provide this basic information. *It constitutes one of the vital tools in the arsenal of free societies.* (From "Behavioral Sciences and the National Security, Report #4," by the Committee on Foreign Affairs, House of Representatives, p. 5r.)

What Is the Purpose of a University?

It is only fair to point out that the University of California generally has not been so easily and consistently seduced as have so many others. It has not had a CIA project since 1962, which must certainly be a national record for a major university, but it did bestow its institutional blessing on the Shah of Iran whom the CIA put into power. Three of its social scientists *did* consult for Project Camelot but the university itself did not become institutionally involved. It *does* provide economic-planning aid to the military government in Brazil through a contract with AID but the project's directors are at least aware that their situation is fraught with moral difficulties and are under no illusions that Castello Branco represents anything like what Wesley Fishel once said Diem did, "one-man democratic rule." But the University of California does preside over the design and manufacture of atomic weapons. Can a university, in this situation, fully dedicate itself to seeking the ways in which knowledge can be transmuted into wisdom?

CHAPTER III

༄

SOUTHERN
CALIFORNIA
COUNTRY

"This is the end, O Pioneer—
These final sands
I watch you sift with meditative hands,
Measure the cup of conquest."
                              James Rorty

A Slight Case of Cultural Confusion*

CAREY MCWILLIAMS

WHEN THOUSANDS of settlers began to trek into Southern California, they came to a land strange and paradoxical concerning which they knew literally nothing and about which no available lore existed. There were no reliable guidebooks, no agricultural manuals, no soil analyses, no weather charts. Furthermore they came bearing a load of previously acquired notions, customs, practices, and concepts which they stubbornly insisted could be applied in Southern California. There was nothing tentative or experimental about their approach to this new and novel environment. What had worked in Kansas would work in Southern California. Newcomers have had to discover the novelties and paradoxes of the region by a painful trial-and-error process. While time and experience have gradually corrected some of their more egregious misconceptions, the process of cultural adaptation has been continuous. Each new wave of migrants has been compelled to discover the region afresh. Heavy and continuous migration has made it impossible for the residents of the region to undertake a thorough exploration of the land and its resources, its limitations as well as its potentialities.

"The story of America," wrote T. K. Whipple, "is the story of the process of interaction between the American country and

* From *Southern California Country* (Duell, Sloan and Pearce, affiliate of Meridith Press, 1946). Copyright 1946, by Carey McWilliams. Used by permission of the publisher.

the foreign heritage of the American people." European cultural practices imported to the Atlantic states could be adjusted to the new environment with comparative ease. A Dutch farmhouse was not only practical in Pennsylvania; it was fairly well adapted to the environment. It seemed to fit the land and the landscape. The same farmhouse probably would not have been altogether out of place in Kansas, assuming that the materials for its construction had been available. But such a farmhouse is unthinkable in Southern California. As the American settlers moved westward, many cultural incongruities did appear, but the discrepancy between the imported cultural practice and the new environment was generally one of degree. A slight variation or modification would bring the particular cultural practice into a workable relation with the new habitat. But once the jump was made to Southern California, across the mountains and the desert, the old practice had to be radically modified or altogether abandoned, for this environment differed in kind and was, furthermore, highly paradoxical. Things nowhere else available, this smiling land offered in abundance. But the newcomers knew literally nothing of the land and they had brought with them, as Stewart Edward White has pointed out, "the mode of existence they learned elsewhere, and have not the imagination to transcend." Most of the other regions of the country were settled by a process of accretion. Settlers gradually filled up Illinois and then overflowed, so to speak, into Minnesota and Michigan. But Southern California has been settled overnight, not by people from neighboring states and similar environments, but by people who have come from all over the world and from every state in the union. Out of this basic experience has come the amusingly confused culture of the region, a culture which has by no means yet succeeded in eliminating the irrelevant, discarding the incongruous, and coming to grips with the physical factors of the environment.

1. Agricultural Adaptation

The first settlers who came to Southern California found a region that had many native herbs, grasses, and shrubs, but the list of trees was small indeed. They looked in vain for the maple, the hickory, the basswood, the chestnut, and other familiar trees. "Oh, for the green pastures," wrote Beatrice Harraden, "for the deep lanes, and forests of trees, for the brooks and rivers, for the grass and ferns and mosses, and for everything in Nature soothing to the eye and comforting to the spirit!" About the only trees were the sycamores and cottonwoods along the stream beds and the beautiful live-oaks that dotted the rolling hills. These lovely live-oaks, dense of limb and leaf, with dark glossy spoon-shaped leaves that never changed color with heat or drought or frost, cast a solid pool of black shade on the ground. "They once covered the valleys," wrote Van Dyke, "with solid green, through which one could ride for miles in almost perpetual shade."

One of the first things the settlers did, of course, was to hack down the live-oaks. So thoroughgoing was the process that the tree soon disappeared from many sections. When the period of settlement began, the foothills were covered with a heavy mantle of shrubs, manzanita, madrona, chokecherry, live-oak bushes, lilac, wild-mahogany, and coffee-berry. All these varieties were termed "brush" or "chaparral." The chaparral provided an excellent cover for the soil and lent great beauty to the landscape. Much of the chaparral was immediately burned; in fact it has been burning ever since. Since there were few native fruits in the region, and most of these were not edible, the settlers promptly concluded that fruit would not grow in the region. The manzanita, coffee-berry, and chokecherry, they said, were only "fit for bears to eat." The fact is, of course, that all known varieties of fruit can be grown in the region. Great herds of sheep introduced in the 'sixties were permitted to stamp out the native bunch-grass and alfileria (burr-clover) before they could seed, thereby destroying most of the range grass.

Since a dry period of two months in other sections was regarded as a calamity, "a drought," the notion persisted for years that Southern California was a desert. Elsewhere the best soils were found along the river bottoms and so these lands were sought out by the first agricultural settlers in the region. It took them almost a quarter of a century to discover that some of the best lands, particularly for citrus crops, were the foothill uplands. When artesian wells were first tapped around 1867, the notion prevailed that these wells were inexhaustible. So many wells were drilled that, at one time, the sparkle of artesian waters could be seen throughout the plains. But within two decades many of these wells had disappeared. While the first settlers knew something about irrigation, they knew literally nothing about the art of irrigation in a semi-arid climate. They wasted water wantonly and with only meager results. In fact, it was only when they began to imitate irrigation methods long practiced in Mexico and elsewhere in the Southwest by Indians that they really learned how to irrigate. They brought with them the Anglo-Saxon doctrine of riparian rights, which worked fairly well in the northern part of the state, but, when applied south of Tehachapi spelled disaster. It was not until pressure from the southern part of the state forced the adoption of the Wright Act in 1887 that the beginning of a better system of water utilization was inaugurated.

The initial success in wheat-farming in Southern California resulted in the enactment of fencing legislation that virtually destroyed the free range and with it the cattle industry. The initial success with sheep-raising resulted in such large herds of sheep that the remaining range lands were destroyed, even for sheep. Since the seasonal variations were so slight, farmers began to bet on the season, going in for large one-crop bonanza farming. All of these early successes, as Van Dyke noted, had a baneful influence on development of the region's agriculture. "Farming" was replaced by "ranching." According to Van Dyke, the principle of ranching was "to do nothing yourself that you can hire any one else to do and raise nothing to eat that you can buy." Because nature seemed to be kindlier here, slovenly farming practices developed. The land was not really plowed; it was "cultivated." "Scarcely anyone from east of the Sierras," wrote Van Dyke in 1886, "knows anything about the lands of Southern California or their management, no matter what he may know of farming or gardening elsewhere. Unless one lays aside all conceit, and learns anew from those who have learned here, one may meet not only vexation, but loss."

Gradually improved farming practices were developed and, after a time, remarkably swift progress was recorded. But the progress did not occur until the settlers had been compelled to abandon their preconceptions. The fact that they were ultimately forced to reconsider established farming practices in this new environment, resulted in discoveries which have had a profound influence on agriculture, not only in California, but throughout the country. For the novel environment of Southern California has sharply challenged anachronistic methods and stereotyped procedures. The old, deep-seated, and widespread belief that a new culture would eventually arise in California, a culture fashioned not on imitation but on functional adaptation, does have this basic experience as its justification. While the idea has been grossly inflated and pompously proclaimed, it does have a core of reality. The nature of this reality becomes more apparent as one turns from agricultural practices to other cultural items.

2. Architecture

One of the first things the settlers did, of course, was to change the style of architecture. To be sure, there was not much in the way of an architectural style to be changed. The Spanish ranch-house, however, was a well-adapted structure. With its interior patio, its lowpitched roof, its kitchen removed, in many instances, from the house itself, and with its wide verandas extending around the house (with all rooms opening on the veranda and the patio), it was certainly a comfortable and livable home. The Spanish ranchhouse, however, largely vanished in the decade after 1880 (twenty-six dilapidated structures are all that exist in Los Angeles County today). The low adobe houses in the towns, with their flat asphaltum roofs, were quickly replaced by "elegant and substantial dwellings," the Mansard-roofed monstrosities of the 'seventies. Churches, hotels, and office buildings of the boom years were all done in the most florid taste of the period. "The blossoming civic vision" of the time, as one historian put it, "inspired from the East and clothed in the fashion of the day," was notable for its "gingerbread and cupolas." In many cases, the effort to eradicate the past as completely as possible was based upon a studied attempt to make the new land look as much like the East as possible. A Santa Barbara historian, for example, writes that the boosters "apparently proceeded on the theory that the Eastern Visitors would be made happiest by finding things here, excepting the climate, as much as possible like what they had left 'back east.'" To make these newcomers feel at home, and to minimize their confusion, even the names of the streets were changed, with Calle del Estado becoming Main Street.

It was not only the architecture that was changed; the physical environment underwent a kind of face-lifting. Since almost any flower, shrub, or tree would grow in Southern California, the boosters went to the far corners of the earth and imported the most heterogeneous assortment of ornamental plants, shrubs, trees, and flowers ever assembled in an environment to which they were not native. By 1880 there was scarcely a town in the region that did not have its particular showplace, an exotic, privately owned garden, in which plants, flowers, and shrubs of all varieties had been assembled and planted side by side for the delectation of the newcomers. Since the environment is highly versatile, many of these importations seemed to fit the landscape. For example, the eucalyptus, although not native to the region, is, next to the

live-oak, the loveliest tree to be found in Southern California today. But other importations, such as certain varieties of the petti-
coated palm tree, have always been an abomination, a blot on the
landscape, hideous beyond description. Today some two hundred
and seventy varieties of trees are planted along the streets of
Los Angeles, of which fully fifty per cent are blackwood acacias,
a tree not particularly well adapted to the environment. Used to
being "wide open in all directions," the Iowa contingent chopped
down trees with gay abandon and trimmed hedges as hedges had
never been trimmed before.

Until a comparatively recent date, the gardening manuals
available in Southern California were importations, written with
an eastern or middle western climate and environment in mind.
Not only were they useless in Southern California, but they contributed mightily to the spoliation of the landscape. Since everything would grow, everything was planted. Failing to understand
that the beautiful coloring of the land is not a reflection of
things, but consists in the peculiar quality of the light itself,
newcomers have indulged in riotously incongruous color schemes.
The misuse of the bougainvillea and the giant red geraniums
(usually placed side by side) is merely one of the more ghastly
examples that might be cited. Even to this day, the landscaping
of the region is incongruous, confused, and shows everywhere the
absence of a developed tradition within the region. In the glare
of the sunlight, certain bright colors become intolerably oppressive and garish. When the hillsides were discovered as likely
building sites, no thought was given to preserving contours or to
obscuring roads and highways by planting shrubs and trees. "The
people got busy with steamshovels," as Frank Lloyd Wright puts
it, and began "tearing down the hills to get to the top in order to
blot out the top with a house." Today the hills around Los Angeles are scarred with roadways, exposed like cuts or gashes,
forming a crazy zigzag pattern, with most of the damage being
well-nigh irreparable.

One of the first things newcomers do in Southern California
is to make themselves feel at home. "We are beginning to feel
quite at home," says a character in a novel by Sidney Burchell,
"having our own things around us. This morning when I woke up,
and saw the old bureau and toilet glass beyond the foot of the
bed, and the window chintzes, I thought for a moment I must be
back in Maine." When the Iowa brigade began to arrive in Los
Angeles, each family, writes Harry Carr, had a home "with a

living room that took the place of our Iowa parlors. Each one
bulged out with a bunion in the way of a bay window. Coming
out nearly as far as the bay window was a tiny porch. The
Iowans had pleasant visions of sitting on the front porch in the
long tropical evenings. They found that night followed day as
suddenly as the dropping of a curtain, without a romantic twi-
light, and that the evenings, even in summer, were so cold that
they would have to muffle themselves in their buffalo overcoats.
Both the baywindow and the front porch were surrounded by a
fringe of what we admiringly called 'art glass,' bilious patches of
yellow, blue and red set in frames around the edges of the window. The front porch opened into a hall and from the hall opened
a front and back bedroom. Back of the living room was a dining
room with an amazing 'built-in' sideboard; and back of the dining
room was a pantry and kitchen. All around the eaves and the roof
ridge of the cottage were 'scroll work,' doodads that looked like
cake frosting."

With no architectural tradition in the region, aside from the
meager fragments from the Spanish period, it is not surprising that
the newcomers should have imported the style of house then prevailing in the particular region from which they came. Since many
of these early settlers came from New England, they dotted
Southern California with typical New England homes, with high
steep roofs to shed the snow that did not fall, with dark interiors
that contrasted nightmarishly with the bright out-of-doors, and
with deep cellars built for needless furnaces. In one booster publication appears a picture of such a home with the explanatory
note, "In Los Angeles the snow-shedding roof is merely for ornament." Throughout the region today one comes suddenly on these
homes, usually in a magnificent setting of orange trees and flower-
ing shrubs, their "gloomy stupidities" standing out in the sharpest
possible contrast with the land.

Fortunately the absence of durable materials, such as marble
and stone, prevented most of these structures from becoming
lasting monuments to the prevailing cultural confusion. But they
have survived in sufficient numbers to give the region an odd appearance of being both old and new, West and South, North and
East. One can still encounter ancient derelict frame structures in
the older sections of Los Angeles positively fascinating by their
incongruity. For in this environment, they are probably the oldest-
appearing houses in America. They look as old as time, as old as
the iron hills. A New England colonial structure built in 1776

appears actually modern, in its environment, by contrast with the gingerbread homes of the 'seventies which survive in Los Angeles.

Around the turn of the century, however, experience with the environment had produced a new and livable home, the California bungalow. In part the bungalow was an outgrowth of what had earlier been called "the California house": a simple structure built of rough redwood boards. But, as finally developed, it was based upon the bungalow originally built by Englishmen for use in tropical countries. British officials had found the bungalow to be a reasonably comfortable home in a tropical environment and, being inexpensive, it appealed to them, for their residence was, in most cases, temporary in character. It was precisely these qualities that appealed to newcomers in Southern California. A low, spacious, airy house, the bungalow could be built by people of moderate means and informal tastes, who were not quite sure that they intended to remain in Southern California and therefore did not want to invest a considerable sum in a home. The great merit of the bungalow was that it minimized the distinction between the exterior and interior walls, that it tended to merge the house with the landscape to which it was definitely subordinated.

Between 1900 and 1915, a few Southern California architects, in particular the firm of Greene and Greene, began to adapt the bungalow form in an interesting way, making it into a year-round home, and giving it a more substantial character while retaining its essential simplicity and absence of decoration. Universally built of redwood, these bungalows of the period 1900–15 are among the few homes in the region that really fit the environment. To encounter one today is still a delight. As the form became more popular, however, a certain amount of gingerbread began to be added. Imitators of Greene and Greene began to use cobblestones for the purpose of converting the bungalow into a "Swiss chalet," while others began to give the bungalow an Oriental appearance by adding upturning roofs and Japanese storm-porches. A Greene and Greene bungalow, however, remains a good home in Southern California.

Unfortunately the bungalow was literally engulfed by the "rash of stucco" that swept over Southern California after 1915. The San Diego Panama–California Exposition of that year was planned several months before San Francisco decided to have, in the same year, its Panama–Pacific Exposition. Learning that San Francisco intended to have a great fair the same year, San Diego at first considered abandoning its own plans. Direct competition with

San Francisco was obviously unthinkable. Then Bertram Goodhue, the architect, suggested that San Diego might give its exposition a special character by designing all the buildings in Spanish Colonial style. There had been "Spanish," and "Mission," and "Mooresque" structures in Southern California before the San Diego Exposition, but the appearance of these structures had never assumed the proportions of an epidemic. After the San Diego Exposition, all Southern California "went Spanish."

The so-called Spanish Colonial home that came out of the exposition, with its walls of white stucco and roof of red tile, was a model easily imitated by commercial contractors. It had the merit of looking a little more like the environment than the models they had been using for so many years. Furthermore, it was called Spanish and could be related, therefore, to the Mission background, and it was simply constructed. It did have one or two definite merits: a considerable amount of plain surface and low lines. By 1920 this neo-Spanish stuccoed home was the building model almost universally used by the large contractors. Southern California was Hispanized in appearance as quickly as, at an earlier date, it had been Anglicized. The style was used for residences, apartments, flats, store buildings, post offices, public structures, filling stations, roadside huts, and mortuaries. Most of Santa Barbara was rebuilt in this style after the earthquake of 1925, and, still later, an ambitious promoter built an entire village, San Clemente, in the same style. Even with some surrounding shrubbery, the glare from this village is still blinding for a distance of three miles. "As there was nothing of the Spanish there to begin with," writes Max Miller, "there is nothing there now—unless one considers the regimentation of white stucco of all the houses and all the buildings as being Spanish."

It seemed to Frank Lloyd Wright in 1934 that "the eclectic procession to and fro in the rag-tag and cast-off of the ages was never going to stop" in Southern California. "It was Mexico-Spanish now. Another fair, in San Diego this time, had set up the Mexico-Spanish as another model—for another run of thirty years." Despite the elaborate effort that went into the scheming to make these houses "original" or "different," they all looked exactly alike. "The same thought, or lack of thought," wrote Mr. Wright, "was to be seen everywhere. 'Taste'—the usual matter of ignorance—had moved toward simplicity a little, but thought or feeling for integrity had not entered into this architecture. All was flatulent or fraudulent with a cheap opulent taste for tawdry Spanish Medievalism." The neo-Spanish style just happened, by pure accident, to be a little more in keeping with the environment than the variety of styles which had been used, and it was awkwardly and clumsily adapted. "The loose rude Spanish-tiled roofs," Wright pointed out, "give back the sunshine stained pink." As far as the occupants were concerned, they felt as out of place in these homes as "the fra himself or a silken Spaniard would have looked in their little Middle-Western parlors." Although the Middle Westerner had been induced to purchase a Spanish home, he had changed but little. He still clung, as Mr. Wright observed, to his straw hat, English coat, trousers and boots long after he had moved to Southern California.

The restoration of the Missions had much to do with creating a popular acceptance of "the stucco rash." All the railway stations of the Southern Pacific Company in California were done in what the company termed the Mission style. The Franciscans who designed the Missions were not architects; they had only a faint memory of Spanish churches when they sketched out the designs for the crude structures the Indians built in California. While the Missions had some merits as structures, and could have been used as a model in the absence of any other, they became a deplorable influence. "More architectural crimes have been committed in the name of the Missions than in any other unless it be the Grecian Temple," wrote Irving Gill. At its best, the Mission style was ecclesiastical, not domestic, and the attempts to adapt it for domestic purposes were wholly grievous in effect. The same phoniness appeared in the so-called Mission furniture which was originally designed by Gustav Stickley, editor of *The Craftsman*. At a fair in 1900, Stickley had exhibited two clumsy chairs, with straight backs and legs made of three-inch posts, which he had labeled Mission. Since the California Missions were exciting much attention at the time, the name immediately became popular and Mission furniture was born. In a sense, the Spanish style of the Mission was as foreign to the region as any of the other styles later used. It was merely by a kind of accident, as Mr. Wright emphasized, that it seemed to be a little more apposite than, say, a New England stone house or a plantation mansion.

Once the Mission and Spanish notions had caught on, builders discovered what Herbert Croly had pointed out, namely, that "Southern California is a country in which almost any kind of house is practical and almost any kind of plant will grow." There then began the wild debauch of eclectism which has continued unabated to the present time and which has excited the wonder and curiosity of all visitors. Even earlier, however, eclectism had been rampant in the region. Harry Ridgway, the Pasadena architect, who specialized in "high-art styles," contended that he never made two buildings alike. He never wanted any man to be able to point to a structure and say, "That's one of Ridgway's structures—it shows the earmarks of his style." True to this prescription, he loved to combine diverse and dissimilar styles in the same structure, using Venetian, Norman, Eastlake, Old Spanish, Old Plantation, Italian, French Mansard, English and Colonial Dormers, Old English Queen Anne, and Old English Elizabethan in such combinations as his fancy dictated. He has had, of course, many imitators in Southern California.

The beginnings of a real architecture in the region date from the work of Irving Gill, a sadly neglected figure in Southern California. Trained in the office of Louis Sullivan in Chicago, Gill worked on the Columbian Exposition of 1893 and, after its completion, came to San Diego. For years he had wandered in his taste, seeking in Grecian, Roman, Italian, and early English models the style that he wanted to find. Finally, as he said, he abandoned all models and returned to the basic forms of the straight line, arch, cube, and circle, in an effort to evolve a new style. Rebelling against all gimcrack ornament, cheap construction, and false effect, he built, in the face of much opposition, the first modern homes in Southern California. Later he took over the idea of the "bungalow court," a Southern California innovation, and by designing the houses so that each had separate entrances, exits, halls and gardens, created some structures, such as the Bella Vista Terrace in Sierra Madre, that have remained wholly charming through the years. Gill used interior walls to capture the exterior light. In all his work, he sought to give real permanence, so as to avoid, as he put it, the appearance of structures erected like sets in a motion-picture studio.

Some of his comments about the architectural problem he sought to solve in Southern California have an interest that quite transcends the issues he discussed. In 1916 he wrote: "The west has an opportunity unparalleled in the history of the world, for it is the newest white page turned for registration. The west unfortunately has been and is building too hastily, carelessly and thoughtlessly. Houses here spring up faster than mushrooms, for mushrooms silently prepare for a year and more before they finally raise their house above the ground. People pour out here as on the crest of a flood and remain where chance deposits them when the rush of waters subsides, building temporary shacks wherein they live for a brief period while looking about for more permanent anchorage. The surface of the ground is barely scraped away, in some cases but a few inches deep, just enough to allow builders to find a level, and a house is tossed together with little thought of permanence, haste being the chief characteristic. The family of health- or fortune-seekers which comes out here generally expects to camp in these poor shacks for a short time and plans to sell the shiftless affair to some other impatient newcomer." A survey of apartment houses, made in Los Angeles in 1938, confirmed this impression by finding that the average tenant occupancy period was six weeks.

It is this lack of a sense of permanency that, in part, accounts for the unreal appearance of the region and the restless character of its population. "Neither was there any permanence here, any roots," observes a character in Myron Brinig's novel, *The Flutter of an Eyelid.* "Houses were literally builded on sand, and if not sand, their foundations were insecurely laid in clay. Men and women were in constant movement, drifting and whirling through the air like toy balloons." It is not merely that many houses are built so flimsily, however, that creates this impression. The same impression is enhanced by the circumstance that the houses have no earthly relation to the environment. They are unreal, as unreal as motion-picture sets. Turning a corner in the Hollywood hills, one comes upon, say, an elaborate Norman-French chateau or a monstrous square home, in no style whatever, built on a curving hillside lot. As much as anything else, it is the lack of a functional relationship between these homes and the land on which they rest that creates the illusion of unreality. And I do believe that the character of the architecture, while reflecting the restless character of the occupants and their recent arrival in the region, also contributes to their rootlessness and their feeling of unreality about the land in which they live. How can they feel at home in such a house in such a land? It may be built of stone and steel, but it is as unreal as though it were made of paper-maché. Underlying these considerations, however, there is still another paradox. Referring to the foothills of the coast range, John Evans writes in his novel, *Shadows Flying,* "There is unrealness, too—a theatrical beauty which is almost unbelievable. Visually very beautiful, but somehow unalive. In summer the swelling masses, full of voluptuous curves and undulations, are burned to a golden brown in the strong sun; there is little or no rainfall in these months. Here and there, sometimes singly and sometimes in small groups, the magnificent oaks, wide-spreading and symmetrical, almost too perfectly formed, press their somber shadows against the blond land. There is too much composition; perhaps there is too much beauty."

Nowadays the seeds of integrity sown by Gill and Frank Lloyd Wright, fertilized by influences from Japan and Europe, have begun to bear fruit in some real homes in Southern California. The first of the modern European architects to reach Los Angeles was R. M. Schindler, who arrived from Vienna around 1922, after a short period spent in the office of Frank Lloyd Wright. He was followed a few years later by Richard Neutra, another Viennese, who, also, had been first attracted to Chicago by the work of Wright and Sullivan. Both Neutra and Schindler have been greatly influenced by Wright and they in turn have had an important influence on some of the younger men of the region, such as Gregory Ain and Harwell Harris, both of whom have worked with Neutra and Schindler. It is not surprising, therefore, that out of a listing of 136 modern homes published a few years ago in *Twice-A-Year* 30 should be located in Southern California or that the architectural magazines should have had so many articles, of recent years, about the extremely interesting domestic architecture that is developing in the region (see, in particular, an article by Talbot F. Hamlin, in *Pencil Points* for December, 1939).

3. "Scenic Arts"

The problem of cultural adaptation, strikingly apparent in architecture, the most graphic and literal of the arts, has also found reflection in the other arts in Southern California. Both in writing and in painting, Southern California has lagged behind the northern part of the state, which, for all practical purposes, is forty years older in point of settlement. The first reaction of the strangers who poured into the region south of Tehachapi was one of intense preoccupation with its scenic wonders and oddities. Both the early painting and writing of the region were largely devoted to the "scenic," the picturesque, the grandiloquent, aspects of the environment. Artists were so preoccupied with the novelty of the environment that they devoted little attention to a close study of what this environment was really like. They tended to see everything through glasses colored by preconceptions and their vision of the land itself was weirdly distorted and often amusingly inaccurate.

Most of the writers who came to Southern California after the

American conquest were, as Hildegarde Flanner has pointed out, "aliens in a land toward which it is impossible to remain indifferent." The poets in particular, she thinks, might well have remained silent throughout the period of "tourist fancy," for it is only after the new and the strange have become an integral part of the poet's experience that he can express his feeling toward the land. "Quite fittingly," writes Genevieve Taggard, "there has never been a poem written about a eucalyptus tree. There could not be, until this special tree has gone into the experience of many people so long and so deeply that when a poet comes to write of it he has no sense of its novelty, but only the feeling of its everlasting uniqueness. Just now the eucalyptus tree is *news*; anything said of it, try as we may, has chiefly a reportorial and journalistic quality." Southern California was not at all like the faint reflection of the region that began to find expression in story, verse, and novel after 1884. For beneath the surface it is, as Miss Flanner has said, "a hard land, if a bright one, and if man cannot find water, he can die, and with less hope of resurrection than the flowers." But Southern California would not permit these newly arrived poets to wait until the land had come into some proper focus; it forced them to burst into print with consequences that have been truly appalling. With Gene Stratton Porter the desire to write poetry had remained a "suppression" as long as she lived in Rome, Indiana. But as soon as she arrived in Southern California, in 1919, "Something in the wonderful air, the gorgeous colour on all hands, and the pronouncedly insistent rhythms, all combined to force utterance."

Poetic utterance has certainly remained "forced" all through the years. The California poets, as Miss Taggard once pointed out, have tried too hard. In a strenuous effort to force some poetry out of the region the three thousand poets of Southern California have banded together into a network of organizations that structurally resembles the National Association of Manufacturers. There are more poets per square mile in Southern California than in any other section of the United States. They have poetry societies, poetry magazines, poetry breakfasts, and poetry weekends. They meet together to chat and to sip tea, to plot and to confer. In Los Angeles, there are poetry lanes, poetry shrines, and poetry gardens. Thumbing through innumerable anthologies of Southern California verse, one can find many poems that deal with familiar scenes and themes of the region. Yet the stuff of the region is wholly lacking in these pallid verses. The few individuals who have done rather well with the land itself have been those who, like Miss Flanner, have had the wit to recognize the existence of a cultural problem: the necessity of creating, little by little, the exterior world in the image of old truths and convictions brought to the land. The imagination of the artist has not yet penetrated this exterior world; it has not become familiar; the period of awkward self-consciousness has not ended. Only within recent years, in fact, have a few poets dropped their sight, so to speak, from the ocean, the mountains, and the desert, and begun to concentrate on what the land is really like. For it is not all "sunshine and poppies."

No region in the United States has been more extensively and intensively reported, of recent years, than Southern California. Within the last decade, a dozen or more novels have been written about Hollywood alone. And yet, offhand, I can think of only four novels that suggest what Southern California is really like: *The Day of the Locust* by Nathanael West, *Ask the Dust* by John Fante, *A Place in the Sun* by Frank Fenton, and *The Boosters* by Mark Lee Luther. In a study of forty-six writers who have written novels about Southern Cailfornia, Margaret Climie found that none had been born in the region and that most of them had only resided there a short time. It is worth noting that the writers who have most vividly captured the feel of the California landscape have been native sons, like John Steinbeck, or long residents like Robinson Jeffers.

"Transport a man to a remote wilderness," wrote T. K. Whipple, "and what happens? He builds himself a log cabin or a sod hut; he works and endures hardship and deprivation; he clears land and plows it; perhaps he prospers. But what happens to the mind of a man thus uprooted, and to his children's minds? The sense impressions of centuries must be obliterated before sounds and sights and smells gather full power and meaning. It will be long before these people have the feeling as a symbol for the goldenrod, say, that they once had for the rose or for heather, for maize as well as for wheat. The still where they make corn whiskey will not at once get the emotional hold upon them that the winepress had. The mockingbird and the hermit thrush will mean less to them than the nightingale had meant. When will the unfamiliar objects begin to get a grip on them and take on a symbolic content. . . . No matter how a transplanted man may thrive in his possessions, his life is to some extent impoverished, even though he may be quite unconscious of the deprivation, though he may have disliked the old and may like the new: he once had a close and vital tie with the world about him, and now he has little or none."

Of recent years there have been some indications that man is beginning to feel at home in the West, that the sense of the "scenic" is being replaced by a feeling of familiarity for the land. Reviewing a new novel by Walter Van Tilburg Clark in the *New Yorker*, Edmund Wilson said: "This book is a Far Western book, and, like the fiction of the Pacific slope, like John Steinbeck and William Saroyan, it does not quite meet the requirements of an Easterner. It seems too easy-going and good-natured, too lacking in organization, always dissolving into an even sunshine, always circumventing by ample detours what one expects to be sharp or direct. There is an element in all this fiction that seems to us 'goofy' or 'corny.' Yet it cannot be said that the East has had lately so much to show that is better; and it is one of the signs of the vitality of writing in the United States that the Pacific coast should be producing a literature of its own, appropriate to its temper and climate, and almost as independent of New England, New York, and the South as it is of current fashions in Europe. . . . The United States faces today toward the West as well as the East, and the West Coast is working out its own culture. The pull of the Pacific is felt in writing as in everything else."

The early landscape painters who began to work in Southern California after 1880, painters such as Elmer Wachtel, William Wendt, and Guy Rose (the only native son of the lot), experienced the same difficulty in seeing the land as did the writers. To the extent that they were successful, as Arthur Millier has pointed out, they had to narrow their sights, "choosing small, rather than grand, subjects and seeking for truth of appearance." In their early work, one can detect "the shock of recognition," as, for the first time, they actually *saw* or began to see, the dry arroyos, the shifting shadows, the foothill chaparral. And it must be admitted that most of them saw the land dimly and imperfectly. One can examine hundreds of these early Southern California landscapes of sunlight flickering through eucalyptus groves, of the flush that swiftly passes over the mountains before the sun falls into the sea, and recognize nothing except the strenuous, largely futile, forced effort that went into the attempt to picture a scene not yet familiar.

Many of these early artists were brought west by the railroads, among others, Fernand Lungren. An eastern-trained artist, Lungren once wrote, "I had to unlearn most of what I had understood as light and color and especially atmosphere, or lack of it." After he had succeeded in freeing his mind, to some extent, of preconceptions, and had begun to paint the land, he was surprised to discover that local critics dismissed his later work as spurious and preferred the earlier "scenes." Another early artist of the region, J. Bond Francisco, complained of "the mocking brilliancy of the sky" and pointed out how he had only discovered, late in life, that "the light was the thing in Southern California; that the light actually changes the texture and shape of the hills." This light completely baffled the first generation of landscape painters. It has only been with the appearance of a second generation that the "quick, fluid fact" of the light has begun to show in the work of such painters as Milford Zornes, Barse Miller, Phil Dyke, Tom Craig, George Post, Dong Kingman, and Millard Sheets. "The quality of California light," writes Alfred Frankenstein, the art critic, "is not a Chamber of Commerce invention but a characteristic subtropical fact." It accounts, he believes, for the extraordinary reception given Van Gogh exhibits in California. "Take a swirl of hills, its grass burned to a golden crisp in the heat and dryness, put in a flame or two of coniferous green and a snarl of clouds in the sky and you have (1) a landscape by Van Gogh, or (2) the view from practically any window in California not hemmed in by city buildings." The early landscapists failed to bring "the California light to paper, in all its brilliance and saturation"; the spirit of the place is simply not in them.

When artists visited Southern California at a later date, after the face of the region had been lifted, they were usually troubled by a feeling that the land was unreal and impermanent. Some of them devised theories, to account for this feeling, that were close to the truth. "Like all irrigated civilizations," wrote Maxwell Armfield in 1925, "the land has a certain air of unreality and impermanence about it . . . all green things grow here with speed, continuity, and abandon, so that a sense of permanency is attained, but it is only a permanancy that is skin-deep. One does not question the display of exotic flowers and trees, the palms and gigantic geranium hedges; the humming birds and gorgeous swallow-tail butterflies; but all the time there is a sense of having strayed into one of Mr. Wells's Utopias." After studying the land for some months he noted that much of the exoticism was superficial. He began to observe "the sparseness of leafage in proportion to the ground," a circumstance responsible "for those exquisite effects of blue and pale purples, with discreet orange and all manner of dim golden hues," which would be quite "vulgar in the midst of greenery." He began to detect that the land was gray and brown and that the illusion of color came with the "golden air tempered for half the year by sea-mist." And, lastly, he shrewdly discerned that the painter lives in Southern California "amidst a riot of colour that is *not* indigenous and yet which *might well* have belonged to the landscape" (italics mine).

No notion is more deeply seated, no idea has echoed more persistently through the years, than the theory that a new and vital culture would some day be born in California. "Here if anywhere else in America," said William Butler Yeats on a visit to California, "I seem to hear the coming footsteps of the muses." The historian Froude, in his book *Oceana*, predicted that a new school of art would some day arise in this rich and beautiful corner of the world, this island on the land. In most cases, the theory has been proclaimed *ex cathedra*, pompously, bombastically, rhetorically. But there has always been a basis for the belief. "The American poet," wrote Hildegarde Flanner, "living there [in California], so haplessly exploited, so rarely left to its own charm is aware not of the exciting pleasure of living in a nation's playground; not of the advantages of climate or place or ease of life. Rather, he is aware that he is part of a great movement, an ancient movement of humanity spreading and reaching out toward what it hopes is a better and happier life. *This movement has gone as far west as it can*—there is the ocean. In sight of that barrier the force of expansion is concentrated, localized, multiplied, and, in the south, we have a great metropolitan area, shut in on one side by the Pacific, on the other by mountains and the desert. *Here is a centering of human energy and desire* . . . here human energy and purpose having reached the limits of physical advance, are bound to flow back upon themselves and in doing so must either stagnate or create."

Physically attached to the West rather than belonging to the West, culturally isolated from the rest of America during decades when it grew 'like a gourd in the night," California has always struggled, however uncomprehendingly, for independent expression. Visitors have sensed this struggle much more keenly than settled residents. "What America is to Europe," wrote Lord Bryce, "what Western America is to Eastern, that California is to the other Western States. It has more than any other the character of a great country, capable of standing alone in the world." Long isolated from what he called "the steadying influence of eastern states," California had been peopled by "a mixed multitude, bringing with it a variety of manners, customs, and ideas." Here on the western shore, a society had been formed that was "more mobile and unstable, less governed by fixed beliefs and principles," than he had found elsewhere in America. "California," he wrote, "is the last place to the west before you come to Japan," a place in which he detected "a sort of consciousness of separate existence."

In the movement of American culture westward, the persistence of those cultural traits imported from Europe has gradually weakened, and, in California, they have tended to disappear under the shock of impact with an environment qualitatively unlike that to be found elsewhere in the nation. It is the last frontier of western civilization, a land where the West faces the East. California, in fact, looks toward the East and toward the West. "You can't live for twenty summers on the hem of the Sierra Madre's magnificent purple garment," wrote the artist Anthony Anderson, "and still keep your Parisian ideals of seeing and doing. You are bound to start, sooner or later, new fashions of your own that are absolutely in keeping with your environment."

"The idea is held by everybody in Southern California," to quote from a magazine article by James M. Cain, "that some sort of destiny awaits the place." Underlying this persistent *mystique* about a renascence of art and culture in California are the cultural realities mentioned in this chapter. I refrain from adding still another prediction to the incredibly protracted list of those who have said that the arts would some day be "entempled" in California, but I do point to the fact that here, in California, when the garment does not fit, it is soon discarded. The family from Des Moines may bring their overstuffed furniture with them to Los Angeles, but, if they stay here long enough, they will discard the trash and buy something usable and comfortable. And what they buy to replace the old will, in most cases, be something that has been designed and manufactured in California.

A nearly perfect physical environment, Southern California is a great laboratory of experimentation. Here, under ideal testing conditions, one can discover what will work, in houses, clothes, furniture, etc. It is a great tribal burial ground for antique customs and incongruous styles. The fancy eclectic importations soon cancel out here and something new is then substituted. The reason the fresh growths are not more conspicuous than they are at present is that the importation-and-discarding process has been continuous. As Max Miller has so shrewdly observed, "Each decade the previous residents once again are outnumbered by a new cyclonic invasion bringing its own idea of how California should be remodeled." Each new wave of migration invariably results in the construction of still more subdivisions made up of eastern and middle western homes, but, as the native life begins to grow, some of the force of this tendency is arrested and a degree of stability begins to develop. The heterogeneous architectural styles to be encountered in Los Angeles (and the same could be said of clothing and furniture) merely reflect the heterogeneous character of the population, recruited from every state in the union and from every class.

In fact, it is the heterogeneity of its population that serves to make Southern California the ideal testing ground for ideas, styles, manners, and customs. "Let anything happen in the rest of the country," writes Idwal Jones, "in Arkansas or Maine, and there is instant repercussion inside the borders of Southern California. It has absorbed the frontier; it has become the national hot-bed and testing ground." No one has described this aspect of the region better than Farnsworth Crowder: "Here American institutions sharpen into focus so startling as to give the effect, sometimes, of caricature. Here the socio-economic class conflict is vividly posed in burning silhouettes against the walls of the factory and the hinterland. Here American scholarship and research are at their best; American cults and quasi-religions are at their shabby and shallow worst; here are America's indignant soap-boxers and pamphleteers, bigots surrendered to some over-simplified ideal, its scared reactionaries and its grim stand-patters; its baronial aristocracy, its patient poor, its sober, good natured, self-centered middle class; its promoters, racketeers, opportunists, and politicians; its fagged-out oldsters and its brash, raw youth. . . . What America is, California is, with accents, in italics. National currents of thought, passion, aspirations and protest, elsewhere kept rather decently in subterranean channels, have a way of boiling up in the Pacific sun to mix in a chemistry of queer odors and unexpected crystallizations: but it is all richly, pungently American and not to be disowned, out of embarrassment and annoyance, by the rest of the nation which is in fact its parental flesh and blood, its roots and its mentor." Here is the land where the Gothic in idea and manner, in style and expression, stands out in sharp relief and, perhaps for the first time, is recognized for what it is. For this land is not merely a testing ground, it is also a forcing ground, a place where ideas, practices, and customs must prove their worth or be discarded.

The Political Culture of Southern California*

JAMES Q. WILSON

A PERSON LIKE MYSELF, who grew up in Southern California, finds it increasingly difficult to understand people who say they understand California. "Explaining California," especially Southern California, has always been a favorite pastime for New Yorkers and Bostonians who have changed planes in Los Angeles, or made a two-day trip to the Rand Corporation, or just speculated on what kind of state could be responsible for Hollywood. Nor need one be an easterner to play the game; living in San Francisco carries with it a permanent license not only to explain but to explain away (*far* away) Los Angeles.

This game might have been regarded as an amusing (though to me, irritating) diversion so long as what was being explained or "understood" was Hollywood and Vine, or orange-juice stands shaped like oranges, or Aimee Semple McPherson, or the Great I Am, or traffic on the Los Angeles freeways. It became a little less amusing when the same "explanations" thought appropriate for Aimee and the poor orange-juice vendors (most of whom, by the way, have disappeared) were applied to the John Birch Society and other manifestations of the far Right. Anybody crazy enough to buy orange juice at such places or to drive on those freeways must be crazy enough to be a Bircher. Let two Birchite loudmouths pop off anywhere else in the country and we rush to

* From *Commentary* (May, 1967). Copyright © 1967 by the American Jewish Committee. Used by permission of the publisher.

our sociology texts to see whether it is alienation or the decline of
the small entrepreneur that is the cause; let two of them say the
same thing in Los Angeles, and we just smile knowingly and mur-
mur, "It figures."

Even this systematic application of the double standard was
harmless enough before Ronald Reagan. Now a striking conservative personality has become governor of the largest state in the
union by an election plurality of over a million votes, most of
which he picked up in Southern California. This Hollywood-actor-
turned-politician ("it figures") has, to the amazement of many,
made a rather considerable impression, not only on the voters of
his state but on Republicans around the country including, apparently, a group of presumably toughminded fellow governors. From
now at least through the 1968 convention we have to take Reagan
quite seriously, and even if he fails to go the distance we must,
I think, take Reaganism seriously. It will be with us for a long
time under one guise or another. We will not take it seriously by
trying to explain it away as if it were something sold at one of
those orange-juice stands or preached from the pulpit at some
cultist church.

I grew up in Reagan country—not Hollywood, but the lower-
middle-class suburbs of Los Angeles. It was a distinctive way of
life. I think I could still recognize another person who grew up
there no matter where I should meet him, just as surely as an
Italian can spot a person from his village or region even though
they are both now in Queens. I am under no illusion that anyone
has the slightest interest in my boyhood (I have next to no interest in it myself), but I do suspect that it may be useful to try to
:xplain what it was like at least in general terms, and how what
it was like is relevant to what is happening there today. Though I
grew up and went to school there, I left a long time ago in order
to acquire some expensive eastern postgraduate degrees and a political outlook that would now make me vote against Reagan if I
had the chance. I do not intend here to write an apology for
Reagan; even if I thought like that, which I don't, I would never
write it down anywhere my colleagues at Harvard might read it.

I

The important thing to know about Southern California is that
the people who live there, who grew up there, love it. Not just
the way one has an attachment to a hometown, any hometown,

but the way people love the realization that they have found the right mode of life. People who live in Southern California are not richer or better educated than those who live in New York; the significant point about them is that they don't live in New York, and don't want to. If they did, they—the average Los Angeleno (my family, for example)—would have lived most of their lives in a walkup flat in, say, the Yorkville section of Manhattan or not far off Flatbush Avenue in Brooklyn. Given their income in 1930, life would have been crowded, noisy, cold, threatening—in short, *urban*. In Long Beach or Inglewood or Huntington Park or Bellflower, by contrast, life was carried on in a detached house with a lawn in front and a car in the garage, part of a quiet neighborhood, with no crime (except kids racing noisy cars), no cold, no smells, no congestion. The monthly payments on that bungalow —one or two bedrooms, one bath, a minuscule dining room, and never enough closets—would have been no more than the rent on the walkup flat in Brooklyn or Yorkville. In 1940, with the Depression still in force, *over half the population* of Los Angeles lived in single-family homes. Only about half of these were owner-occupied, but even to rent a house was such a vast improvement over renting an apartment that nobody looked back; they only looked ahead to the time they could pick up their own mortgage. San Francisco in the same year was another matter. Only a third of the population lived in single-family homes there, the reason being that there were almost no *houses* to rent; if you wanted a house, you had to buy it, and not many people in 1940 could afford to buy.

There has been a good deal of loose talk about "radical" politics (which I suppose means anything to the right of Earl Warren) developing out of a rootless, highly mobile population with no sense of *place*, of continuity, of stability. That may explain radical politics somewhere, but not in Los Angeles. The people who voted for Reagan have lived for years, in many cases decades, in Southern California. And they have lived in houses, not anonymous, impersonal apartment buildings.

Indeed, it was during the period of Los Angeles's greatest population growth that it voted, over and over again, for Earl Warren—the very embodiment (then) of moderation. The explanation, I believe, is quite simple: truly rootless, mobile people are more likely to vote the way established institutions—newspapers, churches, labor unions, business firms—tell them to vote. Revolutions are never made by the last man to get off the train; they are made by those who got off a long time ago and, having put down roots and formed their own assessment of matters, have the confidence, the long-nurtured discontent, and the knowledge of how to get things done sufficient to support independent political action. (Radical politics, I suspect, follows the same pattern as Negro riots: contrary to what the McCone Commission asserted but did not prove, the Negroes who rioted in Watts—or at least those who rioted violently enough to get themselves arrested—were Negroes who had been in Watts for a long time. Over half the teen-age Negroes arrested had been *born* in California; over three-fourths had lived there for more than five years.)

In any case, it is a mistake to try to explain a particular election by underlying social trends. Elections, after all, are choices, and how they come out depends on who the voters have to choose between. That Reagan won last year does not mean that *last year* some ineluctable social force finally surfaced and carried the day. A vote for Reaganism was always possible in Southern California (and had revealed itself in countless congressional and local elections). The point I wish to make is that there has for a long time been a "Reagan point of view" in the Southern California electorate, that this point of view was powerfully shaped by the kinds of people who went to California and the conditions of life there.

The people who in 1940 lived in those hundreds of thousands of detached and semi-detached homes came from all over the country, but primarily they came from the Midwest, the border states, and the "near South." Almost none came from Europe: about 6 per cent, to be exact, had been born in Italy, Ireland, England, Germany, France, Sweden, or Russia; another 2½ per cent had been born in Mexico. (In San Francisco, the proportion of foreign born was twice as large.) But 28 per cent had been born in the American heartland—the dustbowl states (Texas, Oklahoma, Arkansas, Louisiana, Kansas, Nebraska), or the border states (Indiana, Missouri, Tennessee, Kentucky), and the upper plains (Iowa, Wisconsin, Minnesota, the Dakotas). If you add in the nearby mountain and southwestern states (Colorado, Utah, Arizona, New Mexico, Nevada), the total proportion rises to over a third. And if you add in the persons whose parents had been born in these states, the proportion no doubt (there are no figures) exceeds a half. Again, San Francisco is a contrast—only about a tenth of its people in 1940 were from the heartland states. Between 1920 and 1940, during the Depression, over 400,000 persons born in the heartland moved to Los Angeles. *Less than a tenth* as many moved to San Francisco.

Except for Arkansas, Louisiana, and Texas, no southern states are included in these migration figures. This is important to bear in mind—such conservatism as Southern California displays was not imported from the Deep South. In fact, even those who came from southern states were likely to be from places like West Texas, where Confederate sentiment was never very strong.

These migrants were rural and small-town people. And here, of course, another popular explanation of Southern California politics takes the stage. These voters are supposed to yearn for the simpler life and the small-town virtues that they left behind. They are reactionary, it is claimed, in the precise sense: seeking to turn back the clock to a day when life was easier, virtues less complicated, and the Ten Commandments a sufficient guide. Perhaps so—there is no doubt some truth in this. But it flies in the face of the fact that these are people who *left* small-town and rural America (millions more stayed behind, after all)—and left it for jobs in big defense plants and large office buildings. I was never aware of any effort to re-create small-town America in Southern California, unless you put in that category the Victory Gardens people planted to raise vegetables during the war. On the contrary, they adopted rather quickly a suburban style of life, with its attendant devotion to the growing of a decent lawn (how many farms have you ever seen with a good lawn?). Furthermore, it is not the migrants themselves who on the whole have voted for Reaganism, but their children. The migrants voted for Roosevelt and Upton Sinclair and looked on disapprovingly as their children began to adopt the hedonistic mores of Southern California teen-age life. There was as much intergenerational conflict among the Okies and Arkies in California as among the Italians and the Irish in Boston or New York. And yet it was these youngsters who grew up, married, moved out to Orange County or to Lakewood, and voted for Reagan and castigated Pat Brown, the last of the New Deal–Fair Deal Democrats. (To be completely accurate, a lot of the older people voted for Reagan, too, but they, I imagine, found it much harder to let go of their traditional attachment to Franklin Roosevelt and Earl Warren; the young people had no trouble at all.)

This is not to say that the migrants brought nothing with them. On the contrary, they brought an essential ingredient of Southern California life—fundamentalist Protestant individualism. We like to think of the store-front church as being a Negro invention; not so. I remember scores of white store-front churches—mostly of small Pentecostal and Adventist sects—lining the main streets of Long

Beach. Most people, of course, went to established churches, but these were only bigger and slightly more orthodox versions of the same thing—Baptists, Methodists, Mormons, Brethren, Church of God, and so on. Church was a very important part of life, but hardly any two people belonged to the same one. We were Catholics, and we had to drive out into the dairy farming country (I will never forget the way Sunday morning smelled—incense and cow manure, in equal portions) where there were enough Mexican farmhands and Dutch Catholic dairymen to make up a parish. All my friends sang hymns and listened to "preachin'." And the preaching was evangelical, fundamentalist, and preoccupied with the obligation of the *individual* to find and enter into a right relationship with God, with no sacraments, rituals, covenants, or grace to make it easy.

The religious character of San Francisco was strikingly different. In 1936 (the last time the government took a census of church organizations), 70 per cent of the reported church membership of San Francisco, but only 40 per cent of that in Los Angeles, was Catholic. And of the claimed members of Protestant sects, 40 per cent in San Francisco, but only 26 per cent in Los Angeles, belonged to the high-status, non-fundamentalist churches—Congregational, Episcopalian, Unitarian, and Universalist. Both cities had about the same proportion of Jews, but, as will be argued in a moment, the leadership, at least, of the two Jewish communities was rather different. Los Angeles, and even more its middle-class suburbs, was Protestant and fundamentalist Protestant at that.

The social structure did nothing to change the individualistic orientation of life. People had no identities except their personal identities, no obvious group affiliations to make possible any reference to them by collective nouns. I never heard the phrase "ethnic group" until I was in graduate school. I never knew there were Irishmen (I was amazed many years later to learn that, at least on my mother's side, I had been one all along) or Italians (except funny organ grinders in the movies, all of whom looked like Chico Marx). We knew there were Negroes (but none within miles of where we lived) and Jews (they ran Hollywood and New York, we knew, but not many of us had ever met one). Nobody even pointed out to me that I was a Catholic (except once, when a friend explained that that was probably the reason I wouldn't join the Order of De Molay, a young people's Masonic group).

The absence of such group identities and of neighborhoods associated with those identities may be one reason for the enormous emphasis on "personality." Teen-agers everywhere, of course, place great stock in this, mostly, I suppose, because they feel such an urgent need to establish an identity and to be liked by others. But in Southern California, it went far beyond that—there was a cult of personality that dominated every aspect of life. Everybody was compared in terms of his or her personality; contests for student-body office were based on it. To be "popular" and "sincere" was vital. In a New York high school, by contrast, personality would have to share importance in such contests with a certain amount of bloc voting among the Irish, Italians, and Jews, or between "project" people and brownstone people, or even between leftists and far leftists.

Perhaps because of the absence of ethnic and religious blocs which in turn are associated with certain political positions, perhaps because Southern California (then) was very remote from those urban centers where "The Future of Socialism" was being earnestly debated, student life in and around Los Angeles was remarkably apolitical. Most people were vaguely for Roosevelt, though there was a substantial (and growing) group that announced defiantly that while their parents had voted for FDR in '32, and perhaps even in '36, they weren't going to do *that* any more. Registered Democrats who voted Republican were commonplace, but after noting that fact there wasn't, politically, much left to be said. (It was different in downtown Los Angeles where the Jews lived; L. A. High, and later Los Angeles State College, were very political. A considerable Wallace movement flourished in 1948. Many of those people are now in the Democratic club movement.)

Politics for these people came to mean, in later years, expressing directly one's individual political preferences and expecting them to be added up by a kind of political algebra into a general statement of the public interest. "Bloc voting" and group preferences were unheard of and, when heard of, unthinkable. And the idea that political parties ought to do anything besides help add up preferences was most heterodox—the worst thing that could be said about it was that it was "Eastern." The well-known institutional features of California's political system—weak parties, the extensive use of the referendum to decide policy issues, nonpartisanship—were perfectly matched to the political mentality that was nurtured in Southern California.

That nurturing was distinctive but hard to describe. Rural

Anglo-Saxon Protestants have lived in lots of states, but they haven't produced the Southern California style of politics anywhere else. One reason is to be found in what it was like, and to a considerable extent is still like, to grow up in Southern California. Everybody, as I have already noted, lived in a single-family house. There was no public transportation to speak of, so that the movement of people within the city followed no set corridors. People moved about freely and in so doing saw how everybody lived. That movement was institutionalized in the Sunday Afternoon Drive—not to the beach or an amusement park, but just "around" to look at homes, call on friends, or visit distant relatives. A house was, as a Catholic might put it, the outward and visible sign of inward grace. There was no anonymity provided by apartment buildings or tenements or projects. Each family had a house; there it was, for all to see and inspect. With a practiced glance, one could tell how much it cost, how well it was cared for, how good a lawn had been coaxed into uncertain life, and how tastefully plants and shrubs had been set out.

A strong, socially reinforced commitment to property was thus developed, evident in how people treat those homes today. An enormous amount of energy and money is devoted to repairing, improving, remodeling, extending, and landscaping. Even in areas with fairly low incomes, such as those where the elderly and the retired live, houses are not on the whole allowed to deteriorate. A family might buy a house for six or seven thousand dollars with, for the period, a big mortgage, and then spend several times that over a generation or two in home improvements. Those who could not afford it substituted labor for capital. People were practicing do-it-yourself in Southern California long before anybody in the advertising business thought to give it a name. Year-round warm weather made year-round outdoor labor possible—and, of course, year-round outdoor inspection by one's critical neighbors.

Much of this labor was cooperative. The Southern California equivalent of the eastern uncle who could "get it for you wholesale" was the Los Angeles brother-in-law who would help you put on a new roof, or paint the garage, or lend you (and show you how to use) his power saw. A vast, informally organized labor exchange permeated the region, with occasional trades of great complexity running through several intermediaries—the friend who would ask his brother, the plumber, to help you if you would ask your uncle with the mixer to lay the concrete in front of somebody's sister's home. Saturday saw people driving all over the county carrying out these assignments.

Driving. Driving everywhere, over great distances, with scarcely any thought to the enormous mileages they were logging. A car was the absolutely essential piece of social overhead capital. With it, you could get a job, meet a girl, hang around with the boys, go to a drive-in, see football games away from home, take in the beach parties at Laguna or Corona del Mar, or go to the Palladium ballroom in Hollywood. To have a car meant being somebody; to have to borrow a car meant knowing somebody; to have no car at all, owned or borrowed, was to be left out—way out.

Those cars led parents and professional moralists to speak of "teen-agers and their jalopies." They were not jalopies—not to us, anyway. The oldest, most careworn Ford Model A was a thing of beauty. To be sure, the beauty often had to be coaxed out; yet what was life for but to do the coaxing and take credit for the beauty? Beauty, of course, meant different things to different boys. For some, it was speed and power; and so they would drop a V-8 block into the "A" chassis and then carefully, lovingly, bore it out, stroke it, port it, and put two barrels or four barrels on it. For others, beauty was in the body, not the engine, and their energies would go into customizing the car—dropping the rear end, chopping down the top, leading in the fenders, stripping off the chrome (it took Detroit decades to recognize the merits of these changes and then to mass-produce them), and above all painting, sanding, rubbing, painting, sanding, rubbing—for ten or fifteen or twenty coats, usually of metallic paint. Again, warm weather made it easier—you could work outside year round and if you ran out of money before the job was finished (which was most of the time), you could drive around in the unfinished product with no top, primed but not painted, and no hood over the engine. Of late, Mr. Tom Wolfe of *New York* magazine has discovered car customizing and decided it is a folk art. It wasn't folk art in the 40's; it was life.

The sense of property developed by this activity has never been measured and perhaps never can be; I am convinced it was enormous and fundamental. After marriage, devoting energy to the improvement of a house was simply a grown-up extension of what, as a juvenile, one had done with cars. There is, of course, a paradox here: the car was used in great part to get girls. It was a hand-polished, custom-made rolling bedroom, or so its creators hoped. (In this they were as often disappointed as a Harvard man taking a Radcliffe girl into his house rooms during parietal hours; every girl likes to be *seen* in such places, but a distressingly small proportion are inclined to *do* anything there.) But the hedonistic purposes to which the car might be put did not detract from its power to create and sustain a very conventional and bourgeois sense of property and responsibility, for in the last analysis the car was not a means to an end but an end in itself. Shocked parents never got that point: they saw the excess that the car permitted, they did not see the intensely middle-class values that it instilled.

Low-density, single-family homes, a lack of public transportation, the absence of ethnic neighborhoods, and the use of cars combined to prevent the formation of streetcorner gangs, except in very central portions of Los Angeles and one or two older cities. The principal after-school occupation of a teen-age eastern boy from a working class family is to "hang out" at the corner candystore, the icecream parlor, or in front of the drugstore with class and ethnic compatriots. Having a "corner" of your own—or having "turf," in the case of the ambitious and imperialistic—would have made no sense to an equivalent group of young men in Southern California. The eastern life-style produced a feeling of *territory*, the western life-style a feeling of *property*. Teen-agers in Southern California hung out together, to be sure, but not in any fixed spot, and where they did hang out tended to be a place reached by a car, with lots of free parking for other cars. The drive-in restaurant was the premier institution catering to this need. But it was also a very democratic institution, since it was not (and because of its location some distance from one's home, could not become) the "turf" of any particular gang. Rich and poor, Protestant and Catholic, anybody with a car could get there and, barring a losing fight over a girl, stay there. There were rivalries, but like modern warfare they tended to be between large, heterogeneous, and impersonal rivals—one high school against another, not one ethnic group against another.

Can all this explain why Southern California is so different, politically, from Northern California—why it, so much more than the Bay Area, supported Goldwater and Reagan? Perhaps not entirely. And yet I believe the kind of people living there and their life-styles are very important, much more important than, say, the presumed influence of the conservative *Los Angeles Times*. The *Oakland Tribune* is even more conservative, but the East Bay region it serves is more "liberal" in its voting than L.A. And the very liberal McClatchey newspapers in the Central Valley do not seem to have turned back the Reagan tide. On the other hand, San Francisco has Southern-California-style suburbs as well, with bungalows and cars and the like, and the people there are not as conservative as their counterparts in the south. But as we have seen, the people who migrated to San Francisco in the 30's and 40's were different from those who settled in Los Angeles. And once the different life styles of the two cities became apparent, non-Californians must have begun deciding to move to the Bay Area or to Los Angeles on the basis, in part, of what they had heard about those styles. A small but visible difference in the beginning thus became a very large difference in the end.

II

The political institutions and economic character of Southern California reinforced the life style and gave it expression. Politics, as I have said, was nonpartisan, free-swinging, slightly populistic —a direct appeal to the people was to be made on all issues. The major parties for decades were virtually moribund and therefore never performed their customary (and to my thinking, desirable) task of aggregating interests, blurring issues, strengthening party loyalties, and finding moderate candidates. Not that the people wanted immoderate candidates. So long, at least, as the issues were not very grave—before civil rights, and welfare, and Berkeley, and crime—they wanted honest, competent administrators who favored change but in an orderly manner. In Earl Warren they got such a man and he made sure the regular Republican party, whose fat cats were on the whole considerably to his right, would not have a chance to replace him. He built a personal following outside the regular, and cumbersome, party apparatus. Like most personal followings, however, it made no provision for a transfer of power. The obvious Warren protégé—Thomas Kuchel—was in the Senate, Warren's personal following in the state could not be handed to another man, and the party was in no shape to find a candidate of its own. Any man with money and a good smile could take a crack at capturing the nomination on his own, and many did.

Such organization as existed tended to be in the north, rather than the south. San Francisco and Alameda County across the bay had more in the way of party machinery, financed on a steady basis, than the south had, at least until the emergence of the California Democratic clubs. A little organization goes a long way in an organizational vacuum, and the north exercised a disproportionate influence in California politics for some time. The northern Democrats had some old families—many Jewish—who helped pay the party's bills during the long, lean years.

The south had few such persons—or more accurately, it had some very rich, self-made men from the oil business and from the vast agricultural enterprises of the Imperial Valley who were conservative Democrats in the (by now) well-documented tradition of the American Southwest. They may be more visible in Texas today, but twenty years ago they were more influential in California.

Why? There were Jews in Southern California, tens of thousands of them in and around Los Angeles. (Yet looking back on my high-school days, I can think of only one Jew I was personally acquainted with, and he went to another high school across town. Jews were Hollywood, we all knew.) Many of them were in the movie industry and in command of wealth and great resources for publicity. Why didn't they help to finance and lead the Southern California Democratic party? Some did—or tried—at least for a while. A high point of that influence was the 1950 senatorial campaign of the liberal Helen Gahagan Douglas, the movie actress. It wasn't George Murphy or Ronald Reagan who put Hollywood into politics, it was Mrs. Douglas, who lost to Richard Nixon. Two years before, many of her supporters had turned, in frustration, to third-party politics and become important figures in the 1948 campaign of Henry Wallace. It was a disaster. Bolting the party nationally was a far more serious thing than bolting it locally, where it could hardly be said to exist. The Truman Democrats took control in California and, when Communist Party influence in the Wallace movement became too obvious to be denied (Wallace himself was to admit it later), they were in a position to treat the Douglas and Wallace Democrats as thoroughly discredited in the eyes of the voters. Shortly thereafter, the era of McCarthyism descended upon the country, and in Hollywood involvement in politics was for the time being finished. What Mrs. Douglas had begun, Henry Wallace and Joe McCarthy succeeded in ending.

But it was not only that Hollywood Jews had lost power, it was also that Hollywood Jews were different from those in other urban centers. The social and economic heights of Hollywood were commanded, not by German Jews, but by East Europeans; not by old families but by immigrants; not by Wall Street smoothness but by *nouveau riche* entrepreneurship. Such Hollywood money as went into politics was used much as money was then used in the movie industry—impulsively, by dictatorial men used to having their own way, and on behalf of "stars." If the star system worked on the movie lots, why couldn't it work in politics? Thus, a glamorous figure, a big name, and occasionally a conspicuous nut could get *personal* backing for a campaign, but there was little or no money for organization, for routine affairs, or for professional (and necessarily bureaucratic) leadership.

Anyway, the voter wasn't much interested in liberalism even if it *could* be financed. Los Angeles was prosperous, and even greater prosperity seemed just around the corner. The aircraft plants and shipyards had taken tens of thousands of families and given every member, including the mother, a job, thereby putting them, in four years' time, in a wholly different and higher economic bracket. A generation of slow gain was compressed into a few years; progress wasn't around the corner, or something you hoped for for your kids, it was right here and now. War prosperity affected the whole country, but it had a special effect on Southern California—there was more of it, because there was more war industry located there, and it benefited people who only a few years before had been fighting for survival on a dustswept farm in the Texas panhandle. John Steinbeck told us how those farmers and sharecroppers saw California as the Promised Land. But they had only been promised relief checks from the Farm Security Administration; instead, they found overtime checks from Lockheed.

Next to the kind of people who live there, the rate of economic growth of Southern California—and today, of the whole Southwest—is the main key to its political life. Visiting scholars make much of the business domination of Dallas, or the presumed influence of the *Los Angeles Times* in Southern California, or the "Chamber of Commerce mentality" of San Diego. The important thing to understand is that these have not been alien influences imposed from above on the populace—they are merely the more obvious indicators of the fact that business values are widely shared. (Not business *control*; voters are quick to resent that, when it is pointed out to them, in Los Angeles as anywhere. Sam Yorty became mayor by running against the *Times* and other "downtown interests," and he is still very popular in his city, however much ridicule he may take from Robert Kennedy in Washington.) Business values are here meant in the widest sense—a desire for expansion and growth, a high rate of increase in property values, finding and developing mass markets, and keeping capital moving and labor productive.

No one was immune from this psychology. How could he be?

Everyone was buying, or intended to buy, his own home. Many factory workers and salesmen speculated in real estate on the side. A favorite topic of conversation at our dinner table, and I am sure at thousands of dinner tables just like it, was the latest story about the fantastic price a certain parcel had just been sold for and what a shame it was that we passed up the chance to buy it two years ago for peanuts. (We never seemed to have enough peanuts around at the right time.) The purpose of government was to facilitate this growth—open up new land, bring in water, make credit easy, keep the defense plants rolling. Government was not there to keep painfully acquired positions secure by paying out benefits or legislating new regulations. Government was there to help bring in the future, not protect the past.

Not everyone felt this way, of course. Elderly people who came to California to retire had a different view. They wanted pensions, benefits, regulations. They were numerous and visible, but though they come quickly to mind when one thinks back on the shuffleboard and croquet courts at Lincoln Park in Long Beach or on the soapbox orators and bench-sitters in Pershing Square in Los Angeles, they were never representative of the local political ethos. They were the butt of countless jokes and the target for much political criticism: they wanted to hold back tomorrow (it was believed), cash their relief checks, and lie in the sun. That was *wrong,* most working families thought. The Negro, who today is the victim of the anti-welfare sentiment, was actually the second victim; the first was the old folks. They were attacked for moving to California "just to get a pension," told to "go back where they came from," and fought against in countless welfare issues. (About the only thing they were spared were allegations that they constituted a sexual threat. I cannot recall my father, no paragon of tolerance, ever trying to clinch an argument against a liberal by asking him how he would like it if his daughter grew up and married an old man.)

The old folks fought back, but in California it was a *protest* movement. George McLain organized the old folks (nobody ever called them "senior citizens"; they didn't even call themselves that), and made them a potent force in state politics, but it was a force directed *against* the two major parties and their candidates. He won concessions for his followers and now they may be so secure as to be accepted as a political fact of life; what they wanted, however, was never accepted.

Southern California's political culture, including but not limited to what might be called Reaganism, is one which I suspect is characteristic of areas experiencing rapid economic growth and general prosperity, especially if there are few institutions—political parties, churches, labor unions—to frame the issues and blunt popular instincts. People there are concerned about the growth in the size of the economic pie, not (except for the elderly) in preserving the size of their present slice. The attributes in a person to be admired are those which indicate his ability to enhance his position and expand his resources. If I had to cite only one way in which southwestern politics differ from northeastern politics, it would be this: the former region is developmental, future-oriented, and growth-conscious; the latter is conserving, past- or present-oriented, and security-conscious. Note that I say "conserving," not conservative; there is a difference. The Northeast by some measures is less "conservative" than the Southwest, though it is easy to exaggerate the difference. A conserva*tive* is usually thought of as a person who favors limited government, minimized administrative involvement in private affairs, maximum free choice. A conserv*er,* on the other hand, needs *more* government in order to protect present stakes from change, from threats posed by other groups, and from competition.

Before we get carried away with the difference, some qualifications are in order. There are conserving forces at work in Southern California. One is the elderly. Another is the slowly emerging labor movement. For years Los Angeles was a tough city in which to be a trade unionist. There are still people who remember with horror the bombing of the *Los Angeles Times.* But unions are making headway. One is the Retail Clerks, which is organizing in the supermarkets and dime stores; another is the Machinists, active in aircraft and auto assembly plants. And the region's economic growth has not unleashed anything like the hysteria of the Florida land boom.

Even more important as a challenge to the general political culture of the region, with its concern for property, propriety, individual responsibility, economic growth, and limited government, is ideological liberalism. By the time McCarthyism was ending and the blacklists were beginning to lose their grip on Hollywood (perhaps because faced with the competition from television and European producers, Hollywood could no longer afford the luxury of a blacklist), Adlai Stevenson was making his appearance as a force in the Democratic Party. The enormous outpouring of support for him in Southern California has been oft remarked upon, as has the vigorous club movement that grew up in the aftermath of his 1952 and 1956 presidential campaigns. The movement activated a wholly new generation of political enthusiasts and provided a new base of operations for some of the leftovers from older forms of liberal and radical politics.

These clubs did not recruit the people I have been describing in earlier pages, nor have they taken hold in the areas in which these people live. The clubs grew up on the northern and eastern periphery of the region—the Hollywood hills, Santa Monica, Beverly Hills, Pacific Palisades, and out into the college towns, such as Pomona, in the interior. Young Jews, young intellectuals, persons transplanted to Los Angeles from the East (by 1940, about 10 per cent of the population had been born in New England, New Jersey, or Pennsylvania), and older California radicals flocked into the clubs. But the clubs never really took root among the workingclass and middle-class bungalows of Long Beach, Inglewood, or Redondo Beach, to say nothing of Orange County to the Southeast. The Democratic clubs initially had little interest in Southern California; they were interested in national and international issues. (The civil-rights movement has changed that; the clubs are now deeply involved in such matters locally.) They had, at the outset, no real program for California (though they had one for just about everything else), and thus there was no necessary conflict between what they wanted and what those who later voted for Reagan wanted—no necessary conflict, perhaps, but conflict nonetheless. And the most intense kind of conflict, for what was at stake were large and symbolic issues—Red China, capital punishment, world peace, and civil liberties. The Southern California electorate quickly became deeply polarized.

The polarization is not immediately evident in voting statistics. In the aggregate, Southern California elects a mixture of liberals and conservatives much like any other region, and on many of its famous referenda votes for and against public expenditures about like other areas. But these aggregate figures conceal the real symptoms of polarization—several Democrats (not all) are as far to the left of their party as is possible; several Republicans (not all) are as far to the right of their party as possible. And on referenda issues—especially those involving such matters as open occupancy in housing—the returns and the polls suggest that Southern California has both the most intense proponents and the most intense opponents (the latter outnumbering the former; the region as a whole was against fair housing by a considerable margin—in San Francisco, the vote was both less lopsided and, I suspect, based on less intensely polarized views). This is *not* the same thing as saying that Southern California is more "bigoted" than the Bay Area. Because of the way the issue was framed, people were asked to vote *for* the *right* to sell their property to whomever they chose. In Southern California, property rights are vital and freedom in their exercise staunchly defended. There have been, I would guess, fewer attacks on Negro families seeking homes in white neighborhoods in Southern California than in, say, Pennsylvania, Ohio, or Illinois. The housing issue was fought out at a more general level—not over whether one was for or against Negroes, but over alternative conceptions of what freedom requires. And the polarization of opinion on this issue, as on most, was most intense among persons of higher status. The educated, affluent easterners and intellectuals (who work in law firms or the communications media or the universities) are more inclined than their less well-off fellows to support the Democratic clubs and liberalism; the educated, affluent sons and daughters of the midwestern migrants (who now work as engineers and accountants in aerospace and petroleum industries) are more inclined than their less well-off fellows to support Goldwater and Reagan.

III

Is Southern California's political culture unique? Not really—it is but the earliest, most publicized, and most heavily populated example of a pattern now to be found throughout much of the Southwest. It appeared first in Southern California because more people went there and because California's political institutions gave almost immediate expression to it. In other states, the party structure constrained its free expression for a time; the ambitions of rival politicians and factions in Texas and Arizona made the ideology less evident, at least for a while. Goldwater's easy victory at the 1964 Republican convention indicates how widespread are certain aspects of that culture—in fact, it overstates it, because Goldwater himself overstated many features of that culture. The Southern Californians about whom I have written want limited government, personal responsibility, "basic" education, a resurgence of patriotism, an end to "chiseling," and a more restrained Supreme Court. They are not quite so certain that they want an adventurous foreign policy or a high-risk international confrontation with communism. No doubt the militant Goldwater en-

thusiasts wanted such a policy, but they must have mistaken what
the rank-and-file would support. Reagan has not yet made the
same mistake—he took Goldwater's views, stripped away the
foreign policy (except for very general statements) and references
to turning back the clock on Social Security (after all, he wanted
a coalition between the elderly and the young).

But Goldwater, however badly managed his campaign, won
the convention and won it by methods and with supporters which,
in whatever state they were found, could very easily have been
found in Southern California. Amateur political clubs, impassioned
volunteers, appeals to highly moral and symbolic issues—the
Republican party professionals, to their profound irritation, had
to put up with all of it, just as party professionals in California,
Democrats and Republicans alike, have been putting up with it
since the early 1950's.

The Southern California political style is spreading; it seems
to be, at least in the western part of the United States, the con-
comitant of the American success story. There, millions of people
are realizing their ambitions. They are not "rootless" or yearning
for "small-town simplicity" or profoundly irritated by all the
hustle and bustle; they are acquiring security, education, living
space, and a life style that is based in its day-to-day routine on
gentility, courtesy, hospitality, virtue. Why, then, are they so discontent? It is not with their lot that they are discontent, it is with
the lot of the nation. *The very virtues they have and practice are,
in their eyes, conspicuously absent from society as a whole.* Politics
is corrupt—not in the petty sense, though there is that—but in the
large sense; to these people, it consists of "deals," of the catering
to selfish interests, of cynical manipulation and doubletalk. The
universities are corrupt—children don't act as if they appreciate
what is being given them, they don't work hard, and they are
lectured to by devious and wrongheaded professors. And above
all, everywhere they look, somebody is trying to get "something
for nothing," and succeeding.

These views may not be confined only to the political culture
in which they are now articulated. Surveys I have taken, and others
I have read, indicate that the single most widespread concern
of middle-class Americans is over the "decay of values"—evi-
denced by "crime in the streets," juvenile delinquency, public
lewdness, and the like, but going much beyond these manifestations
to include everything that suggests that people no longer act in
accordance with decent values and right reason. In many places,

especially in the Northeast, our political institutions (happily) do not allow such views to play much part in elections. Parties, led by professionals, instinctively shun such issues, feeling somehow that public debate over virtue is irrelevant (what can government do about it?) and dangerous (nobody can agree on what virtue is or that your party has more of it). Powerful non-political institutions tend, also, to keep such issues out of politics or to insist that they be matters of private conscience. For one, the Catholic Church, which draws the religious and moral interests of its followers inward, toward the sacraments and the educational and religious facilities of the Church which must be maintained and served. For another, large labor unions, which have never mistaken a "stamp out smut" campaign for a fifty-cent increase in the minimum wage. And a self-conscious intelligentsia with common ties to prestigious centers of liberal-arts education has, in many regions, especially the East and the Bay Area, an important role to play among local elites. They use their access to the mass media and to officialdom to make certain that other, non-moral issues predominate—after all, the major function of the schools they went to was to induce them to rebel against the "middle-class morality" which, in the modern parlance, is a hangup.

Regional differences will never disappear entirely, and thus the political culture of Southern California will never be *the* political culture of our society. But the strength of all those institutions which resist it is waning, and thus we are likely to have more of it in more places in the future. I happen to think that morality is important and that those concerned about it are decent people (after all, I'm related to a sizeable number of them). But I fear for the time when politics is seized with the issue. Our system of government cannot handle matters of that sort (can any democratic system?) and it may be torn apart by the effort.

"A Journey Through Los Angeles"*

ALDOUS HUXLEY

IT HAD all been arranged by telegram; Jeremy Pordage was to look out for a colored chauffeur in a gray uniform with a carnation in his buttonhole; and the colored chauffeur was to look out for a middle-aged Englishman carrying the Poetical Works of Wordsworth. In spite of the crowds at the station, they found one another without difficulty.

"Mr. Stoyte's chauffeur?"

"Mr. Pordage, sah?"

Jeremy nodded and, his Wordsworth in one hand, his umbrella in the other, half extended his arms in the gesture of a self-deprecatory mannequin exhibiting, with a full and humorous consciousness of their defects, a deplorable figure accentuated by the most ridiculous clothes. "A poor thing," he seemed to be implying, "but myself." A defensive and, so to say, prophylactic disparagement had become a habit with him. He resorted to it on every sort of occasion. Suddenly a new idea came into his head. Anxiously, he began to wonder whether, in this democratic Far West of theirs, one shook hands with the chauffeur—particularly if he happened to be a blackamoor, just to demonstrate that one wasn't a pukka sahib even if one's country did happen to be bearing the White Man's burden. In the end he decided to do nothing. Or, to be more accurate, the decision was forced upon him—as usual, he said

---

* From *After Many a Summer Dies the Swan* (Harper & Row, 1939). Copyright 1939 by Aldous Leonard Huxley. Used by permission of the publisher.

to himself, deriving a curious wry pleasure from the recognition of his own shortcomings. While he was hesitating what to do, the chauffeur took off his cap and, slightly overacting the part of an old-world Negro retainer, bowed, smiled toothily and said:

"Welcome to Los Angeles, Mr. Pordage, sah!" Then, changing the tone of his chanting drawl from the dramatic to the confidential, "I should have knowed you by your voice, Mr. Pordage," he went on, "even without the book."

Jeremy laughed a little uncomfortably. A week in America had made him self-conscious about that voice of his. A product of Trinity College Cambridge, ten years before the War, it was a small, fluty voice, suggestive of evensong in an English cathedral. At home, when he used it, nobody paid any particular attention. He had never had to make jokes about it, as he had done, in self-protection, about his appearance, for example, or his age. Here, in America, things were different. He had only to order a cup of coffee or ask the way to the lavatory (which, anyhow, wasn't called the lavatory in this disconcerting country) for people to stare at him with an amused and attentive curiosity, as though he were a freak on show in an amusement park. It had not been at all agreeable.

"Where's my porter?" he said fussily in order to change the subject.

A few minutes later they were on their way. Cradled in the back seat of the car, out of range, he hoped, of the chauffeur's conversation, Jeremy Pordage abandoned himself to the pleasure of merely looking. Southern California rolled past the windows; all he had to do was to keep his eyes open.

The first thing to present itself was a slum of Africans and Filipinos, Japanese and Mexicans. And what permutations and combinations of black, yellow and brown! What complex bastardies! And the girls—how beautiful in their artificial silk! "And Negro ladies in white muslin gowns." His favorite line in *The Prelude*. He smiled to himself. And meanwhile the slum had given place to the tall buildings of a business district. The population took on a more Caucasian tinge. At every corner there was a drugstore. The newspaper boys were selling headlines about Franco's drive on Barcelona. Most of the girls, as they walked along, seemed to be absorbed in silent prayer; but he supposed, on second thought, it was only gum that they were thus incessantly ruminating. Gum, not God. Then suddenly the car plunged into a tunnel and emerged into another world, a vast, untidy, suburban world of filling stations and billboards, of low houses in gardens, of vacant lots and waste paper, of occasional shops and office buildings and churches—primitive Methodist churches built, surprisingly enough, in the style of the Cartuja at Granada, Catholic churches like Canterbury Cathedral, synagogues disguised as Hagia Sophia, Christian Science churches with pillars and pediments, like banks. It was a winter day and early in the morning; but the sun shone brilliantly, the sky was without a cloud. The car was traveling westwards and the sunshine, slanting from behind them as they advanced, lit up each building, each sky sign and billboard as though with a spotlight, as though on purpose to show the new arrival all the sights.

EATS. COCKTAILS. OPEN NITES.

JUMBO MALTS.

DO THINGS, GO PLACES WITH CONSOL SUPER-GAS!

AT BEVERLY PANTHEON FINE FUNERALS ARE NOT EXPENSIVE.

The car sped onwards, and here in the middle of a vacant lot was a restaurant in the form of a seated bulldog, the entrance between the front paws, the eyes illuminated.

"Zoomorph," Jeremy Pordage murmured to himself, and again, "zoomorph." He had the scholar's taste for words. The bulldog shot back into the past.

ASTROLOGY, NUMEROLOGY, PSYCHIC READINGS.

DRIVE IN FOR NUTBURGERS—whatever they were. He resolved at the earliest opportunity to have one. A nutburger and a jumbo malt.

STOP HERE FOR CONSOL SUPER-GAS.

Surprisingly, the chauffeur stopped. "Ten gallons of Super-Super," he ordered; then, turning back to Jeremy, "This is our company," he added. "Mr. Stoyte, he's the president." He pointed to a billboard across the street. CASH LOANS IN FIFTEEN MINUTES, Jeremy read; CONSULT COMMUNITY SERVICE FINANCE CORPORATION. "That's another of ours," said the chauffeur proudly.

They drove on. The face of a beautiful young woman, distorted, like a Magdalene's, with grief, stared out of a giant billboard. BROKEN ROMANCE, proclaimed the caption. SCIENCE PROVES THAT 73 PER CENT OF ALL ADULTS HAVE HALITOSIS.

IN TIME OF SORROW LET BEVERLY PANTHEON BE YOUR FRIEND.

FACIALS, PERMANENTS, MANICURES.

BETTY'S BEAUTY SHOPPE.

Next door to the beauty shoppe was a Western Union office. That cable to his mother. . . . Heavens, he had almost forgotten!

Jeremy leaned forward and, in the apologetic tone he always used when speaking to servants, asked the chauffeur to stop for a moment. The car came to a halt. With a preoccupied expression on his mild, rabbit-like face, Jeremy got out and hurried across the pavement, into the office.

"Mrs. Pordage, The Araucarias, Woking, England," he wrote, smiling a little as he did so. The exquisite absurdity of that address was a standing source of amusement. "The Araucarias, Woking." His mother, when she bought the house, had wanted to change the name, as being too ingenuously middle-class, too much like a joke by Hilaire Belloc. "But that's the beauty of it," he had protested. "That's the charm." And he had tried to make her see how utterly right it would be for them to live at such an address. The deliciously comic incongruity between the name of the house and the nature of its occupants! And what a beautiful, topsy-turvy appositeness in the fact that Oscar Wilde's old friend, the witty and cultured Mrs. Pordage, should write her sparkling letters from The Araucarias, and that from these same Araucarias, these Araucarias, mark you, at *Woking,* should come the works of mingled scholarship and curiously rarefied wit for which her son had gained his reputation. Mrs. Pordage had almost instantly seen what he was driving at. No need, thank goodness, to labor your points where she was concerned. You could talk entirely in hints and anacoluthons; she could be relied on to understand. The Araucarias had remained The Araucarias.

Having written the address, Jeremy paused, pensively frowned and initiated the familiar gesture of biting his pencil—only to find, disconcertingly, that this particular pencil was tipped with brass and fastened to a chain. "Mrs. Pordage, The Araucarias, Woking, England," he read out loud, in the hope that the words would inspire him to compose the right, the perfect message—the message his mother expected of him, at once tender and witty, charged with a genuine devotion ironically worded, acknowledging her maternal domination, but at the same time making fun of it, so that the old lady could salve her conscience by pretending that her son was entirely free, and herself, the least tyrannical of mothers. It wasn't easy—particularly with this pencil on a chain. After several abortive essays, he decided, though it was definitely unsatisfactory, on: "Climate being sub-tropical shall break vow re underclothes. Stop. Wish you were here my sake not yours as you would scarcely appreciate this unfinished Bournemouth indefinitely magnified. Stop."

"Unfinished what?" questioned the young woman on the further side of the counter.

"B-o-u-r-n-e-m-o-u-t-h," Jeremy spelled out. He smiled; behind the bifocal lenses of his spectacles his blue eyes twinkled, and, with a gesture of which he was quite unconscious, but which he always automatically made when he was about to utter one of his little jokes, he stroked the smooth bald spot on the top of his head. "*You* know," he said, in a particularly fluty tone, "the bourne to which no traveler goes, if he can possibly help it."

The girl looked at him blankly then, inferring from his expression that something funny had been said and remembering that Courteous Service was Western Union's slogan, gave the bright smile for which the poor old chump was evidently asking, and went on reading: "Hope you have fun at Grasse. Stop. Tendresses. Jeremy."

It was an expensive message; but luckily, he reflected, as he took out his pocketbook, luckily Mr. Stoyte was grossly overpaying him. Three months' work, six thousand dollars. So damn the expense.

He returned to the car and they drove on. Mile after mile they went, and the suburban houses, the gas stations, the vacant lots, the churches, the shops went along with them, interminably. To right and left, between palms, or pepper trees, or acacias, the streets of enormous residential quarters receded to the vanishing point.

CLASSY EATS. MILE HIGH CONES.

JESUS SAVES.

HAMBURGERS.

Yet once more, the traffic lights turned red. A paperboy came to the window. "Franco claims gains in Catalonia," Jeremy read, and turned away. The frightfulness of the world had reached a point at which it had become for him merely boring. From the halted car in front of them, two elderly ladies, both with permanently waved white hair and both wearing crimson trousers, descended, each carrying a Yorkshire terrier. The dogs were set down at the foot of the traffic signal. Before the animals could make up their minds to use the convenience, the lights had changed. The Negro shifted into first, and the car swerved forward, into the future. Jeremy was thinking of his mother. Disquietingly enough, she too had a Yorkshire terrier.

FINE LIQUORS.

TURKEY SANDWICHES.

GO TO CHURCH AND FEEL BETTER ALL THE WEEK.

WHAT IS GOOD FOR BUSINESS IS GOOD FOR YOU.

Another zoomorph presented itself, this time a real estate
agent's office in the form of an Egyptian sphinx.

JESUS IS COMING SOON.

YOU TOO CAN HAVE ABIDING YOUTH WITH THRILLPHORM
BRASSIERES.

BEVERLY PANTHEON, THE CEMETERY THAT IS DIFFERENT...

With the triumphant expression of Puss in Boots enumerating
the possessions of the Marquis of Carabas, the Negro shot a glance
over his shoulder at Jeremy, waved his hand towards the billboard
and said, "That's ours, too."

"You mean, the Beverly Pantheon?"

The man nodded. "Finest cemetery in the world, I guess," he
said; and added, after a moment's pause, "Maybe you's like to see
it. It wouldn't hardly be out of our way."

"That would be very nice," said Jeremy with upper-class
English graciousness. Then, feeling that he ought to express his
acceptance rather more warmly and democratically, he cleared his
throat and, with a conscious effort to reproduce the local vernacular, added that it would be *swell*. Pronounced in his Trinity College Cambridge voice, the word sounded so unnatural that he
began to blush with embarrassment. Fortunately, the chauffeur
was too busy with the traffic to notice.

They turned to the right, sped past a Rosicrucian Temple, past
two cat-and-dog hospitals, past a School for Drum-Majorettes and
two more advertisements of the Beverly Pantheon. As they turned
to the left on Sunset Boulevard, Jeremy had a glimpse of a young
woman who was doing her shopping in a hydrangea-blue strapless
bathing suit, platinum curls and a black fur jacket. Then she too
was whirled back into the past.

The present was a road at the foot of a line of steep hills, a
road flanked by small, expensive-looking shops, by restaurants,
by night-clubs shuttered against the sunlight, by offices and apartment houses. Then they too had taken their places in the irrevocable. A sign proclaimed that they were crossing the city limits of
Beverly Hills. The surroundings changed. The road was flanked
by the gardens of a rich residential quarter. Through trees, Jeremy
saw the façades of houses, all new, almost all in good taste—
elegant and witty pastiches of Lutyens manor houses, of Little
Trianons, of Monticellos; lighthearted parodies of Le Corbusier's
solemn machines-for-living-in; fantastic adaptations of Mexican
haciendas and New England farms.

They turned to the right. Enormous palm trees lined the road.

In the sunlight, masses of mesembryanthemums blazed with an intense magenta glare. The houses succeeded one another, like the pavilions at some endless international exhibition. Gloucestershire followed Andalusia and gave place in turn to Touraine and Oaxaca, Düsseldorf and Massachusetts.

"That's Harold Lloyd's place," said the chauffeur, indicating a kind of Boboli. "And that's Charlie Chaplin's. And that's Pickfair."

The road began to mount, vertiginously. The chauffeur pointed across an intervening gulf of shadow at what seemed a Tibetan lamasery on the opposite hill. "That's where Ginger Rogers lives. Yes, *sir,*" he nodded triumphantly, as he twirled the steering wheel.

Five or six more turns brought the car to the top of the hill. Below and behind lay the plain, with the city like a map extending indefinitely into a pink haze.

Before and to either hand were mountains—ridge after ridge as far as the eye could reach, a desiccated Scotland, empty under the blue desert sky.

The car turned a shoulder of orange rock, and there all at once, on a summit hitherto concealed from view, was a huge sky sign, with the words BEVERLY PANTHEON, THE PERSONALITY CEMETERY, in six-foot neon tubes and, above it, on the very crest, a full-scale reproduction of the Leaning Tower of Pisa—only this one didn't lean.

"See that?" said the Negro impressively. "That's the Tower of Resurrection. Two hundred thousand dollars, that's what it cost. Yes, *sir.*" He spoke with an emphatic solemnity. One was made to feel that the money had all come out of his own pocket.

An hour later, they were on their way again, having seen everything. Everything. The sloping lawns, like a green oasis in the mountain desolation. The groups of trees. The tombstones in the grass. The Pets' Cemetery, with its marble group after Landseer's Dignity and Impudence. The Tiny Church of the Poet—a miniature reproduction of Holy Trinity at Stratford-on-Avon, complete with Shakespeare's tomb and a twenty-four-hour service of organ music played automatically by the Perpetual Wurlitzer and broadcast by concealed loud speakers all over the cemetery.

Then, leading out of the vestry, the Bride's Apartment (for one was married at the Tiny Church as well as buried from it)— the Bride's Apartment that had just been redecorated, said the chauffeur, in the style of Norma Shearer's boudoir in *Marie Antoinette*. And, next to the Bride's Apartment, the exquisite black marble Vestibule of Ashes, leading to the Crematorium, where three super-modern oil-burning mortuary furnaces were always under heat and ready for any emergency.

Accompanied wherever they went by the tremolos of the Perpetual Wurlitzer, they had driven next to look at the Tower of Resurrection—from the outside only; for it housed the executive offices of the West Coast Cemeteries Corporation. Then the Children's Corner with its statues of Peter Pan and the Infant Jesus, its groups of alabaster babies playing with bronze rabbits, its lily pool and an apparatus labeled The Fountain of Rainbow Music, from which there spouted simultaneously water, colored lights and the inescapable strains of the Perpetual Wurlitzer. Then, in rapid succession, the Garden of Quiet, the Tiny Taj Mahal, the Old World Mortuary. And, reserved by the chauffeur to the last, as the final and crowning proof of his employer's glory, the Pantheon itself.

Was it possible, Jeremy asked himself, that such an object existed? It was certainly not probable. The Beverly Pantheon lacked all verisimilitude, was something entirely beyond his powers to invent. The fact that the idea of it was now in his mind proved, therefore, that he must really have seen it. He shut his eyes against the landscape and recalled to his memory the details of that incredible reality. The external architecture, modeled on that of Boecklin's Toteninsel. The circular vestibule. The replica of Rodin's Le Baiser, illuminated by concealed pink floodlights. The flights of black marble stairs. The seven-story columbarium, with its endless galleries, its tiers on tiers of slab-sealed tombs. The bronze and silver urns of the cremated, like athletic trophies. The stained glass windows after Burne-Jones. The texts inscribed on marble scrolls. The Perpetual Wurlitzer crooning on every floor. The sculpture. . . .

That was the hardest to believe, Jeremy reflected, behind closed eyelids. Sculpture almost as ubiquitous as the Wurlitzer. Statues wherever you turned your eyes. Hundreds of them, bought wholesale, one would guess, from some monumental masonry concern at Carrara or Pietrasanta. All nudes, all female, all exuberantly nubile. The sort of statues one would expect to see in the reception room of a high-class brothel in Rio de Janeiro. "Oh Death," demanded a marble scroll at the entrance to every gallery, "where is thy sting?" Mutely, but eloquently, the statues gave their reassuring reply. Statues of young ladies in nothing but a very tight belt imbedded, with Bernini-like realism, in the Parian flesh. Statues of young ladies crouching; young ladies using both hands to be modest; young ladies stretching, writing, callipygously stooping to tie their sandals, reclining. Young ladies with doves, with panthers, with other young ladies, with upturned eyes expressive of the soul's awakening. "I am the Resurrection and the Life," proclaimed the scrolls. "The Lord is my shepherd; therefore shall I want nothing." Nothing, not even Wurlitzer, not even girls in tightly buckled belts. "Death is swallowed up in victory"—the victory no longer of the spirit but of the body—the well-fed body, forever youthful, immortally athletic, indefatigably sexy. The Moslem paradise had had copulations six centuries long. In this new Christian heaven, progress, no doubt, would have stepped up the period to a millennium and added the joys of everlasting tennis, eternal golf and swimming.

All at once the car began to descend. Jeremy opened his eyes again, and saw that they had reached the further edge of the range of hills, among which the Pantheon was built.

Below lay a great tawny plain, chequered with patches of green and dotted with white houses. On its further side, fifteen or twenty miles away, ranges of pinkish mountains fretted the horizon.

"What's this?" Jeremy asked.

"The San Fernando Valley," said the chauffeur. He pointed into the middle distance. "That's where Groucho Marx has his place," he said. "Yes, *sir*."

At the bottom of the hill the car turned to the left along a wide road that ran, a ribbon of concrete and suburban buildings, through the plain. The chauffeur put on speed; sign succeeded sign with bewildering rapidity. MALTS CABINS DINE AND DANCE AT THE CHATEAU HONOLULU SPIRITUAL HELPING AND COLONIC IRRIGATION BLOCK-LONG HOT DOGS BUY YOUR DREAM HOME NOW. And behind the signs the mathematically planted rows of apricot and walnut trees flicked past—a succession of glimpsed perspectives preceded and followed every time by fan-like approaches and retirements.

Dark-green and gold, enormous orange orchards maneuvered, each one a mile-square regiment glittering in the sunlight. Far off, the mountains traced their uninterpretable graph of boom and slump.

"Tarzana," said the chauffeur startlingly; and there, sure enough, was the name suspended, in white letters, across the road.

"There's Tarzana College," the man went on, pointing to a group of Spanish-Colonial palaces clustering round a Romanesque basilica. "Mr. Stoyte, he's just given them an auditorium."

They turned to the right along a less important road. The orange groves gave place for a few miles to huge fields of alfalfa and dusty grass, then returned again more luxuriant than ever. Meanwhile the mountains on the northern edge of the valley were approaching and, slanting in from the west, another range was looming up to the left. They drove on. The road took a sudden turn, aiming, it seemed, at the point where the two ranges must come together. All at once, through a gap between two orchards, Jeremy Pordage saw a most surprising sight. About half a mile from the foot of the mountains, like an island off a cliff-bound coast, a rocky hill rose abruptly, in places almost precipitously, from the plain. On the summit of the bluff and as though growing out of it in a kind of stony efflorescence, stood a castle. But what a castle! The donjon was like a skyscraper, the bastions plunged headlong with the effortless swoop of concrete dams. The thing was Gothic, medieval, baronial—doubly baronial, Gothic with a Gothicity raised, so to speak, to a higher power, more medieval than any building of the thirteenth century. For this . . . this object, as Jeremy was reduced to calling it, was medieval, not out of vulgar historical necessity, like Coucy, say, or Alnwick, but out of pure fun and wantonness, Platonically, one might say. It was medieval as only a witty and irresponsible modern architect would wish to be medieval, as only the most competent modern engineers are technically equipped to be.

Jeremy was startled into speech. "What on earth is that?" he asked, pointing at the nightmare on the hilltop.

"Why, that's Mr. Stoyte's place," said the retainer; and smiling yet once more with the pride of vicarious ownership, he added: "It's a pretty fine home, I guess."

The orange groves closed in again; leaning back in his seat, Jeremy Pordage began to wonder, rather apprehensively, what he had let himself in for when he accepted Mr. Stoyte's offer. The pay was princely; the work, which was to catalogue the almost legendary Hauberk Papers, would be delightful. But that cemetery, this Object—Jeremy shook his head. He had known, of course, that Mr. Stoyte was rich, collected pictures, owned a show place in California. But no one had ever led him to expect *this*. The humorous puritanism of his good taste was shocked; he was appalled at the prospect of meeting the person capable of committing such an enormity. Between that person and oneself, what contact, what community of thought or feeling could possibly exist? Why had he sent for one? For it was obvious that he couldn't conceivably like one's books. But had he even read one's books? Did he have the faintest idea of what one was like? Would he be capable, for example, of understanding why one had insisted on the name of The Araucarias remaining unchanged? Would he appreciate one's point of view about . . .

These anxious questionings were interrupted by the noise of the horn, which the chauffeur was sounding with a loud and offensive insistence. Jeremy looked up. Fifty yards ahead, an ancient Ford was creeping tremulously along the road. It carried, lashed insecurely to roof and running boards and luggage rack, a squalid cargo of household goods—rolls of bedding, an old iron stove, a crate of pots and pans, a folded tent, a tin bath. As they flashed past, Jeremy had a glimpse of three dull-eyed, anemic children, of a woman with a piece of sacking wrapped around her shoulders, of a haggard, unshaved man.

"Transients," the chauffeur explained in a tone of contempt.

"What's that?" Jeremy asked.

"Why, *transients,*" the Negro repeated, as though the emphasis were an explanation. "Guess that lot's from the dust bowl. Kansas licence plate. Come to pick our navels."

"Come to pick your navels?" Jeremy echoed incredulously.

"Navel oranges," said the chauffeur. "It's the season. Pretty good year for navels, I guess."

They emerged once more into the open and there once more was the Object, larger than ever. Jeremy had time to study the details of its construction. A wall with towers encircled the base of the hill, and there was a second line of defence, in the most approved post-Crusades manner, half way up. On the summit stood the square keep, surrounded by subsidiary buildings.

From the donjon, Jeremy's eyes traveled down to a group of buildings in the plain, not far from the foot of the hill. Across the façade of the largest of them the words "Stoyte Home for Sick Children" were written in gilded letters. Two flags, one the stars and stripes, the other a white banner with the letter S in scarlet, fluttered in the breeze. Then a grove of leafless walnut trees shut out the view once again. Almost at the same moment the chauffeur threw his engine out of gear and put on the brakes. The car came gently to a halt beside a man who was walking at a brisk pace along the grassy verge of the road.

"Want a ride, Mr. Propter?" the Negro called.

The stranger turned his head, gave the man a smile of recognition and came to the window of the car. He was a large man, broad shouldered, but rather stooping, with brown hair turning gray and a face, Jeremy thought, like the face of one of those statues which Gothic sculptors carve for a place high up on a West front—a face of sudden prominences and deeply shadowed folds and hollows, emphatically rough-hewn so as to be expressive even at a distance. But this particular face, he went on to notice, was not merely emphatic, not only for the distance; it was a face also for the near point, also for intimacy, a subtle face, in which there were the signs of sensibility and intelligence as well as of power, of a gentle and humorous serenity no less than of energy and strength.

"Hullo, George," the stranger said, addressing the chauffeur, "nice of you to stop for me."

"Well, I'm sure glad to see you, Mr. Propter," said the Negro cordially. Then, he half turned in his seat, waved a hand towards Jeremy and with a florid formality of tone and manner, said, "I'd like to have you meet Mr. Pordage of England. Mr. Pordage, this is Mr. Propter."

The two men shook hands, and, after an exchange of courtesies, Mr. Propter got into the car.

"You're visiting with Mr. Stoyte?" he asked, as the chauffeur drove on.

Jeremy shook his head. He was here on business; had come to look at some manuscripts—the Hauberk Papers, to be precise.

Mr. Propter listened attentively, nodded from time to time, and, when Jeremy had finished, sat for a moment in silence.

"Take a decayed Christian," he said at last in a meditative tone, "and the remains of a Stoic; mix thoroughly with good manners, a bit of money and an old-fashioned education; simmer for several years in a university. Result: a scholar and a gentleman. Well, there were worse types of human being." He uttered a little laugh. "I might almost claim to have been one myself, once, long ago."

Jeremy looked at him inquiringly. "You're not *William* Propter, are you?" he asked. "Not 'Short Studies in the Counter Reformation,' by any chance?"

The other inclined his head.

Jeremy looked at him in amazement and delight. Was it possible? he asked himself. Those "Short Studies" had been one of his favorite books—a model, he had always thought, of their kind.

"Well, I'm jiggered," he said aloud, using the schoolboyish locution deliberately and as though between inverted commas. He had found that, both in writing and in conversation, there were exquisite effects to be obtained by the judicious employment, in a solemn or cultural context, of a phrase of slang, a piece of childish profanity or obscenity. "I'll be damned," he exploded again, and his consciousness of the intentional silliness of the words made him stroke his bald head and cough.

There was another moment of silence. Then, instead of talking, as Jeremy had expected, about the "Short Studies," Mr. Propter merely shook his head and said, "We mostly are."

"Mostly are what?" asked Jeremy.

"Jiggered," Mr. Propter answered. "Damned. In the psychological sense of the word," he added.

The walnut trees came to an end and there once more, on the starboard bow, was the Object. Mr. Propter pointed in its direction. "Poor Jo Stoyte!" he said. "Think of having *that* millstone round one's neck. Not to mention, of course, all the other millstones that go with it. What luck we've had, don't you think? —we who've never been given the opportunity of being anything much worse than scholars and gentlemen!" After another little silence, "Poor Jo," he went on with a smile, "he isn't either of them. You'll find him a bit trying. Because of course he'll want to bully you, just because tradition says that your type is superior to his type. Not to mention the fact," he added, looking into Jeremy's face with an expression of mingled amusement and sympathy, "that you're probably the sort of person that invites persecution. A bit of a murderee, I'm afraid, as well as a scholar and gentleman."

Feeling simultaneously annoyed by the man's indiscretion and touched by his friendliness, Jeremy smiled rather nervously and nodded his head.

"Maybe," Mr. Propter went on, "maybe it would help you to be less of a murderee towards Jo Stoyte, if you knew what gave him the original impulse to get damned in just *that* way"—and he pointed again towards the Object. "We were at school together, Jo and I; only nobody called him Jo in those days. We called him Slob, or Jellybelly. Because, you see, poor Jo was the local fat boy, the only fat boy in the school during those years." He paused for a moment; then went on in another tone, "I've often wondered why people have always made fun of fatness. Perhaps there's something intrinsically wrong with fat. For example, there isn't a single fat saint—except, of course, old Thomas Aquinas; and I cannot see any reason to suppose that he was a real saint, a saint in the popular sense of the word, which happens to be the true sense. If Thomas is a saint, then Vincent de Paul isn't. And if Vincent's a saint, which he obviously is, then Thomas isn't. And perhaps that enormous belly of his had something to do with it. Who knows? But anyhow, that's by the way. We're talking about Jo Stoyte. And poor Jo, as I say, was a fat boy and, being fat, was fair game for the rest of us. God, how we punished him for his glandular deficiencies! And how disastrously he reacted to that punishment! Over-compensation . . . but here I am at home," he added, looking out of the window as the car slackened speed and came to a halt in front of a small white bungalow set in the midst of a clump of eucalyptus trees. "We'll go on with this another time. But remember, if poor Jo gets too offensive, think of what he was at school and be sorry for him—and don't be sorry for yourself." He got out of the car, closed the door behind him and, waving a hand to the chauffeur, walked quickly up the path and entered the little house.

The car rolled on again. At once bewildered and reassured by his encounter with the author of the "Short Studies," Jeremy sat, inertly looking out of the window. They were very near the Object now; and suddenly he noticed, for the first time, that the castle hill was surrounded by a moat. Some few hundred yards from the water's edge, the car passed between two pillars, topped by heraldic lions. Its passage, it was evident, interrupted a beam of invisible light directed on a photoelectric cell; for no sooner were they past the lions than a drawbridge began to descend. Five seconds before they reached the moat, it was in place; the car rolled smoothly across and came to a halt in front of the main gateway of the castle's outer walls. The chauffeur got out and, speaking into a telephone receiver concealed in a convenient loophole, announced his presence. The chromium-plated portcullis rose noiselessly, the double doors of stainless steel swung back. They drove in. The car began to climb. The second line of walls was pierced by another gate, which opened automatically as they approached. Between the inner side of this second wall and the slope of the hill a ferroconcrete bridge had been constructed, large enough to accommodate a tennis court. In the shadowy space beneath, Jeremy caught sight of something familiar. An instant later he had recognized it as a replica of the grotto of Lourdes.

"Miss Maunciple, she's a Catholic," remarked the chauffeur, jerking his thumb in the direction of the grotto. "That's why he had it made for her. We's Presbyterians in *our* family," he added.

"And who is Miss Maunciple?"

The chauffeur hesitated for a moment. "Well, she's a young lady Mr. Stoyte's kind of friendly with," he explained at last; then changed the subject.

The car climbed on. Beyond the grotto all the hillside was a cactus garden. Then the road swung round to the northern slope of the bluff, and the cactuses gave place to grass and shrubs. On a little terrace, over-elegant like a fashion-plate from some mythological *Vogue* for goddesses, a bronze nymph by Giambologna spouted two streams of water from her deliciously polished breasts. A little further on, behind wire netting, a group of baboons squatted among the rocks or paraded the obscenity of their hairless rumps.

Still climbing, the car turned again and finally drew up on a circular concrete platform, carried out on cantilevers over a precipice. Once more the old-fashioned retainer, the chauffeur, taking off his cap, did a final impersonation of himself welcoming the young master home to the plantation, then set to work to unload the luggage.

Jeremy Pordage walked to the balustrade and looked over. The ground fell almost sheer for about a hundred feet, then sloped steeply to the inner circle of walls and, below them, to the outer fortifications. Beyond lay the moat and, on the further side of the moat, stretched the orange orchards. "*In dunkeln Laub die Gold-Orangen glühn,*" he murmured to himself; and then: "He hangs in shades the orange bright, Like golden lamps in a green night." Marvell's rendering, he decided, was better than Goethe's. And, meanwhile, the oranges seemed to have become brighter and more significant. For Jeremy, direct, unmediated experience was always hard to take in, always more or less disquieting. Life became safe, things assumed meaning, only when they had been translated into words and confined between the covers of a book. The oranges were beautifully pigeon-holed; but what about the castle? He turned round and, leaning back against the parapet, looked up. The Object impended, insolently enormous. Nobody had dealt poetically with *that*. Not Childe Roland, not the King of Thule, not Marmion, not the Lady of Shalott, not Sir Leoline. Sir Leoline, he repeated to himself with a connoisseur's appreciation of romantic absurdity, Sir Leoline, the baron rich, had—what? A toothless mastiff bitch. But Mr. Stoyte had baboons and a sacred grotto, Mr. Stoyte had a chromium portcullis and the Hauberk Papers, Mr. Stoyte had a cemetery like an amusement park and a donjon like . . .

There was a sudden rumbling sound; the great nailstudded doors of the Early English entrance porch rolled back and from between them, as though propelled by a hurricane, a small, thick-set man, with a red face and a mass of snow-white hair, darted out on to the terrace and bore down upon Jeremy. His expression, as he advanced, did not change. The face wore that shut, unsmiling mask which American workmen tend to put on in their dealings with strangers—in order to prove, by not making the ingratiating grimaces of courtesy, that theirs is a free country and you're not going to come it over *them*.

Not having been brought up in a free country, Jeremy had automatically begun to smile as this person, whom he guessed to be his host and employer, came hurrying towards him. Confronted by the unwavering grimness of the other's face, he suddenly became conscious of this smile—conscious that it was out of place, that it must be making him look a fool. Profoundly embarrassed, he tried to readjust his face.

"Mr. Pordage?" said the stranger in a harsh, barking voice. "Pleased to meet you. My name's Stoyte." As they shook hands, he peered, still unsmiling, into Jeremy's face. "You're older than I thought," he added.

For the second time that morning, Jeremy made his mannequin's gesture of apologetic self-exhibition.

"The sere and withered leaf," he said. "One's sinking into senility. One's . . ."

Mr. Stoyte cut him short. "What's your age?" he asked in a loud peremptory tone, like that of a police sergeant interrogating a captured thief.

"Fifty-four."

"Only fifty-four?" Mr. Stoyte shook his head. "Ought to be full of pep at fifty-four. How's your sex life?" he added disconcertingly.

Jeremy tried to laugh off his embarrassment. He twinkled; he patted his bald head. *"Mon beau printemps et mon été ont fait le saut par la fenêtre,"* he quoted.

"What's that?" said Mr. Stoyte frowning. "No use talking foreign languages to me. I never had any education." He broke into a sudden braying of laughter. "I'm head of an oil company here," he said. "Got two thousand filling stations in California alone. And not one man in any of those filling stations that isn't a college

graduate!" He brayed again, triumphantly. "Go and talk foreign
languages to *them*." He was silent for a moment; then, pursuing
an unexplicit association of ideas, "My agent in London," he went
on, "the man who picks up things for me there—he gave me your
name. Told me you were the right man for those—what do you
call them? You know, those papers I bought this summer. Roe-
buck? Hobuck?"

"Hauberk," said Jeremy, and with a gloomy satisfaction noted
that he had been quite right. The man had never read one's books,
never even heard of one's existence. Still, one had to remember
that he had been called Jellybelly when he was young.

"Hauberk," Mr. Stoyte repeated with a contemptuous impa-
tience. "Anyhow, he said you were the man." Then, without pause
or transition, "What was it you were saying, about your sex life,
when you started that foreign stuff on me?"

Jeremy laughed uncomfortably. "One was implying that it was
normal for one's age."

"What do you know about what's normal at your age?" said
Mr. Stoyte. "Go and talk to Dr. Opispo about it. It won't cost
you anything. Obispo's on salary. He's the house physician."
Abruptly changing the subject, "Would you like to see the castle?"
he asked. "I'll take you round."

"Oh, that's very kind of you," said Jeremy effusively. And for
the sake of making a little polite conversation, he added: "I've
already seen your burial ground."

"Seen my burial ground?" Mr. Stoyte repeated in a tone of
suspicion: suspicion turned suddenly to anger. "What the hell do
you mean?" he shouted.

Quailing before his fury, Jeremy stammered something about
the Beverly Pantheon and that he had understood from the chauffeur that Mr. Stoyte had a financial interest in the company.

"I see," said the other, somewhat mollified, but still frowning.
"I thought you meant . . ." Mr. Stoyte broke off in the middle of
the sentence, leaving the bewildered Jeremy to guess what he had
thought. "Come on," he barked; and, bursting into movement, he
hurried towards the entrance to the house.

A Journey into the Mind of Watts*

THOMAS PYNCHON

THE NIGHT OF May 7, after a chase that began in Watts and ended some fifty blocks farther north, two Los Angeles policemen, Caucasians, succeeded in halting a car driven by Leonard Deadwyler, a Negro. With him were his pregnant wife and a friend. The younger cop (who'd once had a complaint brought against him for rousting some Negro kids around in a more than usually abusive way) went over and stuck his head and gun in the car window to talk to Deadwyler. A moment later there was a shot; the young Negro fell sideways in the seat, and died. The last thing he said, according to the other cop, was, "She's going to have a baby."

The coroner's inquest went on for the better part of two weeks, the cop claiming the car had lurched suddenly, causing his service revolver to go off by accident; Deadwyler's widow claiming it was cold-blooded murder and that the car had never moved. The verdict, to no one's surprise, cleared the cop of all criminal responsibility. It had been an accident. The D.A. announced immediately that he thought so, too, and that as far as he was concerned the case was closed.

But as far as Watts is concerned, it's still very much open. Preachers in the community are urging calm—or, as others are putting it: "Make any big trouble, baby, the Man just going to

---

* From *The New York Times Magazine*, June 12, 1966. Copyright © 1966 by The New York Times Company. Reprinted by permission.

come back in and shoot you, like last time." Snipers are sniping but so far not hitting much of anything. Occasional fire bombs are being lobbed at cars with white faces inside, or into empty sports models that look as if they might be white property. There have been a few fires of mysterious origin. A Negro Teen Post— part of the L.A. poverty war's keep-them-out-of-the-streets effort —has had all its windows busted, the young lady in charge expressing the wish next morning that she could talk with the malefactors, involve them, see if they couldn't work out the problem together. In the back of everybody's head, of course, is the same question: Will there be a repeat of last August's riot?

An even more interesting question is: why is everybody worrying about another riot—haven't things in Watts improved any since the last one? A lot of white folks are wondering. Unhappily, the answer is no. The neighborhood may be seething with social workers, data collectors, VISTA volunteers, and other assorted members of the humanitarian establishment, all of whose intentions are the purest in the world. But somehow nothing much has changed. There are still the poor, the defeated, the criminal, the desperate, all hanging in there with what must seem a terrible vitality.

The killing of Leonard Deadwyler has once again brought it all into sharp focus; brought back longstanding pain, reminded everybody of how very often the cop does approach you with his revolver ready, so that nothing he does with it can then be really accidental; of how, especially at night, everything can suddenly reduce to a matter of reflexes: your life trembling in the crook of a cop's finger because it is dark, and Watts, and the history of this place and these times makes it impossible for the cop to come on any different, or for you to hate him any less. Both of you are caught in something neither of you wants, and yet night after night, with casualties or without, these traditional scenes continue to be played out all over the south-central part of this city.

Whatever else may be wrong in a political way—like the inadequacy of Great Depression techniques applied to a scene that has long outgrown them; like an old-fashioned grafter's glee among the city fathers over the vast amounts of poverty-war bread that Uncle is now making available to them—lying much closer to the heart of L.A.'s racial sickness is the co-existence of two very different cultures: one white and one black.

While the white culture is concerned with various forms of systematized folly—the economy of the area in fact depending upon it—the black culture is stuck pretty much with basic realities like disease, like failure, violence and death, which the whites have mostly chosen—and can afford—to ignore. The two cultures do not understand each other, though white values are displayed without let-up on black people's TV screens, and though the panoramic sense of black impoverishment is hard to miss from atop the Harbor Freeway, which so many whites must drive at least twice every working day. Somehow it occurs to very few of them to leave at the Imperial Highway exit for a change, go east instead of west only a few blocks, and take a look at Watts. A quick look. The simplest kind of beginning. But Watts is country which lies, psychologically, uncounted miles further than most whites seem at present willing to travel.

On the surface, anyway, the Deadwyler affair hasn't made it look any different, though underneath the mood in Watts is about what you might expect. Feelings range from a reflexive, angry, driving need to hit back somehow, to an anxious worry that the slaying is just one more bad grievance, one more bill that will fall due some warm evening this summer. Yet in the daytime's brilliance and heat, it is hard to believe there is any mystery to Watts. Everything seems so out in the open, all of it real, no plastic faces, no transistors, no hidden Muzak, or Disneyfied landscaping, or smiling little chicks to show you around. Not in Raceriotland. Only a few historic landmarks, like the police substation, one command post for the white forces last August, pigeons now thick and cooing up on its red-tiled roof. Or, on down the street, vacant lots, still looking charred around the edges, winking with emptied Tokay, port and sherry pints, some of the bottles peeking out of paper bags, others busted.

A kid could come along in his bare feet and step on this glass —not that you'd ever know. These kids are so tough you can pull slivers of it out of them and never get a whimper. It's part of their landscape, both the real and the emotional one: busted glass, busted crockery, nails, tin cans, all kinds of scrap and waste. Traditionally Watts. An Italian immigrant named Simon Rodia spent thirty years gathering some of it up and converting a little piece of the neighborhood along 107th Street into the famous Watts Towers, perhaps his own dream of how things should have been: a fantasy of fountains, boats, tall openwork spires, encrusted with a dazzling mosaic of Watts debris. Next to the Towers, along the old Pacific Electric tracks, kids are busy every day busting more bottles on the steel rails. But Simon Rodia is dead and now the junk just accumulates.

A few blocks away, other kids are out playing on the hot black-

top of the school playground. Brothers and sisters too young yet
for school have it better—wherever they are they have yards, trees,
hoses, hiding places. Not the crowded, shadeless tenement living
of any Harlem; just the same one- or two-story urban sprawl as
all over the rest of L.A., giving you some piece of grass at least
to expand into when you don't especially feel like being inside.

In the business part of town there is a different idea of refuge.
Pool halls and bars, warm and dark inside, are crowded; many
domino, dice, and whist games in progress. Outside, men stand
around a beer cooler listening to a ball game on the radio; others
lean or hunker against the sides of buildings—low, faded stucco
boxes that remind you, oddly, of certain streets in Mexico. Women
go by, to and from what shopping there is. It is easy to see how
crowds, after all, can form quickly in these streets, around the
least seed of a disturbance or accident. For the moment, it all only
waits in the sun.

Overhead, big jets now and then come vacuum-cleanering in
to land; the wind is westerly, and Watts lies under the approaches
to L.A. International. The jets hang what seems only a couple of
hundred feet up in the air; through the smog they show up more
white than silver, highlighted by the sun, hardly solid; only the
ghosts, or possibilities, of airplanes.

From here, much of the white culture that surrounds Watts—
and, in a curious way, besieges it—looks like those jets: a little
unreal, a little less than substantial. For Los Angeles, more than
any other city, belongs to the mass media. What is known around
the nation as the L.A. Scene exists chiefly as images on a screen
or TV tube, as four-color magazine photos, as old radio jokes, as
new songs that survive only a matter of weeks. It is basically a
white Scene, and illusion is everywhere in it, from the giant aerospace firms that flourish or retrench at the whims of Robert
McNamara, to the "action" everybody mills along the Strip on
weekends looking for, unaware that they, and their search which
will end, usually, unfulfilled, are the only action in town.

Watts lies impacted in the heart of this white fantasy. It is, by
contrast, a pocket of bitter reality. The only illusion Watts ever
allowed itself was to believe for a long time in the white version
of what a Negro was supposed to be. But with the Muslim and
civil-rights movements that went, too.

Since the August rioting, there has been little building here,
little buying. Lots whose buildings were burned off them are still
waiting vacant and littered with garbage, occupied only by a parked

car or two, or kids fooling around after school, or winos sharing a pint in the early morning. The other day, on one of them, there were ground-breaking festivities, attended by a county supervisor, pretty high-school girls decked in ribbons, a white store owner and his wife, who in the true Watts spirit busted a bottle of champagne over a rock—all because the man had decided to stay and rebuild his $200,000 market, the first such major rebuilding since the riot.

Watts people themselves talk about another kind of aura, vaguely evil; complain that Negroes living in better neighborhoods like to come in under the freeway as to a red-light district, looking for some girl, some game, maybe some connection. Narcotics is said to be a rare bust in Watts these days, although the narco people cruise the area earnestly, on the lookout for dope fiends, dope rings, dope peddlers. But the poverty of Watts makes it more likely that if you have pot or a little something else to spare you will want to turn a friend on, not sell it. Tomorrow, or when he can, your friend will return the favor.

At the Deadwyler inquest, much was made of the dead man's high blood alcohol content, as if his being drunk made it somehow all right for the police to shoot him. But alcohol is a natural part of the Watts style; as natural as LSD is around Hollywood. The white kid digs hallucination simply because he is conditioned to believe so much in escape, escape as an integral part of life, because the white L.A. Scene makes accessible to him so many different forms of it. But a Watts kid, brought up in a pocket of reality, looks perhaps not so much for escape as just for some calm, some relaxation. And beer or wine is good enough for that. Especially good at the end of a bad day.

Like after you have driven, say, down to Torrance or Long Beach or wherever it is they're hiring because they don't seem to be in Watts, not even in the miles of heavy industry that sprawl along Alameda Street, that gray and murderous arterial which lies at the eastern boundary of Watts looking like the edge of the world.

So you groove instead down the Freeway, maybe wondering when some cop is going to stop you because the old piece of a car you're driving, that you bought for $20 or $30 you picked up somehow, makes a lot of noise or burns some oil. Catching you mobile widens The Man's horizons; gives him more things he can get you on. Like "excessive smoking" is a great favorite with him.

If you do get to where you were going without encountering a cop, you may spend your day looking at the white faces of personnel men, their uniform glaze of suspicion, their automatic smiles, and listening to polite putdowns. "I decided once to ask," a kid says, "one time they told me I didn't meet their requirements. So I said: 'Well, what are you looking for? I mean, how can I train, what things do I have to learn so I *can* meet your requirements?' Know what he said? 'We are not obligated to tell you what our requirements are.' "

He isn't. That right there is the hell and headache: he doesn't have to do anything he doesn't want to do because he is The Man. Or he was. A lot of kids these days are more apt to be calling him the *little* man—meaning not so much any member of the power structure as just your average white L.A. taxpayer, registered voter, property owner; employed, stable, mortgaged, and the rest.

The little man bugs these kids more than The Man ever bugged their parents. It is the little man who is standing on their feet and in their way; he's all over the place, and there is not much they can do to change him or the way he feels about them. A Watts kid knows more of what goes on inside white heads than possibly whites do themselves; knows how often the little man has looked at him and thought, "Bad credit risk"—or "Poor learner," or "Sexual threat," or "Welfare chiseler"—without knowing a thing about him personally.

The natural, normal thing to want to do is hit the little man. But what, after all, has he done? Mild, respectable, possibly smiling, he has called you no names, shown you no weapons. Only told you perhaps that the job was filled, the house rented.

With a cop it may get more dangerous, but at least it's honest. You understand each other. Both of you silently admitting that all the cop really has going for him is his gun. "There was a time," they'll tell you, "you'd say, 'Take off the badge, baby, and let's settle it.' I mean he wouldn't, but you'd say it. But since last August, man, the way I feel, hell with the badge—just take off that gun."

The cop does not take off that gun; the hassle stays verbal. But this means that, besides protecting and serving the little man, the cop also functions as his effigy.

If he does get emotional and say something like "boy" or "nigger," you then have the option of cooling it or else—again this is more frequent since last August—calling him the name he expects to be called, though it is understood you are not commenting in any literal way on what goes on between him and his mother. It is a ritual exchange, like the dirty dozens.

Usually—as in the Deadwyler incident—it's the younger cop of the pair who's more troublesome. Most Watts kids are hip to what's going on in this rookie's head—the things he feels he has to prove—as much as to the elements of the ritual. Before the cop can say, "Let's see your I.D.," you learn to take it out politely and say, "You want to see my I.D.?" Naturally it will bug the cop more the further ahead of him you can stay. It is flirting with disaster, but it's the cop who has the gun, so you do what you can.

You must anticipate always how the talk is going to go. It's something you pick up quite young, same as you learn the different species of cop: the Black and White (named for the color scheme of their automobiles), who are L.A. city police and in general the least flexible; the L.A. county sheriff's department, who style themselves more of an elite, try to maintain a certain distance from the public, and are less apt to harass you unless you seem worthy; the Compton city cops, who travel only one to a car and come on very tough, like leaning four of you at a time up against the wall and shaking you all down; the juvies, who ride in unmarked Plymouths and are cruising all over the place soon as the sun goes down, pulling up alongside you with pleasantries like, "Which one's buying the wine tonight?", or, "Who are you guys planning to rob this time?" They are kidding, of course, trying to be pals. But Watts kids, like most, do not like being put in with winos, or dangerous drivers, or thieves, or in any bag considered criminal or evil. Whatever the cop's motives, it *looks* like mean and deliberate ignorance.

In the daytime, and especially with any kind of crowd, the cop's surface style has changed some since last August. "Time was," you'll hear, "man used to go right in, very mean, pick maybe one kid out of the crowd he figured was the troublemaker, try to bust him down in front of everyone. But now the people start yelling back, how they don't want no more of that, all of a sudden The Man gets very meek."

Still, however much a cop may seem to be following the order of the day read to him every morning about being courteous to everybody, his behavior with a crowd will really depend as it always has on how many of his own he can muster, and how fast. For his mayor, Sam Yorty, is a great believer in the virtues of Overwhelming Force as a solution to racial difficulties. This approach has not gained much favor in Watts. In fact, the mayor of Los Angeles appears to many Negroes to be the very incarnation of the little man: looking out for no one but himself, speaking always out of expediency, and never, never to be trusted.

The Economic and Youth Opportunities Agency (E.Y.O.A.) is a joint city-county "umbrella agency" (the state used to be represented, but has dropped out) for many projects scattered around the poorer parts of L.A., and seems to be Sam Yorty's native element, if not indeed the flower of his consciousness. Bizarre, confused, ever in flux, strangely ineffective, E.Y.O.A. hardly sees a day go by without somebody resigning, or being fired, or making an accusation, or answering one—all of it confirming the Watts Negroes' already sad estimate of the little man. The Negro attitude toward E.Y.O.A. is one of clear mistrust, though degrees of suspicion vary, from the housewife wanting only to be left in peace and quiet, who hopes that maybe The Man is lying less than usual this time, to the young, active disciple of Malcolm X who dismisses it all with a contemptuous shrug.

"But why?" asked one white lady volunteer. "There are so many agencies now that you *can* go to, that *can* help you, if you'll only file your complaint."

"They don't help you." This particular kid had been put down trying to get a job with one of the larger defense contractors.

"Maybe not before. But it's different now."

"Now," the kid sighed, "*now*. See, people been hearing that '*now*' for a long time, and I'm just tired of The Man telling you, '*Now*, it's OK, *now* we mean what we say.'"

In Watts, apparently, where no one can afford the luxury of illusion, there is little reason to believe that now will be any different, and better than last time.

It is perhaps a measure of the people's indifference that only 2 per cent of the poor in Los Angeles turned out to elect representatives to the E.Y.O.A. "poverty board." For a hopeless minority on the board (7 out of 23), nobody saw much point in voting.

Meantime, the outposts of the establishment drowse in the bright summery smog; secretaries chat the afternoons plaintively away about machines that will not accept the cards they have punched for them; white volunteers sit filing, doodling, talking on the phones, doing any kind of busy work, wondering where the "clients" are; inspirational mottoes like SMILE decorate the beaverboard office walls along with flow charts to illustrate the proper disposition of "cases," and with clippings from the slick magazines about "What Is Emotional Maturity?"

Items like smiling and Emotional Maturity are in fact very big with the well-adjusted, middle-class professionals, Negro and white, who man the mimeographs and computers of the poverty war here.

Sadly, they seem to be smiling themselves out of any meaningful communication with their poor. Besides a nineteenth-century faith that tried and true approaches—sound counseling, good intentions, perhaps even compassion—will set Watts straight, they are also burdened with the personal attitudes they bring to work with them. Their reflexes—especially about conformity, about failure, about violence—are predictable.

"We had a hell of a time with this one girl," a Youth Training and Employment Project counselor recalls. "You should have seen those hairdos of hers—piled all the way up to here. And the screwy outfits she'd come in with, you just wouldn't believe. We had to take her aside and explain to her that employers just don't go for that sort of thing. That she'd be up against a lot of very smooth-looking chicks, heels and stockings, conservative hair and clothes. We finally got her to come around."

The same goes for boys who like to wear Malcolm hats or Afro haircuts. The idea the counselors push evidently is to look as much as possible like a white applicant. Which is to say, like a Negro job counselor or social worker. This has not been received with much enthusiasm among the kids it is designed to help out, and is one reason business is so slow around the various projects.

There is a similar difficulty among the warriors about failure. They are in a socio-economic bag, along with the vast majority of white Angelenos, who seem more terrified of failure than of death. It is difficult to see where any of them have experienced significant defeat, or loss. If they have, it seems to have been long rationalized away as something else.

You are likely to hear from them wisdom on the order of: "Life has a way of surprising us, simply as a function of time. Even if all you do is stand on the street corner and wait." Watts is full of street corners where people stand, as they have been, some of them, for twenty or thirty years, without Surprise One ever having come along. Yet the poverty warriors must believe in this form of semimiracle, because their world and their scene cannot accept the possibility that there may be, after all, no surprise. But it is something Watts has always known.

As for violence, in a pocket of reality such as Watts, violence is never far from you: because you are a man, because you have been put down, because for every action there is an equal and opposite reaction. Somehow, sometime. Yet to these innocent, optimistic child-bureaucrats, violence is an evil and an illness, possibly because it threatens property and status they cannot help cherishing.

They remember last August's riot as an outburst, a seizure.
Yet what, from the realistic viewpoint of Watts, was so abnormal?
"Man's got his foot on your neck," said one guy who was there,
"sooner or later you going to stop *asking* him to take it off." The
violence it took to get that foot to ease up even the little it did
was no surprise. Many had predicted it. Once it got going, its basic
objective—to beat the Black and White police—seemed a reasonable one, and was gained the minute The Man had to send troops
in. Everybody seems to have known it. There is hardly a person
in Watts now who finds it painful to talk about, or who regrets
that it happened—unless he lost somebody.

But in the white culture outside, in that creepy world full of
pre-cardiac Mustang drivers who scream insults at one another
only when the windows are up; of large corporations where Nice-
guymanship is the standing order regardless of whose executive
back one may be endeavoring to stab; of an enormous priest caste
of shrinks who counsel moderation and compromise as the answer
to all forms of hassle; among so much well-behaved unreality, it is
next to impossible to understand how Watts may truly feel about
violence. In terms of strict reality, violence may be a means to
getting money, for example, no more dishonest than collecting
exorbitant carrying charges from a customer on relief, as white
merchants here still do. Far from a sickness, violence may be an
attempt to communicate, or to be who you really are.

"Sure I did two stretches," a kid says, "both times for fighting,
but I didn't deserve either one. First time, the cat was bigger than
I was; next time, it was two against one, and I was the one." But
he was busted all the same, perhaps because Whitey, who knows
how to get everything he wants, no longer has fisticuffs available
as a technique, and sees no reason why everybody shouldn't go the
Niceguy route. If you are thinking maybe there is a virility hangup
in here too, that putting a Negro into a correctional institution for
fighting is also some kind of neutering operation, well, you might
have something there, who knows?

It is, after all, in white L.A.'s interest to cool Watts any way
it can—to put the area under a siege of persuasion; to coax the
Negro poor into taking on certain white values. Give them a little
property, and they will be less tolerant of arson; get them to go in
hock for a car or color TV, and they'll be more likely to hold
down a steady job. Some see it for what it is—this come-on, this
false welcome, this attempt to transmogrify the reality of Watts
into the unreality of Los Angeles. Some don't.

Watts is tough; it has been able to resist the unreal. If there is any drift away from reality, it is by way of mythmaking. As this summer warms up, last August's riot is being remembered less as chaos and more as art. Some talk now of a balletic quality to it, a coordinated and graceful drawing of cops away from the center of the action, a scattering of The Man's power, either with real incidents or false alarms.

Others remember it in terms of music; through much of the rioting seemed to run, they say, a remarkable empathy, or whatever it is that jazz musicians feel on certain nights; everybody knowing what to do and when to do it without needing a word or a signal: "You could go up to anybody, the cats could be in the middle of burning down a store or something, but they'd tell you, explain very calm, just what they were doing, what they were going to do next. And that's what they'd do; man, nobody had to give orders."

Restructuring of the riot goes on in other ways. All Easter week this year, in the spirit of the season, there was a "Renaissance of the Arts," a kind of festival in memory of Simon Rodia, held at Markham Junior High, in the heart of Watts.

Along with theatrical and symphonic events, the festival also featured a roomful of sculptures fashioned entirely from found objects—found, symbolically enough, and in the Simon Rodia tradition, among the wreckage the rioting had left. Exploiting textures of charred wood, twisted metal, fused glass, many of the works were fine, honest rebirths.

In one corner was this old, busted, hollow TV set with a rabbit-ears antenna on top; inside, where its picture tube should have been, gazing out with scorched wiring threaded like electronic ivy among its crevices and sockets, was a human skull. The name of the piece was "The Late, Late, Late Show."

The Battle of Sunset Strip*

EDGAR Z. FRIEDENBERG AND
ANTHONY BERNHARD

.

T HE SUNSET STRIP, of Los Angeles but not in it, is a grimly
prophetic area. Social, political, and demographic factors explo-
sively combined, have established there a persistent pattern of
conflict and hostility which conveys the sinister atmosphere of life
in California today with remarkable economy. The atmosphere of
the Strip is spreading fast, and is toxic. The reagents which generate it are not peculiar to the area—just, at present, more concentrated there. The same peculiar odor now hangs over the University
of California where, optimists say, atmospheric conditions are still
probably sub-lethal except to those in especially exposed positions.

Sunset Boulevard is wide, heavily traveled, and about twenty
miles long. It runs from downtown Los Angeles to the Pacific
Ocean north of Santa Monica, though there are shorter and easier
ways to get there. The portion known as the Strip is about a third
of the way out from town, and owes its existence to a geographical
anomaly.

Where the Strip developed, Sunset Boulevard runs through an
area about two miles wide which, with Beverly Hills adjoining it
on the west, is entirely surrounded by Los Angeles but excluded
from it. Beverly Hills is a separate municipality, but the area in

* From *The New York Review of Books* (March 9, 1967). Copyright
© 1967 by The New York Review. Used by permission of the publisher.

which most of the Strip is located is known as West Hollywood and is not incorporated at all. Lawful authority in West Hollywood is administered by Los Angeles County and represented by deputy sheriffs. Freedom from municipal control permitted the Strip to develop into an area of illicit amusement, violent and vulgar but conventional. But during the past decade its character has changed. It ceased to be violent, while vulgarity has become so characteristic of Los Angeles as to require no special enclave in which to flourish. The night clubs and dance halls became somewhat more sedate, and the Strip began to blend into Los Angeles on the east. Smart, or nearly smart, specialty shops opened; and reputable, if rather garish, apartment buildings and hotels were built. Los Angeles's expensive Restaurant Row developed along the western part of the Strip, near Beverly Hills, and along La Cienega Boulevard where it intersects Sunset.

But business along the now respectable Strip has not been flourishing. Its near suburban façade developed spots of urban decay. There were even vacancies, and businessmen began to worry. Nothing was happening to relieve the Strip's mediocrity: Hollywood had lost much of its allure; Westwood, a few miles further west, was far more elegant; this part of Sunset wasn't even tawdry enough to be exciting. The plight of the Strip is epitomized in two electric signs that still dominate its east end. One urges fun-seekers on to Las Vegas; the other shows two elderly satisfied customers —it is not clear whether they are shades or survivors—smiling with satisfaction at the services they have received from Forest Lawn. In any case, the signs suggest, there could be little reason to remain on the Strip.

At this juncture, and about two years ago, some of the tavern operators came up with a suggestion for improving business. They suggested that Los Angeles County rescind its ordinance forbidding persons under twenty-one from dancing in any place where liquor is served. There could be no question of legalizing the service of liquor to persons under twenty-one, which is forbidden by state law. But rescinding the ordinance would at least permit the owners to admit "teen-agers"—usually for a minimum charge of $2.50 —sell them soft drinks and provide them with the kind of music they enjoy, which would open up a totally new market. This was done, and the response was so promising that many of the tavern operators signed leases on their property for several years.

The youngsters who moved onto the Strip and into the clubs

did no drinking and behaved very well on the whole. But they are the vanguard of Southern Californian youth, where the vanguard is quite far out, like a vanguard should be. Their dress and hair styles are "mod" in the extreme; The Byrds sing their music, and The Buffalo Springfield, and The Peanut Butter Conspiracy, and The Mothers of Invention. Most of the music is beautiful, though some of it is strange; and exactly this may be said of the youngsters themselves.

But as their numbers increased they brought trouble. Traffic along Sunset Boulevard slowed and sometimes halted, especially on weekends, less from the influx of youngsters than because of the curious and hostile tourists and family groups who came to stare—and sometimes to jeer and throw eggs—at them. National newsmagazines published colorful reports on the Strip in which the kids were featured as a new social problem. The local press established a presence with batteries of searchlights and mobile TV units, ready to report any dramatic event or, if none occurred, to incite one. The narrow sidewalks of Sunset Boulevard became crowded with youngsters who wanted to be where the action was but who lacked the funds or the inclination to lay out a succession of $2.50 entrance fees. They lounged and strolled along in a manner that the tourists who glared at them would have enjoyed as picturesque in a Mexican city where the *corso* is established custom; here, their elders enjoyed recoiling from them in a kind of squeamish panic almost as much.

As the situation developed, business began to fall off in Restaurant Row, whose adult customers had trouble driving to Scandia or The Marquis. Local shopkeepers who were not directly affected by the youngsters' presence, since they were closed at night, nevertheless became anxious about the damage they thought the kids were doing to the area's reputation (they had not, apparently, read Jane Jacobs with understanding). But how could the kids be turned off? They had the support of the tavern and coffee-house operators whose livelihood they had become; and these men were bound and protected by their leases. Moreover, at this point, the good behavior of the "teeny-boppers" had become a problem. If they had been drinking or making a public nuisance of themselves they could have been abated easily enough. But they were neither hostile, nor aggressive, nor disorderly in their conduct; except by their sheer numbers and incidental economic impact they bothered nobody except people who are psychically disturbed by the sight of youngsters in long hair and colorful clothing:

> *They only have respect for men in*
> *tailored suits*
> *If you have long hair or are wearing boots*
> *They think you're doing something wrong!*

the kids were to sing, with mournful detachment, when the police moved in and cracked down.

The legal basis on which the Sheriff's Office began to act is County Ordinance 3611.1 which provides that "no person under the age of eighteen years shall loiter about any public street, avenue, alley, park or other place" between 10 P.M. and sunrise unless accompanied by a parent, legal guardian, or spouse over twenty-one years old. The city of Los Angeles has a similar ordinance, and also has an ordinance forbidding loitering without reference to age or time of day; it is posted on a sign that greets every traveler who arrives at the airport. Loitering is defined as "to idle, to loaf, to stand idly by or to walk, drive, or ride about aimlessly and without purpose"—a definition that may well make the entire solar system illegal. Shortly after New Year's, the County Board of Supervisors made the law tougher by adding a $500 fine, six months' imprisonment, or both, applicable to parents or guardians of juveniles.

Through most of last fall, community pressure to crack down on "juvies" and get them off the Strip had mounted more rapidly than police action had responded. The weekly Los Angeles *Free Press*—one of the best and most aggressive of the loosely syndicated "underground press," alleged in a detailed front-page story on October 28 that illustrations for a *Los Angeles Times* story published October 12 called "A Hard Day's Night on the Strip," showing sheriff's deputies questioning suspected juveniles, had, in fact, been staged for the *Times*. The Sheriff's Department, the *Free Press* said, had solicited the article from the *Times* "as an effective local counter to adverse criticism of the Department" in a recent *Life* magazine article devoted to the Strip.

The *Free Press* also dutifully reported that the Sheriff's public relations office had denied its story. In any case, by mid-November, it was surely no longer necessary to stage exhibitions of police zeal. Sheriff's deputies, assigned to the Strip in force, had been forcefully enforcing County Ordinance 3611.1. This ordinance, which I have quoted, presents unusual difficulties. Perhaps because of loose draftsmanship, it fails to forbid persons of youthful appearance to *exist* between 10 P.M. and sunrise and forbids only their loitering in public places. Suspects must therefore be required to produce identification that reveals their age—a demand that has since been declared unconstitutional though juveniles have, in any case, no defensible constitutional rights and may not be affected by this decree. The law does not forbid anyone to attend a private party or any legitimate place of entertainment legally open to persons of their age, or to travel directly between such a place and their home, so long as he does not "ride about aimlessly and without purpose," regardless of the hour. Nevertheless, many youngsters complain, police arrest them for loitering as soon as they leave a coffee house to go to their cars to drive home; and Los Angeles city police did certainly arrest—on a charge of "interfering in an arrest"—the fifty-seven-year-old executive director of the American Civil Liberties Union of Southern California when he attempted to inform a youth that he need not produce the identification demanded. This arrest, moreover, occurred when the police entered a private hall where a rally to protest police action was in progress, in which the loitering ordinance could not conceivably have applied.

Youngsters also frequently allege police brutality in arrests. Whether police action constitutes brutality or merely indignity, what the police do is certainly objectionable. One tactic, repeatedly photographed on the Strip, is to stand behind the victim and thrust the billy club under his chin, grasping it at both ends and using it as a kind of *garrotte* to force his head back. Another, applicable only to long-haired youths, is to grasp their hair and twist their heads into position to be photographed. The following incident described by Malcolm Carter in the San Francisco *Sunday Examiner & Chronicle* of December 11 describes the way it is happening:

The police in action, however, were even more frightening. Seeing a cruiser with two deputies pull a car to the side, then follow the car off the Strip, I became curious. So I watched as the deputies ordered three 16 or 17 year olds out of their car, lean them against the vehicle for a thorough frisk and search the car (presumably for drugs) with a flashlight.

"With all due respect," I said to the deputy watching his partner complete a citation, "but couldn't that be considered an unreasonable search? Don't you have to show cause?"

His answer: "I assume everyone has a weapon. That's how I stay alive."

This conversation took place after the boys, pale and obviously nervous, were lectured about breaking the rules and asked whether their parents knew where they were.

But another conversation was even stranger. On a street overlooking the Strip, Sheriff's men had established a kind of command post. In the first cruiser, sat a deputy peering through binoculars. In a second car sat other men. But the third vehicle was the pivotal one. Their faces made grotesque by a powerful light source bouncing off the roof, four men made plans. Two of them huddled around a makeshift table in back, poring over mimeographed instructions and penciled notations.

"Can I help you?" a voice said. It was an officer eager to rid himself of intruders.

"No," I said, "just looking."

"This is a restricted area," he declared.

"Restricted to whom?"

"To police and press." Since I did not have a Los Angeles press card (Los Angeles does not issue temporary press cards to visiting journalists), he was not interested in my credentials as I stood there on the sidewalk looking at the Strip.

"I'd like to see a superior officer," I said. He pointed to his stripes. So I asked him what constituted unreasonable search.

Through clenched teeth he answered, "I don't interpret the laws; I just enforce 'em."

On Saturday, November 12, real disorder erupted in a throng of at least a thousand people along the Strip who were protesting police action and expressing their anger at being driven from their scene. Considering the intensity of feeling that prevailed, it is remarkable that so little violence or property damage occurred. An adult threw a coke bottle through a liquor store window. There were, according to the *Free Press* of November 18:

. . . a few fistfights between servicemen and Sunset Strip youth that took place at the beginning of the formation of the crowd, most provoked, I understand from eyewitnesses, by the servicemen. A few evaluations can be made. A total of not more than twenty or thirty persons were engaged in fighting or vandalism. There was not the wholesale rioting that the newspapers and mass media implied. The great majority of the teen-agers on the scene, at least one thousand by official count, were orderly and lawful, with the possible exception of creating a traffic jam by congregating in the streets.

But the traffic jam occasioned the only serious property damage—estimated at about $200, or roughly 5 per cent of that done later in the month by active, though clean-cut, university students protesting their football team's failure to get invited to the Rose Bowl—that has yet occurred on the Strip. Two Los Angeles city buses were stalled by traffic on Sunset Boulevard. According to eyewitnesses, TV crews moved in on them then and began shouting to the youths to climb onto the buses and wave their placards so that they could be seen. They did; and the passengers and drivers, understandably disturbed, abandoned the buses. The TV crewmen then began to shout to the kids, "You're not just going to stand there, are you? Do something!" and the youngsters began to rock the bus, scratch slogans on it, and ultimately to attempt—fortunately unsuccessfully—to set one of the empty buses on fire.

This, the most widely publicized incident that has occurred on the Strip, was, in fact, a psuedo-event, involving a small number of youths whose behavior was highly atypical of their fellows on the scene, and whose immaturity had been deliberately utilized by the mass media to create a dramatic incident. But psuedo or not, reaction to the event followed immediately. Police surveillance and harassment tightened. The County Board of Supervisors revoked the order permitting persons under twenty-one to dance in clubs where liquor was served to adults. The license of Pandora's Box, a coffee house owned and operated by former tennis star Bill Tilden, which catered entirely to teen-agers and young adults and had never served liquor, was canceled, and emergency action to condemn and demolish the building was begun, as part of a street realignment program that had been under way. The *Los Angeles Times* of November 30 reports the comments of City Councilman James B. Potter, Jr., who had moved the condemnation ordinance, on his visit to Pandora's Box the previous Saturday evening:

"I found the place (Pandora's Box) dirty and filthy," Potter said. "Businessmen were crying that their rights were not being observed by the mobs. He [the owner of Pandora's Box] made no effort to clear the people from his premises despite the fact that it caused a tremendous traffic problem.

"With all these people congregating there, it provided an explosive situation. It could have been very bad if somebody started something. "Luckily, nobody did."

Outside Pandora's Box on this Saturday evening, November 26, somebody had started something. The people whom Mr. Tilden made no effort to clear from his premises were mostly refugees, rather than customers, who had been driven into Pandora's Box by a police *battue* comparable to a medium-scale military operation. He himself was then arrested and his livelihood was destroyed; but he did not drive the youngsters from his property, which served them as a temporary haven. The scene on the Strip was confused, as the Los Angeles police moved up past Pandora's Box to the county line just west of it while sheriff's deputies swept Sunset Boulevard from the west. The November 28 *Los Angeles Times* reported that 150 Los Angeles policemen and 200 sheriff's deputies had arrested sixty young adults and seven juveniles in an operation that lasted from 9 P.M. till 1:30 Sunday morning; and that those arrested had been protesting "a crackdown on the use of the Strip by youths." It continued:

The baton-wielding deputies executed a new tactic in helping disperse the crowd of 1,500 persons, many of them curious passersby.

They invoked a county loitering ordinance against demonstrators who blocked sidewalks for more than 15 minutes and refused to move on. Previous tactics were to arrest juveniles for violation of the 10 P.M. curfew.

About 200 youths protested the loitering arrests, saying they violated their constitutional rights of peaceful assembly.

But the report broadcast from the scene at the time, by a reporter for Los Angeles radio station KPFK, though harder to follow, presented a less complacent picture. According to this, shortly before 10 P.M. sheriff's deputies cruising in sound trucks began warning juveniles to return home or face prosecution for curfew violation. Meanwhile, Los Angeles police had sealed off Sunset Boulevard at the east end of the Strip. Just after ten, the deputies began checking ID's; draft cards, driver's licenses, or a curious special document Los Angeles juveniles who have neither are required to carry. While official statements maintain that the "curfew" ordinance is not enforced selectively against individuals, observers agree that youngsters with long hair and colorful attire are invariably "busted" first; if there are enough of these to tax

the capacity of the operation the Law has mounted, less conspicuous youths may escape detection.

While the "juvies" were being rousted, and many of the
people on the Strip were crowding around the sheriff's sound
trucks to hear their orders, one side of Sunset Boulevard was
being sealed off, as the east end of the Strip already had been.
Then, over the sound trucks, the people were ordered to "disperse." In fact, they were not even permitted to cross Sunset
Boulevard at most points. Most could not return to their cars;
indeed, the area was so congested that many could not move at
all. Those who were lucky enough to find themselves caught in
front of the property of a sympathetic café-owner forced their
way inside and found sanctuary, as Councilman Potter complained.
But most, of course, did not; some found their way barred from
parking lots and the normally public courtyard of a local, privately supported art museum by armed guards. Some of those
who could not find a way out of the area were arrested for loitering in it; others who could not get across the street in the crowds
before the light changed at the few intersections where they were
allowed to try were arrested for jaywalking.

The Los Angeles *Free Press* for December 2—its first issue
after November 26—also presents a different picture of "the
baton-wielding deputies" referred to in the Los Angeles *Times:*

Suddenly, with no provocation, a mass of Deputies charged the pedes-
trians around the front of the Fifth Estate (a coffee house whose
manager has given his young clients their staunchest support, and
who has also produced a film called *Blue Fascism*, which does not
support his local police). People were viciously clubbed and beaten.
There was no plan or purpose evident in the beatings or the subsequent
arrests. It seemed the handiest people, with no regard given to age,
sex, or social position, were clubbed, kicked, punched and/or arrested.

This episode was witnessed by a large group of major news media
representatives. At the scene, these "working journalists" expressed
great indignation and concern over the behavior of the Sheriff's
Deputies. But their indignation was not conveyed to their audiences,
except in the case of unedited films shown on TV.

But three successive weekends of terror on the Strip had
begun to arouse the city. The American Civil Liberties Union had
sent observers—including, as has been noted, its local executive
director—to the Strip. An informal alliance of clergymen convened by the Reverend Ross Greek of the West Hollywood Pres-

byterian Church, which is located just east of the Strip on Sunset
Boulevard, began going out to stand with the youngsters, listen
to them—though the clergymen hardly understood their language
—and be present as witnesses to their encounters with the police.
Rather to the clergy's astonishment, the kids received them grate-
fully.

Ordinary citizens, and some not so ordinary, also began to
show their feelings. One of us (Bernhard) reported of the taxi
driver who drove him to the Strip early the following Saturday
evening, December 3:

He was the parent of some teenagers who apparently hung out on the
Strip quite often. He identified me immediately because of my hair
which though long is not terribly long and asked me if I was going
to be up on the Strip that night. I said I didn't know—I didn't know
whether anything was happening, and I asked him what he thought.
He said he thought that there wasn't going to be much happening that
night, but that he thought the police were being very unjust and were
taking away the rights of the kids. He wasn't quite sure what rights
were being usurped, but he seemed to feel that in some way the kids
were being gypped of something they deserved. He was speaking as a
parent, and he seemed to have some kind of emotional understanding
of the kids.

So did another parent, encountered on foot on the Strip much
later in the evening: a middle-aged, high-heeled woman with piles
of bleached-blond hair, who teetered valiantly ahead toward
where the action was, her breast thrust forward, partly in determination. "I have a boy along here somewhere," she confided.
"I'm not trying to find him; he'd die if he knew I was here at all.
But I have to see what they're doing to the kids!"

It is hard to say what the total experience is doing to the
kids who, in any case, are of course diverse in their response and
their character. But there is a characteristic air that many of them
seem to share, at least when you meet them on the Strip. There
is hardly any hostility towards adults—even towards the police.
One policeman on duty New Year's Eve in front of the now
derelict Pandora's Box stood looking at a group of "teeny-
boppers" who had nevertheless gathered as usual for a time on the
worn dirt lot in front of it. His face, for some reason, fell suddenly into a warm smile; and the kids at once began to greet
him with equally warm cries of "Happy New Year." But usually
they are neither friendly nor hostile; they are open, but wary,

like deer in a forest which they have learned to assume is dominated, though not exclusively inhabited, by predatory animals.
They are as I imagine Ariel would have become if Caliban had
come to reign instead of Prospero. He has; this is just what has
happened in Southern California, which, since last November's
elections, dominates the whole state and affects the university
system as well. And Caliban is not a very satisfactory embodiment
of lawful authority. As you walk along the Strip on a weekend
evening a sense of terror quietly develops. As it mounts, you
comfort yourself with the thought that comes naturally to anyone
who assumes that what he lives in is a community: if anybody
pushes you around, you can always call a cop. In a moment—
a bad moment—the fallacy of this reasoning comes to mind.
Thereafter, you keep an ear cocked as you stroll along chatting
with the kids, without quite realizing what you are listening for.
But it is a simple sign; when the sound of motorcycles drops, it
means that the police have dismounted and are going through
the crowd on foot, clubs in hand; you look around for friendly
private property.

> *There's somethin' happening here,*
> *What it is ain't exactly clear.*
> *There's a man with a gun over there*
> *A'tellin' me I got to beware—I think*
>   *it's time to*
> *—Stop! Children, What's that sound?*
> *Everybody look what's going down.*
> *There's battle lines being drawn*
> *nobody's right, if everybody's wrong*
> *Young people speaking their minds*
> *Are gettin' so much resistance from*
>   *behind. Families—*
> *Stop! Hey, what's that sound?*
> *Everybody look what's going down.*[1]

sings Stephen Stillis in "For What It's Worth": a poignant, un-
earthly song by The Buffalo Springfield.

Several of the ministers who walk the Strip to watch over the
kids are hardened veterans of the civil rights movement. No one
has been killed on the Strip, as Mr. Reeb was in Alabama; but
in one way the Strip is worse. In Selma, you could always tell

---

[1] Words and music by S. Stillis. © Copyright 1966, Cotillion Music,
Inc., Ten-East Music & Springalo Music. Used by permission.

yourself that things were better at home; but Los Angeles is home. Alabama, one assumes, is the product of a benighted, segregated social system. But Los Angeles is American democracy in action.

American democracy in action has its own process of healing and reconstruction, and some of these are at work along the Strip. Al Mitchell, manager of the Fifth Estate, has organized and is chairman of a militant committee called RAMCOM—Right of Assembly and Movement Committee—to hold demonstrations and inform the public that the youngsters on the Strip are not hoodlums, but fellow citizens whose rights are in jeopardy. RAMCOM, however, has been rather quickly outstripped by the more moderate and much better financed committee called CAFF—Community Action for Facts and Freedom—chaired by Jim Dickson, manager of the Byrds. Fred Rosenberg, owner of The Marquis and president of the Sunset Strip Restaurant Association, has issued conciliatory statements. Members of all three groups have met together under the sponsorship of the Los Angeles County Delinquency and Crime Commission, to implement a truce initiated, rather uncertainly, by RAMCOM, which covered the holiday period when much larger numbers of youngsters than usual might have been on the Strip, heightening the probability of disorder; but also heightening their chances of victory.

The truce was largely successful: there was not much action of any kind on the Strip over the holidays. But the prognosis is not good; disorder may have been averted, but that, it appears, could have been accomplished merely by restraining police action in the first place. And the chances of greater freedom and dignity for the Strippies, which is the major issue, look bad. The meetings held by the Delinquency and Crime Commission were closed. Even the decision to refer the matter to a Commission on Crime and Delinquency rather than to the Human Relations Commission, which was likewise available, prejudices the case against the youngsters. The action of the County Board of Supervisors in toughening the loitering law while the truce was in effect violates the spirit of the truce, which, in any case, has now expired. RAMCOM is planning more demonstrations and not just on the Strip; for the youngsters have been talking about spreading out and moving on into the nearby San Fernando Valley, where the whole cycle will probably begin again with fresh protagonists. Similar events, though on a smaller scale, have been going on around Greater Los Angeles all the while, anyway.

Things will surely get worse unless California develops a system of authority that does more than demand obedience—that commands respect. And it probably won't: the potential just doesn't seem to be present in the culture. Concrete proposals tend to run the other way. A local paper that serves the West Hollywood area has been urging that the district be incorporated, so that it could have its own police who would not be subject to the restraints bureaucracy imposes on the Los Angeles city and county officials and could really rough the kids up; one issue proposed that they be shot down with machine guns. One tends to dismiss this sort of thing as psycho-ceramic nonsense; but at the heart of Governor Reagan's current legislative package is a bill which would rescind existing legislation that forbids any local jurisdiction from imposing more severe penalties for any offense than those provided under state law. The stated purpose of the Governor's bill is precisely to strengthen the hand of local authorities to deal with what they regard as specially severe local problems. No comparable protection for individuals who become the objects of law enforcement is contemplated; though it seems clear that those who become the special focus of police concern sometimes need it; and not only the Strippies. A bartender who was arrested during a raid on his bar by plain-clothes members of the Los Angeles vice squad just after the stroke of New Year's and subsequently booked was so badly injured in the process that he has since died, thus avoiding the necessity of defending himself against the felony charge of assaulting an officer. Mr. Reagan has made his determination to clean up Berkeley and, presumably, the rest of the state clear; but in his own New Year's inaugural statement he also stated that he intended to conduct the affairs of the state as nearly as possible as the Prince of Peace might have done it. Yet the Prince of Peace was sometimes obliged to make professional visits among the despised and rejected of society; and on these occasions He behaved rather differently from the vice squad.

Yet it would be misleading to consider that the present social climate in California affects only the young, the deviant, and those otherwise helpless. What is operative on our scene is a basic disrespect for human dignity, and a capricious and petulant use of power, which cannot be tolerated in any society that hopes to be democratic. Historically, we have taken simultaneous appearance of gross abuses of minorities and gross instability of status to be the very signs of fascism, whether Western or Stalinist.

These social symptoms, when they occur together, transcend in their tragic significance the human weaknesses and possibly confused motives of the individuals involved in them. That the president of the largest university in the world, which lays claim to greatness, should be dismissed after fifteen years of service in that office and previously as chancellor of the Berkeley Campus, without regard to his intellectual distinction, administrative ability, or virtually unquestioning devotion to the policies set down by the Regents is incredible. But that he should be kicked out without so much as a day's notice, without consultation with any member of the university community, whether administrator, faculty member, or student, violates not only his rights and ours, but the very idea of social structure itself, quite apart from the question of Clark Kerr's enormous strengths and few—though occasionally serious—weaknesses.

We are no society here; we are here, as on a darkling plain, swept by confused alarms of struggle and flight. Arnold applies; but the idiom of The Buffalo Springfield is sharper and clearer:

> *Paranoia strikes deep*
> *Into your life it will creep*
> *It starts when you're always afraid*
> *Step out of line, The Man come and*
> *take you away You better—*
> *Stop! Hey, what's that sound?*
> *Everybody look what's going down.*

CHAPTER IV

❧

LIFE STYLES

"I should be surprised if mysticism did not soon make some advance among a people solely engaged in promoting their own welfare. It is said that the deserts of Thebaid were peopled by the persecutions of the Emperors and the massacres of the Circus; I should rather say that it was by the luxuries of Rome and the Epicurean philosophy of Greece."

Alexis de Tocqueville

California: Mecca of the Miraculous*

CAREY MC WILLIAMS

CALIFORNIA PROPHETS, like its geraniums, grow large, rank, and garish. In this state where imported llamas browse on the hillsides near San Simeon, where oranges are sold in Chinese pagodas, and bootblacks, such as the Duke of Hollywood, wear top hats and crimson capes, eccentrics flourish in abundance. Strange influences, occult and psychic, esoteric and mundane, undeniably, are at work. What are these cults that to many are the state's most amazing characteristic? What forms and shapes emerge from the smoke of dreams, the cloudy occultism of California?

None quite compares, in charm and wonder, with Mighty "I AM." A weird brew of Theosophy, Rosicrucianism, New Thought, Buck Rogers, and Superman, the "I AM" ideology—the quotes must *always* be placed around the title—was dreamed up by Guy W. Ballard and his wife, Edna. After a career as paper hanger, stock salesman, and mine promoter, Ballard came to Los Angeles around 1932. Two years later he published under the nom de plume of Godfrey Ray King, a work entitled *Unveiled Mysteries*.

The deity of the cult is the Ascended Master, Saint Germain. As Ballard tells the story, he first met Saint Germain (the "Saint" must *never* be abbreviated) on the slopes of Mount Shasta. Appearing out of the void, Saint Germain offered Ballard a cup of "pure electronic essence." On drinking the essence and chewing

---

* From *Holiday* (January, 1947). Used by permission of the author.

279

a tiny wafer of "concentrated energy," Ballard was enveloped by a "white flame which formed a circle about fifty feet in diameter." Lifted into the stratosphere, Ballard and Saint Germain were whizzed through time and space, visiting, among other places, the buried cities of the Amazon, France, Egypt, Karnak, Luxor, the fabled Inca cities, the Royal Tetons, and Yellowstone National Park. Wherever they journeyed, they found an abundance of the treasure that, as a mine promoter, Ballard had never succeeded in discovering: jewels, Spanish pirate gold, rubies, pearls, diamonds, gold bullion, casks of silver—the plunder of antiquity. Unbelievable as it may sound, this revelation, at $2.50 a copy, sold by the thousands in Southern California. The Ballards were soon ensconced in a great barnlike tabernacle where a blazing neon light flashed word of the Mighty "I AM" presence.

Then the Ballards added to their merchandise: a monthly magazine; books; photographs of Ballard, The Messenger; phonograph recordings of the "music of the spheres," composed by Ballard; lectures; charts of the "Magic Presence" for twelve dollars; a steel engraving of the "Cosmic Being, Orion, better known as the Old Man of the Hills," for two dollars; special "I AM" decree binders; "I AM" signet rings (twelve dollars); a special electrical device, equipped with colored lights, called "Flame in Action" which sold, in varying sizes, for fifty dollars and two hundred dollars. Finally, there appeared a "New Age Cold Cream."

After the death of Ballard, his wife was indicted and convicted in the federal courts of using the mails to defraud. . . . A federal audit revealed that over $3,000,000 had been collected in sales, contributions, and "love offerings." From its beginnings in Los Angeles, the movement spread to Chicago, New York, Salt Lake City, Fort Worth, and Dallas, with an estimated 350,000 converts.

Wishing Makes It So

At the trial it was testified that Mrs. Ballard's late husband, with the aid of K-17, one of the Ascended Masters, had providentially sunk three submarines which Adolf Hitler had dispatched to blow up the Panama Canal. Well groomed, heavily veiled ladies took the stand and confessed their breathless belief in the doctrine of "precipitation"—meaning that if you concentrate hard enough on anything you want, a jewel, an automobile, or an orchid, you can precipitate it.

For months before his death, Ballard had warned his followers that Los Angeles would be destroyed on February 29, 1936. Veteran victims of California earthquakes shuddered and besought The Messenger to intervene with Saint Germain, who, at the zero hour, obligingly averted the catastrophe. A bulletin of the cult contained this terse communiqué: "The inner work of Mr. Ballard's Ascension was completed in Honolulu in 1936, but his Etheric Body did not withdraw until December 29, 1939." Apparently Ballard had been a zombie for three years.

One might think that conviction in the federal courts would have worked some diminution in Southern California's powerful will-to-believe, but the movement actually gained strength by the "crucifixion" of Mrs. Ballard, known in the cult as Joan of Arc, Chanera, Jesus, and Saint Germain. A recent visit to the "I AM" Sanctuary at 1320 S. Hope Street, Los Angeles, convinced me that the Ascendent Master is still doing all right. Classes are conducted from 7 A.M. to midnight every day. One must have first read and approved volume one of the volumes dictated to Ballard by Saint Germain before one can be enrolled in the freshman course.

In the Sanctuary's Temple of Music, recordings of "the music of the spheres" have been played without interruption, for twenty-four hours a day, since June 30, 1945. No word has ever been spoken in the Temple, to which only initiates are admitted. During my interview with a representative of The Messenger, the walls vibrated to the chant of a class in a nearby room. For the "adorations," "affirmations," and "decrees" of the cult are chanted in unison, repeated over and over again, rising to an almost intolerable shrillness and vehemence as the initiates demand radios, automobiles, perfumes, and pressure-cookers of Saint Germain.

Great stress is placed in the "I AM" cult on color vibrations. Followers will not wear red or black, or have these colors in their homes. For black is symbolic of Night, Darkness, and Death; while red signifies Blood, Danger (as witness the red "stop signs" in traffic), and Destruction. Science has even proved, I was informed, that the color has been known to drive people crazy. The only red tolerated in the cult is that of the American flag.

Like so many other California cults, the "I AM" folk are strict vegetarians. Sex, except for procreation, is rigidly proscribed.

Explaining this taboo, my informant pointed to the increasing divorce rate and blithely stated: "Everyone knows that ninety per cent of the divorces are due to the indulgence in sex as a pleasure." Essential to their ideology is the concept of a layer of atmosphere above the earth charged with the evil emanations of mankind. This layer must be "blasted," "exorcised," "lifted" by the magic "I AM" presence. Great stress is placed on words such as "riches," "power," and "jewels"—symbols of wealth and energy. "Blasted" is a key word. Obstructions to the will of the individual must be blasted by the dynamic energy of Saint Germain's "magic Purple ray" and the "atomic accelerator." Almost pure Buck Rogers, "I AM" is, perhaps, the first cult of the atomic age.

En route from San Francisco to Los Angeles, the curious traveler can make the acquaintance of any number of bizarre wayside prophets and hot-dog-stand savants. On the highway between Santa Cruz and San Jose is Holy City, where "Father" W. E. Riker, perennial candidate for governor, "The Wise Man of the West," presides over "the world's most perfect government." Holy City itself consists of a restaurant, a post office, a print shop, and Riker's headquarters over which appears the sign: HOLY CITY—INFORMATION BOOTH—ALL MYSTERIES ANSWERED. Along the highway, Holy City is advertised by signs reading: "If you are contemplating marriage, suicide, or crime see us first," and "Dispel the idea that you are different than God or the other fellow when sifted down."

The magnum opus of "Father" Riker, a former showman and circus barker from the Middle West, is a book called *The Perfect Government,* written in question-and-answer form. Thus: "Question: When was this philosophy established? Answer: In 1908, prior to the great Halley's comet. Question: Are any of your people married? Answer: They are all married to Wisdom." Riker is a typical California prophet in at least three respects: his lack of modesty, his vigorous self-assertion, and his violent rhetoric. As Conrad Aiken once observed, there is about the state "that somewhat specious and stagy largeness which California so impartially visits upon trees, fruits, and prophets alike."

Down the coast, in Atascadero, lives William Kullgren, publisher of *The Beacon Light,* food faddist, and astrologer.

Kullgren, who bitterly opposes sex, smoking, and drinking, asserts that individuals can attain real insight into the mysteries of the cosmos only by the regular intake of his specially prepared foods: the dry herb Kamba; Papaya Tablets; Kelp-Carbon Tablets; Vegex; Alfalfa; Lemon Juice Powder; Kol-N-Zyme; Beet Root Powder; and, above all, raw kelp.

From various "lunations" which he has worked out, Kullgren is convinced that Southern California awaits destruction. Kullgrenites are advised to purchase trailers and stake out possible retreats which should be located at elevations of not less than two thousand, nor more than three thousand feet. "You may think I am crazy," warns the prophet of Atascadero, "but my responsibility ends when I warn you of what I know will come. The religion of the old Piscean Age is crumbling." In a land haunted by fear of earthquakes, such Jeremiahs of the highway can't fail to attract a following.

Where Stars Are Shy

It is one of the paradoxes of Los Angeles that here, where it is almost as difficult to see the stars as it is to see the sun in Pittsburgh, should be located the international headquarters of astrology. For most of the year, the stars are lost in the soft mist of the night skies. Yet crystal-ball gazers, horoscope readers, and other magicians specializing in predicting the future have long flourished. Perhaps the at-times-uncertain future of Southern California has contributed to their prevalence. To be assured that Southern California did have a future—even by an astrologer— must have been comforting. The practice reached such peaks of extravagance that, some years ago, the city of Los Angeles adopted an ordinance making the prediction of the future for a fee a misdemeanor.

Astrology, one of the oldest of the arts, was thus compelled to go underground. But the itch to know the message of the stars did not abate; it became more prevalent. In December, 1945, Mrs. Colby Griffin, formerly secretary of the American Federation of Astrologers, was arrested in Los Angeles, convicted, and fined $100. At her trial, the courtroom was packed with anxious astrologers. Hope ran high that Judge James Pope would hold the ordinance unconstitutional, but it was dashed when word spread that Judge Pope was a Virgo. The three appellate judges who heard the appeal must also have been born under the sign of Virgo, for, in July, 1946, the conviction was sustained and the ordinance upheld.

For practicing astrologers in Los Angeles the motion-picture colony, as one investigator has pointed out, offers "richer diggings than the forty-niners ever found in the Mother Lode." Actors are notoriously superstitious folk, forever jittery about the future. Such stars as Maria Montez and Alan Hale have no hesitancy in expressing their reliance upon astrology. Miss Montez refuses to appear at the studios on days when the signs are not propitious, while Mr. Hale ascribes the success of his marriage of thirty-three years largely to astrological forecasts. It is not at all uncommon for an actor to pay $500 for a single "delineation." Some have contracts with astrologers for the preparation of regular monthly forecasts. One such horoscope that I saw gave the following intimations for a Thursday: "Good for publicity, advertising, business matters, dealings with relatives, especially brothers and sisters, and for all Arian types of interest. Make Hay while the Sun Shines these Beautiful May Days."

Among the favorite teachers of astrology in Hollywood is Mrs. Blanca Gabriella Holmes, wife of Stuart Holmes, star of the silent films. The Holmeses live in a house that once served as headquarters for the Theosophy Society, indicating the curious overlapping of cultic influences in Southern California. Another Hollywood wizard is Carroll R. B. Righter, who calls people by their birthday instead of their name. "Hello, June 18," he will cheerily greet a friend.

Los Angeles is also the headquarters of Llewellyn George, "the dean of American astrologers," who publishes the *Astrologers* as well as the *Astrological Bulletina*. George plants flowers and vegetables in his garden in accordance with a horoscopic schedule: "Vegetables bearing below the ground when the moon is tipped downwards, those bearing above the ground when the crescent of the moon is slanted upwards."

High Priestess of Astrology

The First Temple and College of Astrology, at 736 S. Burlington Street, Los Angeles, founded by James Keifer, an osteopath, has been in operation for thirty-nine years. Presided over by Mrs. Harriet K. Banes and a faculty of eight ebullient ladies, the First Temple offers courses in Ancient and Modern Astrologers, Scientific Embryology Applied to Pre-Natal Astrology, Mundane Astrology, and Horary Astrology.

Californians show chronic interest in cults based upon some phase of sun worship. The oldest is the Mazdaznan cult, which has its international headquarters at 1159 S. Norton Street, Los Angeles. Based on the "ancient Parsee Sun-Worship teachings of Mazda," or Zend-Avesta, this cult was brought to California some thirty years ago by Dr. Otoman Adusht Ha'nish. When I first made the acquaintance of Doctor Ha'nish, he was leading his followers in a chant which went something as follows:

> *I am all in One individually and one in All*
> *collectively;*
> *I am present individually and omnipresent*
> *collectively;*
> *I am knowing individually and omniscient*
> *collectively;*
> *I am potent individually and omnipotent*
> *collectively;*
> *I am Mazdaznan and recognize the Eternal*
> *Designs of Humata, Huhata, Hu-varashta*
> *A-shem, Vo-hu, A-shem, Vo-hu, A-shem, Vo-hu.*

Doctor Ha'nish passed away in 1936, and was succeeded in the role of high priest by Gloria Maude Gasque. Mother Gloria, as she is known in Mazdaznan circles, appears at meetings in a priestly creamcolored silk gown with knotted girdle. Strict vegetarians, the Mazdaznans are in revolt against Angro Mainyus or the spirit of Evil. Flesh-eating destroys the purity of the blood; smoking pollutes the Breath of God; while alcohol interferes with "the Glandular activity upon which the Infinite Intelligence Depends." Man is possessed of extra senses: Transmillion, Telepathy, Spiritual Discernment, Clearsight, and Realization. The elaborate declaration of principles requires an intensity of concentration which, frankly, I have never been able to devote to it. One runs across such passages as the following: "Keeping abreast with the Spirit of the Times, Mazdaznan remains conscious of lumonism, unitism, dualism, trinitism, panism, and polyism, as revealed in the macrocosm and microcosm of the Infinite and Finite, completely over blending but never ending."

Rosicrucianism has always been a fountainhead of the esoteric. The Rosicrucian dispensation, which numbered such occultists as Marie Corelli and Bulwer-Lytton among its European adherents, was brought to California around October, 1911, when its prophet, Max Heindel, established the colony of Oceanside, between Los Angeles and San Diego. It is a beautiful fifty-acre tract, with a vegetarian cafeteria, a temple of healing with murals of the zodiac, a chapel, and a dozen or so cottages for the residents. This branch of the Order of the Rose Cross is devoutly vegetarian, astrological, and esoteric. It believes with Goethe's Mephisto that "blood is a juice of a very special kind." Its magazine, *Rays From the Rose Cross,* offers horoscopes, articles on diet, and learned treatises on the curative power of precious gems. Thus the emerald is a laxative; amber, being highly magnetic, is good for asthma; and red coral, if worn about the body, will eliminate stomach disorders.

This group, which calls itself a fraternal order rather than a cult, claims to have anticipated the atomic bomb in its teachings. When the sun, by reason of the procession of the equinoxes, shall have entered the Sign of Aquarius, the Slavic race will become dominant; but the seventh and final race of the Aryan Epoch will arise in the United States, presumably in Southern California.

The Rosicrucians, like most Californian cults and fraternal orders, are divided into northern and southern branches. The Heindelian sect is highly concentrated in the south, while the Amorc sect has its headquarters in San Jose—AMORC being Ancient and Mystical Order Rosae Crucis. The Amorcs are strictly Egyptian in ritual and symbolism; the Heindelians more on the Anglo-American pattern. Visitors who have traveled along the famous El Camino Real (Highway 101) have doubtless been inspired at the sight of the Amorc headquarters, an impressive upsurge of pure Egyptian architecture in the mocking sunlight of California.

All manner of esoteric outcroppings may be found in the great white sand dunes of Pismo Beach and Oceano—long a favorite hideaway for mystics, occultists, new religionists, poets, and vegetarians. In Pismo Beach is published *The American Vegetarian,* which contains the highly diverting advertisements of the Carey–Perry School of the Chemistry of Life (Hollywood); the Essene School of Life, which sponsors an annual Biochemical Grape-Cure at Tecate; and the Lemurian Ambassador. Never be surprised at what you find in the dunes of Oceano.

Beautiful, sun-drenched Ojai Valley, near Santa Barbara, is the center of Theosophical speculation. Driven from Hollywood by the encroachment of motion pictures and big business, Albert Powell Warrington brought the remnants of his Krotona Colony to Ojai in 1920. It is also the home of Edgar Holloway, termed the Man from Lemuria, who declares that he flew into the valley some years ago in a great flying fish. The beginning of Ojai, however, dates from the publication of an article in the early 20's, by Dr. Ales Krdlicka, the anthropologist, predicting the evolution of a new sixth subrace in California. Prompted by this revelation, Annie Besant came to California and purchased a 465-acre tract in Ojai Valley as a home for Jiddu Krishnamurti, "the vehicle of the New World Teacher, the Lord Maitreya," whose last incarnation, so we are informed, was in the person of Jesus Christ.

Retires From Messiahship

In 1929 [Jiddu Krishnamurti] renounced the messiahship at a great meeting in Hollywood Bowl. But, prior to this renunciation, the annual encampments of the faithful brought thousands of visitors. One can't be in Ojai Valley for ten minutes without becoming conscious that the whole region is alive with cultic vibrations. Robust ladies, in flat-heeled shoes, scurry about with an air of deep metaphysical involvement; while young men, with lilac manners, hold high discourse on things unseen.

Currently Vedanta is making the greatest stir in Southern California. While it is, perhaps, unfair to call Vedanta a cult, there are cultic implications against the background of present-day Hollywood. An outgrowth of the Ramakrishna Mission founded by Sri Ramkrishna (1836–86), Vedanta is based upon the Veda scrolls, the oldest religious teachings. The first swami or monk of the Ramarkrishna Mission to reach America was Swami Vivekananda, who in 1893 attended a religious conference at the Chicago World's Fair. The present high priest of Vedanta, Swami Prabhavananda, followed him to California in 1923. With unerring insight, he concluded that Hollywood should be the center of Vedanta in America, and established it there in 1929.

At first the Vedanta Society made its headquarters in the home of Mrs. C. M. Wyckoff, now eighty-six, a woman of considerable wealth, but the meetings are now held in a $12,000 alabaster replica of the Taj Mahal, at 1946 Ivar Street. Lectures are given every Sunday morning and a class is held every Thursday evening. The interior walls of the temple are painted a dull gray-green and are adorned with pictures of Krishna, Jesus, Buddha, and Confucius. The services open with Swami Prabhavananda slowly walking into the temple in a long, bright yellow robe—the robe of renunciation. Sitting cross-legged on a raised portion of the temple floor, near a shrine brought from India, with a gray shawl over his shoulders the swami meditates in silence for ten or fifteen minutes. Then he chants an invocation in Sanskrit concluding on the words "Peace, peace, peace," gives a lecture on some phase of Vedanta, takes questions from the audience.

Extremely interesting philosophically, the Vedanta creed has won a number of famous disciples. In 1938, Gerald Heard, the British Diogenes, author of such works as *Pain, Sex and Time,* and *The Ascent of Humanity,* came to live in Los Angeles after a period of tutelage in Quaker mysticism in Pennsylvania. He had heard of Swami Prabhavananda in London. After a year of tutoring with the swami, Heard became a disciple of Vedanta and, in turn, induced Aldous Huxley to take up residence in Southern California. Mr. Huxley's initial impressions are to be found in his novel, *After Many a Summer Dies the Swan* (1939), in which Heard appears as the character Propter. Soon Huxley was also a bona fide disciple. Their presence then attracted the brilliant young English writer, Christopher Isherwood, author of *Prater Violet, The Last of Mr. Morris, Berlin Stories.*

No Living Without It

Near the strange temple on Ivar Street is a monastery in which Swami Prabhavananda resides with four or five male disciples. For some time, Isherwood lived here; in fact, it was only recently that he decided not to become a Vedanta swami. He has conducted services in the temple, participated in its ritual, and writes regularly for its magazine. "I cannot imagine living without Vedanta," he is quoted as having said. The society has issued a book called *Vedanta for the Western World,* with contributions by Heard, Huxley, Isherwood, and John van Druten, the playwright. Naturally, the conversion of such sophisticates has given Vedanta a special fillip among the cults of California.

For a time, a main item of gossip in Hollywood was whether Isherwood was the original for the central character in Somerset Maugham's novel, *The Razor's Edge.* Maugham did come to Hollywood to consult Swami Prabhavananda before writing it.

Membership in the Vedanta Society is highly heterogeneous. There are about 115 members at present, including two doctors, a restaurant owner, an architect, four college professors, a banker, and, curiously enough, two Protestant clergymen: a Presbyterian and a Congregationalist. In Mrs. Wyckoff's home the society maintains a school for novitiates who hope to become nuns (present enrollment five). They lead a semicommunal existence, sharing income, eschewing beef in deference to the Sacred Cow of India, and following a severe regimen of meditation, prayer, and study.

The income for this establishment is largely derived from an orange grove near Whittier, which, together with a $250,000 trust fund, was bequeathed the society by the late Spencer Kellogg, Jr., a manufacturer of linseed oil. Swami Prabhavananda himself has an income left by Kellogg. The swami frankly states that "it is, indeed, a goodly sum."

It is to be doubted that Vedanta will ever kindle fires in the angry eyes of Los Angeles' spiritually dispossessed. Its creed is essentially too civilized and urbane for the restive hordes, raised in the belief that some must necessarily be damned; that, without the damned, there could be no elect.

More attractive to Angelinos was the evangelism of Aimee Semple McPherson. Beside Echo Park Lake in Los Angeles stands a twin memorial to her genius for showmanship—Angelus Temple and its elegant parsonage. She arrived in Los Angeles in the early 20's with a broken-down car, $100 in cash, and two children to support. By 1925 she was the most famous women evangelist in the English-speaking world.

Her Four Square Gospel sect achieved a following of thirty thousand devoted adherents whose love for her survived every shock that her capricious behavior imposed upon their credulity. Since the death of Mrs. McPherson in 1945—from an overdose of sleeping tablets—Angelus Temple is merely another church, but there was a time when it was a church-in-a-circus. The antics of Aimee will survive for years in the folklore of the region.

Following the destruction of Hiroshima by an atomic bomb, Southern California experienced a remarkable outcropping of cosmic-ray cults. In the autumn of 1945, thousands of invalids flocked to the Cosmic Research Laboratories in Long Beach operated by Roy Beebe. Several thousand Southern Californians claim to have been cured of a wide variety of ailments, pains, wheezes, and sniffles by Beebe's controlled cosmic ray. During the height of the hegira, the Pacific Electric lines had to add more buses. Each day hundreds of pilgrims sat in the backyard of Beebe's establishment, exposing themselves to the ray which emanated from a "cosmic box" he had rigged up in his laboratory, or consuming slight portions of wheat meal hopped up with cosmic rays.

Mr. Beebe first discovered "the cosmic" while doing research on Halley's Comet in the Arkansas Ozarks back in 1902. "In 1912," he says, "I succeeded in getting it under control where I could emit it out to the good of humanity. I been usin' it ever since."

Not Here to Stay?

Something about Southern California certainly seems to lend an air of verity to its prophets of doom. Perhaps it is the quality, noted by J. B. Priestley, of "a sinister suggestion of transience," of impermanence. In the folklore of the region, this seems to be linked with theories of oil-well depletion and water supply exhaustion; and, of course, with earthquakes. In no other area are visions of doom so quickly seized upon, so rapidly and fearfully accepted.

Various Southern California cultists in recent years have proclaimed themselves the Messiah. The most flamboyant is unquestionably Dr. Joe Jeffers. A guest of the Nazis in Berlin in 1938, Jeffers is a violent anti-Semite and Catholic-baiter. Right now Jeffers is whipping audiences of two thousand people into a lather of excitement over the impending total destruction of Los Angeles by the greatest earthquake of all time. Shouting at them to fast, to prepare for the end, he urges them to sell their earthly belongings, and to give him the proceeds so that a Zion may be established while there is still time. The only hope of salvation seems to lie in a great floating land mass which is rising off the coast.

It was on December 25, 1875, according to prophet Arthur Bell, that a group of men held a secret meeting at which Mankind United was formed. From 1875 to 1919, these men spent exactly $60,000,000 on research into the causes of war and poverty, disease and crime. And by 1934, Bell, known also as "The Voice," was able to publish a remarkable book outlining the nature of the plan of salvation. The program is revealed in the cryptic slogan 4-4-8-3-4—four hours work a day, four days a week, eight months a year, for an annual wage of not less than $3000 for each adult, with four months annual vacation. When precisely two hundred million people have subscribed to this formula, the plan will be put into effect. Then the Universal Service Corporation will be able to provide an annual income of $30,000 for every member, and a $25,000 home with radio-automatic vocal-type correspondence equipment; automatic news and telephone recording service, air-conditioning, fruit trees, vegetable gardens, hothouses, athletic courts, swimming pools, and sundry other appurtenances. Members will speak an international language and travel free to any part of the globe. In one year alone, Bell received $97,500 from the sale of this new bible of Mankind United.

On May 6, 1943, "The Voice" and some of his associates were convicted of sedition in the federal courts. While the case was on appeal, Bell formed Christ's Church of the Golden Rule to carry on the program of Mankind United. According to the attorney general of California, Robert W. Kenny, Bell had collected by March 1, 1944, in love offerings, gifts, sales, and donations, a sum in excess of $2,500,000. When Kenny brought suit to revoke the church's charter, he discovered it owned and operated several office buildings, stores, large hotels, three swanky beach clubs, and a beautiful estate near Burlingame, equipped with sliding panels, secret doors, and other paraphernalia of a house of mystery. Numbers of people had been induced to surrender their worldly belongings to the church and work on its properties for a nonutopian wage. No one knows how many people joined Mankind United between 1934 and 1946, but the attorney general, in his complaint, estimates 250,000.

I don't know what it is about California that stimulates this desperate quest of Utopia. Emma Harding, who wrote a history of spiritualism, concluded that cults thrive on the Pacific Coast because of the wonderful transparency of the air, the heavy charges of mineral magnetism from the gold mines which set up favorable vibrations, and the still-living passions of the forty-niners which create "emanations."

Sociologically they are to be explained as phenomena of migration. Two out of every three citizens of California were born outside the state. Migration severs old ties, undermines ancient allegiances. It creates the social fluidity out of which new cultic movements arise. But migration does not provide the complete answer.

In part the cults of California, with their emphasis on sun worship, vegetarianism, and apocalyptic visions of an ever-impending doom, are an oblique response to the physical environment. Social panaceas flourish in this empire of prodigious crops, Brobdingnagian vegetables, and rose bushes with 200,000 blossoms, because here natural abundance stimulates dreams of plenty. Since 1875—when the mystic Thomas Lake Harris established the Brotherhood of the New Light colony at Santa Rosa—California has pulsed with vibrations of the other-worldly and trembled under prophecies of doom. It is a land of Visions, Dreams, Exaltations, and New Harmonies, this beautiful, sensuous Land of Mu by the Western Sea.

The Beats*

WILSON CAREY MC WILLIAMS

October, 1958

THE "BEAT GENERATION" has managed to stay news. In fact, it has been the subject of so much comment as to fall into the category of tiresome phenomena. Yet somehow, for someone, it must continue to be interesting, and that interest may be as important as the B. G. itself.

The most recent wave of interest began with the belated discovery of the "beats" by the San Francisco *Chronicle,* which ran a Sunday feature "Life and Love among the Beatniks," supercilious, amused, and thoroughly urbane. The *Chronicle's* rival, the Hearst-owned *Examiner* does not take being scooped on its own ground lying down, and the *Chronicle* story inspired a war of sensational stories featuring beatnik crime. The B.G., it appeared, were ghastly and newsworthy: sculptors were falling off roofs; marijuana ripened everywhere; girls were having their throats slit when they were not suffering the fate worse than death.

The sequel was inevitable. Letters to the Editor appeared urging the beats to return to the Slavic land from which they had doubtless come, and various less literate variations on the theme. The San Francisco police, feeling a challenge, stationed cars in North Beach and patrolmen became ubiquitous. The B.G. patriarch, Eric Nord, was pursued with charges of writing bad checks,

---

* Used by permission of the author.

corrupting young women, and failing to pay parking fines. San Francisco's moral leaders among the clergy made their own contribution. Anglicans traced it to the moral decay of the West and suggested that beat poets give due attention to the works of T. S. Eliot. The Presbyterians, whose theological affinity for the beatniks is somewhat greater, have considered opening their own North Beach coffee house. Billy Graham weighed delivering his evangel in North Beach but his advance reconnaissance team decided, after studying Grant Avenue, that the whole affair was beyond anyone's power save, perhaps, the Most High himself.

The B.G. are not without resources. They toured "squareville" making quotable comments and slapping bartenders with roses, while the Co-existence Bagel Shop posted the warning "Pressnikism go home!" Co-existence is not dead, however; on their tour of downtown San Francisco the beats tried to arrange a "symbolic exchange" of bagels with a delicatessen owner.

The upshot is that prosperity has come to Grant Avenue. Financially, if not culturally, the beats have made it. Tourists stream in to be treated to the sight of B.G. members haranguing police on the subject of persecution while those defenders of law attempt a not very successful pose of objectivity. Meanwhile, the sandal shops do business and the talk of the coffee houses drones on. Yet despite its cartoon-like quality, the war of Grant Avenue is putting people in jail, and amusement cannot be allowed to blank out the realization that something is wrong.

The philosophy of the beats is adolescent, consisting in the discovery that man is mortal and proceeding from this scarcely astonishing proposition to the assertion that life is futile. Intermediate steps of logic are not felt necessary; the truth is felt to be self-evident.

In fact, there is nothing new about the B.G. They are a return to Lutheranism, nay, to even more ancient traditions, the pillar saints and the flagellants. For all of these, there is an irrevocable tension between the yearning vision of the mind and the corrupt, fleshly mortality of the world that can be overcome only by eschewing its delights. The old religious asceticism shows through the modern rhetoric: beats clothe themselves in black; live on diets near the level of starvation, and produce well-known voices and visions; avoid feeding the lusts of the flesh by washing, shaving, or other vanities; reject the pursuit of filthy lucre (except that which may be gathered in *by* a principled rejection). Even beatnik sexuality has been conquered by "coolness": it is calm, indifferent, principled, the antithesis of sensuality.

It is also true that the B.G. are part of the hobo-as-hero school of American letters, itself a reflection of other-worldly asceticism. Indeed, like such earlier on-the-bum movements, the beats have produced some significant writing although their general output has revealed little more than an unparalleled talent for plagiarizing the writings of Henry Miller. A few devoted types caught in the contradictions of heresy aside, most B.G. members reject such futile pursuits as writing and painting in favor of less energy consuming and less futile activities.

But the Beat Generation has even more curious analogues. Alexander Herzen wrote of Russian youth in the age of Nicholas I:

> Rampant vanity was combined with a sort of hopelessness, a consciousness of impotence, a weary disinclination to work. Young people became suspicious, worn out, before they were twenty. All were affected with the passion for self-observation, self-examination, self-accusation.

Yet Herzen knew this was the result of the Tsarist police state, of energies denied political expression and become inverted. So too with the beats, who are one with the Silent Generation of respectable suburbia.

Both find politics immovable and incomprehensible; both stress not rocking the boat. Strangely, the organization man is most appealing in contrast to the beats, for his unthinking routines are at least life-affirming though the result comes more from intellectual sloth than from design. The passion for death underlies much of our civilization: the Silent Generation remains silent, mentally passive, because it fears as much; the Beat Generation has merely carried its fears into practice. The two generations are symbiotes, part of a human ecology: if nature produces a mass of selfless production engineers, she balances with enough nonproducing consumers to make some dent on the surplus.

The very commonplaceness of B.G. bohemianism, the classic quality of its left-bankishness, is the greatest source of its appeal. Of course, respectability must be shocked: that is part of the game, part of the delight. No secret titillation without public outrage: the logic is as old as society itself.

The beats are, after all, a "proof" to the respectable that social problems can be conceived in the same old terms. If one must have rebels, better that they should be of the safely conservative variety, fitting accepted categories of thought and posing no menace in action to the established order of things.

In fact, the characteristic rebellion of our times is more pervasive and more difficult for Americans to face: it is not the product of a social vision which sees America as the image of Tsardom, but the product of corporate, affluent, mass pluralism. It is a rebellion which corresponds to that in the more "open societies" of the West in Herzen's times. Irving Howe has described Stendhal's reaction to an era of "cant and reaction" as

Not hypocrisy . . . but ruse, the strategy of having one's cake and eating it, being a rebel and a bon vivant, deceiving society to undermine it and wooing society to enjoy it.

This is the real, covert rebel of our age who secretly admires the B.G. and values them because they detract attention from himself. Outwardly conformist, he seeks personal identity in hidden deviations. Often, those deviations are no more than mental, dream-worlds below the surface, shaped out of a primal innocence, a savage self-centeredness that rejects the limits of reality. In any case, the characteristic rebellion of the times has two expressions: (1) a violent, murderous running amok when the barriers between mind and world, the old stupid dualistic illusions, are finally broken; inexplicable murder, cruelty, suicide, and (2) an equally murderous, but more abstract and respectable crushing of dissent in order to protect one's "cover," strengthening the motives for conformity, or a still more murderous, more abstracted, hatred for outsiders, often expressed in the language of a love so universal as to deny personality to other men, and hence to become their destroyer.

This rebel we do not understand, do not dare to understand, lest we realize a basic disease in society, a snake in the Garden. Indeed, he does not understand himself. The beatnik is recognizable as a caricature of something we have been led to expect, and is welcome because his rebellion is verbal, visible, and harmless: he is a comedy-relief social problem.

The beats reflect, too, the current posture of academia: they are, in fact, its logical extension. Liberalism offers five dollars a year to the ACLU and votes Democratic. Its conscience assuaged, it adopts the "situational conservatism" of Professor Samuel Huntington which is based on the principle that one must hold the line all summer against unidentified but somehow ubiquitous foes. Few academics have gone so far as to adopt the ponderous, dreary feudalities of Russell Kirk and the new conservatism. Yet that might be preferable: the doctrines of Huntington, Seymour Lipset, and their fellows are a stupid tropism whose only logic is drift, a proof that American liberals no longer feel that their past doctrines can be defended by reason; the only line of defense is the demand that they be accepted as "traditional." Herzen wrote

The whole system of public education was reduced to the preaching of blind obedience leading to official position as the natural reward. The naturally expansive feelings of youth were driven inwards, were replaced by ambition and jealous rivalry. Those who did not perish emerged sick in mind and soul.

Like that age of Herzen's, after the Revolution became Bonaparteism, we are disillusioned with the failure of the old dogmas: progress is not a process; public sentiment can err; Marxism is a fraud, and so on, with the ultimate points of rest on Madison or Grant Avenues.

The Beat Generation is refreshing because it opens a door: it is a negative "cosmic meaning" in place of the "best-of-possible worlds" doctrine of official intellectuality. Hegel engendered Schopenhauer, Ricardo, and Malthus. Symbiotes the beats are: they allow officialdom to define nature and the world, point out the shams and follies of the definition, and seek to betake themselves somewhere else.

Alas, there is nowhere else, and the generation which is watching the beats with an open interest may learn that lesson without discarding the truth that life as respectability defines it is a fraud. That is the greatest of the hopes in a time when problems multiply under the lotus-mask of social calm. The message of the beatniks is a simple one, the same that Herzen's generation sent to its successors:

We do not build, we destroy; we do not proclaim a new truth, we abolish an old lie. Contemporary man only builds the bridge . . . the . . . man of the future will walk across it. . . . Do not remain on this shore. Better to perish with the revolution than to perish in holy reaction.

And better still, one might add, to think in new terms of new societies than to perish with either.

Turned-on and Super Sincere in California*

RICHARD TODD

At 3:30 P.M. *he said: "I feel terribly strange." Tom handed him a small toy animal he had played with as an infant.*

Charley cuddled the toy, kissed it, and said: "There's something very reassuring about this." . . . Charley lay with a peaceful look on his face, cuddling the toy animal.

Tom lay down outside on a deck adjoining the bedroom and his face, too, filled with peacefulness.—San Francisco Chronicle, *May 30, 1966*

CHARLEY, the thirty-six-old man cuddling the toy, has taken LSD. He is acting strangely, but his trip will end in a few hours and with luck he will be back to normal. He arouses only your casual interest as you leaf through the *Chronicle,* in which LSD is as much a staple as recipes and rape. But you might listen more carefully to Tom, his observer and "guide," who has not had any acid and is speaking in his own voice:

It was a wonderful few moments for me. I felt very much at one with Charley and I knew he was living for a while as a five-year-old child. . . . The guide grows in this experience of giving. What a privilege it is to be with another person in this way! No words can describe it.

---

* From *Harper's Magazine* (January, 1967). Copyright © 1966 by Harper's Magazine, Inc. Reprinted by permission of the author and Harold Ober Associates, Inc.

These few lines represent with splendid typicality a way of talking that is not at all unusual at the moment here in California. The new idiom is characterized by self-revelation and utter seriousness. It places highest value on private emotions and "interpersonal relations," and considers restraint in talking about these intimate matters a signal of hypocrisy. The remarks of the LSD guide are faithful to these assumptions, and include some lesser, but important notions: for example, that childhood and simplicity are ideal states of being.

If the LSD milieu is particularly conducive to such innocence, the phenomenon is by no means confined to the drug set. Californians of many sorts are in its grip. Bulletins from the soul fill the air; all manner of private data is yours without asking. Telephone-talk-show callers crowd the switchboards for a chance to talk about their personal commitments; young marrieds eagerly discuss the state of their relationship; everyone will share with you the latest information on his "growth." Are you curious about anything? That fourteen-year-old playmate in bell-bottomed hiphuggers lolling down Sunset on the arm of a Beatlesque older man—do you wonder what her parents think? She will let you in on her hang-ups with them. Do you find it odd that the strapping Santa Cruz surfer has peroxided his hair into golden fleece? Talk to him; he will at least let you know that he uses Lady Clairol. The Berkeley girl will tell you that she smokes nickel cigars, lived with her boy friend first semester, works hard, and that "I feel this growing . . . I guess I'm building my own truth."

Even where you would look for exceptions, you discover that the California language of soul holds sway: the academic community and its intellectual suburbs practice the new idiom without a blush. To a surprising degree, California intellectuals, particularly the young ones, have forsaken traditional ironic speech, with its insistence on a certain distance between the speaker and his inner self. As a result, self-deprecation, wit, insouciance—all the cherished intellectual habits—are out of fashion here. If anything, they are taken as a badge of hated phoniness.

A listener unaccustomed to this attitude can experience some discomfort. You go to a party at the house of a young Stanford couple; he is a Ph.D. candidate and teacher. You don't know them well; as you arrive you note that since you saw them last his hair, once a shaggy pompadour, is now combed *à la mode,* draping forehead, ears, and neck. The party is distinctly academic: the air, which smells of beer and wine, is full of obscenities,

"indeeds," and the music of Bobby Dylan, who is taunting some
hapless middle-class lady for not being turned on: "Something is
happening and you don't know what it is, do you, Mrs. Jones?"
Talking over this din, you find yourself in an unexpectedly serious
conversation with your host. He has taken LSD lately and, though
you are not pressing him, he is anxious to tell you about it. The
first time was up on the mountain, just after a rain. They went
walking and . . . "The dripping leaves," he repeats, "the dripping
leaves. It was so beautiful and it was sufficient . . . the forest
seemed vast." But words are running out; the expression on his
face suggests that it was an experience for which no words were
necessary at the time and few are available now. He explains that
they have taken LSD many times since, but always indoors. They
sit on the sofa and talk. "It lasts for about twelve hours, and
we talk the whole time. It has brought us much closer together
than we have ever been before. We've been able to say things
about our relationship that I wouldn't have thought possible. It's
deepened our love. . . ."

There is no adequate response for this kind of speech, delivered in a conversational way by a casual acquaintance; nothing
perhaps, except a similar disclosure. Yet you realize that if there
is embarrassment in the silence that follows, it is entirely your
own, and you suspect yourself of undue squeamishness. After all,
what's wrong with saying what you feel?

For some, to be sure, openness in speech is more than an
occasional matter, even more than a habit: it is a code. The code
not only prohibits indirection, but frowns on the use of the conventional language of social deceit. A successful California dinner
party may suddenly swerve into failure with the conventional
closing lines: "It was nice to see you." Suddenly everyone is on
edge, a social blunder has occurred: the offender was speaking
artificially, not of the self.

The Game of Truth

Sometimes a believer will explain the code in clear and vehement terms. You are on the top floor of a San Francisco apartment house on the edge of the Haight–Ashbury district—the West
Coast, if not the world-wide center for psychedelic experiences.
Cigarette smoke, only lightly laced with pot, thickens the air.
Through the lone window at the end of the room, you can see the
orange lights of the Golden Gate Bridge. Across the table from
you is an authentic Haight–Ashbury denizen, a bearded Dane,

swathed in corduroy, his head a torrent of hair. His wife is next to him, a Roger Vadim girl, with pouting insolent lips. When the Dane speaks, his English is immaculate, so perfect that his accent seems an affectation. But the Dane does not speak often. Indeed, he has sat, silent, sullen, but intense, for most of the evening. Suddenly, despite the late hour and the general grogginess, he whirls upon you. You have made an error, filling in a silence with an empty remark about the hour, the distance home, the necessity of a departure. The Dane exclaims, "Stop playing games. We do not know each other. We could sit here saying these polite things for a century and we would not know each other. Why don't you tell me what you think of me? Of course, you dislike me? Tell me your opinion of me, and I will be candid with you, and perhaps we can get to know one another, but no more of this game."

"The game of truth," his wife exclaims, "the game of truth. Let's play the game of truth."

Now the game of truth is not about to become a favorite parlor game, and people like the Dane are easy enough to dismiss. At best they are trying to substitute a new and clumsy set of manners for the ones that have served fairly well to protect people from one another for centuries. At worst, they are "going through a phase." Taken alone, they are simply a curiosity. And yet they are not an isolated example; if there are few people who would express the code with equal vehemence, there are many who believe in it. They are impatient not just with "polite" language, but with all the old forms of literate speech, which they see as a barrier to feeling.

Could this be a hopeful development? Might the emergence of youthful minds willing to speak with directness suggest the bright prospect of mental energies not wasted on self-defense?

One popular observer (*Look* magazine) thinks so. For *Look,* the "turned-on Californian" is playing "a new game," whose rules include a "surprising openness in personal relations, a new intensity of personal commitment, a radical shift in the morally admissible, an expanded definition of education. . . ." As these futurists get more adept at their game, *Look* says, "Relations between people will gain a new depth and subtlety."

You think of the B.'s and you wonder. They are not native Californians, but unequivocal Californians: "When we came here, we threw away our clocks. We eat when we want to, sleep when we want to, write when we want to, make love when we want to. It's wonderful." Martin B. is jack-of-all-sophisticated trades: he has earned exotic degrees in technological fields, has held postdoctoral fellowships and rich jobs in California industry, but has turned, with equal success, to art—won creative writing fellowships, written a novel, is now rumored to be working on a play of outrageous political satire. Debby B. bakes more than two hundred kinds of bread. The B.'s are always talking about making love, and once said they practice the act each night. You sense that their preoccupation is an emblem of a larger concern: their contemporaneity, their freedom. The B.'s rid themselves of property each two years in a "pot-latch." They have disposed of all books except reference matter, though they make voracious use of the public library. Their house, free of photographs or mementos, furnished entirely in beige and teak, is a monument to the present.

For the B.'s, whom you see from time to time, you suspect that you are a curiosity, and this is what they are to you. You listen to their exuberant conversation, which has a theme with limitless variations. On a night in June you hear them speak of the musicology of the Beatles, the intrauterine device, their friends ("we like anyone who's open . . . people who can share"), the Nike X, the Grand Tetons ("a wonderful place to make love"), model trains, childbirth, and plant chromosomes. Nothing out of the ordinary here.

You are caught off guard, however, when, on the porch as you are leaving, Martin remarks with no lapse in his ebullience, "We feel so close to you people!"

Outside in the air, you discover that you have a distinctly uncomfortable feeling, as if you had been kissed against your will. What Martin said is certainly not true. You do not feel close to the B.'s, it seems preposterous that they could feel close to you; you are somewhat annoyed by the imposition of the remark, which demands a response it is impossible to give. If there is a naïveté to their behavior, it is an insidious sort of naïveté, because it encumbers you, however briefly, in its untidy emotions.

This odd quality of contrived innocence is not limited to private lives; in California it is institutionalized. Experiments in human behavior abound: family therapy, group therapy, "movement therapy" (no one says a word), industrial "think-tanks," Joan Baez's Institute for the Study of Non-Violence.

The Esalen Institute flourishes at Big Sur—a handsome well-endowed cluster of buildings overlooking the sea, that swirls about the rocks in beautiful subtleties of blue, white, and green. The Institute is dedicated to the "potentialities of human existence." It believes "People can change. Their institutions can change. All can change for the better, not just superficially, but deep down." Here you can come and participate in enterprises of self-improvement led by psychiatrists and therapists, for a cost of $67 (for a weekend) or $170 (for five days). Recent seminars included "Psychodrama and the Body" and "Bio-Energetic Analysis," also an arts-and-crafts event called "Down Home with Staff Members." (One of the staff is described as "potter, printmaker, and some-time breakfast cook," and of another it is said, "In addition to his jewelry and sculpture, he is well-known on the West Coast as a sandalmaker.")

There is that sound again: what is there about it that can simultaneously amuse and annoy? We all know that sandalmakers are respectable, and there is no real reason to suspect that "Bio-Energetic Analysis" is not on the up-and-up. And yet somehow these phrases seem inadequate to the exploration of "human potentialities." Perhaps it is the easy assurance, that certain chumminess ("sometime breakfast cook") with the confident implication that all within earshot are believers, that everyone agrees that we can push back the frontiers of human experience this weekend.

"No Complicated Emotions"

It is the same happy assumption that accompanies the activity that has inspired so many contemporary idioms—drugs. The use of drugs, it should be repeated, does not account for the phenomenon in question; not all the "turned-on Californians" are turned-on in the literal way. Yet it is true that drugs are widely used in California, and that they are never far from intellectual circles, and that they define the hip personality, the man who has, as Timothy Leary prescribes, dropped out to turn on. And while drugs are more a symptom than a cause, the function they appear to serve may offer a clue to the way minds are working here. From pot to LSD, all are used for the same ostensible reason: they "expand the mind."

"The music."

"Wo-ow."

"The levels, so many levels."

"I'm up here."

"Don't talk about it; you'll bring it down."

"Did you hear that? 'You'll bring it down.' Oh, fantastic."

This conversation—as the joint of marijuana is passed around —is not so much an intimation of perceptions as an attempt to keep aloft the mystical communion. The most important effect of pot is evident less in the words that are spoken than in the looks on the faces of the smokers, who are most likely to assume a gentle, abstracted, beneficent, open expression; to let down their guard. The mind is expanded, to be sure; it is made large enough to hold in harmony elements of one's life that are in conflict when the high ends. Pot, like bourbon or nutmeg, is used to simplify, not to complicate experience. That the experience can become very complicated indeed when stronger drugs are used does not mean that the goal is different. The air is full of tales of bad trips, the flesh melting away, etc. (One peyote-mescaline-LSD veteran recalled his first experience: "I thought I was all right until I saw a gorilla at the urinal.") The significant point is that the possibility of a good trip, a voyage to simplicity, a glorious regression to the imagination's childhood, is considered worth the risks. One of the *Chronicle's* LSD subjects said of his experience, "I never get insanity or hallucinations anymore—just peace—and I feel love for everybody who is here." Another put the matter precisely; "I found I was young, about fifteen, walking down the streets of Rome. I was an Italian boy with no complicated emotions."

"No complicated emotions" says it well. After the drug scene has died out, been confined to the laboratory or legalized into dullness, the item of enduring interest will be that—for a short time anyway—simplicity of feeling was elevated to the level of an heroic ideal. It is what everyone, not just the acid head, seems to be striving for. You hope, half the time you believe (if you are a participant in this euphoric sensibility), that emotional prosperity is just around the corner. In the meantime, though, you must prime the pump with LSD. Or—the more frequent alternative—you must rely on the symbol instead of the sensation, on the easy, "open" speech that marks you as a man of feeling.

When a society wears its heart on its sleeve, something curious is likely to happen. Berkeley is as good a place as any to search for these consequences. It is, of course, a magnificent place: after Berkeley nearly every other campus feels like Slippery Rock. There is turmoil, controversy, intellectual energy, a fervid unleashing of the mind. There is local color. It is no doubt true that Berkeley suffers from a tendency to appreciate the defiant act in any form, but these are usually harmless. (No one seriously worries about the activities, say, of the East Bay Sexual Freedom

League—including a nude wade-in in San Francisco last year.) Berkeley's present danger is probably not extremism but . . . contentment.

Contentment is a paradoxical word for the university that supported the Free Speech Movement. Any day of the week rows of tables display the trophies and causes of the moment, advertise open-air speakers and a hundred diversions, including the "Cinema Psychedelica." But if you linger around the Plaza, you are likely to discover the peculiar kind of joy that is the result of self-absorption. The happiness of those who roam about the campus, sit dangling their feet in the fountain, or even harangue each other, is the solid pleasure of the craftsman content in his work. You stroll through Sather Gate and take the pamphlet that is modestly proffered. It addresses itself to whether or not God is dead, and ends with the assurance, "We welcome any questions about life."

This is a nice complacency, which says not so much that we will answer your questions, but simply that we are *here,* and you are out there, and you don't dare laugh at us. This sense of rightness perhaps explains the familiar hip gesture of making non-jokes. You are sitting, to give an example, in the kitchen of an apartment on Grove Street. Its old tongue-in-groove boards were painted pink long ago and are now peeling to reveal green. There is almost nothing in the place: a few cans of garbanzo beans on the shelves, some milk and Vichy water in the icebox. You are having breakfast, Cheerios, with Walter, who lives there. The stairs to the apartment above lead through Walter's kitchen and the two tenants from upstairs appear: Blossom and Manny. Manny eyes the Cheerios box on the table, chuckles, and points, "Look." Blossom looks, shakes her head, murmurs, "Fantastic." Manny chuckles, "Cheerios," and shakes his head. Exit. This routine is easily done with any object, the more ordinary the better: a radio, a toy (a plastic Jesus would be excessively obvious). You just stare at the thing in apparent wonder, as if you could see the absurdity of the whole civilization contained within it. You remain wordless, or utter a "fantastic," that word that hippies reserve almost entirely for the banal.

This air of sureness about the world has a kind of charm on the antic level, but it presents certain difficulties when the discourse moves to a higher plane. Think of all those fresh-faced girls who repeat the new categorical imperative with such artless confidence, "I believe anything's moral as long as it doesn't hurt someone else." The ease with which that remark dismisses tradition's offer of advice and asserts its faith in one's ability to weigh the implications of every act—these qualities can find their way beneath the skin. And when this kind of mind turns to matters of life and death, unnatural results can be expected.

A recent issue of the weekly Berkeley *Barb* contained a front-page elegy for a nineteen-year-old boy who died while on an LSD trip. The piece, entitled "Vernon P. Cox: an Elegy—HE DIDN'T QUITE MAKE IT," described the author's relationship with the boy (friends, fellow poets), appraised his talent (real, prolific, sometimes seventy poems a day), and, of course, lamented his death.

It reads in part:

His name is Vernon P. Cox, and he didn't quite make it. A very decent human being, came from a good family of Stillwater, Oklahoma. (What a fitting name, what a still place. Cattle grazing, oil wells, fraternities. Devoid of original thought. Plain, everyday Stillwater.) . . .

So they come to Berkeley. Shaggy Dog adopted Sanders, who shared their two mattresses for a couple of nights. English from N.Y. and two-three girls were also guests there. Pot, nutmeg, always near, a refrigerator with some peanut butter—and nothing else—pregnant fifteen-year-olds, the beat scene. That's where he lived and wrote, and, a shame to say, didn't quite make it. . . .

He has his first LSD trip in company: Shaggy Dog as usual lay down, softly singing to himself. Their other two companions were busy and happy in themselves. Vernon free and exulted beyond belief suddenly realized that the trip to Europe he desired, but was afraid of, is a must. Packed his things to start then and there. His companions argued with, restrained him, and for a while he was quiet. Then knowing that for him nothing is impossible, that physical laws don't bind him, not bothering to use the door he walked through the window-pane. No one there was quick enough to block his way. He fell three stories. . . . It wasn't suicide; he only started for Europe and didn't quite make it.

The truth about this elegy is that it is comic. It is horrible, unconscious comedy, slapstick, a Charlie Chaplin movie rendered in earnest prose. It manages, through the tandem devices of undoubted sincerity and total mindlessness, to make an already senseless death almost irredeemably absurd.

And yet, it is not likely that the *Barb's* elegy—whatever wretchedness it might have caused the boy's Stillwater, Oklahoma, family—disturbed many Berkeley readers. It asserts, after all, unassailable notions: that youth, sensitivity, poetry, love, and freedom are good things. It only disregards the necessity for a double vision; it makes no attempt to imagine this tragedy as it might look to another time, another town, a parent, to the author himself a few years (months?) later. It only fails to throw a sop to a world in which walking through a window to one's death, with the illusion of going on a European tour, qualifies as a bizarre act. It speaks with absolute assurance, an assurance that is oddly justified by the complacency of its audience.

Like Spilt Milk

The "elegy," of course, is a grotesque, a heightened version of unreality—but, like other grotesques, it has its instructive value. In one sense it can be taken as the careless remarks of a young writer, but in another sense it is the product of a culture as well; if ordinary restraints were operating the elegy would not likely have been written; certainly it would not be received with equanimity. In its painful assumptions that you need only feel, be straight, put down hypocrisy, say what you mean, it is utterly faithful to the unchallenged ideas of the intelligent people whose voice rules this coast.

If this intellectual style is not explicable, it at least is somewhat appropriate to the state whose residents—from hippies to systems men—share, if they share anything, a devotion to the moment. What California seems to need is what it clearly wants least: a past. It is possible to grow obsessed with this prescription, perhaps because everything looks like spilt milk. The land is always wrenchingly visible; from the heart of Berkeley, from the midsts of the most hysterical freeway, you can always see the brown hills, their contours too subtle to accept a building gracefully, waiting to be defiled by another onslaught of tract houses.

If your mood is right, of course, you can be bemused, even exhilarated, by the hodgepodge, as you can by its intellectual concomitants. But your mood can change, as quickly as the passing of the sun can transform the landscape itself—surely no place is as ugly as California on a cloudy day—and you are pushed toward visions of a distinctly hideous future for this state.

Whatever is to become of the place, it is no hopeful sign that so many bright voices are celebrating the self and the now and that much of the state is on a sentimental trip; high, indeed out-of-its-mind—not on LSD, but on language: oldest, strongest drug of them all.

The Esalen Foundation: "Joy is the Prize"*

LEO LITWAK

B IG SUR is an eighty-mile stretch of California coast below
the Monterey Peninsula. It is approximately midway between Los
Angeles and San Francisco and difficult of access from either
direction. Before the coastal highway was completed in 1936, the
shore was accessible only by foot. The Los Padres National Forest, one of the largest preserves in the country, extends thirty
miles inland and is two hundred miles long; it occupies most of
the area. Not much land is available for private ownership. There
are only three hundred residents. The rugged terrain of Los Padres
includes redwood canyons, barren mountain ranges, desert flora,
thick forests. It is the province of mountain lions and wild boar.

Stone cliffs rise two thousand feet above the ocean. Beyond a
wedge of meadow, the steeply inclined hillside begins. For great
distances there is no meadow at all and the serpentine coastal
highway hangs on the cliffside. It is a two-lane road, sometimes
impassable after heavy rains. The fog bank wavers off shore.
When it sweeps in, the traveler faces an uncanny trip, guided
entirely by the few white dashes of the center line that are visible.
With hairpin turns, sharp rises and declines, the road can be
dangerous in bad weather. On clear days when the setting sun
ignites dust particles on your windshield you are forced to drive
blind for dangerous seconds.

---

* From *The New York Times Magazine*, December 31, 1967. Copyright © 1967 by The New York Times Company. Reprinted by permission.

Nonetheless, four thousand people traveled this road last year, in disregard of weather, aimed toward the Esalen Institute, famous until a few years ago under a different name, Big Sur Hot Springs. These are unlikely adventurers. They are doctors, social workers, clinical psychologists, teachers, students, business executives, engineers, housewives—or just fun lovers who have come to take the baths.

Big Sur Hot Springs was originally renowned as the Eden discovered by Henry Miller and Jack Kerouac. Joan Baez once lived there. The springs were purchased in 1910 from a man named Slade by Dr. Henry C. Murphy of Salinas. It was Dr. Murphy's intention to establish a health spa. In order to use the mineral waters he brought in two bathtubs by fishing sloop. They were hauled up the cliff and placed on a ledge at the source of the springs. But because of their inaccessibility, the springs did not flourish as a spa. Not until Dr. Murphy's grandson, Michael, assumed operation of the property in the mid-nineteen-fifties did the baths begin to receive attention—attention that has grown with the development of Esalen Institute.

Michael Murphy at thirty-seven appears to be in his early twenties. He is slender and boyish and has a marvelous smile. I took part in a panel discussion at Hot Springs some years ago and I was not impressed either by the topic, my performance or the audience. I did enjoy the baths. I had misgivings about Murphy's program, yet none about him. He seemed to me generous, charming, innocent, credulous, enthusiastic, and enormously sympathetic. A Stanford alumnus who had done some graduate work in psychology and philosophy, he had recently returned from an eighteen-month study of the art of meditation at the Aurobindo Ashram in Pondicherry, India, and he devoted a considerable part of each day to meditation. I believe he had—and still has—in mind some great mission, based on his Indian experience. I am not quite sure what the scope of his mission is. A friend of his told me: "Mike wants to turn on the world." Esalen Institute is his instrument for doing so. It has come a long way from the shoddy panels of a few years ago. Its spreading impact may seriously affect our methods of therapy and education.

In the course of a year, almost one thousand professional persons—social workers, psychiatrists, clinical psychologists—enroll in Esalen workshops. Close to seven hundred psychotherapists have been trained to administer techniques devised by staff members—Frederick Perls, Virginia Satir, Bernard Gunther, and William Schutz. These techniques have been demonstrated at hospitals, universities, and medical schools. This year Esalen has opened a San Francisco extension which in the first two months of operation has attracted an attendance in excess of ten thousand, offering the same workshops and seminars that are available at Big Sur. Esalen-type communities have begun to appear throughout the country, in Atlanta, Chicago, Los Angeles, Cleveland, La Jolla. One has even appeared in Vancouver, Canada. Murphy offers advice and help, and permits use of his mailing list.

Consider some offerings of the Esalen winter brochure. Seminars led by Alan Watts, the Zen interpreter, and Susan Sontag, the camp interpreter. Workshops for professional therapists conducted by Frederick Perls, an early associate of Freud and Wilhelm Reich and a founder of Gestalt therapy. A lecture panel including the psychologist Carl Rogers and Herman Kahn, the "thinking about the unthinkable" man. Some of the titles are: "Kinetic Theater," "Psycotechnics," "Do You Do It? Or Does It Do You?", "Dante's Way to the Stars," "Creativity and the Daimonic," "On Deepening the Marriage Encounter," "Tibetan Book of the Dead," "Anxiety and Tension Control," "Racial Confrontation as a Transcendental Experience."

What principle guides a mélange that consists of dance workshops, therapy workshops, sensory-awareness experiments, the Tibetan Book of the Dead, Herman Kahn, Carl Rogers, Frederick Perls, and Susan Sontag?

Esalen's vice president, George B. Leonard, has written a general statement of purpose. He says: "We believe that all men somehow possess a divine potentiality; that ways may be worked out—specific, systematic ways—to help, not the few, but the many toward a vastly expanded capacity to learn, to love, to feel deeply, to create. We reject the tired dualism that seeks God and human potentialities by denying the joys of the senses, the immediacy of unpostponed life." The programs, he says, are aimed toward "the joys of the senses."

I had signed up for a workshop led by Dr. William Schutz, a group therapist who has taught at Harvard and the Albert Einstein College of Medicine, among other institutions, and has served on the staff of the National Training Laboratories Interne Training Program at Bethel, Me. His latest book, *Joy*, was published in 1967 by Grove Press.

In the brochure description of Dr. Schutz's workshop I read a warning that the experience would be more than verbal: "An encounter workshop with body movements, sensory awareness, fantasy experiments, psychodrama. Developing the ability to experience joy is the workshop's guiding theme."

Joy as the prize of a five-day workshop?

"How can we speak of joy," Leonard has written, "on this dark and suffering planet? How can we speak of anything else? We have heard enough of despair."

It was easy enough to dismiss the language. It seemed naive to promise so great a reward for so small an investment. Joy for $175 seemed cheap at the price, especially since *The New York Times* was paying. I did have considerable anxieties that some of those "body movements" might be humiliating. And what precisely was meant by "sensory awareness"?

Esalen has changed considerably since my previous visit. Rows of new cabins are ranged along terraces on the hillside. The lodge is located at the bottom of a steep incline, in a meadow. The meadow is perhaps 200 yards deep and ends at the cliff edge. The Pacific Ocean is 150 feet below. A staff of fifty operates the kitchen, supervises the baths, cleans the cabins and garden, and works on construction.

I passed hippy laborers, stripped to the waist, long hair flowing, operating with pick and shovel. Dreamy girls in long gowns played flutes near the pool.

I was somewhat put off by what I considered to be an excessive show of affection. Men hugged men. Men hugged women. Women hugged women. These not hippies, but older folks, like myself, who had come for the workshop. People flew into one another's arms, and it wasn't my style at all.

After dinner, thirty of us met in the gallery for our first session. We began our excursion toward joy at 9 P.M. of a Sunday in a woodsy room on a balmy, starry night.

William Schutz, solidly built, with bald head and muzzle beard, began by telling us that in the course of the workshop we would come to dangerous ground. At such times we ought not to resist entering, for in this area lay our greatest prospect for self-transcendence. He told us to avoid verbal manipulations and to concentrate on our feelings.

We began with exercises. A fat lady in leotards directed us to be absurd. We touched our noses with our tongues. We jumped. We ran. We clutched one another, made faces at one another. Afterward, we gathered in groups of five and were given an ambiguous instruction to discover one another by touching in any way we found agreeable. I crouched in front of a strange-looking young man with an underslung jaw and powerful shoulders. I tried unlocking his legs and he glared at me.

When Schutz asked each group of five to select one couple that seemed least close, the young man with the underslung jaw selected me. The hostile pairs were then requested to stand at opposite diagonals of the room and approach each other. They were to do whatever they felt like doing when they met in the center of the room. A burly middle-aged man marched toward a petite lady. They met, they paused, stared, then suddenly embraced. The next couple, two husky men, both frozen rigid, confronted each other, stared, then also embraced. The young man and I came next. We started at opposite diagonals. We met in the center of the room. I found myself looking into the mean-est, coldest eyes I had ever seen. He pressed his hands to his sides, and it was clear to me that we were not going to embrace. I reached for his hand to shake it. He jerked free. I put my hand on his shoulder; he shrugged me off. We continued staring and finally returned to our group.

There was a general discussion of this encounter. Some feared we might start fighting. Nothing, of course, was farther from my mind. I had gone out, intending to play their game and suddenly found myself staring at a lunatic. He had very mean, cold eyes, a crazy shape to his jaw, lips so grim that his ill-feeling was unmistakable. Back in our group he said to me, in a raspy, shrill voice: "You thought I was going to bat you in the face; that's why you turned away." There was a slurred quality to his speech, and it occurred to me that I might have triggered off a madman. I denied that I had turned away and I was challenged to stare him down. I was annoyed that I had been forced into something so silly.

We proceeded, on the basis of our first impressions, to give one another names, which we kept for the duration of the work-shop. My nemesis accepted the name of Rebel. There was a plump, lovely girl we called Kate. A silent, powerful man with spectacles we named Clark. Our fat group leader received the name of Brigitte. A lumpy, solemn man with thick spectacles we named Gary. An elegant, trim middle-aged woman we named

Sheba. A buxom, mournful woman with long hair became Joan. A jovial middle-aged pipe smoker with a Jean Hersholt manner we named Hans. A fierce, mustached swaggerer in Bermuda shorts was Daniel. A quiet man with a little boy's face we named Victor. I was named Lionel. We were addressed by these names at all times.

I considered this renaming of ourselves a naive attempt to create an atmosphere free of any outside reference. Many of the techniques impressed me as naive. It seemed tactless and obvious to ask so blunt and vague a question as: "What are you feeling?" Yet what happened in the course of five days was that the obvious became clarified. Clichés became significant.

I found myself discovering what had always been under my nose. I had not known how my body felt under conditions of tension or fear or grief. I discovered that I was numb. I had all sorts of tricks for avoiding encounter. I didn't particularly like to be touched. I avoided looking strangers in the eye. I took pride in my coolness and trickery. I didn't believe one should give oneself away. It seemed to me a virtue to appear cool, to be relatively immune to feeling, so that I could receive shocks without appearing to. I considered it important to keep up appearances. I'm no longer proud of what I now believe to be an incapacity rather than a talent.

I thought my group rather dull. I saw no great beauty and a great deal of weakness. I felt somewhat superior, since I was there on assignment, not by choice. I hated and feared Reb.

But in the next five days, I became enormously fond of these apparently uninteresting strangers. We encountered one another in violent and intimate ways, and I could no longer dismiss them.

I was convinced that Rebel was insane. He opened our second meeting with gratuitous insults. He referred to me as "Charley Goodguy." When Brigitte, the leader of our group, told him not to think in stereotypes, he sneered at her: "Why don't you shut up, Fats?" It is difficult to convey the nastiness of his tone— an abrasive, jeering quality.

Daniel exploded. He called Rebel a shark and a rattlesnake. He said he wanted to quit the group because he despised this frightening, violent kid. "You scare me," he told Reb. "It's people like you who are responsible for Vietnam and Auschwitz. You're a monster and you're going to suck up all the energy of this group and it's not worth it. I want to get out."

I told Daniel his response seemed excessive. Vietnam and Auschwitz? "He's a little hostile," I said.

Reb didn't want any favors from me. "Hostile?" he sneered. "Say, I bet I know what you are. You sound to me like a professor. Or a pawnbroker. Which are you, a professor or a pawnbroker?"

Schutz intervened. He said to me and Rebel: "I feel you have something going. Why don't you have it out?" He suggested that we arm wrestle, an innocuous contest, but, under the circumstances, there seemed to be a great deal invested in winning or losing. My arm felt numb, and there was some trembling in my thighs. I feared I might not have all my strength, and Rebel appeared to be a powerful kid.

I pinned him so easily, however, that the group accused him of having quit. Daniel was jubilant: "You're a loser. You're trying to get clobbered."

Rebel was teased into trying again. On the second trial, he pressed my left arm down and demanded a rematch with the right hand. We remained locked together for close to twenty minutes. It was unbearable. I lost all sensation in my hand and arm. I willed my hand not to yield. Finally, I hoped he would press me down and get it over with. It ended when Rebel squirmed around and braced his foot against the wall and the contest was called.

Daniel was delighted by the outcome. He felt as though I had won something for him. Schutz asked: "Why don't *you* wrestle Reb?" Daniel despised violence. He probably would lose and he didn't want to give that monster the satisfaction of a victory. Violence was right up that shark's alley. He refused to play his games. Nonetheless, Daniel was on the ground with Rebel a moment later, beet red with strain, trembling down to his calves. Rebel raised his elbow, pressed Daniel down, and the match was called off. Daniel leaped to his feet, circled the room. He suddenly charged Rebel, who was seated, and knocked him from his chair. He then rushed at Schutz, yelling: "It's you I hate, you bastard, for making me do this." Schutz did not flinch, and Daniel backed off. I could see that his impulse was histrionic. I felt sorry for Reb, who mumbled: "I copped out. I should have hit him."

Reb later presented a different guise. Far from being an idiot, he was an extremely precocious twenty-year-old computer engineer, self-taught in the humanities. His father had abandoned the family when he was a child. His mother was a cold customer

—never a sign of feeling. He didn't know where he stood with her. She taunted him in the same abrasive style which he tried with us.

Reb suffered sexual agonies that had brought him several hundred miles in search of a solution. He considered himself perverse and contemptible, the only impotent twenty-year-old kid in the world. He admitted he found women repugnant as sexual objects, and it was hardly surprising that his crude advances were rebuffed. He admitted that his strategy had been to strike out in hope that someone would strike back so that he might *feel*. He was boyish and affectionate outside the group.

My feeling for him underwent a complete reversal. He began to impress me as an intelligent kid, trying with great courage to repair terrible injuries. The monster I had seen simply vanished.

I never anticipated the effect of these revelations, as one after another of these strangers expressed his grief and was eased. I woke up one night and felt as if everything were changed. I felt as if I were about to weep. The following morning the feeling was even more intense.

Brigitte and I walked down to the cliff edge. We lay beneath a tree. She could see that I was close to weeping. I told her that I'd been thinking about my numbness, which I had traced to the war. I tried to keep the tears down. I felt vulnerable and unguarded. I felt that I was about to lose all my secrets and I was ready to let them go. Not being guarded, I had no need to put anyone down, and I felt what it was to be unarmed. I could look anyone in the eyes and my eyes were open.

That night I said to Daniel: "Why do you keep diverting us with intellectual arguments? I see suffering in your eyes. You give me a glimpse of it, then you turn it off. Your eyes go dead and the intellectual stuff bores me. I feel that's part of your strategy."

Schutz suggested that the two of us sit in the center of the room and talk to each other. I told Daniel that I was close to surrender. I wanted to let go. I felt near to my grief. I wanted to release it and be purged. Daniel asked about my marriage and my work. Just when he hit a nerve, bringing me near the release I wanted, he began to speculate on the tragedy of the human condition. I told him: "You're letting me off and I don't want to be let off."

Schutz asked if I would be willing to take a fantasy trip.

It was late afternoon and the room was already dark. I lay down, Schutz beside me, and the group gathered around. I closed my eyes. Schutz asked me to imagine myself very tiny and to imagine that tiny self entering my own body. He wanted me to describe the trip.

I saw an enormous statue of myself, lying in a desert, mouth open as if I were dead. I entered my mouth. I climbed down my gullet, entering it as if it were a manhole. I climbed into my chest cavity. Schutz asked me what I saw. "It's empty," I said. "There's nothing here." I was totally absorbed by the effort to visualize entering myself and lost all sense of the group. I told Schutz there was no heart in my body. Suddenly, I felt tremendous pressure in my chest, as if tears were going to explode. He told me to go to the vicinity of the heart and report what I saw. There, on a ledge of the chest wall, near where the heart should have been, I saw a baby buggy. He asked me to look into it. I didn't want to, because I feared I might weep, but I looked, and I saw a doll. He asked me to touch it. I was relieved to discover that it was only a doll. Schutz asked me if I could bring a heart into my body. And suddenly there it was, a heart sheathed in slime, hung with blood vessels. And that heart broke me up. I felt my chest convulse. I exploded. I *burst* into tears.

I recognized the heart. The incident had occurred more than twenty years before and had left me cold. I had written about it in a story published long ago in *Esquire*. The point of the story was that such events should have affected me but never did. The war in Germany was about over. We had just taken a German village without resistance. We had fine billets in German houses. The cellars were loaded with jams and sausages and wine. I was the aid man with the outfit, and was usually summoned by the call of "Aid man!" When I heard that call I became numb, and when I was numb I could go anywhere and do anything. I figured the battles were over. It came as a shock when I heard the call this time. There were rifle shots, then: "Aid man!" I ran to the guards and they pointed to bushes ten yards from where they had been posted. They had spotted a German soldier and called for him to surrender. He didn't answer and they fired. I went to the bushes and turned him over. He was a kid about sixteen, blond, his hair strung out in the bushes, still alive. The .30-caliber bullets had scooped out his chest and I saw his heart. It was the same heart I put in my chest twenty-three years later. He was still alive, gray with shock, going fast. He stared up at me—a mournful, little boy's face. He asked: "Why did you shoot? I wanted to surrender." I told him we didn't know.

Now, twenty-three years later, I wailed for that German boy who had never mattered to me and I heaved up my numbness. The trip through my body lasted more than an hour. I found wounds everywhere. I remembered a wounded friend whimpering: "Help me, Leo," which I did—a close friend, yet after he was hit no friend at all, not missed a second after I heard of his death, numb to him as I was to everyone else, preparing for losses by anesthetizing myself. And in the course of that trip through my body I started to feel again, and discovered what I'd missed. I felt wide open, lightened, ready to meet others simply and directly. No need for lies, no need to fear humiliation. I was ready to be a fool. I experienced the joy Schutz had promised to deliver. I'm grateful to him. Not even the offer of love could threaten me.

This was the transformation I underwent in the course of that fantasy trip. The force of the experience began to fade quickly, and now, writing two weeks later, I find that little remains. But I still have a vision of a possibility I had not been aware of— a simple, easy connection with my own feeling and, consequently, with others'.

I had great difficulty emerging from my body. I was pinned against my intestines, pregnant with myself. When I finally began to move and restored all the missing organs and repaired those that were damaged, I feared that all this work was temporary, that if I were to leave the heart would vanish, the stomach dry up, the intestines be exposed. Schutz asked if there was anyone who could help me get out. I said: "My daughter." So I invited my daughter to enter my body. She stood near my heart and said: "Come on out, Daddy," and led me out. I ran to a meadow on my chest. I ran through long grass, toward a gate, directly toward the sun. There I lay down and rested.

Occasionally, during my trip, I heard others crying, but I had lost track of the group. I opened my eyes. I had an initial sense of others as darts of candlelight about me. The room seemed to have shifted. It was pitch black outside. Everyone was very close to me—Reb, Daniel, Brigitte, Bill, Joan, Victor, Kate, Clark, Gary, Sheba. Sheba still wept. Brigitte directed us all to lie down and to reach out and touch one another. She turned out the lights and gave us various instructions designed to release us and finally we parted.

It was not easy leaving these people I had met only five days before. Time was distorted and we seemed to have lived years together. It was not easy leaving Big Sur. On the final morning, the entire workshop met to say good-by. Our group gathered in a tight circle, hugging and kissing, and I found myself hugging everyone, behaving like the idiots I had noticed on first arriving at Esalen. I hugged Rebel. I told him he was a great kid and that a few years from now he might not even recall his present trouble. I told him not to envy his peers. He was probably much better than they.

Schutz ended our last meeting by playing a record from *The Man of La Mancha,* "The Impossible Dream." We were at that point of sentiment where corny lyrics announced truths and we could be illuminated by the wisdom of clichés.

The condition of vulnerability is precious and very fragile. Events and people and old routines and old habits conspire to bring you down. But not all the way down. There is still the recollection of that tingling sense of being wide awake, located in the here and now, feeling freely and entirely, all constraints discarded. It remains a condition to be realized. It could change the way we live.

The Nonstudent Left*

HUNTER S. THOMPSON

AT THE HEIGHT of the "Berkeley insurrection" press reports were loaded with mentions of outsiders, nonstudents, and professional troublemakers. Terms like "Cal's shadow college" and "Berkeley's hidden community" became part of the journalistic lexicon. These people, it was said, were whipping the campus into a frenzy, goading the students to revolt, harassing the administration, and all the while working for their own fiendish ends. You could almost see them loping along the midnight streets with bags of seditious leaflets, strike orders, red banners of protest and cablegrams from Moscow, Peking, or Havana. As in Mississippi, and South Vietnam, outside agitators were said to be stirring up the locals, who wanted only to be left alone.

Something closer to the truth is beginning to emerge now, but down around the roots of the affair the fog is still pretty thick. The Sproul Hall sit-in trials ended in a series of unexpectedly harsh convictions, the Free Speech Movement has disbanded, four students have been expelled and sentenced to jail terms as a result of the "dirty word" controversy, and the principal leader, Mario Savio, has gone to England, where he'll study and wait for word on the appeal of his four-month jail term—a procedure which may take as long as eighteen months.

As the new semester begins—with a new and inscrutable chancellor—the mood on the Berkeley campus is one of watchful

* From *The Nation* (September 27, 1965). Used by permission of the publisher.

waiting. The basic issues of last year are still unresolved, and a big new one has been added: Vietnam. A massive nationwide sit-in, with Berkeley as a focal point, is scheduled for October 15–16, and if that doesn't open all the old wounds, then presumably nothing will.

For a time it looked as though Governor Edmund Brown had sidetracked any legislative investigation of the university, but late in August Assembly Speaker Jesse Unruh, an anti-Brown Democrat, named himself and four colleagues to a joint legislative committee that will investigate higher education in California. Mr. Unruh told the press that "there will be no isolated investigation of student–faculty problems at Berkeley," but in the same period he stated before a national conference of more than one thousand state legislators, meeting in Portland, that the academic community is "probably the greatest enemy" of a state legislature.

Mr. Unruh is a sign of the times. For a while last spring he appeared to be in conflict with the normally atavistic Board of Regents, which runs the university, but somewhere along the line a blue-chip compromise was reached, and whatever progressive ideas the Regents might have flirted with were lost in the summer lull. Governor Brown's role in these negotiations has not yet been made public.

One of the realities to come out of last semester's action is the new "anti-outsider law," designed to keep "nonstudents" off the campus in any hour of turmoil. It was sponsored by Assemblyman Don Mulford, a Republican from Oakland, who looks and talks quite a bit like the "old" Richard Nixon. Mr. Mulford is much concerned about "subversive infiltration" on the Berkeley campus, which lies in his district. He thinks he knows that the outburst last fall was caused by New York Communists, beatnik perverts, and other godless elements beyond his ken. The students themselves, he tells himself, would never have caused such a ruckus. Others in Sacramento apparently shared his view: the bill passed the Assembly by a vote of 54 to 11 and the Senate by 27 to 8. Governor Brown signed it on June 2. The Mulford proposal got a good boost, while it was still pending, when J. Edgar Hoover testified in Washington that forty-three Reds of one stripe or another were involved in the Free Speech Movement.

On hearing of this, one student grinned and said: "Well I guess that means they'll send about 10,000 Marines out here this fall. Hell, they sent 20,000 after those fifty-eight Reds in Santo Domingo. Man, that Lyndon is nothing but *hip!*"

Where Mr. Hoover got his figures is a matter of speculation, but the guess in Berkeley is that it came from the San Francisco *Examiner*, a Hearst paper calling itself "The Monarch of the Dailies." The *Examiner* is particularly influential among those who fear King George III might still be alive in Argentina.

The significance of the Mulford law lies not in what it says but in the darkness it sheds on the whole situation in Berkeley, especially on the role of nonstudents and outsiders. Who are these thugs? What manner of man would lurk on a campus for no reason but to twist student minds? As anyone who lives or works around an urban campus knows, vast numbers of students are already more radical than any Red Mr. Hoover could name. Beyond that, the nonstudents and outsiders California has legislated against are in the main ex-students, graduates, would-be transfers, and other young activist types who differ from radical students only in that they don't carry university registration cards. On any urban campus the nonstudent is an old and dishonored tradition. Every big city school has its fringe element: Harvard, New York University, Chicago, the Sorbonne, Berkeley, the University of Caracas. A dynamic university in a modern population center simply can't be isolated from the realities, human or otherwise, that surround it. Mr. Mulford would make an island of the Berkeley campus but, alas, there are too many guerillas.

In 1958, I drifted north from Kentucky and became a nonstudent at Columbia. I signed up for two courses and am still getting bills for the tuition. My home was a $12-a-week room in an off-campus building full of jazz musicians, shoplifters, mainliners, screaming poets, and sex addicts of every description. It was a good life. I used the university facilities and at one point was hired to stand in a booth all day for two days, collecting registration fees. Twice I walked almost the length of the campus at night with a big wooden box containing nearly $15,000. It was a wild feeling, and I'm still not sure why I took the money to the bursar.

Being a "non" or "neo" student on an urban campus is not only simple but natural for anyone who is young, bright, and convinced that the major he's after is not on the list. Any list. A serious nonstudent is his own guidance counselor. The surprising thing is that so few people beyond the campus know this is going on.

The nonstudent tradition seems to date from the end of World War II. Before that it was a more individual thing. A

professor at Columbia told me that the late R. P. Blackmur, one
of the most academic and scholarly of literary critics, got most
of his education by sitting in on classes at Harvard.

In the age of Eisenhower and Kerouac, the nonstudent went
about stealing his education as quietly as possible. It never occurred to him to jump into campus politics; that was part of the
game he had already quit. But then the decade ended, Nixon
went down, and the civil rights struggle broke out. With this, a
whole army of guilt-crippled Eisenhower deserters found the
war they had almost given up hoping for. With Kennedy at the
helm, politics became respectable for a change, and students who
had sneered at the idea of voting found themselves joining the
Peace Corps or standing on picket lines. Student radicals today
may call Kennedy a phony liberal and a glamorous sellout, but
only the very young will deny that it was Kennedy who got them
excited enough to want to change the American reality, instead
of just quitting it. Today's activist student or nonstudent talks
about Kerouac as the hipsters of the '50's talked about Heming-
way. He was a quitter, they say; he had good instincts and a
good ear for the sadness of his time, but his talent soured instead
of growing. The new campus radical has a cause, a multi-pronged
attack on as many fronts as necessary: if not civil rights, then
foreign policy or structural deprivation in domestic poverty
pockets. Injustice is the demon, and the idea is to bust it.

What Mulford's law will do to change this situation is not
clear. The language of the bill leaves no doubt that it shall henceforth be a misdeameanor for any nonstudent or nonemployee to
remain on a state university or state college campus after he or
she has been ordered to leave, if it "reasonably appears" to the
chief administrative officer or the person designated by him to
keep order on the campus "that such person is committing an act
likely to interfere with the peaceful conduct of the campus."

In anything short of riot conditions, the real victims of Mulford's law will be the luckless flunkies appointed to enforce it.
The mind of man could devise few tasks more hopeless than
rushing around this 1,000-acre, 27,000-student campus in the
midst of some crowded action, trying to apprehend and remove—
on sight and before he can flee—any person who is not a Cal
student and is not eligible for readmission. It would be a nightmare of lies, false seizures, double entries, and certain provocation. Meanwhile, most of those responsible for the action would
be going about their business in legal peace. If pure justice pre-

vailed in this world, Don Mulford would be appointed to keep order and bag subversives at the next campus demonstration.

There are those who seem surprised that a defective rattrap like the Mulford law could be endorsed by the legislature of a supposedly progressive, enlightened state. But these same people were surprised when Proposition 14, which reopened the door to racial discrimination in housing, was endorsed by the electorate last November by a margin of nearly 2 to 1.

Meanwhile, the nonstudent in Berkeley is part of the scene, a fact of life. The university estimates that about three thousand nonstudents use the campus in various ways: working in the library with borrowed registration cards; attending lectures, concerts and student films; finding jobs and apartments via second-hand access to university listings; eating in the cafeteria, and monitoring classes. In appearance they are indistinguishable from students. Berkeley is full of wild-looking graduate students, bearded professors, and long-haired English majors who look like Joan Baez.

Until recently there was no mention of nonstudents in campus politics, but at the beginning of the Free Speech rebellion President Kerr said "nonstudent elements were partly responsible for the demonstration." Since then, he has backed away from that stand, leaving it to the lawmakers. Even its goats and enemies now admit that the FSM revolt was the work of students. It has been a difficult fact for some people to accept, but a reliable poll of student attitudes at the time showed that roughly eighteen thousand of them supported the goals of the FSM, and about half that number supported its "illegal" tactics. More than eight hundred were willing to defy the administration, the governor and the police, rather than back down. The faculty supported the FSM by close to 8 to 1. The nonstudents nearly all sided with the FSM. The percentage of radicals among them is much higher than among students. It is invariably the radicals, not the conservatives, who drop out of school and become activist nonstudents. But against this background, their attitude hardly matters.

"We don't play a big role politically," says one. "But philosophically we're a hell of a threat to the establishment. Just the fact that we exist proves that dropping out of school isn't the end of the world. Another important thing is that we're not looked down on by students. We're respectable. A lot of students I know are thinking of becoming nonstudents."

"As a nonstudent I have nothing to lose," said another. "I

can work full time on whatever I want, study what interests me, and figure out what's really happening in the world. That student routine is a drag. Until I quit the grind I didn't realize how many groovy things there are to do around Berkeley; concerts, films, good speakers, parties, pot, politics, women—I can't think of a better way to live, can you?"

Not all nonstudents worry the lawmakers and administrators. Some are fraternity bums who flunked out of the university, but don't want to leave the parties and the good atmosphere. Others are quiet squares or technical types, earning money between enrollments and meanwhile living nearby. But there is no longer the sharp division that used to exist between the beatnik and the square: too many radicals wear ties and sport coats; too many engineering students wear boots and levis. Some of the most bohemian-looking girls around the campus are Left puritans, while some of the sweetest-looking sorority types are confirmed pot smokers and wear diaphragms on all occasions.

Nonstudents lump one another—and many students—into two very broad groups: "political radicals" and "social radicals." Again, the division is not sharp, but in general, and with a few bizarre exceptions, a political radical is a Left activist in one or more causes. His views are revolutionary in the sense that his idea of "democratic solutions" alarms even the liberals. He may be a Young Trotskyist, a Du Bois Club organizer, or merely an ex-Young Democrat, who despairs of President Johnson and is now looking for action with some friends in the Progressive Labor Party.

Social radicals tend to be "arty." Their gigs are poetry and folk music, rather than politics, although many are fervently committed to the civil rights movement. Their political bent is Left, but their real interests are writing, painting, good sex, good sounds, and free marijuana. The realities of politics put them off, although they don't mind lending their talents to a demonstration here and there, or even getting arrested for a good cause. They have quit one system and they don't want to be organized into another; they feel they have more important things to do.

A report last spring by the faculty's Select Committee on Education tried to put it all in a nutshell: "A significant and growing minority of students is simply not propelled by what we have come to regard as conventional motivation. Rather than aiming to be successful men in an achievement-oriented society, they want to be moral men in a moral society. They want to lead lives less tied to financial return than to social awareness and responsibility."

The committee was severely critical of the whole university structure, saying: "The atmosphere of the campus now suggests too much an intricate system of compulsions, rewards and punishments; too much of our attention is given to score keeping." Among other failures, the university was accused of ignoring "the moral revolution of the young."

Talk like this strikes the radicals among "the young" as paternalistic jargon, but they appreciate the old folks' sympathy. To them, anyone who takes part in "the system" is a hypocrite. This is especially true among the Marxist, Mao-Castro element— the hipsters of the Left.

One of these is Steve DeCanio, a twenty-two-year-old Berkeley radical and Cal graduate in math, now facing a two-month jail term as a result of the Sproul Hall sit-ins. He is doing graduate work, and therefore is immune to the Mulford law. "I became a radical after the 1962 auto row (civil rights) demonstrations in San Francisco," he says. "That's when I saw the power structure and understood the hopelessness of trying to be a liberal. After I got arrested I dropped the pre-med course I'd started at San Francisco State. The worst of it, though, was being screwed time and again in the courts. I'm out on appeal now with four and a half months of jail hanging over me."

DeCanio is an editor of *Spider*, a wild-eyed new magazine with a circulation of about two thousand on and around the Berkeley campus. Once banned, it thrived on the publicity and is now officially ignored by the protest-weary administration. The eight-man editorial board is comprised of four students and four nonstudents. The magazine is dedicated, they say, to "sex, politics, international communism, drugs, extremism and rock'n'roll." Hence, *S-P-I-D-E-R*.

DeCanio is about two-thirds political radical and one-third social. He is bright, small, with dark hair and glasses, clean-shaven, and casually but not sloppily dressed. He listens carefully to questions, uses his hands for emphasis when he talks, and quietly says things like: "What this country needs is a revolution; the society is so sick, so reactionary, that it just doesn't make sense to take part in it."

He lives, with three other nonstudents and two students, in a comfortable house on College Avenue, a few blocks from the campus. The $120-a-month rent is split six ways. There are three bedrooms, a kitchen, and a big living room with a fireplace. Papers litter the floor, the phone rings continually, and people stop by to borrow things: a pretty blonde wants a Soviet army chorus record, a Tony Perkins type from the Oakland Du Bois Club wants a film projector; Art Goldberg—the arch-activist who also lives here—comes storming in, shouting for help on the "Vietnam Days" teach-in arrangements.

It is all very friendly and collegiate. People wear plaid shirts and khaki pants, white socks and moccasins. There are books on the shelves, cans of beer and Cokes in the refrigerator, and a manually operated light bulb in the bathroom. In the midst of all this it is weird to hear people talking about "bringing the ruling class to its knees," or "finding acceptable synonyms for Marxist terms."

Political conversation in this house would drive Don Mulford right over the wall. There are riffs of absurdity and mad humor in it, but the base line remains a dead-serious alienation from the "repugnant society" of twentieth-century America. You hear the same talk on the streets, in coffee bars, on the walk near Ludwig's Fountain in front of Sproul Hall, and in other houses where activists live and gather. And why not? This is Berkeley, which DeCanio calls "the center of West Coast radicalism." It has a long history of erratic politics, both on and off the campus. From 1911 to 1913, its mayor was a Socialist named Stitt Wilson. It has more psychiatrists and fewer bars than any other city of comparable size in California. And there are 249 churches for 120,300 people, of which 25 per cent are Negroes—one of the highest percentages of any city outside the South. Culturally, Berkeley is dominated by two factors: the campus and San Francisco across the Bay. The campus is so much a part of the community that the employment and housing markets have long since adjusted to student patterns. A $100-a-month apartment or cottage is no problem when four or five people split the rent, and there are plenty of ill-paid, minimum-strain jobs for those without money from home. Tutoring, typing, clerking, car washing, hash slinging, and baby sitting are all easy ways to make a subsistence income; one of the favorites among nonstudents is computer programming, which pays well.

Therefore, Berkeley's nonstudents have no trouble getting by. The climate is easy, the people are congenial, and the action never dies. Jim Prickett, who quit the University of Oklahoma and flunked out of San Francisco State, is another of *Spider's* nonstudent editors. "State has no community," he says, "and the only nonstudent I know of at Oklahoma is now in jail." At twenty-three, he is about as far Left as a man can get in these times, but his revolutionary zeal is gimped by pessimism. "If we have a revolution in this country it will be a Fascist take-over," he says with a shrug. Meanwhile he earns $25 a week as *Spider's* star writer, smiting the establishment hip and thigh at every opportunity. Prickett looks as much like a Red menace as Will Rogers looked like a Bantu. He is tall, thin, blond, and shuffles. "Hell, I'll probably sell out," he says with a faint smile. "Be a history teacher or something; but not for a while."

Yet there is something about Prickett that suggests he won't sell out so easily. Unlike many nonstudent activists, he has no degree, and in the society that appalls him even a sellout needs credentials. That is one of the most tangible realities of the nonstudent; by quitting school he has taken a physical step outside the system—a move that more and more students seem to find admirable. It is not an easy thing to repudiate—not now, at any rate, while the tide is running that way. And "the system" cannot be rejoined without some painful self-realization. Many a man has whipped up a hell broth of reasons to justify his sellout, but few recommend the taste of it. The problem is not like that of high school dropouts. They are supposedly inadequate, but the activist nonstudent is generally said to be superior. "A lot of these kids are top students," says Dr. David Powellson, chief of Cal's student psychiatric clinic, "but no university is set up to handle them."

How, then, are these bright mavericks to fit into the super-bureaucracies of government and big business? Cal takes its undergraduates from the top eighth of the state's high school graduates, and those accepted from out of state are no less "promising." The ones who migrate to Berkeley after quitting other schools are usually the same type. They are seekers—disturbed, perhaps, and perhaps for good reason. Many drift from one university to another, looking for the right program, the right professor, the right atmosphere, the right way to deal with the deplorable world they have suddenly grown into. It is like an army of Holden Caulfields, looking for a home and beginning to suspect they may never find one.

These are the outsiders, the nonstudents, and the potential— if not professional—troublemakers. There is something primitive and tragic in California's effort to make a law against them. The law itself is relatively unimportant, but the thinking that conceived it is a strutting example of what the crisis is all about. A society that will legislate in ignorance against its unfulfilled children and its angry, half-desperate truth seekers is bound to be shaken as it goes about making a reality of mass education.

It is a race against time, complacency, and vested interests. For the Left-activist nonstudent the race is very personal. Whether he is right, wrong, ignorant, vicious, super-intelligent, or simply bored, once he has committed himself to the extent of dropping out of school, he has also committed himself to "making it" outside the framework of whatever he has quit. A social radical presumably has his talent, his private madness, or some other insulated gimmick, but for the political radical the only true hope is somehow to bust the system that drove him into limbo. In this new era many believe they can do it, but most of those I talked to at Berkeley seemed a bit nervous. There was a singular vagueness as to the mechanics of the act, no real sense of the openings.

"What are you going to be doing ten years from now?" I asked a visiting radical in the house where *Spider* is put together. "What if there's no revolution by then, and no prospects of one?"

"Hell," he said, "I don't think about that. Too much is happening right now. If the revolution's coming, it had better come damn quick."

A Social History of the Hippies*

WARREN HINCKLE

AN ELDERLY SCHOOL BUS, painted like a fluorescent Easter egg in orange, chartreuse, cerise, white, green, blue, and, yes, black, was parked outside the solitary mountain cabin, which made it an easy guess that Ken Kesey, the novelist turned psychedelic Hotspur, was inside. So, of course, was Neal Cassady, the Tristram Shandy of the Beat Generation, prototype hero of Jack Kerouac's *On the Road*, who had sworn off allegiance to Kerouac when the beat scene became menopausal and signed up as the driver of Kesey's fun and games bus, which is rumored to run on LSD. Except for these notorious luminaries, the Summit Meeting of the leaders of the new hippie subculture, convened in the lowlands of California's High Sierras during an early spring weekend last month, seemed a little like an Appalachian Mafia gathering without Joe Bananas.

Where was Allen Ginsberg, father goddam to two generations of the underground? In New York, reading his poetry to freshmen. And where was Timothy Leary, self-styled guru to tens or is it hundreds of thousands of turned-on people? Off to some nowhere place like Stockton, to preach the gospel of Lysergic Acid Diethylamide to nice ladies in drip dry dresses.

The absence of the elder statesmen of America's synthetic gypsy movement meant something. It meant that the leaders of

* From *Ramparts* (March, 1967). Copyright © 1967 Ramparts Magazine, Inc. Used by permission of the publisher.

the booming psychedelic bohemia in the seminal city of San
Francisco were their own men—and strangely serious men, indeed, for hippies. Ginsberg and Leary may be Pied Pipers, but
they are largely playing old tunes. The young men who make the
new scene accept Ginsberg as a revered observer from the elder
generation; Leary they abide as an Elmer Gantry on their side,
to be used for proselytizing squares, only.

The mountain symposium had been called for the extraordinary
purpose of discussing the political future of the hippies. Hippies
are many things, but most prominently the bearded and beaded
inhabitants of the Haight–Ashbury, a little psychedelic city-state
edging Golden Gate Park. There, in a daily street-fair atmosphere,
upwards of fifteen thousand unbonded girls and boys interact in a
tribal, love-free, free-swinging, acid-based type of society where,
if you are a hippie and you have a dime, you can put it in a
parking meter and lie down in the street for an hour's suntan
(thirty minutes for a nickel) and most drivers will be careful not
to run you over.

Speaking, sometimes all at once, inside the Sierra cabin were
many voices of conscience and vision of the Haight–Ashbury—
belonging to men who, except for their Raggedy Andy hair, paisley
shirts, and pre-mod western levi jackets, sounded for all the world
like Young Republicans.

They talked about reducing governmental controls, the sanctity
of the individual, the need for equality among men. They talked,
very seriously, about the kind of society they wanted to live in,
and the fact that if they wanted an ideal world they would have
to go out and make it for themselves, because nobody, least of all
the government, was going to do it for them.

The utopian sentiments of these hippies were not to be put
down lightly. Hippies have a clear vision of the ideal community
—a psychedelic community, to be sure—where everyone is turned
on and beautiful and loving and happy and floating free. But it is
a vision that, despite the Alice in Wonderland phraseology hippies
usually breathlessly employ to describe it, necessarily embodies a
radical political philosophy: communal life, drastic restriction of
private property, rejection of violence, creativity before consump-
tion, freedom before authority, de-emphasis of government and
traditional forms of leadership.

Despite a disturbing tendency to quietism, all hippies *ipso facto*
have a political posture—one of unremitting opposition to the
Establishment which insists on branding them criminals because

they take LSD and marijuana, and hating them, anyway, because they enjoy sleeping nine in a room and three to a bed, seem to have free sex and guiltless minds, and can raise healthy children in dirty clothes.

The hippie choice of weapons is to love the Establishment to death rather than protest it or blow it up (hippies possess a confounding disconcern about traditional political methods or issues). But they are decidedly and forever outside the Consensus on which this society places such a premium, and since the hippie scene is so much the scene of those people under twenty-five that *Time* magazine warns will soon constitute half our population, this is a significant political fact.

This is all very solemn talk about people who like to skip rope and wear bright colors, but after spending some time with these fun and fey individuals you realize that, in a very unexpected way, they are as serious about what they're doing as the John Birch Society or the Junior League. It is not improbable, after a few more mountain seminars by those purposeful young men wearing beads, that the Haight–Ashbury may spawn the first utopian collectivist community since Brook Farm.

That this society finds it so difficult to take such rascally looking types seriously is no doubt the indication of a deep-rooted hang-up. But to comprehend the psychosis of America in the computer age, you have to know what's with the hippies.

[KEN KESEY—I]

Games people play, Merry Prankster Division

Let us go, then, on a trip.

You can't miss the Tripmaster: the thick-necked lad in the blue and white striped pants with the red belt and the golden eagle buckle, a watershed of wasted promise in his pale blue eyes, one front tooth capped in patriotic red, white and blue, his hair downy, flaxen, straddling the incredibly wide divide of his high forehead like two small toupees pasted on sideways. Ken Kesey, Heir Apparent Number One to the grand American tradition of blowing one's artistic talent to do some other thing, was sitting in a surprisingly comfortable chair inside the bus with the psychedelic crust, puffing absentmindedly on a harmonica.

The bus itself was ambulatory at about fifty miles an hour, jogging along a back road in sylvan Marin County, four loudspeakers turned all the way up, broadcasting both inside and outside Carl Orff's Carmina Burana, and filled with two dozen people simultaneously smoking marijuana and looking for an open ice cream store. It was the Thursday night before the Summit Meeting weekend and Kesey, along with some fifteen members of the turned-on yes men and women who call him "Chief" and whom he calls the "Merry Pranksters" in return, was demonstrating a "game" to a delegation of visiting hippie firemen.

Crossing north over the Golden Gate Bridge from San Francisco to Marin County to pay Kesey a state visit were seven members of The Diggers, a radical organization even by Haight–Ashbury standards, which exists to give things away, free. The Diggers started out giving out free food, free clothes, free lodging, and free legal advice, and hope eventually to create a totally free cooperative community. They had come to ask Kesey to get serious and attend the weekend meeting on the state of the nation of the hippies.

The dialogue had hardly begun, however, before Kesey loaded all comers into the bus and pushed off into the dark to search for a nocturnal ice cream store. The bus, which may be the closest modern man has yet come to aping the self-sufficiency of Captain Nemo's submarine, has its own power supply and is equipped with instruments for a full rock band, microphones, loudspeakers, spotlights, and comfortable seats all around. The Pranksters are presently installing microphones every three feet on the bus walls so everybody can broadcast to everybody else all at once.

At the helm was the Intrepid Traveler, Ken Babbs, who is auxiliary chief of the Merry Pranksters when Kesey is out of town or incommunicado or in jail, all three of which he has recently been. Babbs, who is said to be the model for the heroes of both Kesey novels, *One Flew Over the Cuckoo's Nest* and *Sometimes A Great Notion*, picked up a microphone to address the guests in the rear of the bus, like the driver of a Grayline tour: "We are being followed by a police car. Will someone watch and tell me when he turns on his red light."

The law was not unexpected, of course, because any cop who sees Kesey's bus just about *has* to follow it, would probably end up with some form of professional D.T.'s if he didn't. It is part of the game: the cop was now playing on their terms, and Kesey and his Pranksters were delighted. In fact, a discernible wave of disappointment swept across the bus when the cop finally gave up chasing this particular U.F.O. and turned onto another road.

The games he plays are very important to Kesey. In many

ways his intellectual rebellion has come full circle; he has long ago rejected the structured nature of society—the foolscap rings of success, conformity, and acceptance "normal" people must regularly jump through. To the liberated intellect, no doubt, these requirements constitute the most sordid type of game. But, once rejecting all the norms of society, the artist is free to create his own structures—and along with any new set of rules, however personal, there is necessarily, the shell to the tortoise, a new set of games. In Kesey's case, at least, the games are usually fun. Running around the outside of an insane society, the healthiest thing you can do is laugh.

It helps to look at this sort of complicated if not confused intellectual proposition in bas relief, as if you were looking at the simple pictures on Wedgwood china. Stand Successful Author Ken Kesey off against, say, Successful Author Truman Capote. Capote, as long as his game is accepted by the system, is free to be as mad as he can. So he tosses the biggest, most vulgar ball in a long history of vulgar balls, and achieves the perfect idiot synthesis of the upper middle and lower royal classes. Kesey, who cares as much about the system as he does about the Eddie Cantor Memorial Forest, invents his own game. He purchases a pre-'40's International Harvester school bus, paints it psychedelic, fills it with undistinguished though lovable individuals in varying stages of eccentricity, and drives brazenly down the nation's highways, high on LSD, watching and waiting for the cops to blow their minds.

At the least, Kesey's posture has the advantage of being intellectually consistent with the point of view of his novels. In *One Flew Over the Cuckoo's Nest*, he uses the setting of an insane asylum as a metaphor for what he considers to be the basic insanity, or at least the fundamentally bizarre illogic, of American society. Since the world forces you into a game that is both mad and unfair, you are better off inventing your own game. Then, at least, you have a chance of winning. At least that's what Kesey thinks.

[KEN KESEY—II]

The Curry Is Very Hot;
Merry Pranksters Are Having Pot

There wasn't much doing on late afternoon television, and the Merry Pranksters were a little restless. A few were turning on;

one Prankster amused himself squirting his friends with a yellow plastic watergun; another staggered into the living room, exhausted from peddling a bicycle in ever-diminishing circles in the middle of the street. They were all waiting, quite patiently, for dinner, which the Chief was whipping up himself. It was a curry, the recipe of no doubt cabalistic origin. Kesey evidently took his cooking seriously, because he stood guard by the pot for an hour and a half, stirring, concentrating on the little clock on the stove that didn't work.

There you have a slice of domestic life, February, 1967, from the swish Marin County home of Attorney Brian Rohan. As might be surmised, Rohan is Kesey's attorney, and the novelist and his *aides de camp* had parked their bus outside for the duration. The duration might last a long time, because Kesey has dropped out of the hippie scene. Some might say that he was pushed, because he fell, very hard, from favor among the hippies last year when he announced that he, Kesey, personally, was going to help reform the psychedelic scene. This sudden social conscience may have had something to do with beating a jail sentence on a compounded marijuana charge, but when Kesey obtained his freedom with instructions from the judge "to preach an anti-LSD warning to teenagers" it was a little too much for the Haight–Ashbury set. Kesey, after all, was the man who had turned on the Hell's Angels.

That was when the novelist was living in La Honda, a small community in the Skyline mountain range overgrown with trees and, after Kesey invited the Hell's Angels to several house parties, overgrown with sheriff's deputies. It was in this Sherwood Forest setting, after he had finished his second novel with LSD as his co-pilot, that Kesey inaugurated his band of Merry Pranksters (they have an official seal from the State of California incorporating them as "Intrepid Trips, Inc."), painted the school bus in glow sock colors, announced he would write no more ("Rather than write, I will ride buses, study the insides of jails, and see what goes on"), and set up funtime housekeeping on a full-time basis with the Pranksters, his wife and their three small children (one confounding thing about Kesey is the amorphous quality of the personal relationships in his entourage—the several attractive women don't seem, from the outside, to belong to any particular man; children are loved enough, but seem to be held in common).

When the Hell's Angels rumbled by, Kesey welcomed them

with LSD. "We're in the same business. You break people's bones, I break people's heads," he told them. The Angels seem to like the whole acid thing, because today they are a fairly constant act in the Haight–Ashbury show, while Kesey has abdicated his role as Scoutmaster to fledgling acid heads and exiled himself across the Bay. This self-imposed Elba came about when Kesey sensed that the hippie community had soured on him. He had committed the one mortal sin in the hippie ethic: *telling* people what to do. "Get into a responsibility bag," he urged some four hundred friends attending a private Halloween party. Kesey hasn't been seen much in the Haight–Ashbury since that night, and though the Diggers did succeed in getting him to attend the weekend discussion, it is doubtful they will succeed in getting the novelist involved in any serious effort to shape the Haight–Ashbury future. At thirty-one, Ken Kesey is a hippie has-been.

[KEN KESEY—III]

The Acid Tests—From Unitarians to Watts

Kesey is now a self-sufficient but lonely figure—if you can be lonely with dozens of Merry Pranksters running around your house all day. If he ever gets maudlin, which is doubtful, he can look back fondly on his hippie memories, which are definitely in the wow! category, because Ken Kesey did for acid roughly what Johnny Appleseed did for trees, and probably more.

He did it through a unique and short-lived American institution called the Acid Test. A lot of things happened at an Acid Test, but the main thing was that, in the Haight–Ashbury vernacular, everyone in the audience got zonked out of their minds on LSD. LSD in Pepsi. LSD in coffee. LSD in cake. LSD in the community punch. Most people were generally surprised, because they didn't know they were getting any LSD until it was too late. Later, when word got around that this sort of mad thing was happening at Acid Tests, Kesey sometimes didn't give out LSD on purpose, just so people wouldn't know whether they did or did not have LSD. Another game.

The Acid Tests began calmly enough. In the early versions Kesey merely gave a heart-to-heart psychedelic talk and handed LSD around like the Eucharist, which first happened at a Unitarian conference in Big Sur in August of 1965. He repeated this ritual several times, at private gatherings in his home in La Honda, on college campuses, and once at a Vietnam Day Committee rally at

Berkeley. Then Kesey added the Grateful Dead, a pioneer San Francisco rock group, to his Acid Tests and, the cherry on the matzos, the light show atmospheric technique of projecting slides and wild colors on the walls during rock dances. This combination he called "trips." Trip is the word for an LSD experience, but in Kesey's lexicon it also meant kicks, which were achieved by rapidly changing the audience's sensory environment what seemed like approximately ten million times during an evening by manipulating bright colored lights, tape recorders, slide projectors, weird sound machines, and whatever else may be found in the electronic sink, while the participants danced under stroboscopic lights to a wild rock band or just played around on the floor.

It was a fulgurous, electronically orgiastic thing (the most advanced Tests had closed circuit television sets on the dance floor so you could see what you were doing), which made psychedelics very "fun" indeed, and the hippies came in droves. Almost every hippie in the Bay Area went to at least one Acid Test, and it is not exceeding the bounds of reasonable speculation to say that Kesey may have turned on at least ten thousand people to LSD during the twenty-four presentations of the Acid Test. (During these Tests the Merry Pranksters painted everything including themselves in fluorescent tones, and bright colors became the permanent in-thing in psychedelic dress.)

Turning so many unsuspecting people on to LSD at once could be dangerous, as the Pranksters discovered on a 1965 psychedelic road show when they staged the ill-fated Watts Acid Test. Many of the leading citizens of Watts came to the show, which was all very fine except that whoever put the LSD in the free punch that was passed around put in too much by a factor of about four. This served to make for a very wild Acid Test, and one or two participants "freaked out" and had a very hard time of it for the next few days.

After the California legislature played Prohibition and outlawed LSD on October 6, 1966, Kesey wound up the Acid Test syndrome with what was billed as a huge "Trips Festival" in San Francisco. People who regularly turn on say the Trips Festival was a bore: it embodied all the Acid Test elements except acid and, happily for the coffers of Intrepid Trips, Inc., attracted a huge crowd of newspapermen, narcotics agents and other squares, but very few hippies. The Merry Pranksters slyly passed out plain sugar cubes for the benefit of the undercover agents.

Suddenly San Francisco, which for a grown-up city gets excited very easily, was talking about almost nothing but "trips" and LSD. Hippies, like overnight, had become fashionable.

If you are inclined to give thanks for this sort of thing, they go to the bad boy wonder of Psychedelphia, disappearing there over the horizon in his wayward bus.

[HISTORIAN CHESTER ANDERSON—I]

The Ghosts of Scenes Past, or How We got Here from There

Like Frederick J. Turner and Arnold Toynbee, Chester Anderson has a theory of history. His theory is psychedelic, but that is perfectly natural since he is a veteran acid head. Anderson, a thirty-five-year-old professional bohemian who looks forty-five, considers himself the unofficial historian of the psychedelic movement and has amassed enough footnotes to argue somewhat convincingly that the past fifteen years of social change in the United States—all the underground movements, and a significant part of the cultural changes—have been intimately connected with drugs.

If he is going to press his argument all the way, he may have to punch it out with Marshall McLuhan, who no doubt would assert that such phenomena as hippie colonies are nothing but a return to "tribal" culture, an inevitable reaction to our electronic age. And any social historian worth his salt will put it that every society has found some way to allow the sons and daughters of its middle class to drop out and cut up (most hippies by the way, are from middle-class stock, so what's the difference from, say, the Teddy Boys?) Maybe lots, maybe none. But there is no disputing the cultural and artistic flip-flops this country has gone through in the last decade. The jazz musicians' vogue meant something. So did the Beat Generation. So, we suppose, did Pop Art, and Rock and Roll, and so, of course, the hippies. If, in briefly tracing the derivation of the hippies from their seminal reasons in the intellectual uneasiness of the early 1950's, we chance to favor the testimony of Chester Anderson, it is only because he was there.

That was some bad year, 1953. There was a war on in Korea, a confusing, undefined war, the first big American war that wasn't the one to end all wars, because the aftermath of World War II had blown that phobia. And now the Bomb was with us, and with it the staccato series of disturbing headline events that stood for the Cold War; college was the only escape from the draft, but eggheads were becoming unpopular; Stevenson had lost the election and the Rosenbergs had been executed. It was all gloom, gloom, and dullsville, and if you were young and intellectual you were hard-pressed to find a hero or even a beautiful person. The only really alive, free thing, it seemed, was jazz—and the arrival of the long playing record had sparked a jazz renaissance, and with it the first drug heroes: most kids sympathized with Gene Krupa's marijuana busts, the agony of Lady Day's junk hangup was universal, and Charlie Parker had his own drugstore.

Lady Day's way wasn't the way of the new generation, Chester Anderson will be quick to tell you, because she was on "body" drugs. Whatever else body drugs—heroin, opium, barbiturates, alcohol, tranquilizers—may do, they eventually turn you off, and contemporary heads like to be turned on—i.e., senses intensified, stimulated rather than depressed. "Head" drugs, which do the latter, are both cheaper and easier to get than body drugs, and come in approximately eighteen varieties in three different classifications—natural drugs like marijuana, hashish, peyote, morning glory seeds, Hawaiian wood rose seeds, and certain types of Mexican mushrooms; artificial psychedelics like mescaline, LSD, psilocybin and psilocin, and whatever the ingredient is that makes Romilar cough syrup so popular with young heads; and synthetic stimulants which, used in large doses by heads, are known as "speed"—dexedrine, benzedrine, and methedrine.

But in the early 1950's there wasn't such a complete psychedelic medicine shelf to choose from, and the culturally disenchanted pioneers who began to settle new colonies in New York's Village and San Francisco's North Beach had to make do with pot. In a climate dominated by Dwight Eisenhower in the newspapers and Ed Sullivan on television, they also began to turn on to the pacifist, humanist philosophies of Asia—particularly Buddhism, most especially Zen—while Christianity as a workable concept became more meaningless, despite the exemplary efforts of such men as Brother Antoninus and Thomas Merton. American churchmen seemed to have neither the patience nor the fortitude to deal with people who were, well, *unsettled.* Folk music, which had been slowly dying, perked up a little, and there was a new interest in fresh, tuned-in poetry. As the '50's approached middle age and McCarthy went on the rampage, the few signs of life in a stagnant society centered around the disoriented peace movement, the fledgling civil rights movement, the young political Left, jazz and folk music, poetry, and Zen. Most of these followers were, of course, taking pot, while the rest of the country remained on booze and sleeping pills.

(If, in memory of the 85th anniversary of Anthony Trollope's death, we may be permitted an aside to the reader, it would be to say that one of the things that is considered original, but is in fact not, about the hippies is the concept of "dropping out" of society. Without adopting the histrionics of Hogarth crusading against the masses drinking gin, it is true that alcohol is an opiate which serves to help tens of millions of busy businessmen and lethargic housewives to "drop out" of any essential involvement in life and remain political and artistic boors. But alcohol is legal so nobody cares. If pot and LSD were ever legalized, it would be a mortal blow to this bohemia. Hippies have a political posture essentially because of the enforced criminality of their daily dose, and if taking LSD meant no more in society than the commuter slugging down his seventh martini, the conspiratorial magic would go out of the movement.)

Meanwhile, in San Francisco, Allen Ginsberg remembers an evening in 1955 which could stand as well as any for the starting point of what was to become the most thorough repudiation of America's middlebrow culture since the expatriates walked out on the country in the 1930's. The vanguard of what was to be the Beat Generation had gathered at the 6 Gallery on Fillmore Street for a poetry reading moderated by Kenneth Rexroth, a respectable leftish intellectual who was later to become the Public Defender of the beats. Lawrence Ferlinghetti was in the audience, and so were Kerouac and his then sidekick, Neal Cassady, listening to Michael McClure, Phil Lamantia, Gary Snyder, and Philip Whalen read their poetry. Ginsberg was there too, and delighted everyone with a section of the still unfinished "Howl," better known to beats as the Declaration of Independence.

Two distinct strains in the underground movement of the '50's were represented at this salient gathering. One was a distinctly fascist trend, embodied in Kerouac, which can be recognized by a totalitarian insistence on action and nihilism, and usually accompanied by a Superman concept. This strain runs, deeper and less silent, through the hippie scene today. It is into this fascist bag that you can put Kesey and his friends, the Hell's Angels, and, in a more subtle way, Dr. Timothy Leary.

The other, majority, side of the beats was a cultural reaction
to the existential brinkmanship forced on them by the Cold War,
and a lively attack on the concurrent rhetoric of complacency and
self-satisfaction that pervaded the literary establishment all the
way from the *Atlantic Monthly* to Lionel Trilling. Led by men
like Ginsberg and Ferlinghetti, the early beats weighed America
by its words and deeds, and found it pennyweight. They took
upon themselves the role of conscience for the machine. They
rejected all values and when, in attempting to carve a new creative
force, they told America to "go fuck itself," America reacted,
predictably, with an obscenity trial.

The early distant warnings of the drug-based culture that
would dominate the Haight–Ashbury a decade later were there in
the early days of North Beach. Marijuana was as popular as Coke
at a Baptist wedding, and the available hallucinogens—peyote and
mescaline—were part of the beat rebellion. Gary Snyder, poet,
mountain climber, formal Yamabushi Buddhist, and a highly re-
spected leader of the hippie scene today, first experimented with
peyote while living with the Indian tribe of the same name in
1948; Ginsberg first took it in New York in 1951; Lamantia,
Kerouac and Cassady were turned on by beat impresario Hymie
D'Angolo at his Big Sur retreat in 1952. And beat parties, whether
they served peyote, marijuana or near beer, were rituals, community sacraments, setting the format for contemporary hippie
rituals.

But the psychedelic community didn't really begin to flourish
until late 1957 and 1958 in New York, and for that story we
take you to Chester Anderson in the Village.

[HISTORIAN CHESTER ANDERSON—II]

Was the Kingston Trio Really Red Guards?

On Thanksgiving Day, 1957, Chester Anderson was turned
on to grass by a bongo-playing superhippie who went by the code
name of Mr. Sulks. Grass, if you don't know and don't have an
underground glossary handy, is translated marijuana, and from
that day forward, Anderson, who once studied music at the University of Miami so he could write string quartets like Brahms,
became a professional Turn-On and migrated with bohemia, east
to west to east to west, from the Village to North Beach back to
the Village to the Haight–Ashbury, where he can be found today
—a prototype of the older psychedelic type who mixes with the

drifting, turning on kids to form the central nervous system of any body of hippies.

The first psychedelic drug to reach the Village in any quantity was peyote, an obscure hallucinatory cactus bud used by Indians in religious ceremonies. Peyote was cheap and plentiful (it can still be ordered by mail from Laredo at $10 for 100 "buttons") and became highly touted—Havelock Ellis and Aldous Huxley recommended it. The only problem with peyote was that it tasted absolutely terrible, and, as peyote cults sprang up, peyote cookbooks came out with recipes for preparing the awful stuff in ways that would kill the taste. "Man," Chester recalls a head telling him at the time, "if I thought it'd get me high, I'd eat shit." As with most new head drugs, the taking of peyote was treated as a quasi-religious event. The first time Chester took it, he did so with great ritual before a statue of the Buddha.

Peyote was the thing in late 1957, and by the summer of 1958 mescaline, the first synthetic psychedelic, was widely distributed. The heads reacted like unwed mothers being handed birth control pills—they were no longer dependent on nature. Turn-ons could be *manufactured!*

According to Chester's files, LSD didn't arrive in any large, consumer-intended supply in the Village until the winter of 1961–62, and not in the Bay Area until the summer of 1964, but by that time something unusual had happened to America's psychedelic gypsies: they had become formal enemies of the State. Massive harassment by the cops in San Francisco, by the coffeehouse license inspectors in New York, had let the heads and the young middle-class types who came in caravan proportions, to test the no-more-teachers, no-more-books way of bohemian life, to view the Establishment as the bad guy who would crush their individuality and spirituality in any way he could. This is the derivation of whatever political posture the hippies have today. It will be significant, of course, only if the Haight–Ashbury scene doesn't go the way of the Beat Generation—assimilated by a kick-hungry society. For the serious, literary Beats, it was all over but the shouting when the Co-existence Bagel Shop became a stop on sightseeing tours.

In 1962, the Village was pulsating with psychedelic evangelism. LSD was so cheap and so plentiful that it became a big thing among heads to turn on new people as fast as they could give LSD away.

Pot, also, was being used more widely than ever by middle-class adults, and spread from the urban bohemias to the hinterlands by small folk music circles that were to be found everywhere from Jacksonville, Florida, to Wausau, Wisconsin. At the same time, almost the entire Village was treating LSD like it was a selection on a free lunch counter, and a scruffy folknik called Bobby Dylan was beginning to play charitable guest sets in the Washington Square coffeehouses. "Things," Chester said, "were happening more rapidly than we knew."

What was happening, Mr. Jones, was that folk music, under the influence of early acid culture, was giving way to rock and roll. Rock spread the hippie way of life like a psychedelic plague, and it metamorphosed in such rapid fashion from the popularity of folk music, that a very suspicious person might ask if seemingly safe groups like the Kingston Trio were not, in fact, the Red Guards of the hippie cultural revolution.

There was a rock and roll before, of course, but it was all bad seed. The likes of Frankie Avalon, Fabian, and Elvis Presley sent good rock and roll musicians running to folk music. Then absolutely the world's greatest musical blitz fell and the Beatles landed, everywhere, all at once. The impact of their popular music was analogous to the Industrial Revolution on the nineteenth century. They brought music out of the juke box and into the street. The Beatles' ecstatic, alive, electric sound had a total sensory impact, and was inescapably participational. It was "psychedelic music." "The Beatles are a trip," Chester said. Whether the Beatles or Dylan or the Rolling Stones actually came to their style through psychedelic involvement (Kenneth Tynan says a recent Beatles song "Tomorrow Never Knows" is "the best musical evocation of LSD I've ever heard") is not as important as the fact that their songs reflect LSD values—love, life, getting along with other people, and that this type of involving, turn-on music galvanized the entire hippie underground into overt, brassy existence—particularly in San Francisco.

Drug song lyrics may, in fact, be the entire literary output of the hippie generation. The hippies' general disregard for anything as static as a book is a fact over which Chester Anderson and Marshall McLuhan can shake hands. For acid heads are, in McLuhan's phrase, "post-literate." Hippies do not share our written, linear society—they like textures better than surfaces, prefer the electronic to the mechanical, like group, tribal activities. Theirs is an ecstatic, do-it-now culture, and rock and roll is their art form.

[THE MERCHANT PRINCES—I]

Dr. Leary—Pretender to the Hippie Throne

The suit was Brooks Brothers '59, and the paisley tie J. Press contemporary, but the bone-carved Egyptian mandala hanging around his neck, unless it was made in occupied Japan, had to be at least two thousand years old. Dr. Timothy Leary, B.A. University of Alabama, Ph.D. University of California, LSD Cuernavaca, and 86'd Harvard College, was dressed up for a night on the town, but as his devotees say of this tireless proselytizer of the psychedelic cause, it was work, work, work. Tonight Leary was scouting somebody else's act, a Swami's at that, who was turning on the hippies at the Avalon Ballroom by leading them in an hour-long Hindu chant without stopping much for breath. The Avalon is one of the two great, drafty ballrooms where San Francisco hippies, hippie-hangers-on, and young hippies-to-be congregate each weekend to participate in the psychedelic rock and light shows that are now as much a part of San Francisco as cable cars and a lot noisier.

This dance was a benefit for the new Swami, recently installed in a Haight–Ashbury storefront, with a fair passage sign from Allen Ginsberg whom he had bumped into in India. The hippies were turning out to see just what the Swami's *schtick* was, but Dr. Leary had a different purpose. He has a vested, professional interest in turning people on, and here was this Swami, trying to do it with just a chant, like it was natural childbirth or something.

The word professional is not used lightly. There is a large group of professionals making it by servicing and stimulating the hippie world—in the spirit of the Haight–Ashbury we should refer to these men as merchant princes—and Timothy Leary is the pretender to the throne.

Dr. Leary claims to have launched the first indigenous religion in America. That may very well be, though as a religious leader he is Aimee Semple McPherson in drag. Dr. Leary, who identifies himself as a "prophet," recently played the Bay Area in his LSD road show, where he sold $4 seats to lots of squares but few hippies (Dr. Leary's pitch is to the straight world), showed a technicolor movie billed as simulating an LSD experience (it was big on close-ups of enlarged blood vessels), burned incense, dressed like a holy man in white cotton pajamas, and told everybody to "turn on, tune in, and drop out."

In case you are inclined to make light of this philosophic advice you should not laugh out loud. Because Dr. Leary is serious about his work, he can not be dismissed as a cross between a white Father Divine and Nietzsche, no matter how tempting the analogy. He has made a substantial historical contribution to the psychedelic scene, although his arrest records may figure more prominently than his philosophy in future hippie histories.

Since, something like Eve, he first bit into the sacred psychedelic mushroom while lounging beside a swimming pool in Cuernavaca, he has been hounded by the consequences of his act. Since Dr. Leary discovered LSD, he has been booted out of Harvard for experimenting a little too widely with it among the undergraduate population, asked to leave several foreign countries for roughly the same reasons, and is now comfortably if temporarily ensconced in a turned-on billionaire friend's estate near Poughkeepsie, New York, while awaiting judicial determination of a thirty-year prison sentence for transporting a half-ounce of marijuana across the Rio Grande without paying the Texas marijuana tax, which has not been enforced since the time of the Lone Ranger.

If he were asked to contribute to the "L" volume of the World Book Encyclopedia, Dr. Leary would no doubt sum up his work as "having turned on American culture," though his actual accomplishments are somewhat more prosaic. Together with Richard Alpert, who was to Dr. Leary what Bill Moyers was to President Johnson, Leary wrote an article in May, 1962, in, surprise, *The Bulletin of the Atomic Scientists*. The article warned that in event of war, the Russians were likely to douse all our reservoirs with LSD in order to make people so complacent that they wouldn't particularly care about being invaded, and as a civil defense precaution we ought to do it ourselves first—you know, douse our own reservoirs—so that when the reds got *their* chance the country would know just what was coming off. It was back to the old drawing board after that article, but Alpert and Dr. Leary made their main contribution to the incredibly swift spread of LSD through the nation in 1964 by the simple act of publishing a formula for LSD, all that was needed by any enterprising housewife with a B-plus in high school chemistry and an inclination for black market activity. Dr. Leary's religious crusade has been a bust, convert-wise, and not so salutary financially, either, so he announced recently that he was dropping out, himself, to contemplate his navel under the influence. It would be easier to take Dr. Leary seriously if he could overcome his penchant for treating LSD as a patent snake-bite medicine.

An enlightening example of this panacea philosophy is found back among the truss ads in the September, 1966, issue of *Playboy*. In the midst of a lengthy interview when, as happens in *Playboy*, the subject got around to sex, Dr. Leary was all answers. "An LSD session that does not involve an ultimate merging with a person of the opposite sex isn't really complete," he said, a facet of the drug he neglected to mention to the Methodist ladies he was attempting to turn on in Stockton, California. But this time, Dr. Leary was out to turn on the *Playboy* audience.

The following selection from the interview is reprinted in its entirety. Italics are *Playboy's*.

PLAYBOY: We've heard that some women who ordinarily have difficulty achieving orgasm find themselves capable of multiple orgasms under LSD. Is that true?

LEARY: In a carefully prepared, loving LSD session, a woman will inevitably have several hundred orgasms.

PLAYBOY: Several *hundred?*

LEARY: Yes. Several hundred.

After recovering from that intelligence, the *Playboy* interviewer, phrasing the question as diplomatically as possible, asked Dr. Leary if he got much, being such a handsome LSD turn-on figure. Dr. Leary allowed that women were always falling over him, but responded with the decorum of Pope Paul being translated from the Latin: "Any charismatic person who is conscious of his own mythic potency awakens this basic hunger in women and pays reverence to it at the level that is harmonious and appropriate at the time."

Dr. Leary also said that LSD is a "specific *cure* for homosexuality."

The final measurement of the tilt of Dr. Leary's windmill, his no doubt earnest claim to be the prophet of this generation, must be made by weighing such recorded conversations against his frequent and urgent pleas to young people to "drop out of politics, protest, petitions and pickets" and join his "new religion" where, as he said recently:

"You have to be out of your mind to pray."

Perhaps, and quite probably so.

[THE MERCHANT PRINCES—II]

Where Dun & Bradstreet Fears to Tread

Allen Ginsberg asked ten thousand people to turn towards the sea and chant with him. They all did just that, and then picked up the papers and miscellaneous droppings on the turf of Golden Gate Park's Polo Field and went contentedly home. This was the end of the first Human Be-In, a gargantuan hippie happening held only for the joy of it in mid-January. The hippie tribes gathered under clear skies with rock bands, incense, chimes, flutes, feathers, candles, banners, and drums. Even the Hell's Angels were on their good behavior—announcing that they would guard the sound truck against unspecified evil forces. It was all so successful that the organizers are talking about another be-in this summer to be held at the bottom of the Grand Canyon with maybe two hundred thousand hippies being-in.

The local papers didn't quite know how to treat this one, except for the San Francisco *Chronicle's* ace society editor Frances Moffat, who ran through the crowd picking out local socialites and taking notes on the fashions.

Mrs. Moffat's intense interest reflects the very in, very marketable character of San Francisco Hippiedom. Relatively high-priced mod clothing and trinket stores are as common in the Haight–Ashbury as pissoirs used to be in Paris. They are run by hippie merchants mostly for square customers, but that doesn't mean that the hippies themselves aren't brand name conscious. Professing a distaste for competitive society, hippies are, contradictorily, frantic consumers. Unlike the beats, they do not disdain money. Indeed, when they have it, which with many is often, they use it to buy something pretty or pleasureful. You will find only the best hi-fi sets in hippie flats.

In this commercial sense, the hippies have not only accepted assimilation (the beats fought it, and lost), they have swallowed it whole. The hippie culture is in many ways a prototype of the most ephemeral aspects of the larger American society; if the people looking in from the suburbs want change, clothes, fun, and some lightheadedness from the new gypsies, the hippies are delivering—and some of them are becoming rich hippies because of it.

The biggest Robber Baron is dance promoter Bill Graham, a Jewish boy from New York who made it big in San Francisco by cornering the hippie bread and circuses concession. His weekend combination rock and roll dances and light shows at the cavernous, creaky old Fillmore Auditorium on the main street of San Francisco's Negro ghetto are jammed every night. Even Andy Warhol played the Fillmore. Although Graham is happy providing these weekend spiritual experiences, he's not trying to be a leader. "I don't want to make cadres, just money," he said. Graham's crosstown competitor is Chet Helms, a rimless-glasses variety hippie from Texas who has turned the pioneer, non-profit San Francisco rock group called The Family Dog, into a very profit-making enterprise at the Avalon Ballroom.

A side-product of the light show dances, and probably the only other permanent manifestation of hippie culture to date, is the revival in a gangbusters way of Art Nouveau poster art. Wes Wilson, who letters his posters in 18, 24 and 36 point Illegible, originated the basic style in posters for the Fillmore dances. Graham found he could make as much money selling posters as dance tickets, so he is now in the poster business, too.

The posters, at $1 apiece, as common as window shades in the Haight–Ashbury, demand total involvement from the reader, and are thus considered psychedelic manifestations of the existential, non-verbal character of hippie culture.

Haight Street, the Fifth Avenue of Hippiedom, is geographically parallel to Golden Gate Park but several blocks uphill, where rows of half vacant store fronts once indicated the gradual decline of a middle-class neighborhood. But all that changed, dramatically, during the past eighteen months. Haight Street now looks like the Metropolitan Opera Company backstage on the opening night of *Aida*. The stores are all occupied, but with mercantile ventures that might give Dun & Bradstreet cause to wonder. Threaded among the older meat markets, discount furniture stores, laundromats, and proletarian bars are a variety of leather goods shops, art galleries, mod clothing stores, and boutiques specializing in psychedelic paraphernalia like beads, prisms, and marijuana pipes, and of course there is the Psychedelic Shop itself.

The Psychedelic Shop is treated as a hippie landmark of sorts, but the Haight–Ashbury scene was percolating long before the Thelin brothers, Ron and Jay, stuffed a disconcertingly modern glass and steel store front full of amulets, psychedelic books, a large stock of the underground press, and some effete gadgetry for acid heads. The hippie phenomena began to metamorphose from a personal to a social happening around the fall of 1965 after the kids at Berkeley turned on to LSD, Ken Kesey started holding Acid Tests, and The Family Dog staged its first dance.

Instrumental in spreading the word was the *Chronicle*'s highly regarded jazz critic, Ralph J. Gleason. Gleason is read religiously by hippies. Besides explaining to his square readers what is happening, he is also the unofficial arbitrator of good taste in the Haight–Ashbury community. Gleason was quick to tell Ken Kesey, in print, when he was out of line, and did the same for Dr. Leary. Gleason's writings tuned in other members of the *Chronicle* staff, and the extensive, often headline publicity the newspaper gave to the hippie scene (Kesey's return from a self-imposed Mexican exile was treated with the seriousness of a reasonably large earthquake) helped escalate the Haight–Ashbury population explosion.

So there is plenty of business for the hippie merchants, but some of them, like the Thelin brothers, are beginning to wonder where it will all lead. At the prodding of The Diggers, the Thelins are considering making the store a non-profit cooperative that will help "the kids get high and stay high" at low cost. They may also take the same steps with *The Oracle*, the Haight–Ashbury monthly tabloid. The majority of the hip merchants, however, are very comfortable with the ascending publicity and sales, and have as little vision of what they are helping create than did Alexander Bell when he spilled acid on himself.

[EMMETT GROGAN—I]

Will the Real Frodo Baggins Please Stand Up?

Except for the obvious fact that he wasn't covered with fur, you would have said to yourself that for sure there was old Frodo Baggins, crossing Haight Street. Frodo Baggins is the hero of the English antiquarian J. R. R. Tolkien's classic trilogy, *Lord of the Rings*, absolutely the favorite book of every hippie, about a race of little people called Hobbits who live somewhere in pre-history in a place called Middle Earth. Hobbits are hedonistic, happy little fellows who love beauty and pretty colors. Hobbits have their own scene and resent intrusion, pass the time eating three or four meals a day and smoke burning leaves of herb in pipes of clay. You can see why hippies would like Hobbits.

The hustling, heroic-looking fellow with the mistaken identity was Emmett Grogan, kingpin of The Diggers and the closest thing the hippies in the Haight–Ashbury have to a real live hero.

Grogan, twenty-three, with blond, unruly hair, and a fair, freckled Irish face, has the aquiline nose of a leader, but he would prefer to say that he "just presents alternatives." He is in and out of jail seventeen times a week, sometimes busted for smashing a cop in the nose (Grogan has a very intolerant attitude toward policemen), sometimes bailing out a friend, and sometimes, like Monopoly, just visiting. The alternatives he presents are rather disturbing to the hippie bourgeoisie, since he thinks they have no business charging hippies money for their daily needs and should have the decency to give things away free, like The Diggers do, or at least charge the squares and help out the hippies.

Grogan has a very clear view of what freedom means in society ("Why can't I stand on the corner and wait for nobody? Why can't everyone?") and an even clearer view of the social position of the hippie merchants ("They just want to expand their sales, they don't care what happens to people here; they're nothing but goddamn shopkeepers with beards").

Everyone is a little afraid of Grogan in the Haight–Ashbury, including the cops. A one-man crusade for purity of purpose, he is the conscience of the hippie community. He is also a bit of a daredevil and a madman, and could easily pass for McMurphy, the roguish hero in Kesey's novel set in an insane asylum. There is a bit of J. P. Donleavy's *Ginger Man* in him, too.

A few weeks ago, out collecting supplies for The Diggers' daily free feed, Grogan went into a San Francisco wholesale butcher and asked for soup bones and meat scraps. "No free food here, we work for what we eat," said the head butcher, a tattooed Bulgar named Louie, who was in the icebox flanked by his seven assistant butchers. "You're a fascist pig and a coward," replied Grogan, whom Louie immediately smashed in the skull with the blunt side of a carving knife. That turned out to be a mistake, because the seven assistant butchers didn't like Louie much, and all jumped him. While all those white coats were grunting and rolling in the sawdust, a bleeding Grogan crawled out with four cardboard boxes full of meat.

This was a typical day in Dogpatch for Grogan, who has had his share of knocks. A Brooklyn boy, he ran away from home at fifteen and spent the next six years in Europe, working as a busboy in the Alps, and, later, studying film making in Italy under Antonioni. Grogan had naturally forgotten to register for the draft, so when he returned to the United States he was in the Army four days later. That didn't last long, however, because the first

thing Grogan had to do was clean the barracks. His idea of cleaning barracks was to throw all the guns out the window, plus a few
of the rusty beds, and artistically displeasing footlockers. Then
he began painting the remaining bed frames yellow. "I threw out
everything that was not esthetically pleasing," he told the sergeant.

Two days later Grogan was in the psychiatric ward of Letter-
man Hospital in San Francisco where he stayed for six months
before the authorities decided they couldn't quite afford to keep
him. That was shortly after an Army doctor, learning of his film
training, ordered Grogan to the photo lab for "work therapy." It
was a "beautiful, tremendously equipped lab," Grogan recalls, and
since it wasn't used very much, he took a picture of his own big
blond face and proceeded to make 5000 prints. When the doctors
caught up with him, he had some 4700 nine by twelve glossies of
Emmett Grogan neatly stacked on the floor, and all lab machines:
driers, enlargers, developers were going like mad, and the water
was running over on the floor. "What did you do *that* for?" a
doctor screamed.

Grogan shrugged. "I'm crazy," he said.

He was released a little later, and acted for a while with the
San Francisco Mime Troupe, the city's original and brilliant radical theater ensemble. Then last fall, when the Negro riots broke
out in San Francisco and the National Guard put a curfew on the
Haight–Ashbury, The Diggers happened. "Everybody was trying
to figure how to react to the curfew. The SDS came down and
said ignore it, go to jail. The merchants put up chicken posters
saying 'for your own safety, get off the street.' Somehow, none of
those ideas seemed right. If you had something to do on the streets,
you should do it and tell the cops to go screw off. If you didn't,
you might as well be inside."

Something to do, to Grogan, was to eat if you were hungry,
so at 8 P.M., at the curfew witching hour, he and an actor friend
named Billy Landau set up a delicious free dinner in the park,
right under the cops' noses, and the hippies came and ate and
have been chowing down, free, every night since. The Haight–
Ashbury has never been quite the same.

[EMMETT GROGAN—II]

A *Psychedelic* Grapes of Wrath

Every Bohemian community has its inevitable coterie of vision-
aries who claim to know what it is all about. But The Diggers are,

somehow, different. They are bent on creating a wholly cooperative subculture and, so far, they are not just hallucinating, they are doing it.

Free clothes (used) are there for whomever wants them. Free meals are served every day. Next, Grogan plans to open a smart mod clothing store on Haight Street and give the clothes away free, too (the hippie merchants accused him of "trying to undercut our prices"). He wants to start Digger farms where participants will raise their own produce. He wants to give away free acid, to eliminate junky stuff and end profiteering. He wants cooperative living to forestall inevitable rent exploitation when the Haight–Ashbury becomes chic.

Not since Brook Farm, not since the Catholic Workers, has any group in this dreadfully co-optive, consumer society been so serious about a utopian community.

If Grogan succeeds or fails in the Haight–Ashbury it will not be as important as the fact that he has tried. For he is, at least, providing the real possibility of what he calls "alternatives" in the down-the-rabbit-hole-culture of the hippies.

Grogan is very hung up on freedom. "Do your thing, what you are, and nothing will ever bother you," he says. His heroes are the Mad Bomber of New York who blissfully blew up all kinds of things around Manhattan over thirty years because he just liked to blow things up, and poet Gary Snyder, whom he considers the "most important person in the Haight–Ashbury" because instead of sitting around sniffing incense and talking about it, he went off to Japan and became a Zen master. "He did it, man."

This is an interesting activist ethic, but it remains doubtful just what the hippies will do. Not that many, certainly, will join Grogan's utopia, because utopias, after all, have a size limit.

The New Left has been flirting with the hippies lately, even to the extent of singing "The Yellow Submarine" at a Berkeley protest rally, but it looks from here like a largely unrequited love.

The hip merchants will, of course, go on making money.

And the youngsters will continue to come to the Haight–Ashbury and do—what?

That was the question put to the hippie leaders at their Summit Meeting. They resolved their goals, but not the means, and the loud noise you heard from outside was probably Emmett Grogan pounding the table with his shoe.

The crisis of the happy hippie ethic is precisely this: it is all right to turn on, but it is not enough to drop out. Grogan sees the issue in the gap "between the radical political philosophy of Jerry Rubin and Mario Savio and psychedelic love philosophy." He, himself, is not interested in the war in Vietnam, but on the other hand he does not want to spend his days like Ferdinand sniffing pretty flowers.

This is why he is so furious at the hip merchants. "They created the myth of this utopia; now they aren't going to do anything about it." Grogan takes the evils of society very personally, and he gets very angry, almost physically sick, when a pregnant fifteen-year-old hippie's baby starves in her stomach, a disaster which is not untypical in the Haight–Ashbury, and which Grogan sees being repeated ten-fold this summer when upwards of two hundred thousand migrant teen-agers and college kids come, as a psychedelic *Grapes of Wrath,* to utopia in search of the heralded turn-on.

The danger in the hippie movement is more than overcrowded streets and possible hunger riots this summer. If more and more youngsters begin to share the hippie political posture of unrelenting quietism, the future of activist, serious politics is bound to be affected. The hippies have shown that it can be pleasant to drop out of the arduous task of attempting to steer a difficult, unrewarding society. But when that is done, you leave the driving to the Hell's Angels.

The Motorcycle Gangs*

HUNTER S. THOMPSON

Last labor day weekend newspapers all over California gave
front-page reports of a heinous gang rape in the town of Seaside
on the Monterey Peninsula. Two girls, aged fourteen and fifteen,
were allegedly taken from their dates by a gang of filthy, fren-
zied, boozed-up motorcycle hoodlums called "Hell's Angels," and
dragged off to be "repeatedly assaulted."

A deputy sheriff, summoned by one of the erstwhile dates, said
he "arrived at the beach and saw a huge bonfire surrounded by
cyclists of both sexes. Then the two sobbing, near-hysterical girls
staggered out of the darkness, begging for help. One was completely nude and the other had on only a torn sweater."

Some three hundred Hell's Angels were gathered in the Seaside–Monterey area at the time, having convened, they said, for
the purpose of raising funds among themselves to send the body
of a former member, killed in an accident, back to his mother in
North Carolina. One of the Angels, hip enough to falsely identify
himself as "Frenchy of San Bernardino," told a local reporter who
came out to meet the cyclists: "We chose Monterey because we
get treated good here; most other places we get thrown out of
town."

But Frenchy spoke too soon. The Angels weren't on the peninsula twenty-four hours before four of them were in jail for rape,

---

* From *The Nation* (May 17, 1965). Used by permission of the publisher.

and the rest of the troop was being escorted to the county line by a large police contingent. Several were quoted, somewhat derisively, as saying: "That rape charge against our guys is phony and it won't stick."

It turned out to be true, but that was another story and certainly no headliner. The difference between the Hell's Angels in the papers and the Hell's Angels for real is enough to make a man wonder what newsprint is for. It also raises a question as to who are the real hell's angels.

Ever since World War II, California has been strangely plagued by wild men on motorcycles. They usually travel in groups of ten to thirty, booming along the highways and stopping here and there to get drunk and raise hell. In 1947, hundreds of them ran amok in the town of Hollister, an hour's fast drive south of San Francisco, and got enough press notices to inspire a film called *The Wild One*, starring Marlon Brando. The film had a massive effect on thousands of young California motorcycle buffs: in many ways, it was their version of *The Sun Also Rises*.

The California climate is perfect for motorcycles, as well as surfboards, swimming pools, and convertibles. Most of the cyclists are harmless weekend types, members of the American Motorcycle Association, and no more dangerous than skiers or skin divers. But a few belong to what the others call "outlaw clubs," and these are the ones who—especially on weekends and holidays—are likely to turn up almost anywhere in the state, looking for action. Despite everything the psychiatrists and Freudian casuists have to say about them, they are tough, mean, and potentially as dangerous as packs of wild boar. When push comes to shove, any leather fetishes or inadequacy feelings that may be involved are entirely beside the point, as anyone who has ever tangled with these boys will sadly testify. When you get in an argument with a group of outlaw motorcyclists, you can generally count your chances of emerging unmaimed by the number of heavy-handed allies you can muster in the time it takes to smash a beer bottle. In this league, sportsmanship is for old liberals and young fools. "I smashed his face," one of them said to me of a man he'd never seen until the swinging started. "He got wise. He called me a punk. He must have been stupid."

The most notorious of these outlaw groups is the Hell's Angels, supposedly headquartered in San Bernardino, just east of Los Angeles, and with branches all over the state. As a result of the infamous "Labor Day gang rape," the Attorney General of

California has recently issued an official report on the Hell's Angels. According to the report, they are easily identified:

The emblem of the Hell's Angels, termed "colors," consists of an embroidered patch of a winged skull wearing a motorcycle helmet. Just below the wing of the emblem are the letters "MC." Over this is a band bearing the words "Hell's Angels." Below the emblem is another patch bearing the local chapter name, which is usually an abbreviation for the city or locality. These patches are sewn on the back of a usually sleeveless denim jacket. In addition, members have been observed wearing various types of Luftwaffe insignia and reproductions of German iron crosses.[1] Many affect beards and their hair is usually long and unkempt. Some wear a single earring in a pierced ear lobe. Frequently they have been observed to wear metal belts made of a length of polished motorcycle drive chain which can be unhooked and used as a flexible bludgeon. . . . Probably the most universal common denominator in identification of Hell's Angels is their generally filthy condition. Investigating officers consistently report these people, both club members and their female associates, seem badly in need of a bath. Fingerprints are a very effective means of identification because a high percentage of Hell's Angels have criminal records.

In addition to the patches on the back of Hell's Angels jackets, the "One Percenters" wear a patch reading "1%-er." Another badge worn by some members bears the number "13." It is reported to represent the 13th letter of the alphabet, "M," which in turn stands for marijuana and indicates the wearer thereof is a user of the drug.

The Attorney General's report was colorful, interesting, heavily biased, and consistently alarming—just the sort of thing, in fact, to make a clanging good article for a national newsmagazine. Which it did; both barrels. *Newsweek* led with a left hook titled "The Wild Ones." *Time* crossed with a right, inevitably titled "The Wilder Ones." The Hell's Angels, cursing the implications of this new attack, retreated to the bar of the DePaul Hotel near the San Francisco waterfront and planned a weekend beach party. I showed them the articles. Hell's Angels do not normally read newsmagazines. "I'd go nuts if I read that stuff all the time," said one. "It's all bullshit."

Newsweek was relatively circumspect. It offered local color, flashy quotes, and "evidence" carefully attributed to the official report but unaccountably said the report accused the Hell's Angels

---

[1] Purely for decorative and shock effect. The Hell's Angels are apolitical and no more racist than other ignorant young thugs.

of homosexuality, whereas the report said just the opposite. *Time* leaped into the fray with a flurry of blood, booze, and semen-flecked wordage that amounted, in the end, to a classic of super-charged hokum: "Drug-induced stupors . . . no act is too degrading . . . swap girls, drugs and motorcycles with equal abandon . . . stealing forays . . . then ride off again to seek some new nadir in sordid behavior. . . ."

Where does all this leave the Hell's Angels and the thousands of shuddering Californians (according to *Time*) who are worried sick about them? Are these outlaws really going to be busted, routed, and cooled, as the newsmagazines implied? Are California highways any safer as a result of this published uproar? Can honest merchants once again walk the streets in peace? The answer is that nothing has changed except that a few people calling themselves Hell's Angels have a new sense of identity and importance.

After two weeks of intensive dealing with the Hell's Angels phenomenon, both in print and in person, I'm convinced the net result of the general howl and publicity has been to obscure and avoid the real issues by invoking a savage conspiracy of bogeymen and conning the public into thinking all will be "business as usual" once this fearsome snake is scotched, as it surely will be by hard and ready minions of the Establishment.

Meanwhile, according to Attorney General Thomas C. Lynch's own figures, California's true crime picture makes the Hell's Angels look like a gang of petty jack rollers. The police count 463 Hell's Angels: 205 around Los Angeles and 233 in the San Francisco–Oakland area. I don't know about L.A. but the real figures for the Bay Area are thirty or so in Oakland and exactly eleven—with one facing expulsion—in San Francisco. This disparity makes it hard to accept other police statistics. The dubious package also shows convictions on 1,023 misdemeanor counts and 151 felonies —primarily vehicle theft, burglary, and assault. This is for all years and all alleged members.

California's overall figures for 1963 list 1,116 homicides, 12,448 aggravated assaults, 6,257 sex offenses, and 24,532 burglaries. In 1962, the state listed 4,121 traffic deaths, up from 3,839 in 1961. Drug arrest figures for 1964 showed a 101 per cent increase in juvenile marijuana arrests over 1963, and a recent back-page story in the San Francisco *Examiner* said, "The venereal disease rate among (the city's) teen-agers from 15–19 has more than doubled in the past four years." Even allowing for the annual population jump, juvenile arrests in all categories are rising by 10 per cent or more each year.

Against this background, would it make any difference to the safety and peace of mind of the average Californian if every motorcycle outlaw in the state (all 901, according to the police) were garroted within twenty-four hours? This is not to say that a group like the Hell's Angels has no meaning. The generally bizarre flavor of their offenses and their insistence on identifying themselves make good copy, but usually overwhelm—in print, at least —the unnerving truth that they represent, in colorful microcosm, what is quietly and anonymously growing all around us every day of the week.

"We're bastards to the world and they're bastards to us," one of the Oakland Angels told a *Newsweek* reporter. "When you walk into a place where people can see you, you want to look as repulsive and repugnant as possible. We are complete social outcasts—outsiders against society."

A lot of this is a pose, but anyone who believes that's all it is has been on thin ice since the death of Jay Gatsby. The vast majority of motorcycle outlaws are uneducated, unskilled men between twenty and thirty, and most have no credentials except a police record. So at the root of their sad stance is a lot more than a wistful yearning for acceptance in a world they never made; their real motivation is an instinctive certainty as to what the score really is. They are out of the ball game and they know it—and that is their meaning; for unlike most losers in today's society, the Hell's Angels not only know but spitefully proclaim exactly where they stand.

I went to one of their meetings recently, and halfway through the night I thought of Joe Hill on his way to face a Utah firing squad and saying his final words: "Don't mourn, organize." It is safe to say that no Hell's Angel has ever heard of Joe Hill or would know a Wobbly from a Bushmaster, but nevertheless they are somehow related. The I.W.W. had serious plans for running the world, while the Hell's Angels mean only to defy the world's machinery. But instead of losing quietly, one by one, they have banded together with a mindless kind of loyalty and moved outside the framework, for good or ill. There is nothing particularly romantic or admirable about it; that's just the way it is, strength in unity. They don't mind telling you that running fast and loud on their customized Harley 74's gives them a power and a purpose that nothing else seems to offer.

Beyond that, their position as self-proclaimed outlaws elicits a certain popular appeal, however reluctant. That is especially true in the West and even in California where the outlaw tradition is still honored. The unarticulated link between the Hell's Angels and the millions of losers and outsiders who don't wear any colors is the key to their notoriety and the ambivalent reactions they inspire. There are several other keys, having to do with politicians, policemen and journalists, but for this we have to go back to Monterey and the Labor Day "gang rape."

Politicians, like editors and cops, are very keen on outrage stories, and state Senator Fred S. Farr of Monterey County is no exception. He is a leading light of the Carmel–Pebble Beach set and no friend of hoodlums anywhere, especially gang rapists who invade his constituency. Senator Farr demanded an immediate investigation of the Hell's Angels and others of their ilk—Commancheros, Stray Satans, Iron Horsemen, Rattlers (a Negro club), and Booze Fighters—whose lack of status caused them all to be lumped together as "other disreputables." In the cut-off world of big bikes, long runs, and classy rumbles, this new, state-sanctioned stratification made the Hell's Angels very big. They were, after all, Number One. Like John Dillinger.

Attorney General Lynch, then new in his job, moved quickly to mount an investigation of sorts. He sent questionnaires to more than one hundred sheriffs, district attorneys, and police chiefs, asking for information on the Hell's Angels and those "other disreputables." He also asked for suggestions as to how the law might deal with them.

Six months went by before all the replies were condensed into the fifteen-page report that made new outrage headlines when it was released to the press. (The Hell's Angels also got a copy; one of them stole mine.) As a historical document, it read like a plot synopsis of Mickey Spillane's worst dreams. But in the matter of solutions it was vague, reminiscent in some ways of Madame Nhu's proposals for dealing with the Vietcong. The state was going to centralize information on these thugs, urge more vigorous prosecution, put them all under surveillance whenever possible, etc.

A careful reader got the impression that even if the Hell's Angels had acted out this script—eighteen crimes were specified and dozens of others implied—very little would or could be done about it, and that indeed Mr. Lynch was well aware he'd been put, for political reasons, on a pretty weak scent. There was plenty of mad action, senseless destruction, orgies, brawls, perversions, and a strange parade of "innocent victims" that, even on paper, was enough to tax the credulity of the dullest police reporter. Any bundle of information off police blotters is bound to reflect a special viewpoint, and parts of the Attorney General's report are actually humorous, if only for the language. Here is an excerpt:

On November 4, 1961, a San Francisco resident driving through Rodeo, possibly under the influence of alcohol, struck a motorcycle belonging to a Hell's Angel parked outside a bar. A group of Angels pursued the vehicle, pulled the driver from the car and attempted to demolish the rather expensive vehicle. The bartender claimed he had seen nothing, but a cocktail waitress in the bar furnished identification to the officers concerning some of those responsible for the assault. The next day it was reported to officers that a member of the Hell's Angels gang had threatened the life of this waitress as well as another woman waitress. A male witness who definitely identified five participants in the assault including the president of the Vallejo Hell's Angels and the Vallejo "Road Rats" advised officers that because of his fear of retaliation by club members he would refuse to testify to the facts he had previously furnished.

That is a representative item in the section of the report titled "Hoodlum Activities." First, it occurred in a small town—Rodeo is on San Pablo Bay just north of Oakland—where the Angels had stopped at a bar without causing any trouble until some offense was committed against them. In this case, a driver whom even the police admit was "possibly" drunk hit one of their motorcycles. The same kind of accident happens every day all over the nation, but when it involves outlaw motorcyclists it is something else again. Instead of settling the thing with an exchange of insurance information or, at the very worst, an argument with a few blows, the Hell's Angels beat the driver and "attempted to demolish the vehicle." I asked one of them if the police exaggerated this aspect, and he said no, they had done the natural thing: smashed headlights, kicked in doors, broken windows, and torn various components off the engine.

Of all their habits and predilections that society finds alarming, this departure from the time-honored concept of "an eye for an eye" is the one that most frightens people. The Hell's Angels try not to do anything halfway, and anyone who deals in extremes is bound to cause trouble, whether he means to or not. This, along with a belief in total retaliation for any offense or insult, is what makes the Hell's Angels unmanageable for the police and morbidly fascinating to the general public. Their claim that they "don't start trouble" is probably true more often than not, but their idea of "provocation" is dangerously broad, and their biggest problem is that nobody else seems to understand it. Even dealing with them personally, on the friendliest terms, you can sense their hair-trigger readiness to retaliate.

This is a public thing, and not at all true among themselves. In a meeting, their conversation is totally frank and open. They speak to and about one another with an honesty that more civilized people couldn't bear. At the meeting I attended (and before they realized I was a journalist) one Angel was being publicly evaluated; some members wanted him out of the club and others wanted to keep him in. It sounded like a group-therapy clinic in progress—not exactly what I expected to find when just before midnight I walked into the bar of the DePau in one of the bleakest neighborhoods in San Francisco, near Hunters Point. By the time I parted company with them—at 6:30 the next morning after an all-night drinking bout in my apartment—I had been impressed by a lot of things, but no one thing about them was as consistently obvious as their group loyalty. This is an admirable quality, but it is also one of the things that gets them in trouble: a fellow Angel is *always right* when dealing with outsiders. And this sort of reasoning makes a group of "offended" Hell's Angels nearly impossible to deal with.

Here is another incident from the Attorney General's report:

On September 19, 1964, a large group of Hell's Angels and "Satan's Slaves" converged on a bar in South Gate (Los Angeles County), parking their motorcycles and cars in the street in such a fashion as to block one-half of the roadway. They told officers that three members of the club had recently been asked to stay out of the bar and that they had come to tear it down. Upon their approach the bar owner locked the doors and turned off the lights and no entrance was made, but the group did demolish a cement block fence. On arrival of the police, members of the club were lying on the sidewalk and in the street. They were asked to leave the city, which they did reluctantly. As they left, several were heard to say that they would be back and tear down the bar.

Here again is the ethic of total retaliation. If you're "asked to stay out" of a bar, you don't just punch the owner—you come back with your army and destroy the whole edifice. Similar incidents—along with a number of vague rape complaints—make up the bulk of the report. Eighteen incidents in four years, and none except the rape charges are more serious than cases of assault on citizens who, for their own reasons, had become involved with the Hell's Angels prior to the violence. I could find no cases of unwarranted attacks on wholly innocent victims. There are a few borderline cases, wherein victims of physical attacks seemed innocent, according to police and press reports, but later refused to testify for fear of "retaliation." The report asserts very strongly that Hell's Angels are difficult to prosecute and convict because they make a habit of threatening and intimidating witnesses. That is probably true to a certain extent, but in many cases victims have refused to testify because they were engaged in some legally dubious activity at the time of the attack.

In two of the most widely publicized incidents the prosecution would have fared better if their witnesses and victims *had* been intimidated into silence. One of these was the Monterey "gang rape," and the other a "rape" in Clovis, near Fresno in the Central Valley. In the latter, a thirty-six-year-old widow and mother of five children claimed she'd been yanked out of a bar where she was having a quiet beer with another woman, then carried to an abandoned shack behind the bar and raped repeatedly for two and a half hours by fifteen or twenty Hell's Angels and finally robbed of $150. That's how the story appeared in the San Francisco newspapers the next day, and it was kept alive for a few more days by the woman's claims that she was getting phone calls threatening her life if she testified against her assailants.

Then, four days after the crime, the victim was arrested on charges of "sexual perversion." The true story emerged, said the Clovis chief of police, when the woman was "confronted" by witnesses. "Our investigation shows she was not raped," said the chief. "She participated in lewd acts in the tavern with at least three Hell's Angels before the owners ordered them out. She encouraged their advances in the tavern, then led them to an abandoned house in the rear. . . . She was not robbed but, according to a woman who accompanied her, had left her house early in the evening with $5 to go bar-hopping." That incident did not appear in the Attorney General's report.

But it was impossible not to mention the Monterey "gang rape," because it was the reason for the whole subject to become official. Page one of the report—which *Time's* editors apparently skipped—says that the Monterey case was dropped because ". . . further investigation raised questions as to whether forcible rape had been committed or if the identifications made by victims were valid." Charges were dismissed on September 25, with the concurrence of a grand jury. The deputy District Attorney said "a doctor examined the girls and found no evidence" to support the charges. "Besides that, one girl refused to testify," he explained, "and the other was given a lie-detector test and found to be wholly unreliable."

This, in effect, was what the Hell's Angels had been saying all along. Here is their version of what happened, as told by several who were there:

One girl was white and pregnant, the other was colored, and they were with five colored studs. They hung around our bar—Nick's Place on Del Monte Avenue—for about three hours Saturday night, drinking and talking with our riders, then they came out to the beach with us —them and their five boy friends. Everybody was standing around the fire, drinking wine, and some of the guys were talking to them— hustling 'em, naturally—and soon somebody asked the two chicks if they wanted to be turned on—you know, did they want to smoke some pot? They said yeah, and then they walked off with some of the guys to the dunes. The spade went with a few guys and then she wanted to quit, but the pregnant one was really hot to trot; the first four or five guys she was really dragging into her arms, but after that she cooled off, too. By this time, though, one of their boy friends had got scared and gone for the cops—and that's all it was.

But not quite all. After that there were Senator Farr and Tom Lynch and a hundred cops and dozens of newspaper stories and articles in the national newsmagazines—and even this article, which is a direct result of the Monterey "gang rape."

When the much-quoted report was released, the local press— primarily the San Francisco *Chronicle,* which had earlier done a long and fairly objective series on the Hell's Angels—made a point of saying the Monterey charges against the Hell's Angels had been dropped for lack of evidence. *Newsweek* was careful not to mention Monterey at all, but *The New York Times* referred to it as "the alleged gang rape" which, however, left no doubt in a reader's mind that something savage had occurred.

It remained for *Time,* though, to flatly ignore the fact that the Monterey rape charges had been dismissed. Its article leaned heavily on the hairiest and least factual sections of the report, and ignored the rest. It said, for instance, that the Hell's Angels initiation rite "demands that any new member bring a woman or girl [called a 'sheep'] who is willing to submit to sexual intercourse with each member of the club." That is untrue, although, as one Angel explained, "Now and then you get a woman who likes to cover the crowd, and hell, I'm no prude. People don't like to think women go for that stuff, but a lot of them do."

We were talking across a pool table about the rash of publicity and how it affected the Angel's activities. I was trying to explain to him that the bulk of the press in this country has such a vested interest in the *status quo* that it can't afford to do much honest probing at the roots, for fear of what they might find. ·

"Oh, I don't know," he said. "Of course I don't like to read all this bullshit because it brings the heat down on us, but since we got famous we've had more rich fags and sex-hungry women come looking for us than we ever had before. Hell, these days we have more action than we can handle."

Biographical Notes

GERTRUDE ATHERTON (1857–1948) was a native Californian, and the author of several novels and works of local history.

JERRY BERMAN received a law degree from the University of California, Berkeley, in 1967, and is presently practicing law in Washington, D.C.

ANTHONY BERNHARD is a graduate student in the department of sociology at the University of California, Davis.

JAMES LORD BRYCE (1838–1922) was a British diplomat, historian, and political commentator. *The American Commonwealth,* from which the selection in this book was taken, was published in 1889.

CESAR CHAVEZ, chairman of the National Farm Workers Association, was the principal leader of the long strike by vineyard workers in Delano, California, in 1965–66.

EDGAR Z. FRIEDENBERG is a member of the department of sociology at the State University of New York at Buffalo, and is the author of *The Vanishing Adolescent* and *Coming of Age in America.*

HENRY GEORGE (1839–97), journalist, economist, and social philosopher, was a long-time resident of California, and the author of the populist classic, *Progress and Poverty* (1879).

WARREN HINCKLE is an editor of *Ramparts* magazine.

365

DAVID HOROWITZ is the author of numerous articles on education and student politics. His latest book is *The Free World Colossus* (1965).

ALDOUS HUXLEY (1894–1963), British novelist and critic, was the author of *Chrome Yellow, Brave New World, The Doors of Perception, Island,* and many others.

ANDREW KOPKIND is an editor of *The New Republic* and the American correspondent for *The New Statesman.*

ROBERT KUTTNER is a legislative assistant to Congressman William F. Ryan. A former student at the University of California, Berkeley, Mr. Kuttner worked in Robert Scheer's 1966 congressional campaign.

LEO LITWAK is a member of the English department at San Francisco State College, and the author of short stories and several novels.

CAREY McWILLIAMS received a degree in law from the University of Southern California in 1927, and practiced in the Los Angeles area from 1927–38. He served as state Commissioner of Immigration and Housing from 1938–42. His association with *The Nation* began in 1945, and he has been its editor since 1955. Mr. McWilliams is the author of *Ambrose Bierce: A Biography* (1929), *Factories in the Field* (1939), *Ill Fares the Land* (1942), *Brothers Under the Skin* (1943), and many other volumes on American politics, race relations, labor problems, and Western history.

WILSON CAREY McWILLIAMS was born and raised in Merced, California, and received his undergraduate and graduate education at the University of California, Berkeley. He is the author of *The Dilemma of Atomic Power in a Divided World* (1963), and the co-editor, with George A. Lanyi, of *Crisis and Continuity in World Politics* (1966). At present he is a member of the department of political science at Brooklyn College.

BRUCE PAYNE, a former student at the University of California, Berkeley, is doing graduate work in political science at Yale.

THOMAS PYNCHON is the author of *V.* and *The Crying of Lot 49.*

MICHAEL PAUL ROGIN is a member of the department of political science at the University of California, Berkeley, and is the author of *McCarthy and the Intellectuals* (1967).

JOSIAH ROYCE (1855–1916), a native Californian, was the author of several works on philosophy and education, among them *The World and the Individual* and *The Philosophy of Loyalty.*

JOHN SCHAAR is a member of the department of political science at the University of California, Berkeley, and the author of *Loyalty in America* and *Escape from Authority.*

MARK SHECHNER is a former graduate student and teaching assistant at the University of California, Berkeley.

HUNTER S. THOMPSON is a free-lance writer, a frequent contributor to *The Nation, Esquire,* and other periodicals, and the author of *Hell's Angels.*

RICHARD TODD graduated from Amherst College and went to California to continue his studies in English at Stanford. He has returned to the East to become a free-lance writer.

MARK TWAIN (1835–1910) wrote *Roughing It* in 1871–72, during his short period as a journalist in Buffalo, New York. The book is loosely based on Twain's life between 1861—when he left the Confederate Army to journey west with his brother Orion, newly appointed Secretary of the Territory of Nevada—and 1867, when he left California for New York.

DAVID WALLS, a former student at the University of California, Berkeley, works for an anti-poverty project in Kentucky.

JAMES Q. WILSON is the author of *The Amateur Democrat* and *Negro Politics,* and is presently a member of the department of political science at Harvard University.

SHELDON WOLIN, a member of the department of political science at the University of California, Berkeley, is the author of *Politics and Vision.*